W9-BGG-893

Passing Through Transitions

Passing Through Transitions

A GUIDE FOR PRACTITIONERS

Naomi Golan

THE FREE PRESS
A Division of Macmillan Publishing Co., Inc.
NEW YORK

Collier Macmillan Publishers
LONDON

Copyright © 1981 by THE FREE PRESS
A Division of Macmillan Publishing Co., Inc.

All rights reserved. No part of this book may be reproduced or transmitted in any form or by any means, electronic or mechanical, including photocopying, recording, or by any information storage and retrieval system, without permission in writing from the Publisher.

THE FREE PRESS
A Division of Macmillan Publishing Co., Inc.
866 Third Avenue, New York, N.Y. 10022

Collier Macmillan Canada, Ltd.

First Free Press Paperback Edition 1983

Printed in the United States of America

printing number paperback

2 3 4 5 6 7 8 9 10

printing number hard cover

2 3 4 5 6 7 8 9 10

Library of Congress Cataloging in Publication Data

Golan, Naomi.
   Passing through transitions.

   Bibliography: p.
   Includes index.
   1. Crisis intervention (Psychiatry) 2. Adulthood—
Psychological aspects. I. Title.
RC480.6.G63   158'.3   80-70837
ISBN 0-02-912070-5   AACR2
ISBN 0-02-912080-2 pbk.

To my husband, Ezriel Golan, in deep-felt appreciation of the many transitions we have passed through and weathered together

*To every thing there is a season, and a time to every purpose under
   the heaven;*
A time to be born, and a time to die;
A time to plant, and a time to pluck up that which is planted;
A time to kill, and a time to heal;
A time to break down, and a time to build up;
A time to weep, and a time to laugh;
A time to mourn, and a time to dance;
A time to cast away stones, and a time to gather stones together;
A time to embrace, and a time to refrain from embracing;
A time to seek, and a time to lose;
A time to keep, and a time to cast away;
A time to rend, and a time to sew;
A time to keep silence, and a time to speak;
A time to love, and a time to hate;
A time for war, and a time for peace.

—Ecclesiastes (Kohelet) 3:1–8

Contents

PART II   SIGNIFICANT TRANSITIONS IN ADULTHOOD   45

Case Examples of Transitions

Foreword

Two circumstances call for the publication of a book such as this. One is the fact that we live, and breathlessly try to cope, in an era of revolutionary and complex social/psychological change. The other is that the challenges and the trauma, the impacts and disequilibrium, that such changes inject into the lives of adults have only recently begun to be recognized and examined for their inter- and intrapersonal significances. That those professionals who presume to help others weather such social/psychological tempests, quakes, and tremors (at the same time as they struggle to keep their own precarious balance) must recognize the signs and imports of troubles, must further examine them along with the values and means that guide their helping efforts—all this goes without saying. This book offers both some foundations and guides.

Well over a decade ago, in *Persona: Social Role and Personality* I noted the dearth of theoretical constructs, studies, or even isolated clinical accounts of the long development period between late adolescence and old age that bore the catchall label "adulthood." To be sure, Erikson had in his life-stage scheme outlined several adult stages, designating their general character, tasks, and qualities. And sociologists, such as Duvall, had traced the evolution of life tasks and their affective components in adult family life. But compared to the close attention to, documentation of, and resultant conceptions about the development of children, and the consequent useful notions about how to enhance child life, the scripts by which adulthood

xv

might be understood were markedly few and sketchy. It was as if human beings were considered "all done," fixed, upon coming of age. And then, alas, un-made, undone, bit by bit, by the decrements of old age.

What *Persona* proposed was that the tasks and behaviors, the rewards or hurts, the preparation or lack of it, the met or unmet expectations of self and others involved in the vital life-roles of adulthood were all emotionally charged experiences. As such they are potentially moving, since they penetrate into the human being's personality structure and functioning. Thereby they are "developmental" in their import.

My vested interest in this present book by Naomi Golan now becomes manifest. Indeed it is enhanced, because this book has gone considerably further than others have done in detailing the points of emotional involvement in the stressful transitions of adult life.

Within the past few years a number of studies, popularized and scholarly, have begun the exploration of the terrain, climate, and life forces of the long period between adolescence and old age. This book draws upon these studies to apply them and combine them with the live flesh-and-blood clinical observations of social workers. Role transitions constitute only one of the "passages" examined here. Noted for their moving and unsettling powers are other shifts and adjustments common in adult living: geographical migrations, for instance, commonplace as never before in human history, but which, for all their usualness, always demand of the persons involved the ability to change, adapt, cope. There are, further, shifts from one kind of work or career to another, complicated often by bewildering choices; moves out from marriage into singlehood, and then into a second and different marriage that may impose the tasks of step-parenthood; reversals from riding along as the child of caretaking parents to the sudden shifting of gears required on finding oneself to be the caretaker of age-debilitated parents; losses of both means and persons in taken-for-granted support nets.

These are the kinds of changes and transitions that are the subject matter of this book. All are charged with crucialness for the individual person. As Golan points out, many—perhaps most—may be managed, lived through well or badly, by the person himself. But for those who, for one or more of a galaxy of reasons, need the expertise and/or resources of professional help it is essential that the helper understand the particular nature of "unsettling" experiences. Reorganizations of habits, behaviors, and attitudes may all be involved. Thus, to use Havighurst's phrase, a crucial time may be a "teachable moment," since the metal ("mettle" in its variant form) of the personality is likely to be most malleable at such a time, most susceptible to learning and change.

In any profession the point of "knowing" is to enable understanding to be put to use. Thus this book goes beyond delineating the nature and aspects of adult transitional and developmental stages. It deals as well with the available means and methods for helping adults whose transitional crises call for outside interventions.

Throughout the book case materials exemplify and enliven the text. More important, perhaps, is the astonishingly large body of recent research on adulthood, studies which Professor Golan has carefully examined, abstracted, and utilized in support of her own and her contributor–social workers' case observations and experiences. It may fairly be said that in addition to its detailed fine-combing of adult life-changes, this book offers an unusually rich and thorough reference source for anyone interested in adulthood—in its problematic or effective navigation of inevitable transitions, and in the opportunities or obstacles it holds for the development of personal and interpersonal competence and sense of wholeness.

HELEN HARRIS PERLMAN

Preface

This book is a direct continuation of my book, *Treatment in Crisis Situations*, which appeared in 1978. When Gladys Topkis of The Free Press asked me to write another book on crises, I immediately took up the challenge, since at the time I was tied up in one of the "knots" in which practitioners and their teachers periodically entangle themselves. This centered around the question, "When is a crisis *not* a crisis?" I agreed to write the book on the condition that I be allowed to investigate the category of so-called crises which did not appear to fit the same criteria or to proceed in the same way as other time-limited stressful situations did: transitional states.

As an area of practice, treatment during transitional situations is a new sphere of activity for many practitioners, or rather a new coming-to-awareness of what some of us have been engaged in for years. It involves developing a different approach toward clients, many of whom are very close in background, outlook, and vulnerability to the professional himself. It also means changing the focus of traditional forms of intervention so as to become less restitutive and more prospective in direction—doing primary prevention to forestall future disruption.

In this volume we set out to accomplish several things. First, in an effort to clarify the knowledge base, we try to pin down the concept of transitions in the adult life cycle and to offer some theories as to the nature of change and adaptation over the life span. As a way of broadening the theoretical framework for practice, we summarize some of the more salient perspectives

xix

on individual and family development during the adult life cycle and present several of the recent relevant research studies on transitional states.

Next, to learn how this material can be applied in real-life situations, we examine in detail fourteen transitions which can occur during the stages of early, middle, and late adulthood; we trace both their development over time and the points of potential complications, giving actual case examples to illustrate the processes. Finally, we consider the difficulties which can arise during times of transition and we review the various sources and forms of help available to the individual or family, as well as the roles of the various helpgivers. We also offer some tentative guidelines for professional practice during such periods.

This book is intended as source material to be included in curricula of schools of social work, clinical and educational psychology, and marriage and family counseling, to fill a gap in developmental knowledge and practical application that has been found to exist in many programs. Although it stands open to criticism in terms of attempting to present too much and doing so superficially, it was deemed important to cover the entire span of the individual's adult years so that the alternating periods of building up, tearing down, and rebuilding can be seen from a perspective of breadth as well as length. This view of the normal person in his interacting inner and outer worlds, in the process of continuous growth and change, is offered as a sine qua non of the preparation for professional help-giving.

Researching, collecting data, and writing this book have taken the major part of my time and efforts over the past two years. I was helped immeasurably by a large number of friends and colleagues who encouraged, supported, argued with, humored, and provoked me as we went over various pieces of the theory and practice together, thus fueling both my ideas and my struggles to conceptualize and concretize the "bee in my bonnet." Unfortunately, I cannot list everyone who contributed, but I should like to mention a few whose help was vital.

First of all, I should like to thank Helen Harris Perlman, who, since the days when I was her student at the School of Social Service Administration at the University of Chicago, has been a source of inspiration and unfailing support. William Reid also made a valuable contribution by his calm, objective examination of the research issues involved.

I should like to express my appreciation to the faculty and staff at the School of Social Welfare, University of California, Berkeley, where I started this project during the first part of my 1978–79 sabbatical year. Thanks go particularly to Dean Harry Specht, Ralph Kramer, Genevieve Oxley, Tsipora Peskin, Dorothy Turner, Judith Wallerstein, and Katherine Stewart, and to Marjorie Fiske, David Chiriboga, and Harvey Peskin of the University of California, San Francisco. At the School of Social Work, University of Wisconsin–Madison, where I spent the second part of that year,

I am indebted especially to Anne Minahan, Norma Berkowitz, Rosemarie Carbino, Allen Pincus, and Vivian Wood.

In my travels around the country I found these persons particularly helpful: Patricia Ewalt, Eileen Brennan, and Vivian McCoy at the University of Kansas, Lawrence; Hiasaura Rubenstein at the University of Tennessee–Nashville; Anthony Maluccio of the University of Connecticut (Hartford); Sophie Loewenstein of Simmons College, Boston; and Francis Turner, then dean of the school of social work at Wilfred Laurier University in Ontario, Canada. My colleagues and good friends in the field who were very generous in sharing both their ideas and their practice experience include Gertrude Conrad, Shirley Cooper, David Hoffman, Stella Joffe, David Kaplan, Mary Remmel, Gary Rosenberg, Ralph Sherman, and Reva Wiseman. Phyllis Silverman, whose interest in transitions has paralleled and supplemented my own, has contributed immeasurably to my thinking over a number of years. Milton Wittman also added his support.

Space does not permit me to name everyone who contributed case material to this project, and I should like to make it clear that the choice of cases cited was based on the desire to illustrate a particular theoretical or applied point rather than on the material presented or the nature of the practice. Those whose material has been used, even with modifications and switch-arounds, include Seema Allan, Helen Belmaker, Clyde Brown, John Buchler, Mary Connally, Gertrude Conrad, Thomas Flanagan, Sara Fox, Dorothy Gursky, Laura Haward, Edith Jakubowski, Helen Madigan, Dvora Nesher, Betty Russell, Gwen Rowe, Sylvia Schild, Margaret Solberg, Donna Ulteig, Frances Waner, Reva Wiseman, Gwendolyn Williams, and James Williams. I apologize if I have unwittingly offended anyone in my handling of the contributions.

Since my return to the University of Haifa, I have been helped a great deal by colleagues at the School of Social Work who sought to lighten my administrative duties so that I could complete this book. I am particularly grateful to Avraham Sagi, Rachel Kats, and Zvi Eisikovits in this respect. Others who took on additional work uncomplainingly and spurred me on include Nava El-Ad, Anita Weiner, Ariela Loewenstein, Nachman Sharon, Rivka Eisikovits, and Esther Shurka. Trudy Katzenberg, Ruth Pergamenter, and Hannah Shavit helped me test my ideas against the Israeli reality. Gabriel Lanyi, administrative secretary of the school, managed to shoulder many of the routine, day-to-day responsibilities, despite his newness to the position. For this and for his fine arrangements regarding the technical aspects of producing the finished manuscript, I give my sincere thanks. Reva Friedman, my patient and efficient typist, worked uncomplainingly to keep up with my erratic production and to decipher my very rough draft, and thus earned my amazed respect.

Above all, I extend my sincere thanks to my long-suffering family and friends, spread over two continents, who provided me with unfailing comfort and active sustenance as I creaked and groaned my way through the transition of writing. And to Gladys Topkis, who has been invariably supportive in encouraging me to develop my ideas and in arranging opportunities for me to try them out, I feel truly appreciative.

A few explanations at the outset as to the grammatical style. In general, the editorial "we" is used rather than the impersonal "one" or the passive form for the sake of smoothness in narration, even though the ideas are, for the most part, my own amalgam. Where specific individual responsibility needs to be attributed, I use the singular "I."

I struggled mightily with the gender of the third-person pronouns, sometimes using the awkward "he or she" or its equivalent, sometimes resorting to "they," and sometimes falling back on the traditional "he." If anyone's sensibilities are offended, the fault lies not with any unintended sexism but with the limitations of English syntax.

Finally, because the survey of the academic and professional literature covers a number of fields, I decided to use the journalistic style of giving an author's full name the first time it is used, rather than rely on the customary usage of the last name alone or, in the references, on an unidentifiable first initial. If this marks me as a novice, at least I can identify the players on the scoreboard—as, I hope, can the readers.

NAOMI GOLAN

PART I

Viewing the Life Span

The central purpose of this book is to provide professional students and practitioners with an overall view of the transitional processes that shape and transform much of adult life. It aims to map out some of the ways in which normal people with normal problems change and grow over time and how they learn to deal with the key issues that arise within their vital role networks at turning points in their life course. While this process is often handled outside of the professional help system, it constitutes important background information that helpgivers should have at their disposal when they are called upon to intervene in critical situations. It frequently provides the key to defining where the client is when he reaches the point of asking for assistance.

Traditionally, practitioners have tended to view their clients' current life situation through the mirror of past experiences, with an emphasis on early childhood development. In this first section we offer an additional frame of reference: the process that takes place during the bridging periods in the life span as the adult enters new developmental stages, explores uncharted territories, and encounters unfamiliar demands to which he has to adapt. By learning to recognize the links between personality structure and role expectations during periods of heightened change, the professional may learn new ways to view old problems and gain additional insight into how persons and their families learn to deal with them.

We introduce this approach in this section by first discussing the nature

1

of the transitional process and the ways in which change and adaptation take place. We then present a series of perspectives, both theoretical and research-based, by which to examine transitional states. Once this background is established, we can then go on to discuss specific bridging situations.

1

Where Transitions Are Met—and Missed

NORMAL PROBLEMS OF NORMAL PEOPLE

I remember our family's move from the farm to the big city when I was nine. Our parents had decided to make the change months before, and my father had already found a job there. But it all seemed very far away from our everyday life. Then, a few weeks before school ended, my mother started to pack the good dishes and the linens and the ornaments from the parlor whatnot. When my sister Jenny and I saw it was for real, we began to talk about it all the time—at school and at home and with our friends. We had to sort out our toys and books and treasures, to decide which to take with us and which to throw out or give away. We had never been to the city and had only the haziest idea of what was waiting for us.

The day before we left, we brought our calico cat Ginger and Jenny's pet turtle to the kids down the road and made a round of goodbye visits to the barn and the creek and our secret place in the woods. The next morning, when our old sedan was packed to the roof with boxes and bundles and all of the family, we rattled down the lane behind the movers' truck. I still remember the tightness in my throat and the knot in my stomach. I felt sad and glad, excited and scared, all at the same time.

THIS ACCOUNT, recalled forty years later, describes a common experience that all of us go through repeatedly in the course of our lives: the leaving of an old familiar world and the entry into an unknown new one, the passing from one relatively stable state into an interval of strangeness and uncertainty on the way to a new stable state. This interval of passage is a normal yet frequently upsetting life experience. It is often marked by perceptual

3

and cognitive disturbances as well as emotions of confusion, disorientation, and ambivalence. Behavior patterns may become tentative, erratic, and unpredictable as we search for road signs to guide us through unfamiliar territory.

The transition may involve a relatively limited change in one's style of functioning, such as when a couple moves from a ground-floor apartment to a larger one on the third floor. Or it may require a sweeping reorganization of the major networks in one's life, as when a young girl leaves her parental home to get married, move across the country, and start a new job all at the same time. The change may be long-anticipated and even rehearsed in advance by, say, parents who return to couplehood after their last child leaves home. Or it may be entirely unexpected, like the situation of the employee who is suddenly notified that his company has been taken over and he is to be shifted to a new plant on the West Coast. The effects may be transitory and ephemeral for the person who is asked to look after a neighbor's child while the mother goes out of town for the weekend. Or the consequences may be immutable, irreversible, and never to be gotten over for the parent whose own child dies after a lingering fatal illness.

All of these transitions are entirely normal situations that can happen to any of us. Their significant common denominator is that they encompass a bridging period, often marked by feelings of anxiety, loss, and upset, which sometimes erupt into states of active disequilibrium. This period involves an interval of adaptation and reorganization, both in one's inner and outer worlds, during which basic shifts in thinking, feeling, and behaving must be made. Yet, although such transformation is universally experienced, careful attention has been paid to its content and process only recently. Now widespread interest in the phenomenon has moved the topic into the mainstream of professional thinking.

SOCIAL WORK ENCOUNTERS WITH TRANSITIONS

A major part of the activities of family service agencies, marriage and family counseling centers, and physical and mental health clinics and hospitals is concerned with individuals and families in the processes of change. Considerable practice wisdom has accrued over the years in helping this clientele cope with the web of problems which arise, either within themselves or at the interface between their inner selves and their significant others (parents, children, bosses, friends, fellow workers, etc.), at turning points in their life cycle.

Social work practitioners can thus say, with some justification, that they frequently encounter clients/patients/counselees who are in transitional states. For anyone who has worked in such settings, it becomes abundantly clear that assessment and treatment planning in such situations must involve both an etiological examination of what went wrong in functioning during the past and a careful review of what is currently awry. What is often missed is the recognition that upsets during periods of intrapersonal and interpersonal change often follow predictable patterns which can serve as guidelines for both immediate intervention and future planning.

In specialized crisis counseling centers, the acute situational aspects of the case (the precipitating factor) usually take priority. Intervention is usually geared toward focused amelioration or change in the immediate situation. Thus the linkage between, say, a businessman's suicide attempt or a young girl's rape and the underlying, ongoing developmental aspects of the person's life may often be missed or, if noted, not followed up in the structured, time-limited framework in which such crisis services usually operate.

Part of the diagnostic difficulty lies in the paucity of the theoretical material available for use. Traditionally, developmental psychologists have tended to concentrate on the two extremes of the life span. Child psychologists and educational psychologists have examined with meticulous attention the progress of the child from birth through adolescence.[1] More recently, gerontologists and social psychologists have engaged in significant research and theory-building about the aging process.[2] Only within the past decade has pioneering work been carried out on the adult individual as a changing, unfolding personality engaged in a continuous process of growth and change.[3]

In schools of social work, academic courses on personality and socialization have recently begun to adopt this normal-adult-in-the-process-of-change approach.[4] Bibliographies on human growth and individual development sequences have been expanded to include material on normal adult maturational processes and on transitional states. Special summer institutes, continuing education courses, and staff development programs are now being offered to provide practitioners with this "new" material and to help them recast their cases in this framework. Interdisciplinary institutes have been started to specialize in these areas.[5]

Interestingly, in the field of family practice, where no single, strong theory of family pathology undergirds practice, social work theoreticians have long used a maturational perspective to view family problems and stresses. In turn, social work practitioners have begun to operationalize their help to troubled families in terms of developmental stages.[6] A basic shift in theoretical orientation appears to be taking place. In a wide-ranging discussion on various conceptual frameworks for social work practice, Anne Minahan and Allen Pincus recommend that the profession's knowledge base include information on the life tasks that confront *all* people in the life cycle as well as the special tasks that face those with social problems.[7] Carel Germain, in pointing out the parallels between ego psychology and general systems theory, finds that the Eriksonian formulation of *intergenerational cogwheeling*, which emphasizes the reciprocity of tasks for the developing person and his social and physical environment at each stage in the life cycle, meshes well with the ecological approach to practice.[8]

Helen Perlman's *Persona*, which emphasizes the importance of examining vital social roles in work, marriage, and parenthood as part of the adult change process,[9] seemed to have relatively limited impact on the field when it appeared in 1968. Yet today the normative approach to practice directly reflects this stance.[10]

> People commonly, in the course of their lives, acquire roles that are unfamiliar and for which they are unprepared. Parents of new babies often find themselves in this situation, as do young persons entering adolescence, mothers whose children have left home, and couples reaching retirement age. Each developmental phase can be a maturational crisis that places additional strain on coping skills. Moreover, crises such as becoming a divorced parent, suffering a stroke, or facing death may also challenge a person's capacity to assume an appropriate role. Social workers, who are aware of these situational and maturational crisis, are in a good position to offer the counseling, education, and supportive guidance necessary to cope with role assignments for which people are unprepared. [p. 92]

TRANSITIONS AS A PART OF CRISIS THEORY

Psychosocial transitions seem to have become incorporated into the developing body of crisis theory almost by happenstance. In the late 1950s, Erik Erikson, developing his eight-stage epigenetic view of the life cycle, proposed that the individual's ability to solve the key psychosocial crises posed by each developmental level could either enhance or weaken his ability to master crises in subsequent stages.[11] At another point, he defined a psychosocial crisis as a "turning point, a crucial period of increased vulnerability and heightened potential."[12]

Gerald Caplan found that transitional points are usually characterized by

> acute psychological upsets, lasting from about one to four or five weeks, which appear not to have been in themselves signs of mental disorder but rather the manifestation of adjustment and adaptation struggles in the face of a temporarily insoluble problem. Such problems have usually consisted of novel situations that the individual has not been able to handle quickly with his existing coping and defense mechanisms.[13]

John and Elaine Cumming noted that all crises, including transitions, produce a uniform pattern of response: first, a psychological and physical turmoil, including aimless activity or immobilization and disturbances of body function, mood, mental content, and intellectual function; second, a painful preoccupation with the past; and third, a period of remobilization, activity, and adjustment.[14] Lydia Rapoport saw the concept of role transitions and the vicissitudes of role changes throughout the life cycle as one dimension of stress that might precipitate a state of crisis in an individual or a family unit.[15]

Much of the early work on crisis theory, following this line, was applied to transitional situations: widowhood,[16] migration,[17] marriage,[18] parenthood,[19] and retirement.[20] It became apparent, however, that the "fit" to the overall theory was only partial and limited. Several years ago, in an effort to clear up some of the ambiguities, Robert Weiss tried to spell out the relationship between the terms "crisis," "transition," and "deficit."[21] He suggested that it would be most appropriate to use the term "crisis" to refer to a situation of sudden onset, limited duration, and considerable severity in the stress it imposes on those exposed to it. Crises often begin with a brief period in which the individual's emotions seem suspended. At the same time, a sudden mobilization of energy occurs; while the crisis holds, the immediate situation supersedes everything else. The crisis ends either in a return to the pre-crisis situation or in a persisting disruption, which Weiss terms a "transition state." In this latter situation,

> should the crisis end instead in change . . . the individual's emotional organization and his or her other relational arrangements must also undergo change. In addition to having to cope now with new problems, the individual must find different ways of dealing with upset, tension, or fatigue and find new sources of support for security, for feelings of worth, and for other components of well-being. Some previously maintained relationships may fade because they no longer seem approrpiate, while others may be modified to respond to the individual's new needs and relationships not previously existent may now be developed. The individual's concerns and aims may change and with them [his] sense of self. [p. 214]

Weiss notes that the transition state ends with the establishment of a new stable life organization accompanied by a new stable identity. This new life organization may be adequate or may be deficient in some way, which leads to a new stable state of permanent "deficit." The connection, he sees, lies in the fact that the triad of crisis, transition, and deficit often represents the sequelae of loss. He sees crisis as occurring with the first awareness of the imminence of loss; if the loss cannot be avoided, then transition ensues. This, in turn, may give rise to a life organization which is in some respect deficient.

My own interest in the area of adult development stages, and specifically in transitional processes, began some fifteen years ago with my concern over clients in active crisis situations.[22] It became increasingly evident that at certain pivotal periods in their lives, when individuals and families are engaged in making significant changes in the structure and content of their living situations, they become more vulnerable to acute pressures, both externally and internally generated, which they might take in stride in calmer times.[23] At the same time, the high level of tension and severe pain generated by the crisis sometimes catalyzes them into making substantive changes, not only in their immediate stress-connected situation, but in the broader patterns of their lives and their relations with significant others.[24]

Since my colleagues and I had no bank of available knowledge-for-use upon which to draw, outside of Erikson's paradigm of psychosocial crises in the individual life cycle, which is pitched at a high level of abstraction,[25] it took investigation of several disparate transitional situations for us to recognize the similarities and parallels in the process.[26] This in turn has led to burrowing into various pockets of widely diversified theory and research findings and to examining professional accounts of treatment situations in which clients appear to be engaged in making transitions.

The result is by no means a polished conceptualization of how bridging processes develop or how workers self-consciously utilize this approach. Rather, it should be viewed as an early effort to examine more closely a practice area which has, until the past few years, been squeezed willy-nilly into the procrustean bed of crisis intervention.[27] While so-called developmental and transitional crises seem to share some elements in common with other high-stress situations, they also show discernible differences in scope and process.

This book will attempt to examine these similarities and differences and to see how they are operationalized in actual field situations. I hope it will encourage a process of testing and shaping that will, in time, lead to a coherent frame of practice with persons in the process of maturational and transitional change which offers its own theoretical matrix and practice approaches. Furthermore, we may substantiate that during normal developmental bridging periods, as during acute situational crisis, the individual tends to be particularly amenable to help, so that a minimal effort at such a time can prove to be more effective than more extensive help during times of less emotional accessibility. These conclusions can have extensive implications for the structuring and concentration of resources and services in the helping professions.

THE STRUCTURE AND STRATEGIES OF THIS BOOK

This volume is divided into three sections. In Part I we define transitional states, offer some basic concepts relevant to the understanding of how people change during such periods, and examine some recent theoretical frameworks. Part II investigates three developmental transitions which tie together the stages of adulthood and eleven psychosocial transitional situations which can occur during these three adult periods. Part III focuses on intervention in situations involving transitions, the sources and forms such help can take, the roles of the professional, and the nature of the helping process itself.

Several strategy decisions have determined the structure and content of this presentation. First, because of the breadth and depth of the topic, no effort has been made to be either comprehensive or exhaustive in reviewing the literature. Indeed, the disparity and differences in approaches upon which much of developmental theory rests became so unwieldy at times that the temptation arose to forego the search for a master "transitional process" and to concentrate instead on one or several commonly experienced linking periods which could, by inference, be considered characteristic of the phenomenon. It was felt, however, that this would defeat the overall aim of examining differences and similarities in transitional processes over the life span. Thus the material should be viewed as a selected sampling of theoretical, practice, and research findings in this area.

Second, the choice was made to focus on the individual as the primary area of concern. While many of the transitions examined take place within the family system, the dynamics described are primarily those of the person's interaction with his reverberating environment, whether as part of a couple, a parent-child dyad, or an entire family network.

Similarly, at the risk of appearing arbitrary, it was decided to limit the examination of transitional states to Erikson's last three stages of young adulthood, maturity, and old age, covering roughly some sixty years. The first twenty years of life have been extensively studied and documented by educational and developmental psychologists over many decades. In addition, the major part of direct professional practice tends to be carried out with persons in their adult years.

In the original plan for this book, it was hoped that some systematic examination would be made of social class, ethnic group, and sex differences as manifested during transitions. After some months of struggling to make some order out of these aspects, I reluctantly gave up the effort—not because the topics are not crucial, but because I found myself drawn into a number of side issues and tangential interests which were leading me away from my central theme. On the woman's question particularly, I found myself immersed in a number of social-psychological-political positions, each of which could have provided the focus for a chapter in itself. A reluctant compromise was to bring in these variations, which were often a matter of timing ("Working-class women tend to marry earlier than middle-class ones") or emphasis ("In their twenties, many traditional young women support their husband's Dream rather than build their own"), when discussing the specific transitions themselves.

Finally, it would be misleading to offer the case examples and vignettes cited throughout this book as a representative or systematic sampling of practice during transitional states. During an early phase in this study's development, effort was made to design a pilot research project to examine practice in the areas of selected transitional situations. Ruefully, I soon recognized that not only did preliminary assumptions about theoretical approaches and practice commonalities rest on shaky foundations, but a basic lack of knowledge prevented the development of testable hypotheses regarding the activities of either client or worker. It was decided, therefore, as a first necessary step in problem identification, to solicit a "bunch of cases" in order to look, in a preliminary, rudimentary way, at the state of practice at the time of writing.

Some one hundred and twenty-five documented cases in which a normal life transition is involved have been collected and examined. Although a simple case outline was provided as a guide, returned reports ranged in complexity from terse checklists to lavishly detailed process recordings. From these, case examples were drawn to illustrate points in the discussion or to bring out certain practice principles. While respondents were explicitly asked to mask identifying data, I have taken the liberty of switching around details, changing or clarifying actions taken, and even, on occasion, combining similar cases in order to add enriching information to a particular situation.

I hope that out of these anecdotal gleanings certain generalizations can be developed which can provide the basis for future ordered descriptive studies of different types of transitional processes and practice in various settings with various types of clients. In turn, these second-generation types of studies can become springboards for designing and testing controlled experiments in measuring and comparing the relative effectiveness of interventive efforts during these vital periods in the individual's life span. Only in this way can we hope to bring the theory and application of intervention at times of transition into the mainstream of professional practice in an ordered way.

NOTES

IMPORTANT MESSAGE

FOR _____

DATE _____ TIME _____ A.M.
P.M.

M _____

OF _____

PHONE _____

AREA CODE   NUMBER   EXTENSION

TELEPHONED		PLEASE CALL	
CAME TO SEE YOU		WILL CALL AGAIN	
WANTS TO SEE YOU		RUSH	
RETURNED YOUR CALL		SPECIAL ATTENTION	

MESSAGE _____ Michele Hanser _____

_____

_____

_____

_____

_____

SIGNED _____

LITHO IN U.S.A.

TOPS   FORM 3002S

2

The Nature of Transitions
and the Change Process

*All our lives long, every day and every hour, we are engaged in the process
of accommodating our changed and unchanged selves to changed and unchanged surroundings; living, in fact, is nothing else than this process of
accommodation. When we fail in it a little we are stupid, when we fail
flagrantly we are mad, when we suspend it temporarily we sleep, when we
give up the attempt altogether, we die.*

—*Samuel Butler*[1]

DEFINITIONS AND CLASSIFICATIONS

A GOOD STARTING POINT for the investigation of changes in adulthood might
be to try to pin down more precisely what is meant by the term "transition"
when applied to persons in their social situations. The term can be defined
as: "(1) Movement or passage from one position, state, stage, subject, concept, etc., to another; (2) a passage or change of this kind: the transition from
adolescence to adulthood."[2]

James Tyhurst, one of the early social scientists to study this phenomenon, notes that the term "transition" is derived from two Latin words meaning "to go across" and offers an alternate definition: "a passage or change
from one place or state or act or set of circumstances to another."[3] Rhona
Rapoport, a family sociologist who worked with Gerald Caplan and his associates at the Harvard School of Public Health, was one of the first to

11

examine critical transition points in the normal, expectable development of the family life cycle. She noted that these "points of no return" often promote disequilibrium in both the individual and the family systems. However, if handled advantageously, they can result in maturation and new development and offer the opportunity for preventive intervention.[4]

Daniel Levinson, a social psychologist, sees a transition as a bridge, a boundary zone between two stages of greater stability.[5] It involves a process of change, a shift from one life structure to another, terminating the existing one and creating the possibility for a new one. The transitional period involves an ending, a process of separation or loss. In some cases the separation is complete, as when one terminates a job, ownership of a house, or membership in a community. In other instances it is partial, as when contact with a person or group continues but the nature of the relationship changes: a romantic love becomes a modest friendship, or a marriage ends in divorce but the couple maintain their involvement in a new form. Levinson sees a transitional period as a requirement to terminating the past and starting the future.

I find a good working definition to be: "a period of moving from one state of certainty to another, with an interval of uncertainty and change in between." This, of course, does not indicate the range and diversity of transitional phases. Phyllis Silverman, who has worked extensively in this area, has noted:

> Some transitions can be anticipated as the individual predictably matures biologically and moves through various age groups. Other changes are unanticipated, as when a sudden death occurs out of turn in the life cycle or a major illness strikes. The work required in a transition is related to the suddenness of the onset of the condition, the amount or degree of loss to the individual, and how much of his life is touched by the situation. An additional consideration is whether change is total or partial, temporary or permanent.[6]

Transitions may be categorized in different ways. They can be classified by *time periods*, the passages from one chronological stage in the life cycle to another, marked by specific biological, psychological, and social characteristics. They can be differentiated by *role shifts*, the relinquishing of one set of social roles and the taking on of new ones, each calling for a period of adaptation. Or they can be defined by transitional or *marker events*, which serve as the transformation points which start off and shape the period of change.

Various dichotomies have been proposed: gradual or sudden, expanding or contracting, anticipated or non-anticipated, transitory or permanent, reversible or irreversible, internally or externally directed, voluntarily or involuntarily imposed, and so on. Some time ago, in trying to develop a typology of transitions, I found that if one used a *chronological or life-span criterion* some transitions appeared to fall with greater frequency into certain developmental stages and could thus be termed "vertical" or "maturational" in the sense of being stage-related:

YOUNG ADULTHOOD
  Being single to being married.
  Being married to becoming a parent.
MIDDLE ADULTHOOD
  Having one's first child at home to having him start college.
  Having one's last child leave home to resuming life as part of a couple.
LATE ADULTHOOD
  Working to retiring from work.
  Living with one's spouse to having him die and continuing to live alone.

However, not only does there appear to be a wide variation in such age-stage-linked transitions, but other bridging periods seem to be more free-floating, less bound to the biological, psychological, and social "time clocks" described by Bernice Neugarten. Calling them "horizontal" (as opposed to vertical) or "unlinked" does not appear to convey adequately the nature of such intervals as

Separating from one's spouse to becoming divorced.
Leaving one's job to starting a new career.
Moving from one place to another.

In both groupings, moreover, cultural, ethnic, and social-class differences have a profound influence on both the time and the extent of the changes required.

Another effort at classification was to divide transitional periods in terms of *changes in vital social roles*. Here the movement can go in different directions:

Adding on new roles to one's current role cluster, such as

Taking on a part-time job while continuing as a student.
Becoming a parent in addition to being a spouse.
Becoming a foster parent while parenting one's own children.

Some transitions involve a *consolidation of roles*, by giving up one and expanding another:

Stopping part-time work and becoming a full-time supervisor.
Giving up being a researcher while continuing as a teacher and mentor of
  students doing research.

Some require *exchanging one vital role for another* which cannot be carried at the same time:

Giving up being a spouse and becoming a divorced person.

Leaving the confines of an institution and becoming a member of the outside community.

Graduating from being a student to becoming a full-time employee.

Finally, some transitions are concerned with *giving up a vital role that is not replaced by another* (reducing one's role cluster):

Retiring from work without finding a compensatory role in retirement.

Losing one's spouse without remarrying.

Giving up being an active parent without becoming a grandparent or taking a job.

A third classification system might be to view transitions in terms of the *areas of one's life affected.* From this vantage point, some transitions are primarily concerned with *geographical changes:*

Migrating from one country to another.

Moving from the rural south to the urban north.

Moving from the central city to the suburbs.

Others involve *socioeconomic shifts:*

Moving from the lower to the middle class.

Changing from being an ADC mother to being an independent job-holder.

Still others are primarily concerned with *physical and physiological changes:*

From being a sighted to being a sightless person.

From being a wheelchair patient to regaining use of one's legs.

From being grossly overweight to becoming a sylph.

While none of these typologies covers the full range of transitions, what they appear to have in common is the indication that a period of adaptation is involved, not only by the individual undergoing the change, but by his interacting social environment as well. Transitions may be sudden and dramatic or gradual and unobtrusive; they may differ in content and scope; they may have a varying impact on the individual's total life experience. Yet they all involve transformation and change.

CHANGE DURING TRANSITIONS

A great deal has been written in recent years about the nature of the human change process.[7] Helen Perlman notes that one of the powerful stimuli to change in adult life inheres in those circumstances or happenings that are seen as turning points. These may come about as a natural part of the life process, but they are felt with heightened acuity because the person's ability to cope with the needed adjustment in life-style will influence the subsequent course of his life.[8]

She suggests that Robert Havighurst's concept of the "teachable moment,"[9] at which there is maximum inclination to take on new developmental tasks, may be usefully applied in this context. Most teachable moments, says Perlman, occur in the beginning experience of crucialness or in the initial phase of a new set of circumstances, such as the early period of entering college, the first year in a professional school, the first months of marriage or parenthood, the first weeks following migration. At such times, readiness to take in the new ways is strongest. Shifts in role, status, or habitual behavior upset a person's equilibrium and send him groping for new ways in which to cope.

Howard Spierer finds that changes during periods of transition can be viewed from four different aspects: biological, sociological, psychological, and functional.[10] Biologists examine the physiological changes associated with different age levels, particularly the metabolic and hormonal changes which take place. Sociologists concern themselves primarily with social phenomena, with the changes in cohorts (groups of people of the same age) or the shifts in social roles assumed at different stages in the life span. Psychologists often choose a particular personality trait such as "sense of self" or "moral commitment" and follow its transformation over the years. The functional approach concentrates on the combined physical, emotional, and intellectual abilities of individuals to carry out life tasks at different stages in the aging process.

Bernice Neugarten, a developmental psychologist, emphasizes the need to be concerned with the orderly and sequential changes that occur with the passage of time as individuals move from adolescence through adulthood and old age.[11] She sees as one of the salient issues of adulthood the alterations in self-concept and in identity as the individual faces the successive contingencies of marriage, parenthood, career advancement, and decline, retirement, loss of a spouse, illness, and personal death.

Orville Brim points out that studies of life changes often start with the changing physical state.[12] Important shifts in socialization accompany changes in health or the onset of a disability. Individuals and groups vary greatly in the evenness of their lives, in the degree to which they are under pressure to change as they move through the stages of their adult years. Some live simple, undemanding lives, requiring little change in their environment or personalities. Others are beset by a wide array of demands during periods of divorce, family deaths, illnesses, or loss of jobs.

A key element in adult socialization, the process by which one learns to perform his social roles adequately, is the *role prescription* or *expectation* others have for the person, which require changes in beliefs, attitudes, behavior, motives, and values on his part. On the other hand, many demands for socialization changes are self-initiated as persons seek to change themselves in order to become more acceptable in their own (and others') eyes.

The demands to change that stem from others or from oneself are similar in that both encompass either an alteration in a role associated with an existing status or social position or the assumption of a new status and the learning of a new, related role. In the first case, an employer might demand that a worker change his current performance on the production line; in the second, a young woman might pressure her boyfriend to change his role performance once he becomes her husband. Since many persons and groups compete to influence a person's behavior and since he has his own ideas on the subject, the result may be conflict. If all sides desire the same change, the individual and his significant others can cooperate to bring about a gradual, continuing growth on his part. If the demands of others run counter to the wishes of the individual, resistance, antagonism, evasion, or outright revolt may ensue.

As a social interactionist, Howard Becker sees the key to understanding change in the character of the *situation* that requires the individual to act in a certain way.[13] The person's consistency in behavior as he moves from one situation to another depends on the extent of his personal commitment and his ability to pursue a congruous line of activity while rejecting other feasible alternatives. Thus the process of becoming an adult is one of gradually acquiring a variety of commitments which constrains the person into following a consistent pattern of behavior in various areas of life, such as choosing an occupation and starting a family.

Applying this line of thinking to the treatment process, Cornelis Bakker points out that despite the pessimism of professionals, adults tend to be extremely changeable.[14] A person's behavior changes as a function of the situation in which he finds himself. By trying to predict his own and others' role behavior, the individual tries to keep the situation stable and unaltered, thus protecting his own and others' role identity. Yet, when he finds himself in a truly new situation, he is bound to engage in substantially new behavior. The process is basically a circular one: once the person defines himself in a certain way, he seeks situations which are consistent with that definition. Thus the situation itself reconfirms the definition and a feedback loop is instituted.

Peter Marris, a social planner, has examined interacting personal and social changes.[15] He finds that whenever an event occurs which calls for change in established relationships, the will to change has to overcome an impulse to restore the past, to resist the change. He calls this the *conservative impulse*, and it appears more pervasive and profound than simple prejudice or class interest:

> It is as necessary for survival as adaptability, and indeed adaptability itself depends upon it. For the ability to learn from experience relies on the stability of the interpretations by which we predict the pattern of events. We

assimilate new experiences by placing them in the context of a familiar, reliable construction of reality. This structure rests not only on the regularity of events themselves, but on the continuity of their meaning. [p. 6]

Despite the ambivalence and anxiety invoked by venturing into the unknown, the process by which maturation provokes change is not fundamentally disruptive, according to Marris. Different kinds of change can be distinguished in terms of a balance between continuity, growth, and loss. First, many changes are incremental or substitutional; the purposes they seek to satisfy and the pattern of expectations remain essentially the same. Second, some changes may represent growth in the sense that familiar purposes and expectations are not disrupted but are incorporated within a broader range of interests or understanding; they do not threaten the integrity of what has already been learned, and the sense of continuity remains unbroken. Third, other changes may represent loss, either actual or prospective. When patterns of relationships are disrupted in ways for which we are not fully prepared, the thread of continuity becomes attenuated or lost.

The loss may fundamentally threaten the integrity of the structure of meanings on which this continuity rests and cannot be acknowledged without distress. But if life is to go on, the continuity must somehow be restored. When the loss is irretrievable, there must be a reinterpretation of what we have learned. . . . To do this, the loss must first be accepted as something we have to understand—not as just an event that has happened, but as a series of events that we must now expect to happen and a retrospect of earlier events whose familiar meaning has now been shadowed by our changed circumstances. The conservative impulse will make us seek to deny the loss. But when this fails, it will also lead us to repair the thread, tying past, present, and future together again with rewoven strands of meaning. [p. 21]

INNER AND OUTER CHANGE

But what changes in this process? C. Murray Parkes, a social psychiatrist, finds that defining an event as a loss or a gain depends on one's perception of the final outcome of changes in state.[16] Whenever a major change occurs in an individual's life situation, he needs to restructure his ways of looking at the world and his plans for living within it. Effort must be made to give up old patterns of thought and activity and to develop new ones. The crucial factor may be the way in which the person copes with the process of change.

The area in which change occurs, says Parkes, lies first of all in that part of the external world which impinges upon the self, the person's *life space*. He defines this as "those parts of the environment with which the self interacts and in relation to which his behavior is organized: other persons, material possessions, the familiar world of home and place of work, and even the individual's own body and mind, in so far as he can view them as separate from self." [p. 103]

The second area of change is in the individual's internal *assumptive world*, the total set of assumptions and interpretation which he builds up on the basis of his interpretation of past experiences in dealing with the outside world and his expectations of the future. The life space, says Parkes, is constantly changing as novel stimuli, fresh combinations of events, and communications from others are received and assimilated. Since some of these changes fulfill expectations, they require little or no changes in the assumptive world. Others necessitate a major restructuring: the abandonment of one set of assumptions and the development of a fresh set to enable the individual to cope with his new, altered life space. If the change takes place slowly (e.g., a maturational change such as growing in size or gradually becoming older and more frail) and the person has time to prepare gradually for the restructuring, the chances are that it will scarcely be noticed. If, on the other hand, the change is sudden and surprising (e.g., the unexpected loss of a job or a spouse), it is likely to be felt as major.

Parkes uses the term "psychosocial transitions" for the major changes in life space which are lasting in their effects, which take place over a relatively short period of time, and which affect large areas of the assumptive world. In order to cope with these changes, the person is impelled to set up a cycle of further internal and external changes aimed at improving the fit between himself and his environment. At the same time, since he is tied to his assumptive world by affectional bonds (e.g., his view of "his" job or "his" home), he tends to resist change whenever it requires giving up part of his accustomed life space, regardless of whether the net result is advantageous or not.

Since the individual's assumptive world contains models of both the actual world as he perceives it and the ideal world as he thinks (or hopes or dreads) it to be, he becomes aware of the discrepancies between the two. Again, if the gap is anticipated and he has time to rehearse in his mind how he would or should act in the face of change, the transition tends to take place smoothly. If, on the other hand, the change is unexpected or unforeseen, it may open wider the gaps and deficits in his ability to cope with the new situation.

Finally, Parkes notes, the individual is not merely a passive recipient of sensations from his life space; he creates his own unique assumptive world by reaching out into his environment and sampling it. He reacts to his life space by moving within it to keep it the same or to change it. To do so, he needs an intact physical apparatus, knowledge and skills, negotiable possessions (such as money) to obtain the services of others, and the status and role conferred on him by society in order to make use of its potentialities.

Some changes in the person's life space tend to affect his assumptive world more than others. These include the psychosocial transitions leading to changes in personal relationships, such as occur at each stage of the life cycle; changes in loved possessions such as the loss of a home, books, or other articles of sentimental value; changes in familiar environments such as occur during tornadoes or after slum clearances; changes in physical and mental capacities as a result of disease, accident, or the aging process; and changes in social roles and statuses which occur within families or in work groups.

OUTCOMES OF CHANGE

Granting that change, both inner and outer, is an integral part of the transitional process, what forms does it take? Although this question will crop up again and again, it might be well to introduce here four key concepts which are widely used in this context: *adaptation, mastery, coping,* and *defense*. Robert White considers *adaptation* to be the overarching concept, with the other three subsumed under it as strategies of adaptation.[17] He sees *defense* as signifying response to danger or attack, *mastery* as describing behavior in which frustrations have been surmounted and adaptive efforts successfully concluded, and *coping* as dealing with fairly drastic changes or problems which defy familiar ways of behaving and which require the production of new behavior accompanied by uncomfortable affects like anxiety, despair, guilt, shame, or grief. It implies adaptation under relatively difficult conditions.

Adaptation, White points out, means neither a total triumph over the environment nor a total surrender to it; it implies a striving toward an acceptable compromise, carried out by living systems in interaction with their environment. Living systems constantly seek a compromise which not only will preserve them as they are but will also permit them to increase their scope and autonomy.

Strategies for adaptation are usually concerned with behavioral change. They can be divided into (1) obtaining adequate information about the environment; (2) maintaining satisfactory internal conditions for both action and the processing of information; and (3) maintaining autonomy or freedom of movement. Adaptive behavior requires that the person's cognitive field has the right amount of information to serve as a guide to action, that his internal organization retains its balance in the face of external pressures, and that he maintain a range of options of action to give himself space in which to maneuver autonomously.

Some years ago, David Hamburg and John Adams, in reviewing a series of studies of behavior during major life transitions, also emphasized the importance of seeking out and utilizing information.[18] They found that for patients with severe physical injuries, the search for information served to keep distress within manageable limits, maintain a sense of personal worth, restore relations with significant others, enhance prospects for the recovery of bodily functions, and increase the likelihood of working out a personally valued and socially acceptable situation once physical recovery had been attained.

Somewhat later, Adams and Erich Lindemann noted that in crisis situations critical issues arise over the choice of patterns of adaptation.[19] On the one hand, these may be predominantly regressive and defensive, functioning primarily to protect the self from disintegration. On the other hand, they may represent progressive efforts to master the environment, restructure the tasks ahead, and solve the problems of dealing with a novel situation. In most crisis situations, the adaptive process is a complex and changing mix of both regressive and progressive components.

Lois Murphy, who studied children's coping patterns, distinguishes between two types of coping which have definite carry-overs into adult behavior.[20] "Coping I" is the "capacity to cope with opportunities, challenges, frustrations, threats in the environment," while "Coping II" is the "maintenance of internal integration—that is, the capacity to manage one's relation to the environment so as to maintain integrated functioning." [p. 117]

Murphy also offers two new concepts which can have implications for change during transitions: a *continuum of vulnerability* ranging from the most vulnerable person, with all of his frailties, defects, and lack of equipment for survival, to the relatively invulnerable one, who is so robust, adaptable, and resilient that he can survive even severe deprivation, mishandling, and environmental stress.[21] Murphy's second concept is that of *resilience*, the power to recover from disintegrative reactions under stress and return quickly to stable, appropriate functioning.

Important sequelae of recovery are reinforced hope and expectations for the future and a readiness to use support and new constructive defenses. Another important asset is the capacity to mobilize resources under stress, to be strained yet able to put forth extra energy—the "second wind" phenomenon. Still another factor is flexibility in effort and affect: the ability to see and to feel differently in response to new perceptual structuring, and to modify defenses and develop the capacity to change. A final attribute is the *ability to respond to substitutes*, to new objects and opportunities, and to use anxiety and aggression constructively. Resilience thus becomes an active psychophysiological push to restore a satisfying state of being.

In a recent study Aaron Antonovsky, a medical sociologist, asks why some people, faced with tremendous difficulties and obstacles at certain periods in their lives, are able to survive and even to thrive against all rational prognosis.[22] He suggests that this can be understood in terms of their *sense of coherence*, which he defines as "a global orientation that expresses the extent to which one has a pervasive, enduring though dynamic feeling of confidence that one's internal and external environments are predictable and that there is a high probability that things will work out as well as can be reasonably expected." [p. 123]

Persons who possess this sense of coherence tend to perceive their inner and outer environment as foreseeable and comprehensible. Their world has form and structure, is ordered and understandable. As opposed to the person who relies on sheer luck or blind chance to have his needs fulfilled, the person with a stronger sense of coherence is able to see reality clearly and to judge the likelihood of desirable outcomes in view of the countervailing forces operating. While immense effort may be needed to achieve one's goals and while one has to be aware that life involves failure and frustration, such a person has a sense of confidence, of faith that by and large things will work out well.

Antonovsky notes that a radical change in one's structural situation—in marital status, occupation, or place of residence—can lead to a significant modification in one's sense of coherence. Conversely, an individual's sense of coherence plays a significant role in determining his choice of remaining in or changing his life structure. Thus it can become a significant factor to be taken into consideration when examining how persons function during transitional phases in their life. This may very well become the key in determining why some make it to a new stable situation, while others founder and become stuck.

THE TRANSITIONAL PROCESS

material tasks + psychosocial tasks [handwritten annotation]

In order to tie the basic definitions and concepts presented in this chapter to the changes which occur over the adult life span, we introduce at this point the framework which has been developed in previous efforts to examine crises and transitions.[23] This framework, which can be recognized as a variation of the problem-solving paradigm,[24] is cast in terms of two parallel and complementary sequences of tasks which have to be accomplished in order for the person (or family or small group) to pass through the transition successfully.

Material-arrangemental (instrumental) tasks are action-oriented and refer to the obtaining of concrete assistance and the carrying out of substantive arrangements and services. For each of the areas affected by the transition, the person or his agent must carry out the following series of steps:

1. Recognize the lack of supplies and services, the insufficiency or inappropriateness of the old situation, the need to "do something about it."
2. Explore available and potential solutions, resources, and possible new or changed roles; investigate choices and options, weigh alternatives.
3. Make a choice and implement it by applying formally for the solution or resource, taking on the new role.
4. Begin to use the new solution or resource, function in the new role; explore expectations, limitations, requirements, conditions, etc.

5. Go through a period of adaptation and development of increasing competence until performance rises to acceptable norms and pressures decrease to manageable proportions.

At the same time, since individuals tend to react during periods of heightened stress in complex, irrational, and often unpredictable ways, the person may have to engage in the following *psychosocial (affective) tasks*, which are largely thinking- and feeling-oriented:

1. Cope with the threat to past security and sense of competence and self-esteem; deal with feelings of loss and longing for the past.
2. Grapple with the anxieties and frustrations in making decisions or in choosing the new solution, resource, or role and the accompanying feeling of pressure, panic, and ambivalence.
3. Handle the pressures generated in applying for the selected solution or resource, in taking on the new role, and in meeting the stress and frustration in implementation.
4. Adjust to the new solution, resource, or role with all of its attendant shifts in position and status, feelings of inferiority or implied criticism from others, and lack of satisfaction or perceived appreciation from others.
5. Develop new standards of well-being; agree to lessened gratification, diminished satisfaction, and changed self-image until the level of functioning or way of operating rises to acceptable norms and the person feels comfortable in the new situation or role; come to terms with the new, different reality and begin to look for new ways of gratification and sources of enjoyment.

This dual series of tasks will be referred to repeatedly, both in Part II, when we examine the various transitions and attempt to map out their progress, and in Part III, when we consider the roles of help-givers in the intervention process.

3

Change Throughout
the Adult Life Cycle

IN ATTEMPTING TO WEAVE together the strands for a theoretical frame of reference by which to view transitional processes, it is patently impossible to be either comprehensive or thorough. In this chapter we shall briefly mention a small group of theoreticians and researchers whose contributions seem to have direct bearing on developmental and transitional changes in adult life.

Varying Theoretical Perspectives

ANTHROPOLOGICAL APPROACHES

Observers of primitive cultures have long been aware of the unique significance placed on the transitional periods in the personal and collective lives of the members and have recorded the elaborate religious and magical rituals which characterize such bridging phases. Over seventy years ago, Arnold van Gennep, a Belgian anthropologist, defined rites of passage as the ceremonies which accompany what he called the individual's "life crises" of birth, puberty, betrothal, marriage, fatherhood, advancement to a higher class, occupational specialization, and death.[1] Each change in social or religious status involves a shifting of roles: when children are born, married people become parents; when persons die, their spouses become widows or widowers and their children become orphans.

Rites of passage are usually carried out in three phases: *separation, transition,* and *incorporation.* Rituals of separation disengage the individual from his former social status, those of transition gradually remove the barriers to a new status, and ceremonies of reintegration mark his acceptance into tribal life in his newly acquired position. Critical problems of becoming male and female, of relations within the family, and of passing into old age are directly related to the reciprocal devices which the society offers the person to help him achieve his new adaptation and to allow it to adjust to him in his new role.

In describing and classifying these rites, van Gennep distinguishes between secular (profane) and sacred ceremonies. Passage from one physical territory to another, for example, may be accompanied by political, legal, or economic formalities, but the changeover is not as extensive or as ceremonial as the transitions which are magico-religious in nature and are marked by a series of exit, passage, and entry rituals that literally "open the doors." Rites of passage are particularly significant when performed for the first time; thus the rituals marking the *first* birth or the *first* menses are accorded special ceremonies.

Of course, not all societies employ rites of passage to the same degree. Margaret Mead notes, for example, that the tasks of young Samoan girls blend into their adult responsibilities without any abrupt shift. The learning process is a gradual one; initiation rites are not considered necessary, since there is no marked change in attitudes or difference in role and thus no specific point of entry into adulthood.[2]

Mircea Eliade feels that meaningful initiation ceremonies, which once had a place of primary importance in traditional societies, have declined in importance in the modern world. These ceremonies included puberty rites, tribal initiation into secret societies and confraternities, and initiation into a religious or mystical vocation. They were often marked by dramatic or even brutal rituals involving separation of the novice from his mother or the rest of the group and usually contained prohibitions concerning sleeping, drinking, and eating over a certain period of time.[3]

Nevertheless, occasions of birth, marriage, and death are still celebrated in almost all societies by a series of ceremonies in which the individual's new status is underscored and his new position in the community broadcast.[4] Other personal life events, such as initiation into a fraternal order or retirement from a company, may also be marked by specific rituals. Important milestones in the family life cycle, such as the coming of age of a child or entry into grandparenthood, become occasions for celebration within the kinship network and often make up the primary bonding-together activities of the group.

PSYCHODYNAMIC APPROACHES

CARL GUSTAVE JUNG.   Classic psychoanalytic thinking about the life cycle has tended to follow the path set by Sigmund Freud, who regarded adulthood primarily as the period in which early childhood conflicts involving parent figures are reactivated and reenacted. It was Carl Jung, once considered Freud's most brilliant disciple and colleague, who turned his major attention to the dynamics of adult life.

Jung differentiated four stages of life: *childhood*, from birth to puberty; *youth*, from puberty to ages thirty-five or forty; *middle age*, from thirty-five or forty to an unspecified point (about sixty-five) when it merges into *old age*. He felt that the serious problems in life that are consciously struggled with during youth and middle age are never fully solved; meaning and purpose seem to lie not in solving them but in worked at them incessantly and in waging the fight both within oneself and against outside societal forces.[5]

Jung felt that for most persons in the youthful stage, the demands of life put a harsh end to the dreams of childhood. If an individual is sufficiently well prepared, the transition to a profession or career can take place smoothly. However, if the individual clings to illusions that are contrary to reality, problems arise. No one can "take the step into life" without making certain assumptions which may turn out to be false, either in that they show a contradiction between subjective feelings and external facts or because inner psychic difficulties exist, even though adaptation to the outer world has been achieved without apparent effort.

As the person approaches middle age, he begins to feel more certain in his personal attitudes and social positions and to experience more of a sense of having discovered the right course and right ideals. Jung called this third period the stage of adult *individuation*, which he defined as the development process by which a person becomes "more uniquely himself." In the years between thirty-five and forty, the person's character undergoes a change: he begins to find a clearer and fuller personal identity and becomes better able to utilize his inner resources and pursue his own aims. This process of individuation enables the person to develop in a more balanced way his four psychological functions of thought, feeling, intuition, and sensation.

Jung also stressed the importance of the self-regulating psyche—man's ability to reconcile the opposite factors within his own personality: inner and outer reality, reason and emotion, introversion and extroversion, and so on. He saw the goal of human life, particularly in the second half, as the search to integrate these disparate elements and find a balanced whole.

CHARLOTTE BÜHLER.   When Charlotte Bühler began to examine the life histories of older adults, she developed a set of concepts which she called the *basic life tendencies: need satisfaction, adaptive self-limitation* (adjustment), *creative expansion, establishment of inner order,* and *self-fulfillment.* She was one of the first to look for general principles of change over the entire life cycle.

One of Bühler's important contributions is her stress on goal setting and goal restructuring. She sees the self-determination of personal life goals as emerging tentatively during adolescence, becoming more definite and specified during middle adulthood, emerging in later adulthood in a restructured way as a period of self-assessment and a review of past activities, and finally shifting in old age to an experiencing of life with feelings of fulfillment, resignation, or failure.[6]

ERIK ERIKSON.   With the publication of his first book on human development,[7] Erik Erikson started a series of significant works on changes within the life cycle of children, adolescents, and adults that has undoubtedly marked him as the outstanding influence in the field of human development over the past thirty years. His epigenetic formulation, in which he sees each stage as having a time of special ascendancy, has become the classic paradigm for viewing the life cycle.[8] Its most recent version is as shown in Table 3.1.

Erikson sees emerging in each life stage a key *psychosocial crisis*, which he defines as "not a threat or catastrophe but a turning point, a crucial period of increased vulnerability and heightened potential." From the core conflict emerge psychosocial tasks which must be dealt with before passage to the next stage can be effected. The way in which the individual resolves the crisis can either enhance or weaken his ability to master crises in subsequent stages. To Erikson, every acute life crisis also arouses new energies in the person and affords a new opportunity to rework heretofore unresolved critical issues. In another context, he describes the individual's life stages as "interliving"—cogwheeling with the stages of others, which move him along as he moves them.[9]

Although Erikson devotes only three of his eight stages to the adult

Table 3.1.   Psychosocial Crises in the Life Cycle*

Infancy:	Trust vs. mistrust:	HOPE
Early Childhood:	Autonomy vs. shame, doubt:	WILL
Play Age:	Initiative vs. guilt:	PURPOSE
School Age:	Industry vs. inferiority:	COMPETENCE
Adolescence:	Identity vs. identity confusion:	FIDELITY
Young Adulthood:	Intimacy vs. isolation:	LOVE
Maturity:	Generativity vs. self-absorption:	CARE
Old Age:	Integrity vs. despair, disgust:	WISDOM

*Adapted from Erik H. Erikson, *Adulthood* (New York: W. W. Norton & Co., 1976): 25.

years, actually a good deal of his thinking over the past twenty years has been devoted to this period. He postulates that once the crisis of ego identity versus role diffusion has been resolved by late adolescence, the individual must establish intimacy with a person of the opposite sex as opposed to remaining relatively isolated during young adulthood, must become productive or creative (generative) in the areas of work or family relationships or stagnate during maturity, and must achieve ego integrity by feeling satisfied and happy with his accomplishments in old age and accepting responsibility for his own life, as opposed to feeling despair, depression, and fear of death. Through his biographical studies of Luther, Gandhi, and most recently, Einstein,[10] Erikson analyzes how mature individuals recapitulate and replay the key issues which have emerged over the course of their lives. In a complex examination of Ingmar Bergman's film *Wild Strawberries*, he even extends this to an interpretation of the interplay between generations, in which each character is absorbed in his own ascendant maturational crisis yet blends his dialogue and actions to bring out basic social interactions with the generations before and after.[11]

DEVELOPMENTAL APPROACHES

Starting out usually from Erikson's life-stage theories, a number of development psychologists, social psychologists, and sociologists have contributed a series of theoretical and research findings regarding changes in adult life.

ROBERT HAVIGHURST. In an approach which closely parallels Erikson's views, Robert Havighurst postulates a series of developmental tasks which the individual must master if he is to mature successfully and gain life satisfaction. For the three stages of adulthood, he sets up the following groupings of tasks:[12]

EARLY ADULTHOOD (18–35)
Select a mate.
Learn to live with a marriage partner.
Start a family.
Rear children.
Manage a home.
Get started in an occupation.
Take on civic responsibility.
Find a congenial social group.
MIDDLE AGE (35–60)
Achieve adult civic and social responsibility.
Establish and maintain an economic standard of living.
Assist teenage children to become responsible and happy adults.
Develop adult leisure-time activities.
Relate oneself to one's spouse as a person.
Accept and adjust to the physiological changes of middle age.
Adjust to aging parents.

(continued)

LATER MATURITY (60 and over)
  Adjust to decreasing physical strength and health.
  Adjust to retirement and reduced income.
  Adjust to death of spouse.
  Establish an explicit affiliation with one's age group.
  Meet social and civic obligations.
  Establish satisfactory physical living arrangements.

KLAUS RIEGEL.   Klaus Riegel points out two contrasting approaches to the development process.[13] The first sees the life cycle as a process of ongoing development and evolution, a continuous accumulation of bits of experience and information, deemphasizing structural reorganizations. Sudden changes are viewed as disruptions, as "offensive disturbances"; crises are seen as unpredictable disruptions which do not play a significant role in the individual's achievements and development. The second approach sees the life course as progressing through discrete, qualitative leaps and organization of structures, with crises and catastrophes viewed as necessary steps in the process.

Riegel attempts to reconcile these two opposite approaches by proposing a dialectical approach in which changing events within the person's thoughts, actions, and emotions are seen as interacting with and influencing changing events in the outer world of which he is a part, while, conversely, changing events in the outer world influence the changing events within the person.[14]

He divides adult life into six developmental levels. At each level a sequence of events, some of which occur gradually and some of which are sudden, is co-determined by inner-biological and outer-physical conditions (Table 3.2). He draws a distinction between the timing of events that happen to males and those that happen to females and finds differences in the influences of psychosocial and biophysical factors upon each sex. For example, he sees the birth of children as having a strong biological effect upon the mother, while the effect upon the father is mainly social. He also points out that in complex family situations different events may occur simultaneously, each having a reciprocal effect on the members involved, resulting in different structural changes. Most often, gradual changes are triggered by sudden alterations, such as when a person enters college, is drafted into the army, has a child born, and so forth.

BERNICE NEUGARTEN.   Bridging the psychological and sociological approaches, Bernice Neugarten, points out that the salient issues of adulthood change over time.[15] *Youth* (the period comparable to Levinson's "transition to young adulthood") is the time when the ego's major task is confrontation with society, the sorting out of values, and the finding of a "fit" between the self and society. In *young adulthood*, issues relating to intimacy and par-

Table 3.2. Levels and Events in Adult Life

LEVEL (YEARS)	GRADUAL CHANGES				SUDDEN CHANGES
	Males		Females		
	PSYCHOSOCIAL	BIOPHYSICAL	PSYCHOSOCIAL	BIOPHYSICAL	
I (20–25)	college/first job, marriage		first job/college, marriage		
II (25–30)	first child, second job, other children		loss of job	first child, other children	
III (30–35)	children in preschool, move, promotion		children in preschool, move, without job		
IV (35–50)	children in school, second home, promotion, departure of children		children in school, second home		
V (50–65)	unemployment, isolation, grandfather, head of kin	incapacitation	unemployment, second career, departure of children, grandmother, head of kin	menopause	loss of job, loss of parents, loss of friends, illness
VI (65+)	deprivation	sensory-motor deficiencies		widowhood, incapacitation	retirement, loss of partner, death

SOURCE: Klaus F. Riegel, "Adult Life Crises: A Dialectic Interpretation of Development," in Nancy Datan and Leon H. Ginsberg, eds., *Life-Span Developmental Psychology* (New York: Academic Press, 1975): 107. Reprinted by permission.

enthood, and to meeting the expectations of the work world, with its attendant demands for restructuring of roles, values, and sense of self, must be dealt with.

During *middle age*, prominent issues arise related to new family roles: the responsibilities tied in with being the child of aging parents, and the reversal of authority when the child becomes the decision maker for the parent; the confrontation of in-laws who are strangers with the need to establish an intimate relation with each other; and the beginning of grandparenthood. Other issues include the increased introspection and reflection characteristic of midlife; the changing time perspective that becomes restructured in terms of "time left to live" rather than "time since birth"; the personalization of death—which means, for women, the rehearsal for widowhood; for men, the foreshadowing of illness; and for both, increased attention to body monitoring.

In *old age*, issues shift once more. Some concerns are related to renunciation: adaptation to losses of work, friends, spouse, levels of competency and authority. Others deal with reconciliation with family members and personal achievements and failures. Grief must be resolved, both over the death of others and over one's own approaching demise; one's sense of integrity must be viewed in terms of what one has been rather than what one currently is. A final issue is that of one's "legacy," traces of one's self that survive after death.

As an individual grows, says Neugarten, he learns what to anticipate. He is engaged in an ongoing process of socialization during which he is taught what facets of his childhood behavior he must shed to move into adolescence, what is expected of him as he moves from school to job to marriage to parenthood, and what are the approved ways of leaving middle age and growing old.[16]

Adults carry around in their heads a sense of the normal, expectable life cycle, an anticipation and acceptance of the inevitable sequence of events that will occur in the life course, and a recognition that turning points are inescapable:

> From this point of view, the normal, expectable life events do not themselves constitute crises, nor are they trauma-producing. The end of formal schooling, leaving the parents' home, marriage, parenthood, occupational achievement, one's own children growing up and leaving, menopause, grandparenthood, retirement—in our society, these are the normal turning points, the markers or the punctuation marks along the life cycle. They call forth changes in self-concept and in sense of identity, they mark the incorporation of new social roles, and accordingly they are the precipitants of new adaptations. But in themselves they are not, for the vast group of normal persons, traumatic events or crises that trigger mental illness or destroy the continuity of the self. [p. 18]

On the other hand, major stresses are caused by traumatic events which are unanticipated and upset the sequence and rhythm of the life cycle, as when death of a parent comes in childhood rather than in middle age; when marriage does not come at its desired or appropriate time; when a child is born too early or too late; when occupational achievement is delayed; when such events as the emptying of the nest, grandparenthood, retirement, major illness, or widowhood occur off-time and not in their expected sequence. *Timing* thus becomes the key issue.

SOCIOLOGICAL APPROACHES

Some of the sociological material on transitions has been couched in terms of the individual's role changes over time.

RILEY AND WARING.   Mathilda Riley and Joan Waring, in examining the role transitions which punctuate the life course, find two types of difficulties common to nearly all transitions.[17] The first is the strain of *learning the new role* and becoming oriented to the new position, of making the myriad adjustments and resolving the conflicts which grow out of the competing demands of the various roles simultaneously carried by the person. The youth who is making the transition to young adulthood must often cope at the same time with new demands at work, in the family, and in the community. Mature adults engaged in adjusting to the roles of old age must learn to structure the free time imposed on them by retirement, widowhood, or invalidism and to cope with their concomitant sense of devaluation.

The second strain inheres in the *dual nature of the transitional process:* each time an old role is given up and a new one taken on, a double process of learning and adjustment must take place. The person must relinquish the rewards and abandon the investment in the previous role before gaining satisfaction in the new role. Riley and Waring find that each new change in the long chain of transitions over the life course creates a discontinuity with the past. It also demands fresh commitment to a new role, which, in turn, must inevitably be abandoned.

Since role transitions in the life cycle tend to be taken for granted and experienced silently, persons are often unaware that others also find them stressful, posing threats to identity and to feelings of competence and mastery. Wide variations exist in the extent and severity of the problems experienced. Often role shifts become a rich source of new opportunities, challenges, and rewards, offering the promise of heightened self-esteem. On the other hand, they can lead to reactions of failure, hurt, defensiveness, and withdrawal.

While ideally individual and societal expectations should be congruent, in actual practice such conditions rarely exist. Some individuals may not want to assume the new roles prescribed; others may not learn them readily; and very few can master them to perfection. On the other hand, continual social change means that socially defined role expectations may often be unclear, facilities for learning the new role may be inadequate, and no suitable person may be available to model the new role and also express approval when it is performed well. Thus the periods of transition may be marked by feelings of inadequacy, insecurity, betrayal, and loss—creating intolerable strain and, at times, pressures for deviance.

Two conditions are suggested to ease role transitions. First, the new role must be highly valued by both the individual and society. Second, adequate social support must be provided: *instrumental means* (facilities, resources, and teachers) to aid the process of learning, and *emotional supports* proferred by friends and advisers to help release the frustrations and dissatisfactions engendered by the transitional process.

Riley and Waring note that whenever an individual goes through a role transition, others close to him are also affected. The new mother's success or failure in negotiating her role transition will also affect her husband's and new baby's *counterpart transitions*, as they experience their own role changes. When a young man leaves home, the network he leaves behind experiences complementary strains and must learn to relinquish him while the network he enters (college, the army, or his wife's family) must find ways to integrate him.

EVELYN DUVALL.   Family sociologists usually frame adult life transitions in terms of changes in the family life cycle over time. Evelyn Duvall, one of the foremost theoreticians in this area, divides this family cycle into eight stages of varying average lengths of time:[18]

     I. Married couples (without children): 2 years.
    II. Childbearing families (oldest child, birth–30 months): 2.5 years.
   III. Families with preschool children (oldest child, 30 months–6 years): 3.5 years.
   IV. Families with schoolchildren (oldest child, 6–13 years): 7 years.
    V. Families with teenagers (oldest child, 13–20 years): 7 years.
   VI. Families launching young adults (first child gone to last child gone): 8 years.
  VII. Middle-aged parents (empty nest to retirement): 15± years.
 VIII. Aging family members (retirement to death of both spouses): 10–15 ± years.

Duvall points out that a clearcut sequence of stages occurs only in families with a single child; in families with more than one child, an overlap of several years can be found at the various stages, with each subsequent child causing the family to repeat its interactions. Nevertheless, it is the oldest child who takes the family with him (or her) out into the "growing edges of family experience." In addition, some individuals do not fit into this typology: those who never marry; those who marry but do not bear, adopt, or rear children; and those who engage in other forms of intimate relationships (homosexual pairs, group marriages, communes, and other types of households.)

Duvall proposes the concept of *individual developmental tasks*—those that arise at or near a certain time in the person's life, the successful achievement of which leads to happiness and to success with later tasks, and the failure of which leads to personal unhappiness.[19] She points out that when an individual takes on a given developmental task, he must engage in four interrelated operations: (1) perceiving new possibilities for his behavior by reflecting upon what is expected of him or what he sees others accomplishing; (2) forming new conceptions of himself; (3) coping effectively with conflicting demands upon him; and (4) being willing to achieve the next step in his development by working towards it.

Parallel to and intermingling with the individual's tasks, says Duvall, are the *tasks of the family* at different stages in its developmental career. These are defined as the growth responsibilities that arise at a certain stage in the family's life, the successful achievement of which leads to present satisfaction, approval, and success with later tasks, and the failure of which leads to familial unhappiness, disapproval by society, and difficulty with later family development tasks.

Duvall sees critical developmental tasks as emerging whenever the family enters each new stage of its career. Critical transitional events (markers) such as being married, bearing children, releasing them as teenagers or young adults, and continuing as a couple through the empty nest and old age periods each necessitate new adaptations and impose new responsibilities, and at the same time open up new opportunities and pose new challenges. These tasks are listed in Table 3.3.

JOAN ALDOUS.   The personal role transitions of the individual members as they interact with the others within the family bring about sufficient disruption in behavior patterns to force change in the entire family's functioning. Joan Aldous observes that these new patterns are not established immediately.[20] A transitional period occurs during which the family flounders, searches for and tries out new ways of reacting and interacting before it sets up new modes of operation. These intervals serve to demarcate the stages in the family cycle or "career" and often become "points of no return."

Aldous sees a family developmental task arising at any point in its career when the needs of one or more family members converge with the expectations of society in terms of family performance. Generally, such tasks occur in five areas of family functioning: physical maintenance of family members, socialization of family members for roles in the family and other groups,

Table 3.3. Stage-critical Family Developmental Tasks Through the Family Life Cycle

STAGE OF THE FAMILY LIFE CYCLE	POSITIONS IN THE FAMILY	STAGE-CRITICAL FAMILY DEVELOPMENT TASKS
1. Married couple	Wife Husband	Establishing a mutually satisfying marriage Adjusting to pregnancy and the promise of parenthood Fitting into the kin network
2. Childbearing	Wife-mother Husband-father Infant daughter or son or both	Having, adjusting to, and encouraging the development of infants Establishing a satisfying home for both parents and infant(s)
3. Preschool-age	Wife-mother Husband-father Daughter-sister Son-brother	Adapting to the critical needs and interests of preschool children in stimulating growth-promoting ways Coping with energy depletion and lack of privacy as parents
4. School-age	Wife-mother Husband-father Daughter-sister Son-brother	Fitting into the community of school-age families in constructive ways Encouraging children's educational achievement
5. Teenage	Wife-mother Husband-father Daughter-sister Son-brother	Balancing freedom with responsibility as teenagers mature and emancipate themselves Establishing postparental interests and careers as growing parents
6. Launching center	Wife-mother-grandmother Husband-father-grandfather Daughter-sister-aunt Son-brother-uncle	Releasing young adults into work, military service, college, marriage, etc., with appropriate rituals and assistance Maintaining a supportive home base
7. Middle-aged parents	Wife-mother-grandmother Husband-father-grandfather	Rebuilding the marriage relationship Maintaining kin ties with older and younger generations
8. Aging family members	Widow/widower Wife-mother-grandmother Husband-father-grandfather	Coping with bereavement and living alone Closing the family home or adapting it to aging Adjusting to retirement

SOURCE: Evelyn Duvall, *Marriage and Family Development*, 5th ed. (Philadelphia: J. B. Lippincott, 1977): 179. Copyright © 1957, 1962, 1967, 1971, 1977 by J. B. Lippincott Company. Reprinted by permission of Harper & Row, Publishers, Inc.

maintenance of family members' motivation to perform family and other roles, maintenance of social control within the family and between family members and outsiders, and addition of family members through adoption or reproduction and their release when mature.

ALICE ROSSI.   Looking at family careers from a different angle, Alice Rossi calculates that a typical young college-educated woman who married at age twenty-two a man two years her senior, worked for three years after marriage, then had two children two years apart, became a widow at age sixty-five, and finally died herself at age seventy-four will probably have spent her fifty-six years of adulthood in the following way:[21]

> Thirteen years (25 percent) will be lived without a husband: four years of school and employment prior to marriage and nine years of widowhood.
> Twenty-three years (41 percent) will be spent with a husband but with no children under age eighteen: her first three postmarriage years and the twenty years after her youngest child reaches his majority.
> Twenty years (36 percent) will be lived with a husband and at least one child under age eighteen. Of these twenty years, probably only seven will be devoted to full-time mothering, when her children are of pre-school age.

Most young women can (but rarely do) anticipate that they will actually spend almost twice as many years without a husband or fully dependent children as with them, notes Rossi. Almost two-thirds of their adult life will be lived either alone or with just their husbands; only 12 percent will be spent as a full-time mother.

SOCIAL WORK APPROACHES

Social work theoreticians also use a dual perspective from which to view life-span development. In 1971, Frances Scherz described certain "psychological tasks for the family and the individual" that parallel each other, interrelate, influence each other's development, and are repeated at different stages throughout the life cycle.[22] She saw these universal family tasks as centering around three issues: (1) emotional separation versus interdependence or connectedness; (2) closeness or intimacy versus distance; and (3) self-autonomy versus other responsibility. They parallel the individual tasks of (1) separation and the working out of dependency needs; (2) closeness and the establishment of sexual identity; and (3) autonomy and the development of self-control and self worth.

More recently, Sonya Rhodes has offered a typology that adds a systems approach to the way in which the family and the individual life cycles link onto each other.[23] She sees the "cogwheeling" concept as central to the interpretation of the processes of change over time for the family and its members. The family life cycle is divided into seven stages, each with its key transactional tasks and core issues:

Stage 1. Forming a couple relationship: intimacy vs. idealization or disillusionment. This struggle deals with the building of a viable and durable relationship which involves efforts to achieve intimacy based on a realistic perception of the partner as a whole, rather than the idealization of the partner as a romantic image. The fundamental task involves assuming responsibility for oneself in the relationship, negotiating differences and conflicts, resolving unrealistic expectations of one's partner, and finding mutually satisfying ways to nurture and support each other.

Stage 2. The childbearing preschool years: replenishment vs. turning inward. The major struggle entails the development of nurturing patterns among family members so that emotional "food" is available to adult suppliers as well as to the helpless offspring. This depends on the presence of both inner resources and a responsive, caring environment that provides opportunity for refueling the adults as well.

Stage 3. The school-age years: individuation of family members vs. pseudomutual organization. Families at this level must shift the foci of their energies from family concerns to individual interests. The major struggle for the parents is to prepare for an identity not defined by one's roles and responsibilities within the family, once the children's increasing self-sufficiency and competence propel them out into the neighborhood and the community.

Stage 4. The teenage years: companionship vs. isolation. The rising sexuality of teenage children and the surfacing of separation themes arouse intense feelings for all family members, with the major crisis revolving around their ability to develop companionship within and without the family—with the children turning to peer group social networks and the parents revitalizing their marital relationship.

Stage 5. The years when the children are leaving home: regrouping vs. binding or expulsion. The essential task in this stage is to allow the children to depart as a natural outcome of their growth and maturity. Because the separation process is so intense and conflictual for all family members and because the children's disengagement from their family of origin results in major, sometimes sudden modification in the family composition, this phase is often particularly difficult. The core issue is the family's ability to foster and support individuation and the coupling process on the part of the children.

Stage 6. The first post-parental phase: rediscovery vs. despair. Although a period of disequilibrium of traditional coping patterns may follow the departure of the last child, the durability of the marriage depends at this stage on the adaptations sought to reestablish a satisfactory marital balance. The task of rediscovery refers both to a revival of interest in one's marital partner and a mutual attempt by parents and their young adult children to renegotiate their relationship on an adult-to-adult basis.

Stage 7. The second post-parental phase: mutual aid vs. uselessness. In this stage, which lasts from the parents' retirement to their death, the major task is to develop a mutual aid system which can combat generational disconnectedness and feelings of uselessness without loss of dignity. The adaptive capacity of aging parents and their mature adult children to achieve their developmental tasks—which involve spheres of competency, acceptance of real and psychological needs, and the ability to give and to get— depends on the interlocking roles of the generations. It also encompasses social responsibility and meaningful participation within neighborhoods, communities, and the larger society.

Recent Research on Transitions

Within the last few years, an increasing number of research studies on the adult life span, and more particularly, the transitional processes that mark the life cycle, have appeared. University-based teams at Berkeley, Chicago, Duke, Harvard, Johns Hopkins, and San Francisco have begun to report findings in their longitudinal projects on how normal individuals function and develop over long periods of time. New and intriguing projects have been instituted—at Yale, at UCLA, and at Michigan—to "flesh out" earlier theories of adult personality.

Reflecting the varied interest in the area, we briefly review five recent studies on development, and more particularly, transitional processes in adult life, each of which offers a different approach to the subject.

THE LEVINSON STUDY

One of the most interesting—and probably the most controversial—of these studies is the one carried out by Daniel Levinson and his team of researchers in Yale University's Department of Psychiatry.[24] Through intensive interviews carried out over several months, biographical and other data were collected on forty New England men in their thirties and forties. This was supplemented by a battery of psychological tests and by interviews with the men's families, friends, and even employers. From this the researchers developed a thought-provoking "anatomy of the life cycle," which builds upon and adds to Erikson's stages of ego development by centering more on the interaction between the self and the external world (see Figure 3.1).

Levinson proposes dividing the life cycle into five eras of twenty to twenty-five years each, with an overlapping transitional period of about five years binding each era to the next one. (Actually he collected data on only

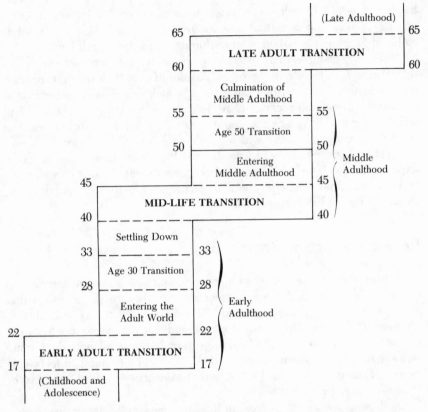

FIGURE 3.1.   Developmental periods in adult life span. SOURCE: Daniel J. Levin-son, *The Seasons of a Man's Life* (New York: Alfred A. Knopf, 1978): 57. Copyright © 1978 by Daniel J. Levinson. Reprinted by permission of Alfred A. Knopf, Inc., and the author.

the two central stages of early adulthood and middle adulthood.) Each era is made up of a six- to eight-year period of relative stability, during which the person's life structure is laid down and developed; then a five-year mid-era transition, during which the first structure is altered in response to the man's changing developmental needs; and then again another six- to eight-year period of stability and growth.

The primary task of each stable period, says Levinson, is to build a life structure by first making key choices, then forming a structure around these choices, and finally pursuing goals and values within the new structure. The primary task of each transitional period is to question and reappraise the existing structure, explore the various possibilities for change within oneself and one's social world, and move towards commitment to the crucial choices which form the basis for a new life structure in the ensuing stable period.

Choices made during a transitional period may lead to moderate or dras-tic changes in the person's life structure. These transitions are often characterized by periods of crisis during which the person has great difficulty in carrying out the developmental tasks posed by the period; he finds his present life structure intolerable yet feels unable to form a better one. Making a choice is often accompanied by a specific *marker event* (such as a divorce or major job change), which may last only a few days or weeks but which is embedded within a process of changes that may have started some time before and may continue for some time to come. The significance of the event varies considerably, depending upon the age at which it occurs and the tasks with which the person is engaged at that time. (For example, divorce at twenty-two would be very different in content and process from, say, divorce at fifty-two.)

A transitional phase comes to an end, not when the particular marker event occurs or when a developmental sequence is completed, but when the tasks of questioning and exploring choices have lost their urgency and the person makes his crucial commitments and is ready to start building, living within, and enhancing a new life structure.

As a corollary to the Levinson project, Wendy Ann Stewart investigated the life structures of women in their adult years.[25] She found that women during the age-thirty transition, show greater variability in the way they accomplish their developmental tasks than do men. This appears to be related to whether the woman forms a stable marriage and family life in her twenties or remains single and/or pursues a career during this time. Women's development during early adulthood starts out as practically identical to Levinson's description of men's, with separation from the family of origin and formation of a dream as the critical tasks for this period.

Those women who remain single and/or choose an occupation, tend to seek a relationship with a Mentor who serves as a model for realization of their Dream, as do men. However, for those women who follow a more traditional female pattern during their twenties, this period proves to be less provisional and the formation of a Mentor relationship less significant than the formation of a relationship with a Special Man, who creates a world within which this type of woman can live out her Dream. The mentoring function in such cases appears to be retained by the woman's mother or even by other women in the family of origin.

During the age-thirty transition, women who did not form a satisfactory home base by their late twenties tend to feel an increased sense of urgency to stabilize their lives. On the other hand, women who married and bore children during their twenties now tend to seek a less dependent, more egalitarian, and more intimate relationship with their husbands and begin to consider expansion of their interests outside of their familial roles, sometimes at the expense of stability and security.

THE VAILLANT STUDY

A more comprehensive and methodologically orthodox study than Levinson's is reported on by George Vaillant, a Harvard psychiatrist, who presents data on a group of ninety-five men who graduated from Harvard in the years 1942, 1943 and 1944; this is part of the larger W. T. Grant Study, one of the oldest longitudinal projects on adult development in the country.[26] Data were collected periodically on broad facets of the men's lives: family relations, friendship and work patterns, sport and leisure activities, politics, personal aspirations and satisfactions, and so forth. The men were interviewed in depth ten years later, and then by Vaillant himself twenty years after that.

Findings tend to focus on personality characteristics, processes of adaptation and adjustment, and the use made of ego defenses throughout the trajectories of the men's lives, Vaillant finds evidence that the Grant Study men, now in their mid-fifties, confirm the adult patterns in young and middle adulthood outlined by Erikson in terms of *intimacy* and *generativity*. However, he adds another dimension:

> In their early thirties, men seemed to be too busy becoming, too busy mastering crafts, too busy ascending prescribed career ladders to reflect upon their own vicissitudes of living. Equally important, they were too colorless, too conforming, to attract the attention of other observers at other ages. At thirty-five, the men of the Grant Study could not wait to step into the driver's seat. At fifty, they were far more concerned about those who worked for them and with them. In short, between Erikson's stage of *Intimacy* and his stage of *Generativity*, appeared an intermediate stage of *Career Consolidation*—a time when they, like Shakespeare's soldier, sought the "bauble Reputation." This maturational pattern of identity to intimacy to career consolidation to generativity has been confirmed for both men and women by the major American studies of adult development. [p. 202]

While he has not yet confirmed it through hard evidence, Vaillant already predicts from his subjects' comments that another intermediate stage will be found to be interposed between Erikson's *generativity vs. stagnation* stage and his *integrity* (which he calls *dignity*) *vs. despair* stage. This appears in the mid-fifties: *keeping the meaning vs. rigidity.*

Vaillant feels, like Neugarten, that events which occur at the appropriate time in the individual's life cycle rarely assume crisis proportions. Events are anticipated and rehearsed, grief work completed, and reconciliation accomplished without shattering the sense of continuity of the life cycle. It is only when life events are too sudden, too late, or too early that they become traumatic.

THE GOULD STUDY

Roger Gould, a practicing psychoanalyst at the UCLA Neuropsychiatric Institute, became interested in the patterns by which adults live out their lives.[27] He questioned some 524 white, middle-class persons (not psychiatric patients) who were divided into seven age groups: 16-17, 18-21, 22-28,

29–36, 37–43, 44–50, and 51–60. He collected data on their relations to their parents, friends, children, and spouses and on their own personalities, jobs, and sexual behavior.

Findings indicated that the late twenties were the most interesting and active period among the respondents, with marriages reflecting many of the stresses and strains of the period. During the thirties, Gould found a clear focus on the family, with considerable psychological changes and a rise in discontent over lack of money. In the 37–43 category, personal comfort decreased and marital comfort remained low; the early forties were held to be an unstable and uncomfortable time. Later in the forties, life seemed to settle down, with both friends and loved ones becoming more important and money less so. This stability continued into the fifties, with couples making the effort to reconcile themselves to limitations. Health issues also emerged at this time.

Gould sees the precise age at which adult life changes occur as a product of an individual's total personality, life-style, and subculture. *How* these changes are expressed and dealt with varies considerably from person to person; *what* they face is the common denominator. He is convinced that the primary task of adulthood is to correct some of the unrealistic idealized images that the child carries with him as he grows up. The adult must be able, throughout the stages of his adult years, to engage in an ongoing confrontation with his own "angry demons" and thus learn to view the world in a more realistic, self-determined way.

THE LOWENTHAL STUDY

A fourth study should be mentioned, although only the first round of data has been reported. Marjorie Lowenthal, Majda Thurnher, and David Chiriboga, of the Human Development Program in the University of California, San Francisco, Department of Psychiatry, began a longitudinal study in the early 1970s of how adults pass through, and adapt to, significant psychosocial transitions in their lives.[28] Some 216 men and women, largely white and of middle- or lower-class origin, were interviewed extensively as they were *about* to enter significant transitions in their lives. The sample included 52 high school seniors about to graduate, 50 newlyweds, 54 middle-aged parents, and 60 pre-retirees. The first two groups were considered to be facing incremental transitions, characterized by role gains and expansions; and the last two, decremental transitions, characterized by imminent losses or changes in familial and work roles (Table 3.4).

Questions covered a wide range of topics including the respondents' personal hopes and aspirations, their relations to their families, their friendship patterns, their self-concepts, their values, their feelings of happiness, their coping patterns, their past stresses, and their future expectations. The researchers found distinct differences between persons' time orientation

Table 3.4.   Principal Transitions (percentages)*

	HIGH SCHOOL		NEWLYWED		MIDDLE AGED		PRE-RETIREMENT	
	Men	Women	Men	Women	Men	Women	Men	Women
Work	16	30	16	8				
Education	72	36	40	8				
Marriage	4	30						
Parenthood	0	0	40	84				
Military	4		4					
Empty Nest					30	59	0	10
Retirement of Self					59	0	100	50
Retirement of Spouse					0	30	0	40
No "Main" Transition	4	4	0	0	11	11	0	0

SOURCE: Marjorie Fiske Lowenthal, Majda Thurnher, David Chiriboga, and Associates, *Four Stages of Life: A Comparative Study of Women and Men Facing Transitions* (San Francisco: Jossey-Bass, 1975): 203. Reprinted by permission.

*Empty cells indicate that the event was not coded for that group.

(whether they were past-, present-, or future-oriented), and between men and women. In the two earlier life stages men were considerably more involved in sociopolitical issues than women, but in the two older groups the position was reversed. Newlyweds were concerned most about the personality characteristics of their mates, but middle-aged men and women described them in operational (role) terms: e.g., the husband was the "boss." Marital dissatisfaction was greatest among the middle-aged women; they also described their mothers in largely negative terms but their fathers in overwhelmingly positive ones (in contrast to their descriptions of their husbands).

Men and women at all the stages differed markedly in their friendship ties: men tended to emphasize shared interests and activities, while women were more concerned with affect and reciprocity. Men showed an increasing mellowness, social ease, and comfort with the self as they grew older, but middle-aged women were almost as conflicted and negative as the high school seniors, both boys and girls. Women of all ages reported more stressful life experiences than men, but middle-aged men were worried about work-related problems and economic security and were bored with their jobs.

Men in all the four stages were more positively oriented towards the future, while women were divided: the psychologically less complex women seemed to be aging more contentedly, drawing upon their stress-avoidant feminine family roles and self-concept, while the more complex, better educated, and more intelligent women relied more on their sense of competence and more aggressive handling of stress. The newlyweds reported more stress experiences in their immediate past than did the older groups. The happiest men at pre-retirement were those who valued ease and contentment rather than more expansive goals.

Among the youngest group, the boys were much more likely to feel in control of and to plan for their coming transition than were the girls, while the middle-aged men felt least able to influence the conditions and circumstances of the changes ahead of them. Among women, it was found that planning was minimal and almost nonexistent among all stages; since few of them felt in control, they seemed to be relying on a "muddling through" process.

THE SHEEHY REPORT

Gail Sheehy is primarily a journalist rather than a social scientist, but her book *Passages* has aroused considerable interest (and discomfort) in academic and professional circles.[29] Writing in an informal, personalistic style, she intersperses her own interpretations with a broad range of material drawn from Freud, Erikson, Levinson, Margaret Mead, Judith Bardwick, and other psychoanalytic, psychological, and sociological theoreticians.

Over a period of three years, she taped interviews with about 115 men and women, aged eighteen to fifty-five, who belong to what she calls America's "pacesetter group," in order to discover what inner changes took place, to compare the developmental rhythms of men and women, and to examine the "predictable crises for couples." From this she attempts to generalize as to the different ways in which individuals and couples carry out their life tasks and develop their unique life-styles, and at which points they become bogged down.

Her report is a potpourri of virtually all the personal and social issues which have faced men and women in the last decade. Its chief virtue seems to lie in the tremendous interest and stimulation it has generated in adult life passages.

While different in form and content, the above studies all stress the sense of change and adaptation over the adult years. Having thus set the stage, we can now go on to consider particular transitional periods throughout these years.

PART II

Significant Transitions in Adulthood

In this part we shall look briefly at fourteen types of transitions which appear to affect significantly the individual during his adult life cycle, illustrating each by case examples taken from records of practitioners. Three of these passages—the *transition to early adulthood*, the *transition to mid-adulthood*, and the *transition to late adulthood*—can be considered "vertical" in the sense that each links together two developmental stages. These are comparable to Levinson's three major transitional periods, which he describes as "structure-changing"; each terminates a previous life structure and creates the possibility for a new one (see Chapter 3, pp. 37–39). During such bridging intervals, the underlying developmental pressure to grow vies with the equally innate resistance to change. We find that at times the inability to master successfully the psychosocial tasks from an earlier developmental level prevents the individual from proceeding smoothly into the next maturational stage, even though chronologically he may be well into the period.

The other eleven "psychosocial" transitions tend to be more specific and overt in their scope and effect. They may occur during a period of broad reorganization of one's life or emerge during a relatively stable period. They usually start out with a "felt difficulty" in a role network or area of social functioning that almost always involves some type of loss or separation from a person, place, or object (see Chapter 2). Though subjectively experienced, such transitions are often characterized by the need to adapt to some overt marker event, which triggers and focuses the push for change. The transitions we shall consider are:

Work, career choices and shifts
Transition to marriage/couplehood
Transition to parenthood
Geographic moves and migrations
Separation, divorce, remarriage
Untimely widowhood
Transition to post-parenthood
Retirement as a bridge
Health impairment
The path to institutionalization
Death of a spouse and survival of the mate

These specific transitions have been grouped loosely under each of the three general developmental ones, since it was initially hypothesized that a particular transition would occur during a specific developmental interval or within the next maturational stage. It soon became evident, however, that some transitions—such as those involving career shifts, geographic moves, and divorce—are not limited to any one age-stage. Some problems in classification appeared when it became evident that marriage at twenty-three, for example, is different in content and process from marriage at forty-five, or sixty-seven; the question arose as to whether we were dealing with the same transition. In fact, in the case of loss of a spouse, it was decided to differentiate completely between being widowed "before one's time" and losing a mate during the terminal stage in the individual's life cycle. Similarly, leaving one's job in early adulthood will be treated separately from officially retiring from the work world.

It became equally evident that the relationships between the intrapersonally defined developmental transitions and the more objectively discernible psychosocial transitions are inextricably interwoven. Indeed, as has been suggested, the tie may vary well be a spiral one: the internal and external pressures for the individual and/or family to carry out developmental tasks bring about changes in status, role relationships, or place, which in turn call for new tasks to be worked on, and so forth. Conversely, the inability to engage in these tasks may prevent the individual or family from making the called-for changes in status, role, or place, leaving them fixated at, or regressed to, a "stuck" position.

The classification of a specific case situation as involving one particular type of transition may seem, in some cases, to be quite arbitrary and artificial, often reflecting the orientation of the setting or the interest of the practitioner. During the 1978–79 academic year, while dividing my time between the University of California, Berkeley, and the University of Wisconsin–Madison, I visited a number of cities to present workshops, give lectures, and hold discussions on transitional states with practitioners in a wide variety of professional and academic settings. As a followup, participants were asked to submit case material from their practice illustrating such situations, the only stipulations being that some adult transitional issue had to be involved and that all identifying information was to be masked.

As indicated in Chapter 1, some one hundred twenty-five case accounts were compiled, from twelve types of settings: family service agencies, mental health centers, general hospitals, student counseling services, children and adolescent settings, public welfare offices, crisis clinics, special services for new immigrants, the deaf, and the aged, guidance clinics, and private practice. Interestingly, as noted above, similar situations were labeled variously as "transition to young adulthood," "work and career change," or "separation and divorce," depending on the source. For clarity's sake, at times it seemed expedient to reclassify a case, since the guiding principle was *not* the nature of the presenting problem but rather the underlying developmental issue with which the client appeared to be struggling.

The general procedure in each chapter will be, first, to recapitulate and present the theoretical framework for viewing the transition; then, to illustrate separate points with available case material. It will be noticed that sometimes the case situation will be sketched in as a vignette; in other instances, the entire treatment process will be included in summary form. Stress will be placed in this section on the transitional process; in Part III we will discuss strategies and techniques of treatment.

The focus in analyzing each transition will be on the *developmental tasks* which have been defined for each period. Wherever possible, we will attempt to view the bridging process in terms of the continua of material-arrangemental and psychosocial tasks outlined at the end of Chapter 2.

Finally, although it is dangerous to set an unequivocal timetable, in order to anchor our discussion of developmental stages, we suggest the following tentative time sequence for the adult years:

	AGE SPAN*
Transition to Early Adult Years	18–22
Early Adulthood	22–40
Transition to Mid-Adult Years	38–42
Mid-Adulthood	42–62
Transition to Late Adult Years	60–65
Late Adulthood	65–85+

*Unlike research categories, the overlap of years is intentional.

4

The Early Adult Years:
Laying the Foundations

Transition to Early Adulthood

THE POINT AT WHICH an adolescent becomes an adult is open to many interpretations. Some theoreticians have suggested that adolescence itself is a transitional status from childhood to adulthood.[1] Others have recommended a sharp differentiation between early and late adolescence. Kenneth Kenniston has even suggested that a new stage in the life cycle, after adolescence but before full asumption of adult status and responsibilities, be called *youth*,[2] while Peter Blos speaks of "postadolescence."

Blos points out that adolescence does not terminate according to some sharply defined criterion. The gradual decline of the typical adolescent mood swings, the sharing of emotions selectively with friends and lovers, the increased predictability of behavior and motivation over time; the stabilization of character formation, and the emergence of a life plan that involves reasonably attainable goals are all indices of the closure of the adolescent struggle. Added to these, says Blos, are the gradual change in the nature of relationships, personal and communal, in the direction of discriminatory involvements and commitments.

He sees four developmental tasks which lead the adolescent into adulthood: recapitulation of the individuation process for the second time; development of ego continuity through formation of a personal view of one's past, present, and future; mastery of residual trauma from childhood; and the formation of sexual identity as the base for the future establishment of stable, adult human relations.[3]

Beatrix Hamburg says adolescence ends when changes in social status occur, including the achievement of an adult work role. Ideally, she feels this would include pursuit of goals in which talents are used, interests focused, and a sense of efficacy established. Generally, it takes place in the context of autonomy and a renegotiation of the young person's relationship to his nuclear family.[4]

Levinson sees this period, the *early adult transition: moving from pre- to early adulthood,* as a developmental bridge between the eras of pre-adulthood and early adulthood. It presents two major tasks: (1) to terminate the adolescent life structure and leave the pre-adult world; and (2) to take a preliminary step into the adult world: to explore its possibilities, to imagine oneself as a participant in it, and to make and test some tentative choices before entering it fully. The first involves a process of *termination;* the second, a process of *initiation*—both essential to a transitional period.[5]

LEAVING THE PRE-ADULT WORLD

In regards to the first task of leaving the pre-adult world, Levinson sees as a major component the need to separate from the family of origin. This may proceed along many levels. Externally, it may entail moving out of the familial home, becoming financially less dependent, entering new roles, and developing autonomous living arrangements. Internally, this task may involve an increasing differentiation between the person and his parents, greater psychological distance from them, and reduced emotional dependency on parental support and authority. The older teenager may have physically left his family far earlier (through death of a parent, placement in a group home, being sent away to a boarding school), or he may still, for tactical reasons, continue to live within the confines of the parental home; in any case he must remove the family from the center of his life and begin the process of change leading to a new home base. Although he continues his attachment to his family, the nature of the relationship changes.

In addition, the older teenager must modify or give up relations with other important figures such as members of his active peer group, and must take a new stance toward the pre-adult aspects of his internal self and the social prerogatives of adolescence as an age-stage in society. For Levinson, as for other theoreticians in the field of transitions, this termination process involves experiencing a sense of loss, a need to grieve for what is being given up, and a fear that the future will not make up for past satisfactions.

The following case vignette illustrates this first aspect of the transition.

TERRI (#110)

Terri, age 18, a freshman in her first quarter at the university, came into the counseling center asking for immediate help. When seen on an emergency basis, she

appeared tense, anxious, agitated, and on the verge of tears. She looked very dis-
heveled and tired and spoke in a hurried, disjointed fashion. Her presenting problem was that she could not write an essay for her first English course; she felt
immobilized and thought she was "going out of her mind" with the pressures of
school. She had fallen behind in all of her classes and couldn't see any way out of the
immediate mess. She feared she was losing control and had worked herself up into
such a frenzy over the piled-up assignments that by now she felt she was driving her
family crazy as well as herself.

Terri was the second of three girls; she lived at home with her parents and
younger sister. She recalled feeling, as a little girl, that both her older and younger
sisters had special positions in the family and she did not. In the third grade, it was
discovered that she could not read, and she was labeled a "learning disability." From
then on, she received special help in a learning center; in addition, each day her
mother would set aside some time and close the others out while she sat alone with
Terri, helping her to read. They continued to work together into high school, when
her school difficulty shifted so that she became upset about having to write papers.
Again, her mother sat and helped her with her work.

This term, with her entrance into the university, her mother decided to withdraw
her help. She began to refuse to sit with her, told her that she would have to work on
her papers by herself, and said that her behavior was too upsetting and she (the
mother) could no longer deal with it. Terri became both furious and frightened at
her mother's pulling away and felt sure she could not do any school work on her own.
She let all of her course work slide drastically.

The counselor and Terri agreed to start working on two levels: to figure out which
of her courses could be salvaged by her efforts and to try to understand what this
writing difficulty represented, what was frightening her, and what the mother-
daughter relationship meant to her. Terri determined that her best chance was to
concentrate on the two courses related to her major. She felt that she was too mixed
up about writing papers and wanted more time to understand herself, that she
needed immediate relief from the paper-writing pressure. She decided to drop the
English course, and on her own, very effectively negotiated with one of the deans to
do this without getting a grade deficiency, even though the deadline had passed. She
caught up in her two remaining courses and completed them with grades of A and
B+.

In her work with the counselor, Terri recognized that she had clung to the picture
of herself as "disabled" because it gave her an identity, made her feel helpless and in
need of being rescued, and brought her a lot of attention. She began to grasp some of
her underlying anger towards her mother as well as her dependency and fears of
disconnecting herself from her. By the end of the quarter she decided to move out
of her parents' home and applied for housing on campus. The focus in treatment
broadened: to try to help her grow up, feel better about herself, and learn how to
manage her schoolwork on her own.

ENTERING EARLY ADULTHOOD

As mentioned above, Levinson sees the second major task of this transitional period as the formation of a basis for living in the adult world. It
involves the translation of a person's vague, ambiguous hopes and fantasies

about his future life into more clearly defined options and firmer choices. During this period, many young people are in college or other schools of advanced training; others have joined the armed forces or have taken first jobs. Levinson found that the majority of the men in his sample formed lives substantially different from that of their parents. Few of the men strongly rejected their roots, but the great majority maintained only tenuous ties to their family's ethnic and religious background. Half of his sample were married during this transitional period, as part of the process of separation from the parents and entrance into adult life.

Marker events which occur during this process of entering the adult world can have a crucial effect on the young adult's emerging life. The following case illustrates the influence of such an incident on a young Israeli soldier just back from the front.*

YOSSI (#217)

Yossi, age 19, seen in a hospital ward of wounded soldiers during the first week of the 1973 Yom Kippur War, was small, dark, and wiry, with a cap of close-cropped black curls. Half of his face and most of his upper body were swathed in bandages and he spoke in a slow, dragging voice. He said his front-line unit had been surrounded and was finally evacuated by helicopter when its position had become untenable. Most of his friends had been killed or seriously wounded. The doctors told him that his own injuries weren't too bad but he'd have to spend some weeks in bed.

Although it was hard for him to talk, Yossi managed to tell his story. He had been born and grew up in a two-and-a-half-room shack in one of the rundown slums of South Tel Aviv, the fifth in a family of thirteen children. His father had worked for years in a textile plant but developed asthma and had become partially disabled. For the past few years he had served as night watchman at the plant, and the family eked out a marginal existence from his meager earnings, disability allotment, and whatever the four oldest children, all married, could spare. They were poor, Yossi recognized, but had a warm, close-knit family who "looked out for each other." He had studied welding in a trade school before starting his army service, but now he didn't think he'd go back to it; in fact he didn't know what he'd do once he got out of the army. He felt disjointed and rootless, still somewhat dazed.

The attack on the unit had come as a total surprise; and it had been necessary to leave everything behind, including Yossi's most prized possession, a small transistor radio usually turned to the army's pop music band. He sounded very depressed when he told me of his good friends in the unit who had died; those who survived were now hopelessly scattered. He felt it would never be the same. As I left, one of the volunteers, a girl who had been waiting in the corner, came over to straighten out his bed. .

When I came back the next day, Yossi's mood had completely changed. He was sitting up in bed, while the same young girl was spooning him ice-cream. On the

---

*Going through three years of compulsory army service is part of the normal, expectable age-linked activity of people aged eighteen to twenty-one in Israel today, and it certainly can be viewed as a rite of passage to young adulthood in this society. That it erupted into active war during his service was a predictable hazard in Yossi's life.

bedside table, prominently displayed, was an impressive-looking radio–tape re-corder. He couldn't wait to tell me his good news. Yael, the volunteer, had heard him tell me about losing his transistor, so last night she told her father about it and they went downtown to his appliance store, where they picked out the latest recorder on the market. This morning she and her father brought it to Yossi as a gift of thanks for what he and the other soldiers had done for them "back at home." Mr. Meron even told Yossi to come to see him about a job once he got out. Yossi couldn't believe that other folks could care that much about him.

For the rest of the week, until he was transferred to a base hospital, Yossi was the life of the ward. Tape recorder on his lap, he made the rounds of the floor in a wheelchair, talking and joking with the other men. He kept repeating the story of his wonderful gift and said that now his life had taken a new direction and purpose.

Although this incident may appear to be unusually dramatic, the young man's quick "bounce back" is characteristic of his age-stage. Despite his own painful injuries and his preoccupation with the loss of his friends and the breakup of his unit, he was able to reequilibrate quickly, and with a new surge of hope and adaptation, begin to concentrate on the business of becoming a young adult.

As part of the bridge to early adulthood, and continuing throughout the twenties and even beyond, Levinson stresses the importance of the transitional phenomenon he calls the *Dream*:

> Many young men develop a conflict between a life direction expressing the Dream and another that is quite different. A man may be pushed in the latter direction by his parents, by various external constraints, such as lack of money or opportunity, and by various aspects of his personality, such as guilt, passivity, competitiveness, and special talents. He may thus succeed in an occupation that holds no interest for him. . . . Those who betray the Dream in their twenties will have to deal later with the consequences. Those who build a life structure around the Dream in early adulthood have a better chance for personal fulfillment. [p. 92]

Once a person enters early adulthood, which we set tentatively as encompassing the years twenty-two to forty, he enters a new developmental stage. It should be recalled that in Chapter 3 Havighurst lists the developmental tasks of early adulthood very tersely: (1) select a mate; (2) learn to live with a marriage partner; (3) start a family; (4) rear children; (5) manage a home; (6) get started in an occupation; (7) take on civic responsibility; and (8) find a congenial social group.

White, in discussing his longitudinal case studies of adult personalities, observes that natural growth during young adulthood tends to occur in five different areas: the stabilization of ego identity, the freeing of personal relationships, the deepening of interests, the humanizing of personal values, and the expansion of caring.[6]

Such changes are most observable in the carrying out of have been called the three major roles of adulthood: *work, marriage,* and *parenthood.* Each will be examined in terms of the transitional phases leading to entry into each role network.

Work and Career Choices and Shifts

Significant transitions in the work cycle occur at three periods in adult life: *when the adult first enters the work/career arena, when he changes from one occupation to another, and when he formally stops working and gives up his role as employer/employee.* Since the last will be covered as part of retirement, this section will concentrate upon the initial entry and the shifts that occur during the early adult years before settling down to one's major occupation. Middle-years work changes will be considered as part of the overall changes in mid-adulthood.

ENTRY INTO THE WORK WORLD

The choice of an occupation or career does not begin in young adulthood; its roots reach far back developmentally. Perlman points out that the young adult has already been conditioned by almost two decades of work required in school and by his relations with his family, friends, and school-mates. Work habits have been formed in the primary-school years, when the issue that Erikson calls "industry vs. inferiority" has been raised and faced.[7]

Theodore Lidz, in tracing the development of the individual,[8] views the choice of an occupation as the product of a long process that starts in early childhood when the three- or four-year-old begins to voice his diffuse and unrealistic aspirations to be, say, a fireman or a nurse. In his play he tries out various work roles, and occasionally one will "stick" and somehow become reinforced, develop into a favored game or fantasy, and eventually lead to an occupational decision. During the juvenile period the child dreams of follow-ing in the path of his various idols—space pilot, movie star, or some other glamorous figure whom he rarely knows personally.

Once the youth reaches his teens, he may settle on a work choice as part of his desire to be like (or different from) a parent or to emulate some idealized figure on whom he plans to model his life. Later on, he sets tentative goals and tests them out through summer jobs or part-time work; often during this period he may become imbued with idealistic plans to reform the world. If he goes on to college or technical school, contact with teachers with whom he may identify and peers against whom he can measure himself broadens his horizons. Eventually, says Lidz, he enters into a realis-tic phase in which he attempts to take stock of his own capacities and needs as well as the possibilities open to him. He weighs such considerations as what is most important to him, how much he hopes to earn, how much preparation he will need, and how this will mesh with other plans such as marriage or travel abroad. He crystallizes his goals by committing himself to a specific vocation, and then chooses his particular interests within the field, which means the acquisition of specialized skills. Lidz sees the young adult's choice of occupation as influencing profoundly his subsequent way of life and personality.

A number of theories as to how vocational choices are made have been developed, often within the framework of vocational and counseling psychology.[9] While discussion of these theories lies outside the framework of this chapter, it should be noted that Donald Super, one of the foremost theoreticians in this area, propounds five long-range developmental tasks: crystalization of a vocational preference (14 to 18 years), specification of a vocational preference (18 to 21 years), implementation of a vocational preference (21 to 24 years), stabilization within a vocation (25 to 35 years), and consolidation of status and advancement (35 years and over). He also proposes a series of specific problem-solving steps by which vocational choices are made: anticipation, awareness of the need to choose among alternatives, acceptance of responsibility for the choice, awareness of factors to be considered, knowledge of sources and resources, crystalization, use of resources for exploration and information, clarification, awareness of the consequences of the choice, specification, synthesis of information and choice, implementation, action on the choice.[10]

When our own hierarchy of tasks (listed at the end of Chapter 2) is applied to entry into the world of work, steps 1 and 2—recognition of the "need to do something about it" and the exploration of available and potential solutions—are closely interwoven. Often, because of the wide range of occupational choices possible and the shifting, evolving demands of the labor market, the young person may have had little opportunity to start to prepare for his specific occupational role during childhood and adolescence. Training for a specific job may vary from a few weeks for a supermarket clerk or an assembly line worker to ten years and more in the case of a physician.

During the occupational search and training phases, say Barbara and Philip Newman, the individual must evaluate the match between his own personal characteristics and learnings and the four central components of the work situation: *technical skills, authority relations, unique demands of the job,* and *interpersonal relations with peers.*[11] Most occupations require both an initial degree of aptitude and skill and, once on the job, a continuing upgrading of technical expertise. Thus in taking step 3—making a choice and applying for a position—the person must consider not only whether he has the ability to start the job but whether he has the potential capacity and technical means to improve himself successfully as he continues. An allied consideration at this time is whether he will derive pleasure and satisfaction from this learning process.

In steps 4 and 5 of the transition process—beginning to function in the new role and going through a period of adaptation—it should be noted that each job has its own particular status and its own place in the hierarchy of decision-making relations among people. An important aspect of job adjustment is determining who evaluates one's work, what criteria are used for making judgment, and what are the limits of job autonomy. The unique occupational demands of a particular job, whether it be welder or occupational therapist, include norms of self-presentation, productivity, and availability. The individual's task is to assess how well he fits into the required pattern and whether he can set up a match between his own capabilities and the specifications of the new occupational role.

Finally, the person must consider the nature of his relations with his fellow employees or peers in the work setting. He may find a relaxed atmosphere, with friends to share the joys and tribulations of the setting, who can work together, gripe together, and share common feelings of accomplishment that offset the stresses endemic to the job. Conversely, he may find he is entering into a work situation engineered to stimulate competition rather than cooperation—a situation in which "getting ahead" becomes the primary objective, often accomplished at the expense of fellow workers. The individual testing out a new job will have to decide whether the particular occupation or setting suits his own needs, demands, and vulnerabilities.

The following vignette illustrates the difficulties experienced by a young man in trying to explore, prepare for, and make an occupational choice. Although the original request for help was framed in terms of a marital crisis, the developmental issue of being stuck at a point in the transition to the world of work was quickly uncovered.

JAMES (#218)

James Baker, age 26, tall and lanky, with thin brown hair, dark-rimmed heavy glasses, and a sober expression, was seen by the intake worker in a family service agency on a high-priority basis after he called frantically that morning to ask for help in "bringing back his pregnant wife." He explained that Betty had left home that morning at dawn after an all-night argument, which started when he announced that he had been dropped from the city work-training program. The cause was a fistfight with his supervisor, who had bawled him out in front of the other trainees. Betty accused him of deliberately throwing away a good chance for a secure future in the city park service after her father had pulled considerable strings to get him into the program. Now she told him she was through; she was sick of working to support both of them while he "tried to find himself."

Background Information. The Bakers had been married for almost two years. They met at a student mixer at the community college which both attended. James said this was the fourth school in which he had enrolled. He had spent almost eight years searching to find a suitable "work line." Until he was a high school senior, he had planned to go on to study accounting and then join his father, a well-known tax expert in the community, in his office. That year, however, his father became embroiled in an unsavory scandal involving fee kickbacks and tax-dodge schemes.

James had been a rather sheltered only child, whose social and physical activities

were limited because of an early bout with
impaired vision and an unspecified "weak he
very upset at the time of his father's arrest an
attend classes. Finally, through the interventi
his exams during the summer and received h
rolled, again with the minister's help, in an
distance from home. After two years, he was
school, who felt he had no religious calling; inst
of the helping professions.

James started at the state university, plann
school level. However, he found the prelimina
and dropped out after one semester. He spent tl
the country. While living in a commune in n
severe case of pneumonia and returned home to live with his mother, who had by
that time divorced his father. He decided to enroll in the local technical college to
train to become a master carpenter. After two months in the program, while working
with a heavy power saw, he caught his right hand in the machinery and severed
several tendons. (Although his injury was repaired, he now has only limited fine-hand
movements. He uses a special hand strap to grasp a pen or a knife.)

Once more James left the program. Several months later, he enrolled in the city
community college with the goal of becoming a street-gang worker. It was at this time
that he met Betty, who was taking a part-time fine arts program and also working as a
secretary. When they decided to get married, they agreed that he would continue
school full-time while she worked to support them; then he would become the
breadwinner while she finished her studies. They moved into a small apartment and
apparently the arrangement worked fairly well for the rest of the year, although
James's grades were rather low, since, he said, he had "gotten out of the study habit."

Six months before James sought help from the agency, Betty discovered that she
was pregnant. They recognized that she would have to give up her job eventually,
and he decided to give up his plans for college. Betty's father, anxious to insure her
future, offered to take James into his contracting business, but after two months they
mutually agreed that he was not cut out to be a builder. His father-in-law then offered
to get him into the special training program which would lead to a city civil service
job and security. And now, James miserably admitted, he had "blown it" once again.

Intervention Plan. James and the worker agreed that Betty's leaving him was the
last straw in a string of discouraging events which needed closer examination. A
two-pronged program was suggested: that he and Betty come in together to work on
trying to make their marriage "jell," and that he be referred to the vocational testing
and counseling service of his previous college to see whether he could find an
appropriate work area compatible with his needs and abilities. At the worker's
suggestion, James called Betty at her parents' home, and an appointment to see both
of them together was set up for the next day.

WORK SHIFTS AND CHANGES

Levinson sees the initial choice of an occupation as just the tentative first
step in a complex sociopsychological process which extends throughout the

.[12] The transformation of interests into occupational
simple or direct process. He finds that the young man who
, easy commitment, without sufficient exploration of external
inner preferences, often comes to regret it later. On the other
he waits until the thirties to make a commitment or never makes
e is deprived of the satisfaction of doing enduring work that is suitable
himself and valuable for society. Occupational choice is seen as part of the
process of going through the "novice" or "apprentice" stage in order to
become a full-fledged adult.

In this connection, Levinson introduces his concept of the psychosocial
ladder.[13] During a person's twenties and until the early thirties, he creates
the foundation on which the ladder can be built. Gradually he climbs the
rungs and moves upwards:

> The ladder may have many rungs or few. The ambitions may be vast and
> burning or modestly realistic. The ladder may lead toward realization of the
> Dream or in another direction. It has both external and internal aspects and a
> man's course along it is shaped by both external and internal forces. Exter-
> nally, it may involve such things as status in an organizational hierarchy (labor
> grade, managerial or academic rank) and reputation in the community or
> occupation. The occupation usually provides a rough timetable for reaching
> various levels of advancement. If a man falls behind the timetable, he is afraid
> that further advancement is unlikely and the entire enterprise may be in
> trouble. Internally, the meaning of the ladder is colored by a man's concerns
> with fame, creative achievement, power, human welfare, the superiority or
> inferiority of his class or ethnic or regional origins, and parental injunctions
> and rejections from the distant past. [p. 142]

The typical adult, during his first years in the labor force, shifts from one
line of work to another, from one job to the next, until he finds a compatible
one. It should be pointed out that the original choice of occupation, like the
subsequent shifts, is not always a rational process. The part that the elements
of happenstance, luck, or "being in the right place at the right time" play in
such choices is an oft-noted but rarely studied phenomenon. (There is also
the associated factor of "knowing the right person in the right place.")

During this trial period, the person gradually builds up the knowledge
and skills suitable for his more mature occupational choice and enters into a
career line that he is likely to continue for the next thirty years. However,
even after settling down into an occupation and developing beginning skills,
he probably will face during his working life periodic demands to learn new
kinds of skills and deal with different materials, different applications of his
knowledge, and/or different markets for his particular training. The individual may be promoted to a new kind of work, reassigned to a different job,
or even discarded as obsolescent. At times, he may resist disruptions and
changes in his occupational world, feeling that the demands of promotion or

reassignment are greater than the concomitant rewards. Some people may even accept promotion and then decide to go back to their earlier, easier, already learned jobs.

The following case excerpt illustrates the ripple effect of a job change on both self-esteem and the social networks in a young adult's life:

DANIEL (#109)

When Daniel, age 24, called the psychiatric clinic of a large city hospital, he said he had problems at work and with his marriage. In his initial interview, he gave as his presenting complaint a generalized feeling of depression and boredom, an inability to involve himself in work, friends, or anything else. He had been going to bed at 9:00 P.M. and had missed work several times because he didn't feel like getting up in the morning. He said he felt negative about everything, which was not like him. These symptoms had started about two months ago, but he didn't know how to "snap out of his down feelings"; he asked for help in getting to the root of his problems.

Further discussion brought out that Daniel was involved in a number of vital life changes at the time his symptoms started. First, he was promoted from his previous job of messenger—a job with a good deal of peer social contact, appreciation for his services, and the chance to move about freely in the city—to an office job with only telephone, rather than in-person, contact with others and considerable supervisory responsibility. Second, a month before he sought help, he and his wife had moved out of the crowded apartment that they shared with another couple into a place of their own, which turned out to be unsatisfactory, and where their landlord was giving them trouble. Third, Daniel's original career plan, to work for about a year and then enroll in law school, had not worked out. Some months previously he had decided, after much soul-searching, not to become a lawyer as he had always planned. The decision was confirmed formally a month before he came to the clinic, when he told his parents and in-laws about his change in plans and the last date for filing his law-school application passed. A career as a lawyer had been part of Daniel's life plan; it had motivated him to work his way through college and had given him a sense of direction. Now, the giving up of this goal seemed to rob his life of coherence. The feeling of a lack of purpose to his life seemed to affect all his social roles: worker, husband, and friend.

Since Daniel appeared to be stuck on the need to find another meaningful occupational plan, treatment focused on this issue, along with the associated problems of autonomy, authority, and power. He engaged in some grief work over his lost career and began to consider reasonable alternatives. During this time, he began to make significant changes in his life structure: at work he was able to replace some incompetent subordinates, and he started to find his job less "hassling." He and his wife moved from their apartment to another one in a less depressing neighborhood. He began to see his friends again and do things with them.

By the end of the fourth session, Daniel reported that he was no longer going to bed early or missing work and his earlier lethargy and depression seemed to have lifted; he appeared very active and energetic. At this point, he decided that he could handle his life situation on his own and refused further treatment. While his problems were by no means resolved, the acknowledgment that a problem existed seemed to be enough to change his mood and "recharge his batteries." He left feeling that he had "more of a handle on things"; interestingly, he never got around to talking about his marital problems.

EFFECTS OF CLASS AND/OR ETHNIC GROUP
ON WORK PATTERNS

The influence of membership in a specific socioeconomic class and/or ethnic group on the person's work patterns, particularly during periods of transition, deserves brief mention here.[14]

THE EFFECT OF CLASS ON THE WORK CYCLE.   Emanuel Kay has contrasted the work life cycle of blue-collar and white-collar workers.[15] He notes that the young high school graduate who enters the blue-collar work force finds himself in a highly structured environment where, at the start, he is assigned the lowest-rated and simplest tasks to perform. He is paid the least and is the first to be discharged during economic pullbacks. Slowly he climbs up the work ladder, waiting out the years until, by his mid-thirties, he has achieved some security, is not as strongly affected by economic fluctuations, and has moved closer to the skilled, well-paying jobs which offer him opportunity for personal satisfaction. By his forties he may feel fairly well boxed in, but any change would mean giving up the seniority and job security for which he has worked all these years. Although he finds few options within his plant to make significant career or job switches, he settles down, in his forties and fifties, to a comfortable, secure routine until he is ready to retire.

The young white-collar worker starts out at a later age, since he first has to go on to college to receive specialized training in his chosen occupation. He enters the work force with high expectations as to his own worth and the progress he can make in terms of career development, status, and compensation. Initially, he may experience some disappointment, but since his profession is portable ("between his ears"), he tends to move around until he finds a place of work where he feels his skills are being utilized satisfactorily. The first years are quite exhilarating as he searches for opportunities to apply and develop his particular abilities. By the mid-thirties, he may find himself well up on the career ladder, at the middle management or professional level, earning a good salary and being recognized as a "real comer" with high potential in his field. The midlife crisis hits him hard, since by this time he has become highly specialized, with relatively inflexible job boundaries. He has two alternatives: to break out of the pattern or remain at the same level, increasingly uncomfortable and dissatisfied, feeling pressured by the new waves of ambitious young professionals who are pushing up from below.

In her searching study of fifty white working-class families, Lillian Rubin found a somewhat similar but less optimistic picture.[16] Men who were interviewed spoke of moving restlessly in their early years from job to job, seeking not only higher wages and better working conditions but some kind of satisfaction and meaning. By age twenty-five, many of the interviewees had held as many as six to ten positions, starting out in unskilled, low-paying jobs and gradually—in some cases—finding spots that still demanded hard work but also provided some sense of mastery and competence. At age thirty, about half the men were settled into jobs at which they had worked for five years, starting the long stretch of relatively secure and stable work years. The other half were still floating from job to job, their future problematic because they were unprotected by seniority and had chaotic, spotty work histories to warn off prospective employers. For them, transitional instability had become a way of life.

ETHNIC EFFECT ON WORK PATTERNS.   While the influence on work patterns of being part of a minority group is undeniable, it becomes extremely difficult to disentangle the effects of being, say, black, Puerto Rican, or Korean from those of being less educated, less socialized into the work ethic, and more prone to economic discrimination. The person's work history tends to be unstable, the intervals between jobs last longer—and he may sink rapidly into the apathy of the hopeless and helpless chronically unemployed. However, even after all of these negatives are acknowledged, developmental and transitional issues rising directly out of divergent ethnic socialization patterns still occur.

The following two brief case examples show the influence of cultural norms on two young people, attempting to break out of familial ethnic patterns during the transition of entry into the work world:

CLAUDINE (#136)

Claudine, age 23, was a slender, attractive young black woman whose underlying depression was evident despite her dramatic, defiant air. She had been referred to a family counseling worker from the consumer budgeting department, where she has asked for help regarding her compulsive spending. She now said she felt very frustrated over her inability during the last two years to break into her chosen profession of journalism; she disliked her present job in a book bindery.

Claudine is the older of two children. She was born in Philadelphia and recalls that since her early childhood her father had been hospitalized for long periods with a diagnosis of schizophrenia. Her mother tried to keep the family together but was also ill frequently. When Claudine was 14 they moved to Cleveland, to be near her mother's family. Here she did well in high school and became fiercely determined to change the pattern of her life. She left home at 17 to attend college on a scholarship.

Since her mid-teens, Claudine had worked sporadically at various part-time jobs but left each after a short while when she became bored and dissatisfied. After completing her college course and receiving her journalism degree, she had tried to find work in this field but so far had only been given brief, unsatisfying assignments. She felt far from her goal in her present job and was already considering moving elsewhere to "try her luck."

Counseling focused on providing Claudine with considerable support, helping her stabilize her external situation, and keeping her from trying to manipulate the worker as she had done with significant others in the past. During this process, she decided to give up her bindery job, contacted the local newspaper, and was given a part-time reporter's job. She moved to a better apartment and showed the first signs of beginning to gain control of her life.

In this next situation, the combined effects of leaving a traditional, structured setting and entering a new work world with unfamiliar demands made the transitional period very difficult.

SAMI (#208)

Sami, age 19, was a fresh-faced, good-looking young Christian Arab from one of the remote villages in northern Galilee. He was referred to the university counseling center by his dormitory houseparent two months after the fall term started because he said he was unable to concentrate, didn't know how to study, and felt he was going to fail in his schoolwork.

When first seen, Sami appeared very depressed and on the verge of tears. This was the first time he had been away from home for more than a day, and he felt bewildered and overwhelmed by the openness and lack of structure at the university. His father, a prosperous building contractor in the region, was determined to keep his first son firmly under his control. He already had picked out a spot in their village, near his own house, where he would build him a home; he had already chosen a bride for him when he would be ready to settle down; and he had a job waiting for him "under his eye." Sami, who was influenced by an older cousin who escaped the traditional pattern and attended the university, was determined to start off on his own but felt the strong counterpressure from his large family pulling him back. He felt lonely, unprotected, and confused.

Since Sami was in danger of being dropped from his program if he did not perform in his work role (as a student), treatment concentrated primarily on this area. Tutoring arrangements were made and he was helped to learn new study habits so that he could absorb the unfamiliar course material. He was also placed in a peer group with fellow students to help him find his way through the complex organizational network of the university. He was encouraged to cancel two courses and to concentrate on the others so that he could pass them by the end of the term. A benign, supportive atmosphere was provided so that he could deal with his difficulties in adjustment during the transitional period of his first year.

WOMEN IN THE WORK WORLD

The unique difficulties encountered by women in their work role as they pass through the life span are pinpointed by Havighurst when he says that, whereas the central role in adult life for men has traditionally been the worker role, women have been primarily wives, mothers, and homemakers.[17] The man is free to concentrate, as part of his transition to early adulthood, on preparing himself for his work career, and he spends most of his twenties and early thirties testing out and shifting jobs until he finds a suitable occupation; but the woman faces many more intervals of transitional uncertainty as she moves in and out of the labor market while juggling priorities in her primary roles.

Three main patterns among working women have been ascertained:[18]

Conventional: the woman drops her career when she marries or has children and concentrates on being a housewife with no intention to return to work.

Interrupted: the woman may drop work for a period when her children are small but intends to resume it eventually.

Continuous: the woman interrupts her work only minimally or not at all if she has children.

Probably one of the most significant trends among young women in recent years has been the increasing tendency to choose the third alternative: to combine full-time careers with marriage or a significant relationship (see Chapter 5), while often postponing having children until the early or mid-thirties.

Actually, a woman's work pattern has usually been shaped since childhood by her socialization into her feminine role, which may be affected by such factors as her parents' hopes and aspirations for her, her peers' values, the influence of her school setting, and even the messages sent out by the women's magazines she favors and the television programs she listens to.[19] Often her vocational decisions are constrained by the occupations which are open to her and considered appropriate for her by her social milieu. Certainly one of the most exciting social changes in recent years has been the affirmative action programs and equal rights legislation that have opened to women many fields previously considered sacrosanct to men. Unfortunately, the issue of a "woman's proper role" has often become obscured by irrelevant political and societal pressures.

In 1971, Cynthia Epstein put the young woman's work dilemma in a nutshell:[20]

The woman who has proved her capabilities in training cannot generally count on society for encouragement or her colleagues for fair treatment. She faces a difficult decision in weighing whether to begin a career that almost inevitably will involve her in a conflict with traditional images of her place in society and, perhaps, with her own images of personal fulfillment. Once past the initial barriers, she may be forced repeatedly to review her decisions as she faces successive conflicts between her personal life and her career. She will also have to decide whether to aim for the rewards men would expect as a matter of course: money, prestige, power, and work satisfaction.

Since then, although hard data are still sparse, an increasingly visible tendency has become evident: many of the earlier issues fought for by the women's movement have been internalized by young women, who have come to regard the building of their own work career as one of the primary tasks of early adulthood. Still, the young woman in her twenties often finds herself surrounded by pressures and counterpressures as she attempts to carry out this developmental task. Stewart, already mentioned in Chapter 3, found two diverging patterns.[21] Some of the women she studied chose to remain single throughout their twenties, pursued an occupation, and sought a relationship with a mentor who served as the model for the realization of their personal dream. By their early thirties, these women felt an increased sense of urgency to stabilize their lives and settle down by getting married and having children. On the other hand, the women who followed the more traditional pattern of marrying early, having children, and facilitating their Special Man's Dream began to feel dissatisfied by the time they reached their thirties. They then started the task of "opening up," pursuing their own occupations, and switching to their own individualistic dream. In either case, both groups of women, who had entered the transition to early adulthood with aspirations and life structures very similar to men's, had developed far more complex life structures by their mid-thirties.

Lucile Duberman sees the primary difference in work patterns among women during this stage as not a question of marriage, but a question of having children. She points out that women with children have a higher probability of an interrupted work history:[22]

> With the advent of children, women are likely to curtail if not discontinue their work lives. As the children grow older, or when women divorce or are widowed, the tendency is to return to work. . . . Typically, females work full-time between the ages of twenty and twenty-three. At this point they either give up work completely or hold part-time jobs. At the age of forty, they return to work.

The woman who chooses the second alternative listed above, that of interrupting (or never starting) her work career with the advent of marriage and parenthood, often finds the decision precipitated by some type of crisis or increased stress. Myrna Weissman and her colleagues, in studying the plight of the educated woman who attempts to reenter the work network after having been a housewife and mother, found that the search for work often occurred (1) during a period of transition associated with a recent move; (2) in connection with the giving up of another job; or (3) as part of a conscious effort to overcome the boredom, depression, and social isolation felt as a housewife. For many of the women, reentry into the work world was tied to their children's starting school. They were not only looking for a job, but were seeking emotional encouragement and support during a period of reassessment of skills and interests, often accompanied by a change of career and further training.[23]

Whatever the woman's reasons for wanting to reenter the work world, it

has been found helpful to view the reentry process as a series of stages—
which closely corresponds to the steps in the transitional sequence sketched
in Chapter 2.[24] This model is used in group vocational counseling work with
adult women:

Stage 1. Vague Discontent. Many women experience a confusing sense of
discomfort about their present life; they feel bored and depressed but
are unable to pinpoint the difficulty.

Stage 2. Inner Preparation. The potential reentry woman tentatively
decides she wants to become involved in new roles outside of the home
and applies for counseling.

Stage 3. Intensive Family Involvement. Before fully committing herself to
serious exploration of her options, she needs to share her new thinking
with her family in order to prevent later conflicts and to help her make
a decision.

Stage 4. Assessment. She undergoes a process of identifying her abilities
and interests, including skills used in family management and volunteer activities.

Stage 5. Generating Alternatives. With a clearer assessment of her
abilities and interests, she is now ready to generate options and engage
in dreams and fantasies to help raise her aspirations level and
"stretch."

Stage 6. Narrowing Alternatives and Clarifying Values. The woman now
begins to reduce her options through clarifying life and work values,
using the guiding question, "What alternatives will allow me to implement my preferred life-style?"

Stage 7. Implementation and Goal Setting. She is helped to define both
her overall long-term goals and her manageable short-term goals, and
begins to implement them with continuous support from the counselor
and her peers.

In this type of program, the focus is specifically on helping the woman
pass through the uncertainty of the reentry transition and developing a
sound base for her activities in the latter part of the early adult life stage. The
transition to the work scene assumes a completely different aspect when
considered as part of the empty-nest transition in mid-adulthood, as will be
discussed in Chapter 8.

5

Transition to Marriage/Couplehood

IN THIS CHAPTER WE TURN to the first two processes by which the individual attempts to deal with the central issue of young adulthood, intimacy vs. isolation, through the formation of a partnership with another person in a committed relationship. Getting married is a critical role transition period for couples who are doing so for the first time.* It involves two people moving out from their families of orientation to the unfamiliar husband-wife relationship.[1] Typically it occurs during their early or mid-twenties, and despite the rising divorce rates and "alternate" patterns of couple relationships, it constitutes the predominant framework for adult living in today's society.

The transitional process that starts with the choice of a marital partner and then goes on to the trial period of the engagement, which leads up to the wedding ceremony, the honeymoon, and the first period of marital adjustment, has been studied extensively as the first stage in family development and as an important milestone in the individual's life cycle. With this, the

---

*When I first began to speak about marriage, I was pointedly reminded by my students that the development of a lasting relationship does not necessarily imply a formal wedding ceremony. I must make it clear, therefore, that I am speaking not about any particular religiously or civilly sanctioned ritual but about a joint commitment over time between two people, usually implying the establishment of a common household, the sharing of living and financial responsibilities, and the interweaving of personal life-styles into a single unit.

marital role network, which will continue to function for most of the couple's life until death, divorce, or separation disrupts it, will become operational.

THE DECISION TO MARRY

The transition from single to married status usually starts with what has been termed the state of "marital readiness." Theoretically, a person would be ready for marriage or couplehood when he/she feels able to enter into a shared intimacy that includes sexual enjoyment and commitment; shows a capacity for tenderness and affection for the other person; displays interest in that person's emotional condition and personal adjustment; indicates a readiness to merge personal plans for the future; is willing to share economic problems and be realistic about ability to contribute to the maintenance of the joint household; and is able to delay immediate personal gratification in order to meet the needs of the other and to build the relationship. In practice, since many young adults still have to complete previous developmental tasks left over from earlier stages, particularly those related to the issues of individuation and identity-formation, difficulties often emerge throughout the transitional period.

Needless to say, the decision to marry is a complex, many-layered judgment, which merges into the question of the choice of a partner. Factors associated with the individual's previous situation (what he is "marrying from"), his current reality, and his anticipated condition (what he is "marrying to") carry varying weights. Lidz points out that the child's early wish to marry a parent becomes transformed during early adolescence into fantasies about parental substitutes such as teachers and older family friends, or into crushes on idols of the peer group. These later give way to trial behavior with adolescent peers themselves, while the young person is still daydreaming of the perfect mate. In late adolescence, dating begins to assume the significance of courtship experiences, including "going steady," testing out sexual compatibility, and experimenting with living together for a period. With the entrance into early adulthood, the person descends from romantic dreams to more concrete reality, but through the process of "falling in love," magnifies his/her reasonably prosaic choice of a partner into "the most wonderful person in the world."[2]

William Lederer and Don Jackson, in their iconoclastic appraisal of the "being in love myth," quote Harry Stack Sullivan's definition of love: "When the satisfaction or the security of another person becomes as significant to one as is one's own satisfaction or security, then the state of love exists." They then go on to point out some actual reasons why people get married: because they lose most of their judgment during courtship, because they feel society expects it of them, because their parents have pressured or maneuvered them into it prematurely and carelessly, because they have an unconscious desire to improve themselves, because their own neuroses pressure them, or because they miss their father or mother and seek a person who will take the parental role for them.[3]

Aldous notes that earlier studies on mate selection posited the operation of a filtering process by which limited linkages in interaction episodes eventually led to greater commitment based on the need for "complementarity." Those pairs who lacked this ability to meet each other's needs dropped the relationship and were filtered out of the selection process. More recent studies, however, show that current couple relationships seem to progress more quickly than in the past, with a greater emphasis on "co-orientation," attachment, and joint activities. Instead of partner similarity being the critical factor in the courtship process that leads to marriage, it is the construction of a "pair community" that is significant.[4]

The desire to leave home at any cost, the social pressures of peers ("All of my friends were getting married and it seemed the thing to do"), unanticipated pregnancies, and the timing of specific events such as graduation from high school or college or the getting of a first job are forces that can escalate the decision. Rubin found that among working-class families the desire to escape the grind of poverty, the pressure of parents fearful that they will lose control of their children (who will end up "on the streets" or in jail), and the urgencies in children from broken homes, born of the need to find a place in which to feel safe and to belong, precipitate young people to marry at an early age.[5] On the other hand, sometimes marriage has to be postponed because of the obligation to support a widowed mother or a retired father.[6]

From their research on 2,000 couples, largely white and middle class, Robert Ryder, John Kafka, and David Olson developed a profile of the phases in the transition to marriage in early adulthood.[7] They delineated the steps in the *courtship* phase.

1. *Initiation.* The first meeting, almost always arranged by friends through parties, double-dates, or even deliberate matchmaking, is usually recalled as uneventful.

2. *Latency.* The couple feels free and uninvolved, able to drop the relationship with no great effort. Friends and relatives maintain a benevolent attitude toward them, often facilitating meetings and providing continued opportunities for activities together.

3. *Precommitment.* The moment of truth for the couple arrives when they have to face the serious implications of their involvement. It may lead to open or covert struggles, including facing the opposition from others, and may often be provoked by some indicator of seriousness which forces the need to decide whether to continue or to break up. Friends who previously abetted the relationship may now obstruct communication or try to separate the couple. Parental opposition, particularly from mothers, may emerge and escalate at this time.

4. *Commitment*. By this time, opposition has died down and there is general acceptance of the relationship. Concerns shift from *whether* the marriage will take place to *how* it can best be managed: Who will arrange the wedding? How will income and property be distributed? What will be done about children? The individuals feel themselves part of an inevitable sequence of events, swept along by an inexorable social process. Parents and friends now engage in confirming activities; they treat the pair as a couple and give showers and bachelor parties as reinforcing rituals.

5. *Transition point*. The culmination of the process is the wedding, when friends and relatives offer reassurance in case of last-minute misgivings. The couple feels that the event has been taken out of their hands, that it is external to their own feelings and must be "made the best of."

In a perceptive and sensitive study of the *getting-married* process which was carried out some years ago and is still considered a landmark in this area, Rhona and Robert Rapoport differentiate three subphases: the engagement period, which ends with the rite of passage of the wedding ceremony; the honeymoon interval; and the early marriage period. For each phase, they outline specific intrapersonal and interpersonal tasks that have to be carried out.

THE ENGAGEMENT

INTRAPERSONAL TASKS.   During the engagement period each person has to deal with three intrapersonal tasks: making oneself ready to take over the role of husband or wife; disengaging oneself from, or altering the form of, other close relationships that compete or interfere with commitment to the new marital relationship; and accommodating patterns of gratification of premarital life to patterns of the newly formed couple relationship.[8]

The first task corresponds to the question of how ready is each one of the couple, as an individual, to enter into the new status of being married and to perform adequately in the marital role. Indicators can be found in the man's preparations to take on the roles of worker, breadwinner, and supporter, and in the woman's acceptance of the roles of homemaker, helper, and enhancer.*

As for the second task, some individuals deal with the question of disengagement from previous relationships—whether they be with a parent, a sibling, a friend, an associate at work, or a peer group—*before* they become engaged, while others need to focus on this distancing process *during* the engagement period. The third task, accommodating the competing gratifications of premarital life to the new relationship, deals with the shift

---

*The sample was drawn from a lower-class and lower-middle-class population, which tended to be more traditional in its outlook and roles than other socioeconomic strata.

from self-oriented pleasures prior to the marriage to couple-oriented mutuality by the end of the engagement period.

INTERPERSONAL TASKS.   The second set of major engagement-period tasks involves the couple's interpersonal preparation for marriage: establishing a couple identity; developing a mutually satisfying sexual adjustment and agreement as to family planning; setting up a reliable system of communication between themselves; working out mutually satisfactory patterns of behavior in regard to relatives, friends, work, and decision making; and making specific plans for the wedding, honeymoon, and early months of marriage.

In today's world, where premarital sexual intimacy and living together for varying periods of time is common practice, couples often forego the formality of an announced engagement, although this varies considerably with social custom and geographic location. In many instances, the cohabitation interval serves as a transitional process during which the two young adults test out their growing commitment and adjustment to each other. In other situations, this interval becomes a mutually compatible arrangement that allows for flexibility of career and other social involvements, continuing until one or both partners decide either to escalate or to terminate the relationship.

THE HONEYMOON

In an exhaustive examination of the honeymoon that usually follows the wedding ceremony,[9] Rapoport and Rapoport define it as a "phase of partial physical and social withdrawal of the newly married couple from the rest of the world, particularly the world of their prior social relationships." It may take a variety of forms: the lovers' nest in specially designated places, the automobile trip, the vacation filled with diversions—all aimed at affording the newlyweds a period of enforced relaxation and seclusion in order to develop intimacy and meld them into a married unit.

The convention of the honeymoon seems to serve a unique function in the development of a couple's relationship. It often acts, together with the wedding ceremony itself, as a definitive rite of passage which marks the change in the nature of the bond. Even today, when many couples have lived together for quite a while, they frequently mention their decision to go away together for varying lengths of time or to isolate themselves from the rest of their social world as a ritual to signal their newly married state.

INTRAPERSONAL TASKS.   The Rapoports posited two intrapersonal tasks to be carried out during this interval: developing competence in engaging in appropriate sexual relations with the partner and learning to live together in a close, formal, socially sanctioned association. Most young couples tend to be concerned about their sexual performance and the honeymoon offers each partner the maximal opportunity to test out fears: the woman's worries about frigidity and the man's about impotence. They will have the chance to try out different sexual techniques at leisure, and to indicate their preferences concerning position, initiation, frequency, and the nature and desirability of orgasm.

The second task is more prosaic but equally as important. Previous intervals in dwelling together with others, such as a roommate at school or even a member of the opposite sex in a casual relationship, do not directly prepare the person for the beginning of living very intimately with a marital partner. This experience often stirs up strong feelings about the issues of autonomy, dependency, unity, and separation. The honeymoon provides the chance to test out each person's reactions to sharing the same bed, using the same bathroom, undressing freely in front of each other, and engaging in other intimate acts of daily living.

Again, even when the partners have previously shared the same living quarters, they frequently report, "It's different now that we are married." Thus the honeymoon allows them a "running in period" to work out the new structure of their living arrangements and develop new patterns of role sharing or solidify old ones. The honeymoon often tests the extent to which each can give up part of his/her independence in favor of adaptation to living with the other.

INTERPERSONAL TASKS. Following from the above, the first task in this area, according to the Rapoports, is to develop the basis for a mutually satisfactory sexual relationship together. The honeymoon can provide the couple with both the uninterrupted time and the unprecedented opportunity to deal with discrepancies in expectations and performance, so that they can understand more fully each other's sexual needs and preferences, and increase the degree of their pleasure and satisfaction with the other.

The second task is to gain a mutually satisfactory shared experience which will act as the basis for developing the husband-wife relationship. The honeymoon provides both an experience in cooperative living and a sense of predicting what the couple's future joint life will be like. The feeling of harmony gleaned from their shared activities and the degree to which the experience is seen as memorable serve to crystallize either a positive emotional tone made up of feelings of trust, relaxation, security, and admiration or its negative counterpart. In either case, the experience often sets the mode for the entire marriage.

Ideally, the honeymoon is designed to give the newly married pair privacy in which to discover one another and the joys of being married. In actuality, according to accounts of young couples, it rarely seems to work out as smoothly as anticipated. Even when they are familiar with each other's personal and sexual patterns and have lived together for a time, the constraints of the marriage contract and their past unresolved conflicts often put a damper on the quality of their relationship. The following excerpt from a private practitioner's casebook illustrates this point.

SHIRLEY (#153)

Shirley, age 23, was referred by a friend who became worried because she had not left her apartment since she and her new husband, Gil, returned from their honeymoon three weeks ago. She seemed to spend most of her time either sleeping or crying. When seen, she appeared very unhappy, although she was visibly trying to control her tears. She said that nothing had gone right since the wedding a month ago; Gil was being very patient with her but she knew she was "driving him out of his mind." She was unable to stop crying, except for the long hours she spent sleeping, sometimes up to fifteen hours a day, and she felt unable to return to her job as receptionist in a dentist's office.

Shirley, pretty, dark, and dramatic, was the oldest of three children. Her father, an engineering consultant, had died three years previously of a heart attack, in his late forties. Her mother, 45, managed a travel agency; one brother, 21, was a senior in college, and a younger sister, 17, was a senior in high school. Shirley, "no great brain," elected not to go on to college, despite her parents' disappointment, and she had held a series of "unimportant jobs" over the past five years. She had moved out of her parents' home into an apartment with two girlfriends four years ago.

At this point in the interview, Shirley began to cry. She said she had always been her father's favorite but had given him "nothing but trouble." She used to fight with her mother all through her teens, but her father would take her part and tell her mother to stop picking on her. Even after she left home and had a series of relationships with young men, he would tell her to take her time and not be hasty in her choice. Shortly before his death she had moved in with a steady boyfriend, of whom her parents disapproved. Her mother "ranted and raved" but her father said very little; nevertheless, after his death, her mother blamed Shirley for having caused his heart attack.

Shortly after her father died, Shirley broke off with this boyfriend and moved back home. Nothing was the same, however; her mother had become very bitter, accusing her of having ruined her (the mother's) life. Finally, "to keep her sanity," Shirley left home again two years ago. She tried enrolling in college but it didn't work out. A year ago she met Gil, who was in engineering school; she saw him as quiet and supportive, much like her father. Her mother again opposed the match, feeling Shirley could do better for herself, and Gil's parents felt they should wait until he graduated and was established. But Shirley felt very lonely and depressed and envied her friends who were already married, so they decided to marry between semesters. They had a small wedding, since finances were limited, and then went off for a week's honeymoon to a nearby ski resort.

Again Shirley broke down during the interview, saying the marriage was a "disaster." Both of them had been exhausted after having made all the wedding arrangements themselves and moving her things over to his place. After the ceremony, they drove directly to the resort, only to find that the heating system had broken down and their room was freezing. Although it was repaired the next day, this put a damper on the whole week. Gil kept getting quieter and more remote and she began to feel it was all her fault. Sexual relations were constrained and "no bells were ringing." She refused to go out on the ski slope and he'd leave her for hours while she stayed in their room crying; on his return, she'd start to chatter, as she usually did when she got nervous, and he wouldn't even answer her. They stuck it out for the week, but she began to feel they had made a terrible mistake. The worst thing was that they no longer seemed able to talk to each other freely as they used to do. Now, since their return, Shirley had been afraid to visit her mother or friends; she was sure everyone would know the situation and tell her that it served her right.

THE FIRST MONTHS OF MARRIAGE

With the return of the couple from the honeymoon, their life as a formal married pair begins in earnest. They must find a way for each to continue his/her personal development and various individual roles with the minimum of friction; to reorganize the behavioral patterns that each has learned in the family of origin, which may involve widely differing ethnic and social customs; and to develop ways of establishing a harmonious mutuality to cushion the inevitable strains of the first months. Lidz describes what the period is like when the marriage gets off to a good start:[10]

> Life becomes a new adventure filled with opportunity to live out what has long been imagined. Each partner relishes having another person so interested in his or her well-being and feels secure in being the center of the spouse's interest and love. Activity, thought, and fantasy have a tangible and legitimate focus which gives a new coherence to one's life. . . . The freedom of sexual intimacy and mutual exploration lends excitement which, in turn, leads to a newfound calm. Each partner makes mistakes and is apt to misunderstand, but evidence of love negates any intent to hurt. The glow of the first months of marriage, with its romantic and even unrealistic overassessment by the spouses of each other, can provide an opportunity for the couple to gain a true familiarity with one another, to gain reciprocal roles, to learn how to share their lives. [p. 435]

During this period, three sets of interlocking developmental tasks must be carried out: his, hers, and theirs. The new husband needs to continue to develop as a young adult and to become established in his occupation (see Chapter 4); to assume his share of the responsibility for support of the family, both for the present and projecting toward the future; to develop competence in his role as sex partner; to begin to share his intimate thoughts and feelings with his wife; to participate in setting up and running the household; and to engage in mutual social and leisure-time interests and activities.

The new wife, in addition to continuing her own personal development, usually takes on major responsibility for running and managing the household and learns or improves her homemaking skills. Furthermore, she often is expected to carry her share of financial responsibility by starting or continuing work. She also needs to develop her own competence as a satisfactory sex partner, learn to communicate effectively and intimately with her husband, develop relations with her in-laws and the husband's extended family, and expand her competence in handling mutual social and leisure-time activities.

Together, the married pair must establish their marriage as a functioning unit by starting on their basic developmental tasks as a family, which overlap and interweave with the individual tasks of each member of the pair: to find, furnish, and maintain their home; to establish mutually satisfactory ways of supporting themselves; to allocate household responsibilities that each partner is able and willing to assume; to establish mutually acceptable personal, emotional, and sexual roles; to interact with in-laws, relatives, and the community; to plan for possible children; and to maintain their motivation and morale even when obstacles and disagreements arise.[11]

In the first few months of marriage, almost all young couples claim to be independent of their parents. Actually, Ryder, Kafka, and Olson found that separation was greater in word than in deed; a high level of contact was maintained even during the honeymoon.[12] If parents lived in the same location, the couple "dropped in on them" as often as four or five times a week, and even if they lived thousands of miles away, visited once or twice in the first months. The wife would telephone her mother at least once a day and the pair would continue to borrow the parents' car and use their washing machine. (In a study on newlyweds carried out in Israel, parents were found to be the chief source of financial assistance, for both ongoing expenses and "big" purchases.[13])

The young couple were often given advice by both sets of parents, although they tended to be closer to the wife's family than to the husband's, with the father-in-law often proferring advice on financial or business matters. The bride received guidance from both her mother and mother-in-law on housekeeping matters and on how to manage her husband, with the husband's mother often complaining that her son was not being treated properly.

Friendship ties were found to be consistently lower in the first months after the wedding. Before the marriage, friendships had almost all been individual to one of the pair; now such friendships became separative in function and tended to be temporarily or permanently discarded or attenuated. Couple friendships, on the other hand, were considered a desirable—even, at times, an obligatory—means of bringing the pair closer. At times, compromise arrangements were worked out so that some individual friendships were maintained, but under new conditions and rules.

What are some of the difficulties that can arise at this time? A full inventory would probably include difficulties in carrying out each of the personal and couple tasks enumerated above, ranging from feelings of sexual inadequacy or incompatibility to problems of personal hygiene and interference from in-laws. Often a young woman becomes so preoccupied with finding a suitable mate that she tends to give up her own educational and vocational interests to become "just a married woman"; this may lead later to boredom,

irritation that the husband does not continue to
even a premature desire for a child before the m
stance.

Moreover, when one spouse ceases to gain sa
tion, and affectional warmth from the other's fe
difficulties may arise between them. Efforts to ga
gaining, gamesmanship, or subterfuge replace
tween the two. When each retains different :
families of origin concerning marital roles and po.....
crepancies may accelerate into differences and active conflict.

Since most individuals' relationship to their parents forms the foundation for the way they relate to significant others, conflict may arise when the spouse is seen in the image of an absent parent rather than as he or she really is. Unintentional behavior is interpreted in the light of past experiences—such as when the husband takes a second drink or the wife burns the soup. This exacerbation may be just a hair's-breadth away from the legitimate role that marriage partners have in compensating for lacks in the family of origin, and in the capacity of a spouse to be protectively and affectionally parental and to provide solace and comfort during times of stress, disappointment, or loss.[14]

Arthur Leader observes that persons sometimes enter into marriage in the attempt to work through their old problems and defects, not so much through the marital partner as through his or her family—particularly one of the parents-in-law.[15]

The complex of interwoven transitional issues, some rooted in the past and some rising out of the current husband-wife relationship, can be seen reflected in the following marital counseling situation, typical of a whole group of similar cases in the first stage of marriage:

MARY AND JOHN (#116)

Although both Mary and John were expected for counseling, Mary appeared alone, saying her husband refused to come in. She said that during the past three weeks he had become withdrawn and distant, spending most of his evenings out with a group of single boyfriends. A week previously he had not returned until 2:30 A.M., when he confessed that he had been out with a teenage girlfriend of hers. They had tried to have sexual relations, but, he said, he could not attain an erection because he was thinking of Mary. He said he felt terribly guilty but added that he was tired of being married and wanted some variety in his sex life. He decided to move out and she helped him pack.

John was gone for four days, during which time he called Mary daily. He had moved back three days before the interview but remained sulky and withdrawn. Mary complicated matters during his absence by telling both sets of parents and all of their friends about his involvement with this other girl. She explained that they were a very close family and always confided in each other.

and Information. Mary and John had been married a year previously, was 18 and he was 21. They had met on a blind date while he was in the air d had dated for four or five months while he was stationed nearby. When he ed he was being transferred to Spain, he wanted her to marry him at once, but er father refused and they had to wait four more months. They spent the first few months of their marriage in Spain, where, Mary said, they had a good time, traveling and enjoying themselves and each other.

On their return, Mary enrolled in a medical technicians' program and John drew unemployment compensation for a while and then became assistant manager of a small restaurant. He was unhappy at his job, hating his long hours and the fact that he had to work nights and weekends, but he did not know what he wanted to do instead. Meanwhile, in time, Mary started to work and was earning more money than he. She also opened her own checking and savings accounts for the first time.

During counseling, Mary was helped to see that recent events had upset the balance in their marriage. She was no longer dependent on John, felt good about herself, and had become more confident. John, on the other hand, was no longer sure of his assumed role as a husband and breadwinner and doubted whether she needed him any longer. In addition, his unhappiness at his work, plus the fact that she had cut off all of his support from family and friends, had increased his feelings of inadequacy and lack of confidence. After several sessions, Mary reported that she was able to apologize to John and he had cried and become less withdrawn.

After several weeks, Mary announced that John and she were seriously thinking of moving to New Orleans, where he planned to enroll in college to major in electronics. She recognized that their problems were partly due to living so close to their parents and decided she could retain her family ties without "telling all." Both of them realized that they were no longer single and able to do the same things with their friends that they had done as teenagers. She said they now felt they had different interests as a married couple and wanted to work at them.

COUPLEHOOD WITHOUT MARRIAGE

Throughout history, a few stalwart souls have always defied tradition and societal norms by living together "outside of the sacred bonds of wedlock." Census figures, undoubtedly understated, show a marked increase in the number of "living together" couples in recent decades. For the young adult, struggling to carry out the developmental tasks of his age-stage, this arrangement seems to have particular significance. Both clinicians and observers of the American social scene have recognized that an increasing number of young people start to live together in a nonmarital couple relationship, either as a transitional phase en route to formal commitment with a marriage contract or as an alternative life-style.* Observers seem to agree that this is a largely middle-class phenomenon and is particularly prevalent among, although by no means exclusive to, college student populations.[19]

*Since we are discussing heterosexual couple relationships here, I shall not address myself to other alternatives to marriage, such as remaining single without a serious attachment,[16] living in a multiple-family or communal arrangement,[17] or single-sex relationships.[18]

Davidoff sees the current phenomenon of large numbers of young couples living together, particularly on campus, as stemming from many societal and psychological forces: a longer adolescence, the advanced technology of contraception, the sexual revolution, the sharp discontinuity between childhood and adulthood, the separation-individuation process, the struggle toward autonomy and interdependence, and the need for women to seek their own identity and the fulfillment of their sexual needs.[20]

The following case vignette, although describing two young "kibbutzniks" living together in Israel contains many developmental issues characteristic of young people on campuses throughout the world:

TAMAR AND OREN (#154)

Tamar came into the counseling center saying she was in despair, in a crisis. She had spent the night hiding in one of the classrooms, crying until she was exhausted, because she felt she couldn't go home any more. She felt under tremendous pressure and wanted desperately to get married, to find a place for herself. But her boyfriend, with whom she had been living for four months, insisted he wasn't ready and warned her to stop pushing him or he would leave. I agreed to meet the two of them together the same day.

Tamar, 26, small, quick, and bouncy, had a piquant, triangular face and short black hair. Oren, 25, who reluctantly came in with her, was tall and shy, with a curiously deliberate manner of speaking. He felt he had to get some things straight in his mind before he could make a decision. We agreed to meet on a time-limited basis to help them decide whether or not to continue their relationship.

Background Information. Tamar and Oren were born and reared in different kibbutzim and met when they came to the university. The oldest of three girls, she described her father as strict and distant, often absent from home for months on official business. Her mother was sketched as immature and overdemanding, insisting on knowing every small detail of her daughters' lives and bitterly resenting her husband's neglect.

After her army service, Tamar had hoped to study architecture but was not accepted at the Technical Institute. She was tremendously disappointed, since she had wanted "to escape." Instead she became involved with a Dutch volunteer on the kibbutz. When he returned to Holland, she followed him and lived with him and his family for six months. The affair was a big disappointment; although Rolf seemed a glamorous figure in Israel, in Holland he turned out to be just a provincial, not-too-bright "mama's boy."

The 1973 War gave Tamar an excuse to return to Israel. Once back, her mother repeatedly rubbed in the disgrace she had brought them in the eyes of the kibbutz. After the war ended, she came to Haifa, where she found a job in a computer firm and enrolled in the university, majoring in computer science.

Oren, from a kibbutz on the northern border, had been a leader in his age group until he was about 15. Then, for the next six years, he said, he stopped growing physically and felt "retarded," left behind by the others both physically and socially. He grew increasingly shy and never had the courage to approach a girl, although all of his friends had paired off. As the third of four children, he had always been considered the "quiet, deep one" at home. He spent his army service in the Golan Heights and became an officer. This, plus the fact that he finally started growing again, restored his self-confidence. He volunteered for the permanent army, although this meant he had to spend four years on active duty. Upon his discharge, he was offered a responsible position in the kibbutz but was determined to go to the university first, enrolling as a philosophy and history major.

At the university, Tamar did well in her studies but found the social life disappointing. Most of the young men seemed immature and inexperienced, and she saw her fellow workers as far more interesting, although most were older and already married. Oren, on the other hand, remained painfully shy, immersing himself in his books. Quite by chance, they met at the beginning of the school year when each rented a room in the same student apartment. They were immediately attracted to each other and within a month moved in together, at Tamar's initiative. Her natural vivaciousness and openness bridged the gap, and Oren found himself losing his reticence as the relationship developed.

Tamar taught Oren all that she knew sexually and they became very absorbed in each other. One issue, however, began to loom as increasingly important: Tamar, who had had a number of previous relationships, said "this was it"; she now felt ready to marry and settle down. Oren, on the other hand, clung to the idea that he had missed out on something over the past ten years and was determined to "catch up" before he took the final step.

As we talked, it became clear that they had reached an impasse. In separate sessions, Tamar and I concentrated on her rejection by her own father, her mother's hectoring and nagging, her feelings of low self-worth, and her frustration that she had so much to give but had been repeatedly disappointed. She saw Oren's reluctance as another slap in her face. She couldn't understand his need to "balance" their experiences, his hesitations and doubts. Crying bitterly, she said she had had such high hopes but now felt rejected once again.

With Oren, we concentrated on his feelings of having been left behind, his stubborn insistence that he had "missed something" by not having had multiple sexual experiences, his inability to relate easily to girls. He saw no inconsistency in saying that he loved Tamar and felt she satisfied him sexually and emotionally but wondered whether it would be the same with other women.

In our joint sessions we concentrated on their relationship, on what each saw in the other, what each gave and took from the other, and on the need to arrive at some decision by the end of the school year, when each would return to their respective kibbutzim. Disaster occurred in the third joint session when Oren told Tamar openly that he loved her and wanted to marry her—and then followed it up by saying that he was "cutting out of himself" something important. Tamar burst into tears and ran out of the room, saying she was finished, this was it!

I was sure the situation was irreparable, but surprisingly, they came in for the next session glowing. The fight had cleared the air, and Oren had taken the initiative to seek out Tamar at a friend's. They talked throughout the night and finally decided to marry by the end of the term. They would go to her kibbutz the next weekend to tell her family and planned to spend spring vacation at his kibbutz, where his family had already met and welcomed her into their warm circle.

Although many of the basic deficits in each of their life patterns had not been resolved or even investigated in depth, they seemed to have reached an important turning point, both in their personal development and in their relationship, and had made, for the first time, a significant commitment to each other.

The young adults from working-class families whom Rubin observed in her study rarely could allow themselves a period of sexual experimentation and search for identity, either before or after their marriage. Premarital sexual relations usually resulted in an unplanned pregnancy and a precipitate (but expected) marriage. This, plus the constant pressure of poverty and intermittent employment at low-paying jobs, took much of the dreaming and joy out of the first months of marriage. Since most of the couples married very young, with little understanding of what they were getting into, the dream faded quickly before the harsh and tedious realities of everyday life.[21]

Once a young pair has passed through the transition to marriage/ couplehood, the next significant milestone in the stage of young adulthood is the enlarging and changing of their two-person marital system to allow their first offspring to enter. This transition is the subject of the next chapter.

6

Transition to Parenthood

As the second process related to the issue of intimacy vs. isolation, the transition into parenthood for the young adult heralds passage to a new developmental level. The arrival of the first child changes a spouse into a parent and turns a marriage into a family. In this chapter we will consider separately the four sequential phases in this bridging interval: the decision to have a child, the pregnancy itself, the birth of the child, and the first post-natal adjustment period.

Early interest in the entry into parenthood developed within the crisis framework through a series of key studies by family sociologists. In the mid-1950s, E. E. LeMasters interviewed young, middle-class couples to determine whether they viewed their adjustment to the recent birth of their first child as a crisis situation.[1] He found that 83 percent reported the experience as an extensive or severe crisis, although most of the pregnancies were wanted and planned and the majority of the marriages were considered adequate. Some years later, Everett Dyer replicated the same study using individual questionnaires and found that 53 percent of the couples who responded fell into the extensive or severe crisis category.[2] Those couples whose marriage was considered stronger and who had more resources to draw upon experienced less crisis.

A third study along the same lines was carried out by Daniel Hobbs, using a random sample of white middle-class and lower-class couples.[3] Unlike LeMasters and Dyer, he found that 87 percent of the couples experienced parenthood as only a slight crisis, while none found it to be of extensive or severe proportions. Ten years later, in 1975, to repeated the same study and obtained essentially the same results, with over 97 percent of the subjects falling in the moderate or lower levels of crisis.[4] (Interestingly, significantly fewer of the couples in 1975 than in 1965 viewed having a baby as being important to their marital happiness—a substantive change in attitudes toward marital and parental roles.) In a similar study, Hobbs and Jane Wimbish found that black parents seemed to experience slightly greater difficulties in adjusting to their first child than did white parents.[5] Both black and white parents of both sexes felt that the interruption of their previous life-styles was the single most bothersome aspect of beginning parenthood.

By this time the focus had shifted from viewing entry into parenthood as a crisis to defining it as a transitional stage. Alice Rossi was the first to propose that becoming a parent can be considered a part of the adult socialization process and to suggest that a more fruitful point of departure than the crisis model would be to examine it as a developmental phase.[6] She notes that previously, when pregnancy was likely to occur shortly after marriage, the major transition point in a woman's life was marriage itself. More recently, with the development of efficient contraceptive methods and the tendency for the woman to continue to work for a period after the marriage, the first big shift in status occurs with her first pregnancy.

THE DECISION TO HAVE A CHILD

Although Perlman views the beginning of parenthood as reaching back into the person's own childhood, to his observations and experiences with his own parents,[7] for our purposes we shall view the transitional process as starting with the decision, voluntary or nonvoluntary, to have a child. Rossi points out that while men are culturally expected to secure their adult status by working, considerable social pressure is exerted upon women to consider maternity as necessary for the fulfillment of their adult role. Moreover, while the decision to marry and the choice of a mate are usually voluntary acts, once a child is born the commitment to parenthood is irrevocable: we can have ex-spouses and ex-jobs, but no ex-children.[8]

Lidz finds the act of conception to have multiple roots at different levels.[9] It is one of mutual creativity during which the boundaries between the self and the other are temporarily obliterated to a greater extent than at any time since infancy. The envisaged infant is seen as a physical fusion of the two parents; both their personalities and their physical traits will unite within the child and he will become the focus of their mutual hopes and responsibilities, a continuing bond forged by and between them.

For many women, their creativity as a mother becomes a central issue that provides meaning and balance to their lives:

With the choice given them, perhaps fewer women will wish to disrupt their careers, or take the risk of becoming a single parent through divorce, or overcome various residual fears of pregnancy and parturition; but for many women . . . birth of a child turns a wife into a woman by setting her on a par with her mother. Her love for the husband who has made such completion possible deepens. . . . To some extent the baby is herself loved by a benevolent father. The process carries residua of the little girl's envy of the mother who could produce a child with and for the father. The husband who is loving permits the woman to complete an old but very important fantasy. [pp. 470–471]

The man, too, usually has strong desires for a child and can be transformed by it. The baby provides a continuity of himself into the future that mobilizes his ambition and offers an important proof of his own virility. It secures and heightens his masculine self-esteem and allows him to realize both the masculine function of protection and support for his family and the feminine aspect of nurturance derived from his early identification with his mother. He is now able to gain the position and status of father that he envied and desired since early childhood.

Other reasons for conceiving may be less constructive. The decision to have a child in order to hold a marriage together or make up for an estrangement between partners, whether consciously expressed or implied, has been found to produce dubious results; at the most it can become a dragging fetter that may become an intolerable burden for both parents and child. The wife's desire to compete with other women, to keep herself busy, to find a central meaning and purpose to her life, and/or to gain an extra card in the power game of her marriage often brings negative side-effects which later become directed against the child itself.

Perlman notes that many women are ambivalent about their pregnancy:[10]

They want a baby, but also want "freedom"; they love children, but want more time; their husbands (or mothers or mothers-in-law) want a baby but—; to have a baby, one must be pregnant—but my figure will be ruined." Some women want pregnancy . . . but are not so sure they want what follows. Pregnancy and childbirth may bring them status and admiration in the eyes of husband and relatives, may bring them privileges of care and protection, but once the child is there the care and protection and admiration shifts over to the baby, and the mother is expected to become not the "cared for" but the "care-giver."

The decision for parenthood touches off in the woman a nostalgia for her own mother, a desire to relive in the union with her future child a reversal of the original mother-child symbiosis; from being child to her mother, she will become mother to her child. Pregnancy may awaken unconscious anxieties, fears, and phobias. Yet women still give birth, knowing in advance that someday their children will leave them, accepting the pains, anxieties, drudgery, and possible tragic losses in store for them. They find the courage, endurance, and capacity to forego monetary pleasures and comforts for the sake of future gratifications.[11]

Recent writers have pointed out the differences between biological, cultural, and social motivations for women to bear children. Nancy Chodorow, for example, maintains that women's capacities for mothering and their abilities to gain gratification from it are strongly internalized and psychologically enforced and are built into the feminine psychic structure. Women are prepared for mothering through the developmental situation in which they grew up and in which women have mothered them.[12]

Similarly, Nancy Russo points out that the "mandate to mother" is historically based on biology and enforced by social and cultural institutions which require that a woman have at least two children and raise them herself. This is increasingly being challenged, however, by the role conflict experienced when a woman attempts to balance the relative rewards and costs of children as opposed to work.[13] On the other hand, some career women in their late thirties, faced with the inexorably moving hands of their biological clock, will frantically opt to have a child, in some cases without the benefit of marriage.

A husband and wife may decide to postpone having children for various reasons: to await their readiness to assume the economic, social, and psychological responsibilities of parenthood, to concentrate on their own career advancement, or even to help curb the world's spiraling population growth. The proliferating field of family planning devotes a considerable part of its counseling efforts to helping couples consider alternatives and develop a planned progression of increases in family size. Efficient contraception methods, on the one hand, and advances in increasing the probability of fertility, on the other, have made the choice of having a child a much more viable decision than in previous times.[14]

Part of the decision to have a child may be based not only on the couple's ability and desire to have one and at what point they wish to do so, but whether, in fact, they *should* have a child. Through genetic counseling, would-be parents can be informed of the medical, social, and genetic facts related to hereditary disorders that may be prevalent in the family background of either person. Counselors can help to establish the risk of a disorder's occurrence, to interpret this risk in meaningful terms, to aid the couple in weighing alternative outcomes, and to support them in the decision they make.[15]

As already noted, sometimes the decision to have a child is not a matter of choice; it comes as an accident, unwanted and unplanned by both husband and wife. This may mean simply a shifting of priorities and attitude of "Well, we hadn't planned it so soon, but now that it's happened, we'll make the best of it." On the other hand, it may come, as Perlman points out, as a shock to the woman, a sickening realization that she is "caught" in an inexorable process. She may try to blot out realization that she is pregnant until physical manifestations make it impossible to deny. She may make active efforts to abort the embryo and endure the expense, humiliation, and pain involved while dealing with the often-negative reactions of husband, relatives, well-meaning friends—and community agencies.

If the process is further complicated by the woman's having become pregnant without being married, the situation becomes enmeshed in a host of social and psychological factors which are outside the purview of this discussion.[16] Rubin's observations on the role that unexpected pregnancy plays in accelerating marriages in working-class families have already been noted. In general, when faced with an unplanned pregnancy, couples frequently choose marriage as the preferred alternative to abortion, placing the child for adoption, or having the mother raise the child alone.[17]

THE PERIOD OF PREGNANCY

WOMEN'S REACTIONS.   Pregnancy, says Therese Benedek, is a critical phase in a woman's life in that it is a biologically motivated step which requires both physiological and psychological adjustment leading to a new level of developmental integration.[18] It is beyond the purpose of this book to specify in detail the physiological, biological, and endocrinological changes which take place during the nine months of the pregnancy cycle, although a general knowledge of the processes is certainly helpful to the prospective parents.[19] Pregnancy in the life of a woman can be considered a period that is biologically special although not abnormal—a period of symbiosis in which the heightened hormonal and metabolic processes necessary to maintain the normal growth of the fetus augment the woman's own vital energies.

In one study, the reactions of women throughout pregnancy were charted.[20] During the first trimester, the subtle body changes are usually the focus of attention: the swelling of the breasts, nausea, morning sickness, aversion to or craving for certain foods; and a general weakness, fatigue, and indolence. Inexplicable mood swings, irritability, and easily hurt feelings make most women feel "not the same person anymore."

By the second trimester, a sudden shift occurs with the quickening, the experiencing of fetal movements, which are perceived as having a delicate, stroking quality, "like holding a butterfly in your hand." For most women, this period is one of fulfillment and delight, although some ambivalence towards the fetus may be noted. Eating becomes an issue: most women feel they must eat for two and become very hungry, yet they are warned by their obstetricians against gaining weight. Some lose enthusiasm for and the capacity to become involved in sex; they worry that intercouse might harm the baby, despite medical assurances to the contrary.

The body begins to lose its familiar shape, and the woman gives up her usual clothes (part of her identity) to wear maternity dresses—which makes her proud but also distressed, since she fears she is no longer attractive to men and will lose her husband's love. She often lacks the support of her extended family and the traditional customs which guided pregnant women in the past. Haunted by vague anxieties and fears, she feels stranded and alone, tending both to idealize her absent mother and to struggle against identifying with her.

With the start of the third trimester, the woman's body feels increasingly awkward, embarrassingly distorted in shape. Frequency and urgency of urination, constipation, and hemorrhoids may be some of the disagreeable side-effects with which she must now contend. Frequent medical checkups and natural-childbirth classes occupy much of her time. The fetus now feels like a giant; its movements are disruptive, and at times painful. The woman begins to experience an increasing attachment to her husband as they impatiently await the day of delivery when they can finally see the baby. At the same time, the approaching delivery may initiate fantasies of death and rebirth.

Benedek points out that a woman whose personality organization makes her a "natural" mother may enjoy the narcissistic state of pregnancy with vegetative calm, while another type of woman may need to defend herself, often consciously, against this type of experience. Many neurotics feel free from their anxiety states during pregnancy; in spite of morning sickness or the realistic apprehensions caused by the pregnancy, they become stable and in good spirits.

Some women carry through their pregnancy with ease and confidence, supported by their husband's sense of pride and anticipation. Others, weighed down by fears and insecurities rooted in economic worries or unhappy ties with husband or family of origin, may find the period more arduous. The inner-directed psychological stage during pregnancy has a regressive pull which brings about mood swings from calm elation to a depressive state of deep-seated insecurity. Under certain circumstances, "regression in the service of the ego," to use Ernst Kris's phrase, occurs. The integrative task of pregnancy, particularly with the first child, is far greater biologically and psychologically than the woman has ever faced before.

During her months of pregnancy, the expectant mother is absorbed in feelings of self-concern and self-care, with anticipations fostered by husband and relatives that she will be protected and indulged. She may engage in fantasies about her future child, which may range from being reality-oriented to pure wish fulfillment—fantasies shaped by her personal needs, by her fears and hopes, and by the expectations and attitudes of the persons who are currently important in her life.[21] Some women report intense anxieties and fears, even in areas which heretofore had been conflict-free, such as their concerns about their future roles and responsibilities and their marriage and career plans. They also begin to shift their own generational perspective to that of mother, and now see their own mothers as prospective grandmothers.[22]

As the day of birth approaches, the young wife begins to engage in "nesting" procedures in preparation for the coming event. If the couple has been living in a small apartment, in some transient arrangement, or even with one set of parents, she may wish for a home of her own; if she is employed, her interest in her job lags. Often she engages in a flurry of activity: moving to larger quarters, fixing up the home, and preparing the baby's room and play area. If she has had little prior experience with infants, she now begins to read voraciously about babies, talk with friends and other young mothers, and hold endless discussions with her husband on the subject. She may become caught up in a round of baby showers and "women only" affairs where the chief topic is, inevitably, childbirth and aftercare advice.

MEN'S REACTIONS.   The expectant father also undergoes a period of psychological preparation for the birth of his first child, although the topic has not been given the same attention as the mother's reactions. Perlman notes that husbands fantasy, together with their wives or alone. For the first child a man usually desires a son who will fulfill his dreams by either following in his footsteps or by being just the opposite and thus achieving the love, admiration, fame, or happiness which the father has longed for but has not known.[23] In addition, the husband may be asked to provide reassurance and love for his wife when her fantasies and anxieties spill over on to him. Benedek notes that often the husband is unable to empathize with his wife's incomprehensible, regressive reactions, and he may begin to resent her feelings, since they deprive him of his own gratification in his virility at having impregnated her.[24]

Among reactions reported are the man's fears of losing his wife and/or child and his doubts as to his ability to function as a future father. As the fetus quickens and the wife grows in size, some men report a slow decrease in sexual activity, ostensibly for fear of harming the fetus, although a few mentioned their negative reactions to their wives' physical appearance. The pregnancy can serve to frustrate a man's own sexual needs and act as a potential focus for marital conflict.

At the same time, many husbands show increased solicitude towards their pregnant wives by performing many household tasks. Nurturance becomes more prevalent as they begin to take care of their wives instead of the frequent reverse pattern. According to one study carried out, husbands seemed even more willing to do household tasks customarily done by their wives than the latter were to have them do so.[25]

In another study of expectant fathers, men were found to fall into three categories: those with a *romantic orientation*, those who were *career-*

oriented, and those who were *family-oriented.* The first group had a casual approach to parenthood, and becoming a father for them was largely a maturational experience, accompanied by marital crisis and conflict with relatives. The second group regarded prospective fatherhood as a burden which would interfere with their work responsibilities or leisure activities; they denied the need for an identity shift. The third group accepted the new responsibilities easily and experienced fulfillment at the prospect of becoming a father and "family man"; they had already begun the transformation into fathers even before the first pregnancy.[26]

Laurence Barnhill, Gerald Rubenstein, and Neil Rocklin investigated the process of transition to fatherhood by interviewing husbands who were attending childbirth preparation classes with their wives.[27] They found that the process of becoming a father could be divided into developmental tasks, four of which cover the period of pregnancy:

1. Decision Making. Initially the father must decide to have a child or accept the reality *ex post facto* that he is going to have one. This decision has both personal implications for the man and ramifications for his relationship with his wife.

2. Mourning. The prospective father, in taking on the role, also undergoes substantial loss in terms of personal freedom. His wife's time and attention becomes increasingly limited, lessening the "looseness" and flexibility within the marital relationship. From conception to delivery and through early infancy, fathers often report having felt "discounted," although these losses may not have been noticed or mourned until much later.

3. Empathic Responding. One of the most potentially satisfying tasks of the father-to-be is his tender support of his wife during her pregnancy and labor. This responsiveness can be tangible and concrete, allowing him to carry out actual tasks and experience successful coping as a way of combating his own sense of helplessness; it also is often time-limited to the pregnancy period.

4. Integrating. At the end of pregnancy, the concrete reality of the child's arrival must be integrated into the spatial, temporal, and social life space of the developing family. The father needs to maintain his acceptance of the child while taking a second, or at least a different, place in his wife's priorities.

Until recently, the role of the expectant father has received little attention in professional or academic literature.[28] Yet practitioners have long been aware of both the positive and negative effects of his attitudes on his wife's reactions to her pregnancy, on his own perceptions of his role as a father-to-be, and on the dynamics of the family in formation. In the following case summary, we see how unfinished developmental tasks from earlier stages of maturation became aggravated by the pregnancy process, which threatened to upset a precarious marital balance.

BRUCE AND BETTY (#180)

Bruce, age 24, and Betty, age 21, asked for counseling because of increasing conflict in their two-year-old marriage. Betty's recently established pregnancy, which was unplanned but accepted, heightened her anxiety; she worried about their having a baby in such a turbulent situation and had doubts as to whether she was ready and able to be a good mother. Other problems also surfaced, notably Bruce's relationship to his widowed mother and Betty's ties with her parents. The couple was seen together in weekly counseling sessions.

At the outset, the marital picture was conflictual. Bruce tried to control the situation, as he tried to control both himself and his external environment, but Betty would become infuriated and continuously challenged his right to do so. In addition, he would act out in typically passive-aggressive ways, such as *not* taking out the garbage or *not* doing any housework. This, too, would upset Betty, since she was feeling nauseated and miserable much of the time.

Although he had an M.A. in business administration, Bruce was struggling to establish himself as an insurance salesman, a job he disliked, and finances were extremely tight. Betty complained angrily that he refused to let her know how things stood financially and she mistrusted his judgment in money matters, since he tended not to pay bills for months at a time yet would splurge wildly on occasion.

Bruce struggled with his anger that his wife trusted him so little and that his mother treated him, her only son, like a "bad boy." As he spoke, his underlying depression surfaced and he began to cry as he acknowledged how little he had ever received from his mother, who had always been stingy towards him. He recalled bitterly that when he had damaged his ear in a boyhood accident she refused to agree to an operation to restore his hearing. Now he was scheduled to enter the hospital soon for this same operation and had to demand her help in paying for it.

Betty, a medical secretary, came from a large, financially secure family in which she had been petted and overindulged as a child. Her parents were very generous and she still felt tied to them, but she resented having to turn to them to be "bailed out" financially now that she was married.

As treatment progressed, the overt conflict was reduced somewhat by having Bruce and Betty focus on their own needs and their expectations from each other. In a pivotal session, Bruce poured out some of his pain and anger over having been deprived as a child of his father, who died when he was very young, a suspected suicide. Now he wondered what he had to give to *his* future son and whether someday his son would feel the same way about *his* father.

Both Betty and Bruce began to show an increased ability to empathize with and support each other, although their own pain, anger, and susceptibilities often got the better of them. As her pregnancy progressed, Betty began to lean more on Bruce and to turn to him for help and reaffirmation, but he was frequently too angry and overwhelmed by the sense of "having things coming to him" to pay heed. In our sessions he was given a good deal of nurturance so that he was able in turn to see what he was doing to her at a time when she needed him.

At one point Bruce finally acknowledged his inability to provide for his growing family as he wanted to and became very downcast over his lack of self-worth. He surrendered control over the family finances to Betty, who seeemed more competent to balance their checkbook and schedule payments as they furnished their second bedroom as a nursery. He became seriously depressed over his inability to live up to the promise of his student years; his lack of self-confidence and sense of injustice kept him from making gains professionally. Betty continued to press him to take better care of her and to let her share in family decisions, which he kept trying to handle unilaterally.

The birth of the baby in March brought something of a lull in the marriage conflict. Both Betty's parents and Bruce's mother were delighted with their first grandson and were very generous, which temporarily eased the young couple's financial stress. Betty stopped working and became engrossed in the baby, while Bruce found himself relating to the infant for the first time as a real person. Both continued to struggle with their own unmet dependency needs and the necessity to delay immediate gratification in view of their new position as parents.

THE BIRTH OF THE BABY

Sooner or later the long-awaited event finally comes to pass. The contractions start and the couple rush to the hospital. Once there, the expectant mother is taken in hand by the obstetrical team and the anxious father is left to wait his turn, among his peers, to hear the news of the outcome of the labor and delivery.

Labor and birth are fairly well explained processes which most couples have read up on during the months of pregnancy.[29] The woman has probably heard detailed accounts of deliveries from her mother, sisters, and friends and has been primed by women's magazines as to what to expect. Yet personal reports reveal that virtually none of the couples in first pregnancies were able to anticipate completely the nature of the event. Even in modern obstetrical practice, which encourages husbands to participate with their wives in prenatal courses and instructions prior to delivery and even become active observers in delivery rooms, few couples seem ready for the reality of the hospital and the maternity floor.

The process of childbirth occurs in three stages.[30] The first stage begins with the earliest signs of labor and ends with the full dilation of the cervix. During this stage, which may last for days and even weeks, the woman may experience back pains and irregular uterine contractions and may come to the hospital with what sometimes turn out to be false labor pains. She is usually kept a few hours and then returns home. Even after she is taken to the labor room, she may have to wait. When she finally experiences contractions every three to four minutes, she is taken to the delivery room.

The second stage of labor begins with the full dilation of the cervix and continues until the fetus is expelled from the mother's body, usually head forward, through the birth canal. Although many women request general anesthesia during the later stages of labor, they are usually encouraged to agree to spinal or local anesthesia so that they can participate actively in at least the first part of the birth process. When respiration and independent blood circulation have been established in the infant, the umbilical cord is cut and clamped.

The third stage consists of the delivery of the placenta ("afterbirth") a few minutes following the birth of the baby. If an episiotomy was performed to enlarge the vaginal opening, it is now repaired and the mother is sent to the recovery room until she is ready to return to her own room in the hospital. Meanwhile, the father, who may have participated in or observed the process or may have been expelled to the waiting room, is notified of the outcome and begins to spread the news and pass out cigars.

In the majority of deliveries, the trusting relationship which the woman has developed with her obstetrician becomes a critical factor in lessening her anxieties; if he puts in a belated appearance or substitutes a less familiar colleague, it sometimes triggers panic reactions. Positive attitudes and active involvement by maternity nurses are becoming an increasingly important factor in maternity services. Some efforts have been made in recent years, largely influenced by the women's movement, to introduce changes in the birthing process such as the development of "alternate services," which enable the woman to give birth in her room, often assisted by a nurse-midwife, with a doctor standing by in case of need. In other cases, women are being encouraged to give birth at home, with the active participation of their families and close friends.[31] Nevertheless, most women still give birth in maternity homes or in the obstetrical wards of general hospitals.

Several versions of preparatory courses for "natural" childbirth are growing in popularity in the United States. The Read method, introduced by the English physician Grantly Dick-Read, is based on the elimination of the vicious circle of fear–tension–pain–fear during the labor process. After learning about pregnancy, labor, and birth, the woman is trained, starting at about the fourth or fifth month, in muscle-control techniques, deep chest breathing, and exercises to achieve a state of relaxation during labor. The Lamaze method, first developed in Russia and continued in France by the French physician Fernand Lamaze, relies upon reeducating the woman to dissociate pain sensations from labor. Women are taught techniques of breathing, or "panting," and are trained to become aware of their body sensations so that they can adjust their activities while becoming actively engaged in the labor process. Participants in these courses, both wives and husbands, generally seem to agree that it helped them feel more "in control" during childbirth, as well as improve their relations toward each other.[32]

COMPLICATIONS IN THE BIRTH PROCESS.   The large majority of pregnancies result in the birth of normal, healthy, full-term infants. Nevertheless, since cases seen by professionals often start with crises brought out by birth anomalies or special situations, it might be well to keep in mind that the normal transitional process of becoming a parent can become deflected and thrown off course by complications at this point. Some of the difficulties may be temporary and remediable; others can be serious enough to stop the process in its tracks. A stillbirth is an irremediable and irreversible event that cannot be "played over" no matter how guilty or remorseful the parents feel.

Birth of a severely retarded or physically abnormal child may demand immediate decisions regarding possible institutionalization, surgical intervention, or the use of complex life-support systems that may have extensive financial and practical implications, to say nothing of the emotional and mental drain on the young parents and their family, friends, and work networks. It takes highly skilled intervention to help upset, angry, depressed, and/or grieving parents, often in a condition of acute shock, to make the necessary immediate judgments on which further action must be based, and, on the other hand, to refrain from taking hasty, impulsive steps that will be regretted later on.

The important issue, in the context of the parents' transitional process, is that this, the first pregnancy, for whatever reason, has turned into an acute crisis. Unless they are helped to deal not only with the present stressful situation but with the underlying maturational issues, they will experience great difficulty in continuing their normal adult development as individuals and their joint life as a married couple who expected to start a normal, healthy family. The following private-practice case illustrates this point.

HEIDI (#215)

Heidi, age 25, came into my office without an appointment. She was pale and distraught, with tear-rimmed eyes. In a low, trembling voice, she said she had to speak to someone before she fell apart. She had borne twins ten months earlier, but both died shortly afterwards. For a while she thought she had gotten over it, but for the past two months she had been feeling increasingly depressed. Don, her husband, had been pressing for them to have another child, and they had been trying, but she hadn't been able to conceive. She felt it was her fault. She couldn't bear the thought of another pregnancy that would end disastrously. At the time the babies were born the hospital social worker had told her that she should talk to someone about them, but she hadn't been able to even *think* about them until now.

She immediately began to talk about the event. She had been in her eighth month of pregnancy and was alone that evening, since her husband was working nights. When she began to feel strong contractions, she tried first to reach Don and then her doctor but couldn't contact either one. She took a cab herself and was shuttled from one hospital to another, finally ending up at the city hospital, where she knew no one, since she was registered to go to a maternity center. It was the beginning of a twenty-four-hour nightmare: she felt completely isolated; no one knew where she was; her husband couldn't even be located until the next morning. Her doctor turned out to be out of town at a medical convention, and all she saw were faceless white coats who kept coming in to examine her and to tell her to bear down. They tried to induce labor, but something "was stuck" and she felt herself growing weaker and weaker. At one point, she remembered, she got down on her hands and knees and begged the nurse to help her, but she was told she'd have to try harder herself.

Finally labor started in earnest and the first baby was born; at that point they realized she was carrying another one, something even her own doctor hadn't discovered. They put her to sleep then, and the next thing she knew she was in an ambulance being transferred to the maternity hospital with the two wrapped-up bundles, since the city hospital didn't have any incubators available. She saw the babies just for a moment before they were taken away; both were dark like Don.

At first everyone kept coming in to congratulate her, even after the head nurse came in to tell her that one of the boys, the smaller one, had died of breathing complications. When Don came that evening to see her, happy and excited, she had to break the bad news to him. Her parents called and were shocked to hear about the little one who had died. Her mother offered to come and stay with her, but they lived three thousand miles away and she had to work and to take care of the younger kids at home.

Heidi and Andy, the other baby, went home at the end of the week. She tried to nurse him but he kept crying, she had to throw her milk away and give him a special formula that the pediatrician ordered. He kept growing worse and finally one night they brought him back to the hospital. He was put in an incubator but kept getting weaker .The pediatrician told them that he had been born with a certain serious defect, and that if he lived he probably would be physically damaged.

She spent all of her time next to his "box," but one night, a week later, after she had gone home to get some sleep, the hospital called to say he was sinking. The nurses took him out of the incubator and she held him in her arms for a while until they told her he was dead.

Afterwards, Heidi said, she "went crazy" for a while. She became so depressed she couldn't even talk to anyone; she'd just sit in the rocker in the baby's room, looking at the empty crib. Her older brother came out for a week, but all she'd do was cry.

After three months at home she roused herself enough to go back to work. She worked as a student counselor in a high school, and during the day she was busy enough so that she didn't have time to think. Meanwhile, Don finished his studies and was sent away for a special training program by the company that hired him; it meant she was left alone at night a lot. She didn't even go out with her girlfriends or have them over for coffee; she just sat by herself watching TV, with the sound turned off.

Heidi said she had been trying to become pregnant but hadn't had her period since the delivery, although she had been taking estrogens in massive doses. She was worried about herself, afraid that something was wrong with her. She said that Don came from a large family and his parents had twenty-one grandchildren; she was the only daughter-in-law who was childless. At this point, she put her head down on her arms and began to sob bitterly.

POSTNATAL ADJUSTMENT

From the moment that the woman returns from the delivery room, the process of "becoming a mother" takes on reality. The man, too, goes through a similar role transformation from the time he sees the child and hears its first birth cry. Several phases in this process can be observed: (1) the *baby honeymoon*, while the mother and child are still in the hospital or maternity center; (2) the *immediate post-hospital period*, during which parents and child struggle to establish a mutual routine; and (3) the gradual *adjustment to the changed pattern of living* as a threesome, which may take up to four or five months.

THE BABY HONEYMOON.   The length of the first phase after birth, while mother and child are still in the hospital, has been increasingly cut down from a week in years past to three or two days, or even one. Under normal conditions the woman recovers rapidly from the trauma and fatigue of labor and delivery, emerging with a feeling of relief and accomplishment: "It's over; I did it!" She accepts the congratulations of family and friends with a sense of complacency or even euphoria. Her husband looks at her with awe and tenderness, at the same time that he is beaming down at the visible evidence of his virility and ability to procreate. Former differences with parents become submerged as all share pridefully in the sense of becoming part of the chain of generations. Active debates are held as to whether the boy baby's ears are shaped like Uncle Harry's or whether the girl's eyes will turn blue like Aunt Mildred's. Endless lists of names are pored over until the right one falls into place.

If the mother has the baby in the room with her, she wakens at the least sound or movement, and a dozen times during the day and night unwraps the blanket to see whether he/she is really complete and perfect. If the baby is brought in to her, she checks on it even before she starts to nurse, and spends hours at the nursery window, comparing her own infant with others. She struggles to nurse and worries that the first colorless drops of liquid are not the rich, endless flow of milk she envisaged. But behind her euphoria lies the haunting question: will she be able to become a good mother?

RETURN HOME FROM THE HOSPITAL.   With the return of the new parents home, laden with gifts, supplies, and baby, the family begins to adapt to their new life together. In some middle-class families, the homecoming may be cushioned by the hiring of a baby nurse for a short interval, while the new mother "gets back on her feet." In other families, both middle and lower class, a mother or mother-in-law will come to stay for a week, or if she lives nearby, will spend a good part of each day helping the young mother fit into her new role. If neither arrangement is available, the young father may have to give up some of his non-working activities or arrange his working hours so that he can take over some of the shopping and household chores until his spouse learns to fit her customary household tasks into the ever-demanding routine of baby care.

Sooner or later, however, the young mother has to put aside the fluffy peignoirs she wore in the hospital and don her workday housecoat with its big pockets for bottle, extra diapers, pins, and other impedimenta of her new role. For the next few months she will have to struggle, with varying degrees of gratification and desperation, with the baby's seemingly insatiable demands, which usually center around the issues of sleeping and feeding. Until the infant's growth needs become adjusted, her primary focus will be on 2:00 A.M. feedings, colic, spitting up, green stools, air bubbles, and uninterpretable periods of crying.

Some mothers find this period one of increasing satisfaction, as they and their infants settle in to a mutually pleasurable symbiosis, often most directly felt during breast-feeding times.[33] Others move about in a chronic fog of fatigue and lack of sleep, while they struggle to keep up with the round-the-clock schedule at a time when they are still recovering from the physical drains of pregnancy and childbirth.

A common reaction during this period may be a *postpartum depression,* often called "after-baby blues." The young mother, struggling to cope with the unfamiliar problems of infant care, sometimes becomes overwhelmed with her own sense of unsureness and inadequacy and experiences feelings of ego depletion, letdown, and surges of panic. She may sense that she is falling apart and unable to cope with more than the most immediate details of living and caring for her child. Minor inconveniences become major traumas, and she feels conflicted about whether she can meet the tasks and responsibilities pressing down on her.[34]

Women's reactions during these first weeks cover a wide spectrum, ranging from transient periods of mild depression to severe bouts of increased irritability and crying spells. They report feelings of inability to concentrate, fantasies of running away, anger towards the baby and husband, helplessness, inability to cope, lethargy, and overall fatigue.[35] In a relatively few instances, the depression may balloon into a severe emotional disorder or postpartum psychosis requiring medical treatment or even temporary hospitalization.

With all this, at some point within the first week, the bonding between mother and infant begins to "jell." Often a woman feels surprise and concern that she immediately did not experience a surge of love and tenderness for the baby, and she begins to worry about her emotional deficiencies as a mother. Yet usually, at some point—while nursing, bathing, or changing—a poignant awareness floods her: this is her child; she is its mother!

The young mother's situation at this time may become either complicated or mitigated by the reactions of the young father. Since the first baby often arrives while husband and wife are still working to establish their relationship as a married couple, he may feel unaccountably let down and experience unacknowledged pangs of jealousy as he watches her and the baby become mutually absorbed in each other. He may tend to react with sharp irritation to the continuous interruptions of meals and sleep. Even when he tries to take over some of the child care chores, he may feel clumsy and out of place as he struggles with diapers and nursing bottles. The core difficulty often lies in his ability to share his wife intimately with the new baby who now claims such a major share of her attention. The twosome has suddenly given way, not only to a third, but to one in which he can easily feel himself as the odd man out.

The research on new fathers reported earlier notes that the birth of the baby necessitates his role transitions in three major areas: *his relation to his new child, to his wife,* and *to the outside world.* The first has to do with the learning of new skills of fathering. The second involves dealing with the role strains and stresses related to sharing and receiving less of his wife's attention in their marital relations. The third addresses itself to his determining the extent to which the nuclear family's boundaries are kept intact, and to the way in which he integrates himself and his new child into his extended family where he has now become both a father and a son.[36]

Many of the new family's concerns are practical ones of adapting housing and living arrangements to the new infant. The unexpectedly high cost of childbearing tends to come as a shock and often occurs just at the time when the couple is still struggling to pay off costs of housing, furniture, and a car and the second income earned by the wife has been cut off. The husband may attempt to cover this by taking on an extra job, which results in additional strain, fatigue, and irritability. Thus a vicious circle is established, since the arrangement leaves the wife to struggle with the never-ending tasks of housecleaning, cooking, laundry, shopping, and baby care without the husband's help and support.

Communication becomes centered at this stage around the newborn infant, who makes his needs known immediately through crying and other nonverbal means, and deals less with the relations between the couple themselves. Reestablishment of marital roles, including resumption of sexual relations, often proceeds slowly, with the wife insisting that she is too tired or that her stitches still bother her, while the husband remains fearful of hurting her through his insistence.

FINAL ADJUSTMENT.   Gradually the transitional period draws to a close as the baby becomes stabilized around a fairly predictable schedule and learns to sleep through (most of) the night. The woman's strength slowly returns as she sleeps for longer stretches and becomes more adept in caring for the infant. In time she takes a good look at herself in the full-length mirror and begins to do the prescribed postpartum exercises to reduce the "flab" of her abdominal muscles and breasts. She finally packs away her washed-out maternity clothes, rummages through her depleted wardrobe, and decides to go on a buying spree to make herself more attractive to her husband, signaling him that she is once again ready to resume sexual relations. The baby becomes more responsive and both parents begin to rejoice as the series of wondrous firsts unfolds: the first genuine smile, the first "swim" in the bath, the first raising of the head, the first rollover, the first backward locomotion in the crib, the first trip to the park, the first proud inspection at a family gathering, and so on. Father, mother, and baby now settle down to being a family.

LOWER-CLASS FAMILIES.   The transition to parenthood takes on a different tempo and emphasis in lower-class families. Rubin found in her study that the financial problems of the young couples she interviewed were exacerbated by the fact that the first child was born just months after the wedding.[37] The young parents were quickly confronted with the economic realities which colored every facet of their marriage, including the birth of their child:

> Indeed, children born just months after the wedding added emotional as well as economic burdens to the adjustment process. Suddenly, two young people, barely more than children themselves, found their lives irrevocably altered. Within a few months—too few to permit the integration of the behaviors required by new roles in new life stages, too few to wear comfortably even one new identity—they moved through a series of roles: from girl and boy to wife and husband, to mother and father. [p. 79]

For most of these young couples, the fun and good times that had brought them together were gone, replaced by a crying, demanding infant and the fearsome responsibilities of parenthood. They no longer felt free to run around with the old crowd, to go to the movies, bowl, or go partying when they felt in the mood. Both husbands and wives suddenly realized that instead of the freedom they had sought in marriage, they had exchanged one set of constraints for another. They felt stuck, abruptly thrust into adulthood and facing the fear that their youth was behind them.

When the telescoping of marriage and parenthood is complicated even further by a parental background of material and emotional deprivation, the normal processes of parenting become even more skewed, as seen in the following case situation, familiar to many social workers in public welfare settings.

THERESA (#160)

Theresa, age 21, a young mother recently separated from her husband, with one son, Eddie, age 4 months, was referred to the Family and Children's Service unit from the Income Maintenance Division of the County Welfare Department for counseling. She had applied to them for emergency aid, saying that her husband had kicked her and their new baby out of their apartment, and that she had no place to live, no money, and a new baby that she didn't know how to care for. By the time we saw her she had found temporary refuge with some acquaintances but could only stay there until the end of the week. She did not want to reconcile with her husband, who had married her under pressure eight months ago and who had been drinking heavily since the baby was born. She wanted, instead, to file for divorce.

Theresa is a small, very thin young woman with sallow skin and heavy makeup. Her chief feature is her heavy, glossy black hair, which she wears in an elaborate, stiff "beehive." Her own background is a very deprived one. Her mother was part of a large Mexican family of migrant workers who had been coming to the area every summer for years. Her father, of mixed Irish-American Indian background, was a truck driver for a large papermill. Theresa was born of a casual relationship when her mother was 15; her father acknowledged her as his child but refused to pay for her support. Her mother continued to take her and her younger sister along with the family as they "worked the crops" in various areas; then, when Theresa was 10, her mother ran off to California and severed all ties with the two girls. Her father was given custody of the two girls and they were placed in a series of foster homes.

When Theresa was 16, she finally dropped out of school and spent the next three years hitchhiking around the country. A year before we saw her she returned to the city, found a room for herself in "Shantytown," and took a job in the pea-canning factory. Since then, her center of activity had been the bowling alley–tavern near her house. Here she met her Polish-American husband, who drove a long-distance truck up and down the Mississippi Valley. For a while she traveled around with him on his rig; then, with the approach of the baby's birth, they set up house in a small apartment. Her husband borrowed money from her father to buy his own truck but spent it instead drinking. Since then, her father had "washed his hands" of them, and her younger sister, married to a farmer in the area, refused to have anything to do with her.

Current Situation.   Theresa appears to be scared, confused, and frustrated at suddenly being saddled with the care of a baby for whom she does not know how to care and who cries a good deal of the time. She never talks to Eddie or calls him by name; there appears to be no emotional bonding between them. She herself is socially isolated, relying on the tavern for whatever social contacts she has. She vacillates between wanting to terminate her parental rights to the baby and wanting to keep him. She speaks vaguely of having him adopted some day but refuses to give him up if it would mean that Eddie would go to his father, whom she regards as an alcoholic who never cared for either of them. She also refuses to place Eddie in foster care, even temporarily, although she needs hospitalization for some unspecified complaint as a result of having been "torn up inside" from a previous abortion. She says he is the only thing that is really hers, but admits that she has spanked him very hard on his buttocks when he refuses to eat and continues to cry.

Help for Theresa and Eddie has primarily taken the form of meeting her material needs through finding her heated housing quarters, providing food stamps and funds for winter clothes and furniture, arranging for instruction in basic childcare from the visiting nurse, and offering her a good deal of emotional support. We have returned periodically to discuss adoptive placement for Eddie, but Theresa feels far too deprived and needful herself to think of giving him up. Instead, we have concentrated on meeting her own needs, so that she can see how things could be different for her child.

As young parents pass through the transition of the birth of their first child, they often set the pattern for their feeling, thinking, and acting during subsequent pregnancies and births. While generally they report that they feel more relaxed and knowledgeable in bearing further children, the first experience remains a significant milestone in their maturation as parents.

7

Geographic Moves and Migrations

Moving can be an occasion of joy, of gaining a new lease on life, or it can be a challenge and, for some, a source of deep distress. Consider the young woman who grew up in the country or a small town moving to the big city for the first time. She asks herself: Will I find a job? Will I be able to make friends? Will I be unbearably lonely? Will I be safe? Or put yourself in the position of the career person looking for bigger and better opportunities: Will things, in fact, be any better there? I wonder how I'll manage not seeing my family and friends very often? Lastly, imagine the immigrant from another country: How will those foreigners accept me? Will I ever be able to learn the language so I can get along? Who will there be to help me if things go wrong? What if I want to come back and don't have the money?[1]

AMERICA IS A COUNTRY of movers. Since World War II, between 18 and 20 percent of the population has moved annually; thus, in any given year, about 37 million persons change their place of residence.[2] Some merely exchange one house or apartment for another in the same community; others move from inner city to outer suburb or from rural farm area to congested city neighborhood; still others migrate considerable distances within the country's borders or beyond.

In this chapter we shall consider only one small aspect of the multifaceted subject of migration, with its complex economic, social, and political ramifications. We shall limit ourselves to examining the transitional process which

the individual and his family pass through as they move from place to place.*
This process of geographic change and adaptation goes on throughout the life
span—it has been estimated that each of us will have moved an average of
fourteen times during his or her lifetime. Nevertheless, we include it in this
section on young adulthood because young adults tend to move more often
than those at other life stages as they prepare to set down roots and establish
themselves on their life course. The moving of older adults to retirement
communities or old people's homes will be considered as part of the aging
process, while the special aspects of moving as part of divorce or widowhood
will be discussed within those frameworks.

Moving as Transition

The period of geographic moves or migrations certainly falls within our
overall definition of a time-limited interval of heightened stress and disruption that links together two relatively stable states. However, it differs markedly from other transitions in that, first, it usually involves a family unit and,
second, it is primarily concerned with the *external* adaptation of the family to
new living conditions in a new community. The balance of social roles within
the family network is less affected, even though members' handling of their
roles may be decidedly altered by the demands of the new social and physical
situation in which the family finds itself.

Brim, who sees moving as part of the normal adult socialization process,
points out that when an adult's work or family causes him to move to a
particular community, both social and geographic mobility are involved.
Change may be required in social activities, consumption patterns, alloca-
tions of leisure time, mode of dress, political attitudes, childcare practices,
and many other aspects of the individual's and family's life-style.[3]

The moving process may involve a single person, a family unit, or even a
three-generational extended family. It may be planned in the sense of a
family's deciding to move in order to provide better schools and play space
for the children or it may be unplanned in the case of a family's being evicted
without notice to make room for a slum-clearance project. It may be local
and limited in nature, so that although the address is changed, the persons
involved still shop at the same supermarket, listen to the same radio stations,
and read the same newspaper or it may involve such long distances that
comprehensive changes in customs, cultural patterns, or even language are
required. It may be temporary, such as a person's going on a year's exchange
fellowship, or permanent in the sense of a family's deciding to uproot itself
from the snow-bound climate of North Dakota and reestablish itself in the

*Technically, the U.S. Census Bureau has drawn a distinction between "moving," which takes
place within the borders of a county, and "migrating," which involves crossing county lines. We
shall, however, use the terms flexibly and sometimes interchangeably.

dry heat of southern Arizona. It may be purely pleasure- and comfort-bound in the case of a couple's moving to Marin County in the San Francisco Bay area or grimly political, as in the case of Russian Jewish immigrants or Vietnamese refugees. Yet each move involves the changing of social roles, the taking on of different social statuses, and the developing of new social relationships.[4]

Moves may take different directions in terms of social mobility. Robert Constable found that in moving upward occupationally, middle-class people tended to become familiar quickly with available resources; however, such a move places heavy pressure on the family, resulting in the aggravation of long-standing problems and the development of new ones. Lower-class families may feel the same strains plus additional ones brought on by their lack of knowledge of resources and their separation from friends and kin. Moving downward is usually associated with other breakdowns, such as family separations, loss of income, and so forth.

The actual move is often symptomatic of other, more serious problems. In moving away, families are sometimes forced to leave by stress-producing conditions in the original neighborhood, such as urban renewal projects, neighborhood changes, or a deteriorating school system. Moving toward an area, on the other hand, usually depends on some attraction in the new neighborhood, such as special recreational facilities or school services. Finally, some people and families expect to be transient as part of their way of life, as in the case of military families, engineers, and migrant workers.[5]

Frequently the process of moving is interwoven with other transitional processes and thus becomes part of both the problem and the solution. In the following excerpt from a family agency's records, moving, though planned to improve an economic condition, becomes the precipitating factor that leads to a disruption in the family's functioning.

SUSAN AND JERRY (#176)

Susan, age 26, telephoned for an appointment, explaining that she and her husband, Jerry, age 30, were returning to this city in a few months after an absence of five years. They had left town immediately after their wedding and she now had come back for a few days to find a place for them to live. Since she sounded very upset, an appointment was made for the next day.

When Susan came in, it was obvious that she was pregnant; she said she was in her fifth month. She and her three-year-old daughter, Nancy, were staying with her parents, but she felt unable to mobilize herself to start to look for a place for the family to live. She had become frightened by her inability to take care of the matter for which she had come to town and hoped I could help her find out what was "holding her down."

Susan and I agreed that we were dealing with two separate transitional issues which had become intermingled: the move back to town and the expectation of her second child. Both aspects were weighing heavily on her. Although they were planning to move back because there were better vocational opportunities for Jerry here, she had serious qualms about returning since she did not get along well with her husband's parents and felt dominated by her own mother. In addition, she was worried about her ability to mother. Nancy was a strong-minded, willful child who could not be controlled easily back home; here at her grandmother's she had become even more difficult to handle. Susan felt that her own inadequacies had become obvious to her parents, and she spent most of her time trying to "hold Nancy down."

As we discussed the various stresses she was feeling, Susan experienced some relief and lifting of her depression through verbalization of her negative feelings relating to both of these issues. She saw herself as being "caught in the trap" again after having escaped from her mother's harassment through her marriage and move out of town. In addition, by returning, she was letting herself open to the disapproval of Jerry's family, who did not think she was good enough for him.

I did not see Susan again for several months, until she called to make another appointment. She came in looking less depressed but more pregnant; she said she expected her baby in several weeks. Since I had last seen her, she had found a townhouse to rent located at a distance from both sets of parents. On her return east, she had discussed the issues we had raised with her husband, and they had agreed to limit their involvement with their respective families at this time. They had just made the formal move back to this city and Jerry was starting his new job on Monday.

Susan came in for a series of four individual interviews and one joint one with Jerry before the birth of the baby. The coming of the new baby was very anxiety-provoking for her, as she still had grave misgivings about her ability to handle both Nancy and the new infant. During our individual sessions, she dwelt on her negative feelings about her own mother, who had always been very critical and controlling of her. She described her father as "kindly and good" and said her husband was much like him. As she was helped to deal with her feelings on a more mature level, Susan's depression and fears began to lift and her functioning as a mother improved. In our joint session, Jerry was supportive of Susan's mothering efforts and cooperative about where and how they would live in this new location.

Throughout this time, Susan and Jerry were settling down in their new home and making the necessary adaptations in their family patterns. Nancy was placed in a nursery school and Susan began to prepare the new baby's room. Both she and Jerry felt that the relationship issues with their parents were still unresolved, but decided to postpone further consideration until they were both more settled and less pressured with their own affairs.

Stages in the Moving Process

As with other transitions, the process of moving and migration can be divided into various phases. Myrtle Reul, a social worker, was one of the first to analyze in depth the common patterns in what she calls the "migration episode."[6] The basis of her personal experience in traveling with and interviewing migratory workers as they transversed the country showed that the process could be divided into four stages: (1) making a decision; (2) breaking with the past; (3) carrying out the move; and (4) making an adjustment. (Note the similarity to other transitional stages.)

DECISION MAKING

The decision to move or to migrate, says Reul, is usually a family decision, even if all may not be involved in the move. The family member who originates the idea may not necessarily be the actual decision maker, whose identity may be determined by the family's culture, class, and structure. It may be an aged matriarch, a respected great-uncle, or even the neighborhood "wise man." Until the decision maker hears the suggestion and accepts the plan, migration cannot take place.

Determination to migrate may be inspired by the need for a better job, for more security, money, prestige, recognition, or freedom. It may be impelled by the search for a different way of life, the need for personal gratification, or the desire to be close to relatives or friends. However, to become activated, the individual (or family) must counter the tendency to preserve the status quo, the pressure to adhere to the familiar and known.* Overcoming this inertia involves exerting a double presure; the *push force*, which presents the personal or financial disadvantages of remaining in the place of origin; and the *pull force*, which embodies the advantages of the place of destination.

Items going into the decision to move include many varied aspects of the community being considered, such as climate, topography, cost of living, life-style, government policies, business conditions, and health and recreational facilities. Since every decision always involves a balancing of gains and losses in relation to the network of subsystems that make up an individual's existence, the decision maker must reckon with the trade-offs involved in the projected move: its effect on family relationships, children's education and welfare, social ties, proximity to aging relatives, and so forth.

Often the primary reason people move, says Reul, is the ability to find a better work situation. The pulls may include the following considerations: increased salary; recognition from superiors or peers; the possibility for personal growth and additional education or the chance to work with a recognized authority in the field; enhanced interpersonal relations with superiors, subordinates, and/or peers; advancement through a change in status, rank, or position; delegated responsibility; variety in work assignments; job security through tenure or company stability; and better work conditions such as a private secretary, private office, or company car.

Francine and Douglas Hall, in analyzing the working couple's dilemma in deciding whether or not to move when one of them is offered a job elsewhere, see that the family has four basic options: (1) to turn the offer down; (2) to accept it and relocate the whole family; (3) to accept it and relocate only the person offered the job, who will see the spouse and children when it can be arranged; or (4) to come up with a creative alternative to satisfy the person, his employer, spouse, and children. They suggest the device of

*See the discussion on Marris's term "conservative impulse" in Chapter 2.

setting up an "expectancy table"—including the listing of all possible outcomes and the weighting of the probabilities of each event occurring—to
help the family consider all of the consequences associated with either the
"yes" or "no" decision.[7]

THE BREAK WITH THE PAST

Once the decision to move or migrate has been made, the person and/or
family must go through the leave-taking phase of breaking with the past in
order to plan for the future. The process of packing, of sorting out stored-
away mementos and outgrown, old-fashioned clothes, brings back a flood of
earlier memories that often is very distressing:

> As he cancels his newspaper delivery service, says good-bye to friends and
> family, resigns from his job, or packs his belongings, these physical actions
> are accompanied by the realization that he will be losing many familiar situa-
> tions and relationships. Since all of the familiar things around him—even
> unpleasant ones—are part of his sense of identity, this sense of loss creates
> conflict for the migrant that may be seen in some form of separation anxiety.[8]

This core anxiety may lie at the heart of much of the individual's "busyness"
as he prepares for the move. Although the excess energy required in handling all the physical arrangements for leaving the old home and arriving at
the new one is often blamed for the person's psychic distress at this stage, it
frequently serves to cover up the underlying anxiety over leaving the familiar past and moving to an uncertain future.

The problem becomes, of course, exacerbated when the decision to leave
is not a voluntary one. Some twenty years ago, Marc Fried investigated the
effect of forced dislocation from the slums of Boston's West End, as part of
Erich Lindemann's program to examine the effects of various types of crisis
situations.[9] He found that the predominant reaction among the persons he
interviewed two years after the move was that of *grief*. This was manifested
in feelings of painful loss, continued longing, and a generally depressive
tone; frequent symptoms of psychological, social, or somatic stress; a sense of
helplessness; occasional expressions of direct or displaced anger; and tendencies to idealize the lost home.

In his analysis of the grief patterns manifested, Fried found a strong
association between positive feelings toward the old area and severe grief.
He concluded that grieving for a lost home shows most of the characteristics
of mourning for a lost person. Two of the important cognitive components of
the reactions were the fragmentation of the sense of *spatial identity* and the
sense of *group identity* that depended on stable, familiar social networks.
Tied to these were the affective qualities of loss of feelings of security and
commitment and depressive reactions. For the working-class population affected by the disruption, the sense of continuity had been fragmented.

Identity—socially especially disrupted
Disruption of social bonds & networks
Even if move is @ voluntary — People
a different respond differently — hardest
pt adolescents

The problem, however, is not limited to migrant farm workers or urban slum dwellers. Maxine Gaylord, who investigated the impact of geographic moves on middle- and upper-middle-class corporate employees and their families, observes that regardless of the reason for a family's move, it entails a built-in sense of loss for all.[10] Each family member, in his or her own way, will experience this, and periods of depression are unavoidable. Children from the ages of three to five often experience emotional difficulties, primarily caused by misinterpretations arising from the fantasy world in which they live. In addition, they frequently see the move as a punitive, hostile act on the part of powerful parents.

Adolescents from fourteen to sixteen, on the other hand, suffer from social frustrations. Since they are in a developmental stage when self-doubt and uncertainty are already high, any added pressure may exhaust their adaptive energies. Acceptance and confirmation of the individual by his/her peers are essential for proper emotional and intellectual growth. The issue of a transfer of identity thus become crucial to the adolescent whose family is planning to move, and sometimes is resolved by having him remain behind with friends and relatives when the family moves. In the experience of families migrating to Israel, the teenage family members were frequently found to be most opposed to the move and suffered the greatest difficulties in their social adjustment.

Myrna Weissman and Eugene Paykel, in their study of depressed women patients at a New Haven mental health clinic, found that a number of them had undergone geographic moves in the recent past.[11] Although the women attributed their depressive symptoms to other factors such as financial problems, increased loneliness, aggravated marital friction, problems with children, career frustrations, and identity confusion, it was found that these events were, in most cases, the byproducts of faulty adaptation to the stresses and changes created by the moving process.

In some cases, it was found that the move had been the last straw in a series of stressful events and interpersonal difficulties; in other cases, moving represented an unsuccessful attempt to resolve financial or marital problems. However, at times the move itself created new stresses and interpersonal difficulties which had not existed earlier.

ACTUAL MIGRATION

The third phase in the transition of moving is the actual physical transfer from the old to the new location. Carlos Sluzki notes that migration is a transition with little or no prescribed rituals. In most cultures and circumstances, migrants are left to deal with the act by the private procedures they work out.[12] Moving takes many forms. The entire family may pile into the overloaded family jalopy to cross the country together to find a new home (as did the dust-grimed Okies of the 1930s portrayed in John Steinbeck's *Grapes of Wrath*). On the other hand, it may be a carefully planned and executed maneuver that may cover a considerable period of time from the place of origin to the place of destination, with a number of intermediate stops. It may even be characterized by a lack of predetermined final destination, with the person or family trying out a number of places before making a definitive choice.

Sluzki finds that the mode or style of the migratory act varies considerably:

1. Some families "burn bridges" behind them and their migration takes on the character of a final and unchangeable act. Others say they are moving for "just a while" even though their return to their place of origin is unlikely.
2. Some families migrate blindly and *en bloc*, with no previous exploration of the field. Others organize more cautiously and send some members ahead as "scouts" to prepare the terrain, secure jobs and housing, and make preliminary arrangements.
3. Some families decide *a priori* that the place they have chosen will be "it," while others explicitly plan on trial periods in various places in order to decide among destinations.
4. Some families migrate legally and have access to institutions of the country (or place) of adoption, while others migrate illegally, thus enhancing their mistrust of and alienation from mainstream institutions.

The person (or family) during this phase can be considered to be "in between systems," having left the stable life of the past and not yet a part of the new world ahead. He may have spent some time on the road, perhaps dawdling along and enjoying the trip, or hurry to reach his goal by a prescribed deadline. Earlier anxieties and doubts have now been closed off; he is on his way.[13]

When the individual finally reaches his destination, the holiday feeling of euphoria continues as he finds temporary lodging, unpacks his hand luggage, and begins to look around: for a job, a place to live, shopping facilities, a laundromat, and "people like himself" who can help him settle in. His first reaction is to observe and evaluate the new situation, to try to absorb new impressions and make sense of what is going on around him. He attempts to understand it by comparing it with his former world, by trying to figure out how he, with his own values, hopes, and experiences, can fit into the unfamiliar scene. Judith Shuval describes these processes graphically in her study of immigrant transit camps during the first years of the State of Israel.[14]

The most common difficulty at this time, says Reul, is the feeling of *dissonance* that results from experiencing situations that produce cognitive inconsistency. Dissonance, defined as "a negative drive state which occurs

*Dissonance between expectations
& reality - inconsistent ideas & opinions*

whenever an individual simultaneously holds two cognitions (beliefs, ideas, opinions) which are psychologically inconsistent,"[15] often rises out of the gap between what is hoped for and what is found.

A person may experience dissonance in various aspects of the migration scene. He may find a sharp discrepancy between his own expectations of physical conditions in the new place and what he actually finds there. He may sense a difference between his own opinions and attitudes and those of the significant others in the group he is preparing to join. He may note a difference in role expectations and role patterns from what he has been accustomed to, and this may threaten his sense of identity or self-esteem.

Because of the many uncertainties and anxieties inherent in this phase, the newcomer often reacts to the discrepancies "between what was and what is, and between what is and what he had hoped would be" by viewing the new world selectively, by denying even obvious faults and drawbacks, and by becoming indiscriminately enthusiastic about the new situation.

An interesting observation, noted by Reul, is that persons who select their own new place in which to live and work experience more dissonance than those who had little or no choice. Conversely, persons who feel they had no control over the decision to move or the selection of destination tend to feel less dissonant—as in the case of evicted families, corporation employees ordered to relocate, or political refugees. Here the urgency of the need to resettle lessens or even removes entirely any dissonance or immediate negative reaction. In Israel, the factor of *ein breira* ("no alternative") has been a significant determinant in helping immigrants from some countries adjust to the economic and social difficulties of the new country of settlement.

THE ADJUSTMENT PERIOD

The third phase imperceptibly melds into the final adjustment period of the migration process. Adjustment occurs when the migrant begins to recover from the initial shock of being in a new environment and proceeds with the long, hard, and purposeful task entailed in becoming part of a new social system. Reul finds that, instead of merely reacting emotionally to his new situation, as he did in the previous phase, the individual now begins to follow a plan of action in order to change either himself or his environment to suit his needs.

Some years ago, when immigration was examined as a transitional state, we viewed it as consisting of two complementary processes: the newcomer's integration into the community and the community's absorption of the immigrant into its midst.[16] Six potential problem areas in which adaptation would have to take place were delineated: income management (earning and spending), health, housing, education, leisure-time activities, and citizenship.

In each of these areas, as already indicated at the close of Chapter 2, two sets of tasks were outlined along the two dimensions of the *material-arrangemental* axis, which dealt with the practical, action-oriented steps that both individual and community had to carry out in order for adaptation to take place, and the *psychosocial* axis, which dealt with the more subtle and less tangible cognitive and emotional changes that had to occur. Table 7.1 shows how these two axes have been worked out in one of the six problem areas, *income management*. Similar tables can be developed for the other problem areas, with specific attention to the unique nature of the move under consideration.

A series of research studies have attempted to gauge retrospectively the effects of geographic mobility on families. Particularly relevant is the one carried out by Stella Jones, who examined the responses of 256 women whose husbands were in managerial or professional positions.[17] She found a pattern of husband and wife working together to make the major decisions concerning the move. Availability of information regarding the new community—particularly about schools and the cost of living—prior to the move and the making of exploratory trips before the final transfer were considered important. Informal learning mechanisms, such as experience gained in previous moves and personal contacts, were felt to be more helpful than a formal structured course on the moving process.

The wives felt that moving did not impede the development of a small number of good, intimate friends and that the moving experience helped them to increase their ability to cope with stress, made them more flexible and adaptable, gave them a broader range of interests, developed their skills in meeting people, and helped them to understand and accept other people, cultures, and customs.

Another study found that in a sample of 159 families with 318 children between the ages of three and eighteen who had made long-distance moves in the recent past, 80 percent of the children made friends easily in the new community and 75 percent reported that school changes were not difficult.[18] The problem became somewhat greater for adolescents, since one-third were reported to be having school difficulties.

Robert Constable, a school social worker, feels that the school is in a crucial ecological position to help the family who moves.[19] The successful adjustment of a child will depend largely on the school and peer group, which are interrelated. When there is a single-parent family or when both parents are employed, the role of the school and of the peer group in the child's socialization becomes dramatically increased. It takes on primary importance for the latency-age and older child.

Most children adjust to a change in environment without involvement of the school social worker, who can focus his concern on those children for whom the process will not succeed. Constable advocates the use of a "distant early warning system" made up of the school nurse, the principal, and other personnel who might be sensitive to the child's special needs.

Sluzki feels that the adjustment period should be divided into the short- and long-range effects of migratory stress.[20] During the first months of the initial "honeymoon," a task-oriented overefficient approach seems to be employed. Often a decided split between the instrumental and affective roles within the family becomes evident. During this period, the most obvious differences between the place of departure and the place of arrival are examined and analyzed in a detached, rational manner, without awareness being displayed of the underlying stressful nature of the immigration experience or of its cumulative impact. Previous family styles of functioning may be continued and even exaggerated. If family members had been close physically and affectively before migration they become even closer now; if they had been mutually distant, they now increase their distance even though the lack of extended networks may force them to spend more time together. Conflicts or individual pathology tend to remain dormant.

Months and even years afterwards, the additive effects of the strengths and weaknesses of the family's coping mechanisms may find expression full-blast. The ineffectiveness of applying old family rules and values to the new culture and society will force a choice between changing or maintaining them. This in turn will call for changing the distribution of roles, norms, and mores which encompass every member of the family. On the other hand, maintaining the old rules may lead to development of an alienating split between the inner world of the family and the outer world in which they live.

During the migration process, some families can manage to mourn what has been left behind and integrate their memories constructively into their own reality. In other cases, however, what was left behind becomes increasingly idealized and idolized, making adaptation to the new life more difficult. Alternatively, it may become denigrated to such an extent that mourning and working through the loss becomes an impossible task. In most cases, coping patterns of the individual members and of the family as a whole become stretched to the limit under the impact of the new demands, and at times they may collapse altogether.

Extreme levels of enmeshment or split can be observed, as well as high levels of intrafamilial confrontation, with some members representing the values of the country of origin, and others, those of the new society. In almost all cases, observes Sluzki, these are accompanied by a distortion of remembrances of the "good old days." Factionalization will appear as tension and overt conflict between spouses or between parents and children, with a tightening of intragenerational coalitions. These conflicts will reach a peak and then progressively fade away, build up into a major interpersonal crisis, or crystallize into medical or psychiatric complaints.

Table 7.1. Material Arrangement Tasks in Integration-Absorption Process: Income Management

TASK FOR IMMIGRANT	TASK FOR COMMUNITY
1. Explore available income sources: work, pension, social security, transfer payments, stipends, special grants, loans, private resources (savings, relatives, and so on); investigate shopping facilities, banking arrangements, investment opportunities, alternate ways of handling money.	1. Compile and make available a directory of job opportunities, data on social security, welfare payments, special benefits, union qualifications, income tax waivers, and so forth; canvass community for potential positions for hard-to-place persons; set up shopping and savings arrangements familiar to and convenient for newcomers.
2. Select job opportunity in which interested; learn qualifications; obtain proper preparation; check eligibility, local regulations regarding money transfers, banking arrangements, credit union, check-cashing, and so forth.	2. Specify qualifications for various jobs and eligibility regulations; set up orientation and training programs for jobs, purchasing, investment, tax information, and money management; train community residents in spending and purchasing habits of the newcomers.
3. Apply for job, social security, stipend, and so forth; arrange for credit, bank accounts, buying of food, clothing, household needs; join union, professional organizations.	3. Accept job applications and bring together employers and potential employees; process applications for credit, banking services, and currency transfers; induct applicants into unions and professional groups.
4. Begin to develop new working skills and work patterns; start adjusting to new conditions, shopping hours, purchasing habits, spending and saving patterns; learn new ways to keep house, cook, use domestic help, and so forth.	4. Adjust working arrangements to make use of newcomers' skills and to accommodate new working styles; make accommodations regarding newcomers' shopping hours, purchasing habits, salaries, childcare needs; develop new opportunities for investments; open new facilities for buying and spending.
5. Arrange for and accept supervision; enter into apprenticeship programs until productivity and income rises to acceptable norms; solicit periodic help from neighbors and friends in adapting to local ways of buying and spending, seasonal needs, and the like.	5. Arrange for and set up supervisory or apprenticeship programs until newcomers' productivity and income rise to acceptable norms; set up periodic demonstration projects and follow-up programs on buying and spending.

Psychosocial Tasks in Integration-Absorption Process: Income Management

Task for Immigrant	Task for Community
1. Cope with threat to past job security, levels of work performance, earnings, income limitations, and accustomed ways of handling money.	1. Cope with threat to prestige and job security of present job incumbents, previous levels of work performance, salary scales, customary ways of handling money, and sources of income.
2. Grapple with anxieties and frustrations in transitional state while investigating job opportunities and struggling with unfamiliar currency, modes of shopping, bill payments, check-writing, and so forth.	2. Grapple with anxieties and frustrations of potential employers, unions, and the like in arranging for training programs; explain need for unfamiliar regulations and procedures.
3. Handle feelings of stress and insecurity generated by applying for job, social security, admission to professional group, and the like; deal with worries regarding currency arrangements, credit loans, and financial security.	3. Tolerate the stress and negative attitudes of employers and job incumbents; accept stress reactions of newcomers in applying for jobs, money transfers, setting up currency arrangements, and so forth.
4. Adjust to new work roles (e.g., from self-employed to worker); redistribute family statuses (from housewife to breadwinner, husband to student); take on new family roles for shopping, childcare, and so on to accommodate to new conditions.	4. Redefine old roles in employer-employee relations, redistribute statuses (from worker-oriented to middle-class society) to accommodate to new values in income management, permit newcomers to participate and rise in economic hierarchy.
5. Develop new standards of "good" job, "necessary" living arrangements, and acceptable range of buying and spending until integration process is completed.	5. Develop new standards of "acceptable" job performance, reduce pressures and demands on newcomers, live with reduced expectations and increased anxiety engendered by new competitors until absorption process is completed.

Source: Naomi Golan and Ruth Gruschka, "Integrating the New Immigrant: A Model for Social Work Practice in Transitional States," Social Work 16, 2 (April 1971): 85–86. Copyright 1971, National Association of Social Workers, Inc. Reprinted with permission, from Social Work, Vol. 16, No. 2 (April 1971), pp. 82–87.

Sometimes the conflict raised by the migration transition can become attenuated or subside for years, only to emerge when the second generation, raised in the country of adoption, picks up what the first generation has heretofore avoided and makes it the theme of a clash between generations. Sluzki notes that this process can be seen particularly in families whose cultural groups have been "ghettoized in their country of adoption, since this closed environment buffers and slows the adaptation."[21]

It is often difficult to predict how successful the adjustment process will be, since the factors inherent to the moving situation are superimposed on basic personality factors. In the following two cases, both involving Russian-Jewish families who migrated to the United States, one unit ended up very well integrated, while the second made only a limited acclimatization. Both were referred to the local Jewish Family Service for help in adjusting to the community to which they had been assigned.

MIKHAIL AND LYDIA BOROKOV (#178)

Mikhail and Lydia Borokov arrived in town with their son, Boris, age 12, coming from Moscow to join their cousin and a more distant relative who had settled here earlier. Their primary motive for immigrating was to insure educational opportunities for their son, since they felt he had no future in the USSR. On a more practical level, they wanted to insure their own safety. Both husband and wife were dentists. They had been salaried government employees, and in addition did private work after hours—a widespread practice that was not officially sanctioned and could put them in danger if the Soviet officials chose to "take measures." They also strongly disliked the Soviet system of government, they said; although they were giving up a comfortable, secure existence there, they had dreamed for years of freedom here.

Mikhail, 42, was tall, slender, and well-groomed, with an open, outgoing manner and quick sense of humor. Lydia, 31, was attractive and vivacious, already quite American in her style of dress. Both were very eager to improve their limited English and become Americanized; they seemed eager to discard their past and talked of their new life zestfully. They already spoke Russian, French, and some German and did not anticipate difficulty in learning English. The Borokovs had already had their first interview at the Vocational Service. Mikhail understood that he would have difficulty receiving a license and entering the dental profession and was prepared to work in a dental laboratory for the time being. Their plan was for Lydia to return to dental school and take her professional degree while he supported the family; then she would work and it would be his turn to qualify. Eventually they hoped to open an office together, as they had done in Moscow.

The primary needs for the Borokovs, they said, were first to find a place to live and second to learn English. They were temporarily living at a medium-priced hotel but were eager to find permanent housing. They planned to look for an apartment in the Marshall High School district, since they wanted Boris to attend a good school with a high reputation and special educational features. They were being tutored privately in English but planned to enroll in the special classes which would open next month at the vocational school. The family would receive limited financial assistance until Mikhail started to work. They had taken a scientific approach to handling their budget and started to visit various stores to do comparison shopping, in order to find the best buys.

The family was seen as primarily needing informational and directional services, and it was expected that they would shortly be able to manage on their own. Several issues were raised concerning their Jewish identity, but they preferred to put them aside until they were settled.

In contrast to the Borokovs, the immigrant described in the following case example was older, had no spouse to support him, and had limited knowledge of the English language. His inappropriate work expectations as well as his basic inflexibility and inability to size up his new situation realistically made his adjustment to his new community far more difficult.

PAVEL GRINBURG (#125)

Dr. Pavel Grinburg, age 53, a heavy, dark-browed widower, arrived in New York with his son, Armin, age 19. He had been chief of neurosurgery in a large government hospital in Leningrad for some twenty-five years. In coming to the United States, he was confident that he could continue in his profession, and he looked forward to working with American surgeons. He was soon installed in a midtown hotel and immediately came to the Vocational Service to arrange to take his qualifying examinations. The counselor felt somewhat dubious, in view of Dr. Grinburg's age and limited specialization, but hoped that his drive, apparent intelligence, and impressive work credentials might, in the end, enable him to achieve his goals.

The first obstacle was his lack of English. A relatively high level of language proficiency was required to pass the English portion of the Educational Council for Foreign Medical Graduates (ECFMG) examination, a prerequisite to taking an internship. Since Dr. Grinburg was not adept at languages, he learned very slowly and it took him a long time to prepare for this examination.

At the same time, in order to help him gain a better understanding of American medical knowledge and techniques, Dr. Grinburg was enrolled in a three-month full-time medical review course aimed at preparing foreign physicians to take the ECFMG exam. Throughout the program, he expressed confidence that his many years of medical experience and his training at a respected Soviet medical institute would ensure his passing the examination.

Upon completion of the medical review course, Dr. Grinburg submitted his application. A traumatic series of events then occurred; on three separate occasions, he failed the ECFMG, both the medical and the English parts. With hindsight, it became clear that his many years of surgical practice had enabled him to function well in his specialty but had removed him from the more general field of medical practice. As a result he had lost his "feel" for basic medicine. In addition, his underlying difficulty in mastering English prevented him from taking full advantage of the medical review course.

By his third failure, Dr. Grinburg was demoralized. Extensive counseling was needed to help him face up realistically to his situation. In time, he came to grasp the fact that it was crucial that he find work—any type of job—in order to become self-supporting. After contacting a number of hospitals, the counselor was finally able to locate a position for him as a darkroom technician who developed X-rays.

At last contact, Dr. Grinburg remained a solitary, deeply embittered person, his dreams of achieving eminence as an American surgeon shattered. Nevertheless, he gained some comfort in knowing that at least he was able to maintain himself independently. His one sustaining hope was that at least his son, who was now enrolled in a premedical program at a local university, would have the opportunity to make full use of his potential here.

These two migration cases, while concerned specifically with emigration from the Soviet Union, can be considered characteristic of the adjustment difficulties of large groups of socio-geo-political displaced persons who have come or have been brought to "countries of refuge" within recent years. Without going into the broader policy and planning issues involved, it becomes apparent that a thorough appreciation of the transitional aspects of the individual's or family's struggle to adapt becomes an integral precondition to working in this area.

8

The Mid-Adult Years: Adjusting and Changing

Midway in the journey of our life I found myself in a dark wood, for the straight way was lost. Ah, how hard it is to tell what that wood was, wild, rugged, harsh; the very thought of it renews the fear! It is so bitter that death is hardly more so. But, to treat of the good that I found in it, I will tell of the other things I saw there.

—*Dante*, The Divine Comedy[1]

WHEN DANTE ALIGHIERI, at age thirty-seven, was banished from Florence in approximately the year 1300, he went through a dark and difficult period until he was able to emerge, prolific and creative again, in his mid-forties. This opening passage from his greatest work is often quoted as expressing the quintessence of the midlife crisis. Similar breaks in continuity and direction have been noticed in the lives of other great creative figures.[2]

Within the last few years, a tremendous flow of articles, books, films, plays, and television programs have used this struggle as the central theme. A growing volume of literature, some based on personal experience and some on research studies of others' behavior, is emerging.[3] In reviewing this material, it soon becomes apparent that few authors agree on even the time span involved. Richard Kerckhoff finds that although the United States Census Bureau defines middle age as lasting from forty-five to sixty-four, research on the middle years may use an onset-age of as early as thirty and a

115

minal age of as late as seventy.[4] The Social Science Research Council demarcates middle age as lasting from forty to sixty and refers to the special stresses of the midlife crisis as apparently occurring throughout that span of time.[5] Neugarten, too, sees the entire period of middle age as one of "heightened sensitivity to one's position within a complex environment, with reassessment of the self as a pervailing theme."[6]

While Erikson assigns to his seventh stage of maturity (which presumably corresponds to the period of middle adulthood) the central task of resolving the *generativity vs. self-absorption* dilemma,[7] Robert Peck suggests that middle age should be viewed as the start of the second half of living.[8] He sees it as a period of psychological change and adjustment during which four major tasks must be mastered:

1. *Valuing Wisdom vs. Valuing Physical Powers.* Although an inescapable consequence of aging is a decrease in physical strength, stamina, and attractiveness, the sheer experience that longer living brings can make the middle-aged person accomplish more than younger persons through the use of wisdom, the ability to make the most effective choices among the alternatives which intellectual perception and imagination present for one's definition. Peck found that those who age most successfully at this stage are those who put the use of their heads above the use of their hands.

2. *Socializing vs. Sexualizing in Human Relationships.* This is interpreted as the opportunity brought on by the sexual climacteric to take on a new kind of value in which men and women are redefined as individuals and as companions rather than primarily as sex objects.

3. *Cathectic (Emotional) Flexibility vs. Cathectic Impoverishment.* This implies the capacity to shift emotional investments from one person to another and from one activity to another. Individuals at this stage, when their parents die, their children grow up and leave home, and their circle of friends and relatives begins to be broken up, need the capacity to shift their interest to other ties in their community and vocational worlds and to develop new relationships and pursuits.

4. *Mental Flexibility vs. Mental Rigidity.* At this time, the question of whether one can gain control over one's own life or must be driven by external events and experiences emerges. Some people learn to utilize their experiences to achieve a degree of perspective and use them as guides to solve new issues, while others tend to grow increasingly inflexible in their opinions and actions and are closed to new ideas.

Rather than consider the entire period of middle adulthood, we are limiting our discussion to two separate key transitions which may or may not be fanned into crises. Although the time spans may vary and in some cases may overlap and merge, their scope and processes are quite different—distinctions which have implications for treatment. The first, the transition to mid-adulthood, refers to the lead-in to the new developmental stage, lasting from about age thirty-eight to forty-two, give or take a few years at either end. This is the second of the three vertical transitions described at the start of this section, and it binds together early and mid-adulthood; it is essentially intrapsychic and existential in nature.

The second transition may begin as early as the late thirties but peaks approximately ten years later. I have termed it "the transition to post-parenthood," and it embodies both the social role passages incurred in moving from the emptying to the restructuring of the family nest and the physical changes involved in the climacteric and menopausal phases. Before starting this discussion, however, a point should be made about gender differences.

In a study of 100 men and women, Neugarten found that both men and women tended to see life during middle age as restructured in terms of time-left-to-live rather than time since birth.[9] She also noted a growing "interiority," a turning inward to the self, with a decreased emphasis on assertiveness and mastery of the environment. Both sexes saw themselves as a bridge between generations, although women tended to define their age status in terms of the timing of events within the family cycle, while men, on the other hand, perceived the onset of middle age by cues presented outside of the family context, often in the area of work or career. "Body monitoring" was used to guard against a new sense of physical vulnerability for men; women were more concerned with their husband's body monitoring and their own "rehearsal for widowhood." While the men reported increased job pressures and job boredom, the women felt an increased sense of freedom and the beginning of a period in which their latent talents and capacities could be put to use in new directions. In the light of these differences, effort will be made, in discussing the two transitions, to distinguish between the reactions of men and women.

Transition to Mid-Adulthood

Almost fifty years ago, the journalist, Walter Pitkin optimistically declared, "Life begins at forty!" Since then, a number of observers have recorded a wide range of reactions to this fateful birthday. Barbara Fried was one of the first to call the transitional period between early adulthood and middle age the "middle-age crisis."[10] She reported that women seem to go through this period between the age of forty and forty-five. She, as well as others, uses the term "middlescence" to describe the individual's reversion to behaviors, thoughts, and feelings which parallel those of adolescence (both their own, retrospectively, and their children's, currently).

MEN'S REACTIONS

To learn men's reactions to the midlife transition, Joel Davitz interviewed a number of men in their early forties.[11] He found that the average man may feel a twinge of apprehension as his fortieth birthday approaches but is confident that the dolorous stories told about this period don't apply to him. He may hesitate briefly but soon continues his energetic climb upward with even renewed energy and ambition.

Gradually and almost imperceptibly, however, the seams begin to weaken. He becomes more sensitive to body aches and pains, grows tired faster, and seems to take longer to recover from illnesses. Music doesn't have its usual rich appeal to his sensitive ear, and he learns that his iron stomach and regular bowels no longer can be depended on. His hair begins to gray and grow thin, and he becomes angry when faced with evidence of weight gain. He may start to have problems in the world of work, and the rise to the top no longer seems inevitable or even possible. He finds himself thinking that he might not get to write that brilliant novel, paint that truly great picture, make a million dollars. In small and subtle ways he passes from the status of the "young man on the way up" to that of the "senior man holding his own." He becomes more realistic, down-to-earth, practical—and more responsible. He begins to work longer hours and becomes concerned about setbacks that once seemed trivial. Perhaps for the first time, he finds it difficult to meet his and his wife's sexual expectations. Faced with the shifting standards of his adolescent children, he begins to brood about his role as a husband and father and to question his own and his wife's moral code. Since he cannot readily blow up at work or with his friends, he finds it safer to explode at home, complaining bitterly about stifling routines and responsibilities imposed upon him by his wife and children.

(It should be recalled from the discussion in Chapter 4 that, chronologically, this time often corresponds to the period when wives in their mid- and late thirties return to school or begin to work. Often this adds to the upset in the family's role equilibrium and increases the husband's discontent.)

Elliot Jaques, the British psychoanalyst, in his influential paper,[12] sees the midlife transition as evident in some form in everyone. After tracing its manifestation in the creative work of great men carried out in their middle and late thirties, he finds that the crisis may take three forms: the creative career may simply come to an end, either through the drying up of creativity or in actual death; it may begin to show and express itself for the first time; or a decisive change in the quality and content of creativeness may take place.

The key lies in the arrival at the midpoint of life, as the individual stops growing up and begins to grow old. With family and occupation established and children on the threshold of adulthood, he enters the prime of life and paradoxically finds that beyond life lies the shadow of death. Jaques maintains that this fact, the intrusion of the reality and inevitability of one's own eventual personal death upon the psychological scene, is the central and crucial feature of the midlife phase. While in early adulthood successful activity can obscure or conceal depressive anxiety, the midlife crisis thrusts it forward with great intensity, resulting in compulsive attempts to remain young, hypochondrical concerns over health and appearance, emergence of sexual promiscuity in order to prove youth and potency, lack of genuine enjoyment of life, and absorption in religious concerns.

Probably the most comprehensive analysis of the male transition to mid-adulthood has been made by Levinson and his associates. [13] He feels that when a man experiences a developmental crisis in his late thirties, it stems from his overwhelming feeling that he has not been able to accomplish the tasks of the previous period, the "settling down" phase of the mid-thirties. He then enters a new period of structure-changing, during which he must work on three major tasks: *to terminate the period of early adulthood, to take the first steps into mid-adulthood, and to deal with the polarities which are the sources of deep division in his life.* He found that some 80 percent of his subjects were engaged in moderate to severe life upheavals during this bridging period in their adult cycle.

The initial focus at this time is on a reappraisal of the past, as the man begins to ask himself:

> What have I done with my life? What do I really get from and give to my wife, children, friends, work, community—and self? What is it I truly want for myself and others? What are my central values and how are they reflected in my life? What are my greatest talents and how am I using (or wasting) them? What have I done with my early Dream and what do I want with it now? Can I live in a way that combines my current desires, values, and talents? How satisfactory is my present life structure . . . and how shall I change it to provide a better basis for the future? [p. 192]

Levinson sees the process of "de-illusionment" as central to this phase, as the man begins to lose or reduce the illusions of early adulthood in an appropriate yet painful fashion. This may evoke diverse feelings of disappointment, joy, relief, bitterness, grief, wonder, freedom—and, above all, the sense of suffering an irreparable loss.

Gradually, the emphasis shifts from the past to the present and future. Some men make significant alterations in the external aspects of their life structure at this time: they become divorced, remarry, change their occupations and life-styles—with an accompanying decline in functioning or upsurge in creativity and social mobility. Others make fewer and less visible external changes but engage in significant internal modifications as they work on the urgent developmental issues which have emerged.

The process of *individuation*—in the sense of forming clearer boundaries between oneself and one's external world—becomes paramount.* This process, according to Jung, begins at midlife and continues throughout the remaining years. Levinson uses Jung's approach to present four tasks of individuation which he phrases in terms of the polarities which have to be

---

*This is sometimes referred to as the third individuation process, following the first individuation, or separation of the infant from his mother, and the second individuation of the adolescent from his family.

resolved: young/old,   destruction/creation,   masculine/feminine,   and attachment/separateness.

YOUNG/OLD POLARITY.   As early adulthood comes to an end, a man is beset by new fears of loss of his youth and the sense of aging. The decline in his physical and psychological powers is an important aspect of this process; he feels he cannot run as fast, lift as much, do with as little sleep as he once could. His hearing and sight are less acute; he remembers less and finds it harder to retain quantities of specific information. He is more prone to aches and pains and may undergo a serious illness during this period which threatens him with impairment or even death. Even though the decline may be quite moderate and normal, he experiences it as catastrophic. The more frequent illnesses, deaths, and losses of others around him reinforce his sensitivity; he notices and reacts to problems in others more because he is trying to come to terms with his own mortality, as Jaques has indicated.

In terms of his own achievements, the man usually reaches a turning point at which he has to change the focus of his earlier ambitions and aspirations. Levinson finds that the ability to give up the intense preoccupation with success is especially difficult if the man has not achieved his earlier goals. His task is to deal with his bitterness towards others, his contempt for himself, and his lost illusions over what might have been. When his sense of frustration is tied to his realization that he is going to die someday, he becomes concerned with the meaning of his life and the need to leave something behind, to establish a *legacy* which he hopes to pass on to future generations.

This legacy may consist of material possessions, creative products, enterprises of various kinds, or influence on others. Often it is viewed in terms of raising his children and maintaining a familial-tribal continuity. Whereas during early adulthood, the man took pleasure in begetting children and having them develop in accordance with his own image, he now shifts to viewing them as an extension of his own labors. Their lives, personal satisfactions, accomplishments, and contributions become an essential part of his legacy; he will live on through them. While such feelings, when held in moderation, enrich his relations with his children, in excess they may become the base for the struggle between him as a parent and his adolescent and young adult offspring.

A man may also see his legacy in terms of the work component of his life structure—his unique creation, which he will leave after he is gone. He becomes more interested at this time in making charitable contributions and helping worthy causes and develops a new altruism toward his community.

DESTRUCTION/CREATION POLARITY.   As the man becomes more aware of his own mortality, he also becomes more aware of destruction as a universal process, says Levinson. His developmental task in this area becomes to understand what part this has played in his own life, to reappraise his own experiences with other persons who have in some way damaged his self-esteem, hindered his development, or kept him from seeking and finding what he wanted most. He must also recognize the part *he* played in causing hurts to others, including his loved ones, and come to terms with his feelings of guilt and remorse.

Much of this reworking of painful feelings and experiences may be at an unconscious level. Many men have no awareness that they have done harm to others or might wish to do so; others feel so guilty over the real or imagined damage they have inflicted that they cannot see the issue of destructiveness in its true perspective. Still others gain, in time, some understanding that one can both feel love and hate toward the same person. During the midlife transition, men often go through intense periods of suffering, confusion, rage against others and against themselves, and grief over missed opportunities and lost parts of themselves.

MASCULINE/FEMININE POLARITY.   Those aspects of gender identity which include the man's sense of who he is as a man, who he wants to be, and who he is terrified of being assume vital importance during the midlife transition. The men in Levinson's study were concerned with such issues as their own feelings of homosexuality (overt or latent), their stress on body prowess and toughness, their pressures for achievement and ambition as an expression of their masculinity, their drives to get ahead and make their fortune for the sake of self and family, their need to wield power by controlling others, and their separation of *thinking* as a masculine trait from *feeling* as a feminine one. From this finding he deduces that each man must come to terms with the basic meaning of masculinity and femininity, which may involve a shift in his relations with his own mother and father (both real and internalized) and in his love relationships with peer women—caring about them for themselves rather than for what they give to complement him. Facing this issue makes the task of becoming a mentor to younger protégés easier and more rewarding, since he can now view them with more compassion and less competitiveness.

ATTACHMENT/SEPARATENESS POLARITY. Levinson expresses this dichotomy in terms of being engaged, involved, "plugged in," seeking, and being rooted, as opposed to being alone, immersed in one's inner world, and engaged in meditation and reverie. During the midlife transition, the man needs to reduce his heavy involvement in the external work world so that he can turn inward to discover the source of his turmoil. He must separate himself from his striving ego and external pressures so that he can "hear his inner voices." His internal self becomes as important as the external world, and he places less value on possessions, rewards, and social approval. His major developmental task in this area is to find a better balance between the needs of the self and of society.

During this transition the man must make substantive changes in several components of his life structure. For example, he must reappraise the nature of the dream he developed during early adulthood, which, with its illusions, sense of omnipotence, and heroic drama, has also become tyrannical. Now he has to rework it by reducing its excessive power and making its demands less absolute. He must also modify the meaning of the ladder symbol. Since by age forty or so he has reached the top rung of his early adult ladder, he needs to reappraise the basic meanings of success and failure. He thus becomes less driven by ambition as he emphasizes more the quality of his experiences, the intrinsic value of his work and products, and their true meaning to himself and others.

Levinson holds that part of the process is related to the shift in generational outlook. As he passes forty, the man finds that he has become a generation ahead of the young men with whom he is in contact. While initially he may feel disappointed at having been ejected from the youthful generation, he gradually finds that he, too, is changing. He enters a new world of work, family, and community life in which his most immediate ties are with other people in their forties and fifties.

He may also at this time become acutely dissatisfied with his marriage, but his dissatisfaction is rooted in his *own* failure to meet his illusions about himself rather than in his wife's shortcomings.

Levinson found five sequences by which the men in his study passed from the settling-down period to middle adulthood:

1. *Advancement within a stable life structure.* Over half of the men had achieved moderate or considerable success and awaited some culminating event to mark the efforts of "becoming one's own man" (e.g., receiving a promotion). However, the great majority found this event to be a failure or flawed success, with the outcome "good enough" but not meeting the hopes they had in mind.

2. *Serious failure or decline within a stable life structure.* A group of the men had been doing poorly for some time; now, with the start of the midlife transition, they had to face honestly the bleak reality of their lack of achievement of their dream and to consider alternate possibilities. Some of the men never recovered from the feeling of defeat and entered a decline with all the marks of failure and hopelessness. Others used the transition to form the basis for a new life, to get out of the rut and free themselves from unrealistic commitments. They began to define the ladder more broadly and find external success and failure less important than the quality of their total life.

3. *Breaking out: trying for a new life structure.* Some men found their previous structure untenable and broke out through such overt acts as leaving their wives, quitting their jobs, or moving to another region. They then tried to build a new structure more in accord with their values and aspirations. However, they found it extremely difficult to make a radical change at this time in life and the new structure often had to be a compromise.*

4. *Advancement which itself produces a change in life structure.* A few of the men moved upward in ways that produced qualitative changes in their lives and had major consequences for their future life course, particularly during their transition to midlife.

5. *Unstable life structure.* Several subjects had seemed unable to achieve any form of stable life structure and to resolve the contradictions in their life course during the settling-down period. During the midlife transition, they continued to feel the pressures of their unstable life structure as increasingly heavy burdens.

The following case summary by a private practitioner is characteristic of the bind in which some hard-driving men find themselves as they approach mid-adulthood.

HARRY WAGNER (#168)

Harry Wagner, age 40, asked for help with a number of stressful problems that had been "ganging up on him" lately. After eighteen years of marriage his wife, Marie, age 38, had grown increasingly sullen and uncooperative, and he suspected she had been doing a lot of drinking when he was not at home. Their oldest son, Kenny, 17, was rarely at home and refused even to eat with the family. Their two daughters, Patty, 15, and Sally, 14, were immersed in their own rock-music world and bickered constantly with each other and with their mother. He had been working at two jobs as an industrial chemist in order to meet the ever-rising financial demands of his family and of his parents, of whom he has been the chief supporter. This past year he had been having a series of stress-related health problems—peptic ulcers and recurrent blackouts—which were growing worse. He knew he'd been drinking too much, and further, for the last four months he had been carrying on an affair with his boss's young secretary, which was turning out to be more serious than he anticipated.

When seen, Mr. Wagner appeared explosively angry, yet with an undercurrent of depression; he felt he had created trouble for himself in every area of his life. He asked for specific help in handling his growing estrangement from his wife and the family's escalating debts. He wanted to leave his wife but didn't see how he could afford it, and he worried over what would happen to the children. It became apparent that he was really struggling with the unpalatable reality that no matter how he tried to maneuver, he found himself in a "no win" situation. The gap between what he wanted and needed and what he was getting seemed to be growing wider and he felt himself immobilized.

*Richard Krantz describes such efforts to find alternative frameworks in his study of men who left established careers to settle in the Sante Fe area during midlife.[14]

We began to look at his current situation, the various roles he carried, the options available to him, and the probable outcome of each. He appeared stuck at the "sorting out" phase, so that he was unable to put the components in a proper perspective. Our goal in working together was set as helping him become more responsible for his own needs; separating out the conflicts in his roles as husband, parent, and son; and developing a set of realistic priorities for dealing with the situation.

Over the year that we worked together, Mr. Wagner learned first to set and then to deal with appropriate limits on himself and on the others in his various networks. With my support, he was able to come to constructive decisions; after trying to set up marital counseling and/or individual treatment for his wife, which she adamantly refused, he decided that they had come to the end of the road, and divorce proceedings were instituted and eventually finalized. Shortly after we started, he broke up with his girlfriend ("She kept on bugging me, just like my wife!") and began to date a number of women. He was able to work out a realistic plan with his younger brothers and sister to share equally in their parents' support. He gave up his "moonlighting" job and began to spend more time at his office; as a result he received a raise and promotion from his company.

As his relations with his children, his parents, his siblings, and his employers improved, so did his health: his ulcers cleared up when he cut down on his drinking and his blood pressure went from a potentially dangerous level down to the normal range. The most difficult area for him to handle was developing realistic financial plans regarding his wife and children; once he left the home, he kept struggling to meet their unrealistic demands, regardless of the cost to himself. A major turning point occurred when he connected his chronic anger and frustration to his inability to set limits on what others could expect from him. Slowly he began to learn to say "No" when he found the request excessive and to deal with the other's anger and then reluctant acceptance. As a result, he was able to cope successfully with a whole series of stressful situations and to identify where he still had to learn to develop new coping patterns. In time he came to see himself as offering support but not having to take care of others entirely on his own.

Currently Mr. Wagner lives alone and calls only occasionally to "consult" with me. He has recently initiated a relationship with a 35-year-old woman, and for the first time in his life, is planning to go away on a three-week vacation. He visits his children and parents frequently and has found a whole new network of friends, both male and female, now that he has taken up tennis in his leisure time. He continues to try to establish a working relationship with his former wife so that they can make joint decisions concerning the children, but recognizes that it is largely a "lost cause."

WOMEN'S REACTIONS

Unfortunately, although a great deal has been written on women in midlife, no definitive interpretation of women's transition to mid-adulthood has been made in the same thorough way that Levinson and his colleagues did for men. Lois Davitz, however, did a survey of how women reacted to becoming forty (parallel to the study on men).[15] She found that the thirty-nine-year-old woman turns forty with mixed emotions, feeling confident of her experience and competence to meet everyday problems, yet vaguely apprehensive and tense because of the birthday's extensive connotations of the "socio-psychological leap" into middle age. She has been taught that society has age-role expectations of her: now that she has passed her youthful days, she must become settled, mature, and wiser—yet also duller, less buoyant, less flexible, and less attractive to others.

Physically, her body gains weight or at least changes its fat distribution to concentrate around her waist and hips. She has to focus grimly on dieting and exercise to maintain her figure and bodily vigor, to pluck out the first gray hairs, and to search for clothes that "do something" for her. She becomes vulnerable to her husband's sexual rejection of her, even as she tries to understand the developmental crisis *he* is going through. At work she starts to be treated with respect rather than camaraderie by her youthful male colleagues, some of whom are being promoted over her head, despite her competence. As she proceeds up the ladder, promotions grow harder to attain, with the step into upper-echelon management the steepest of all.

If she has not married, her single status is emphasized by her married friends, who tend to cut her out of their social life. (See discussion of this point in the chapters on divorcees and widows.) She feels alone at times and worries about the loneliness ahead of her once her parents die and she grows older.

With the children growing up the forty-year-old married woman may decide to enter or return to college or the work world, or to become active in community affairs and volunteer activities. She may engage in an extramarital affair, often in response to her husband's lack of interest and a need to reaffirm her own sense of desirability. On the whole, she tends to ward off the sense of acute crisis that her husband is suffering. Davitz finds that the stresses encountered at this stage often lead to a period of significant psychological growth, because the woman responds actively and thus develops new interests and skills and enhances her sense of self-worth and zest for living—strengths that she will need to meet the crises ahead.

Sheehy sees the woman's crossing into midlife as occurring earlier, at around thirty-five, when the time pinch sets off a "last chance" sense of urgency. She begins to seek answers to questions about the roles and options which she has already chosen or set aside.[16] In response to her reaching her sexual peak around this time, she may desire and seek out new sexual experiences. She may reenter the labor force, largely because of the need to help meet the current high costs of living and also to help the family move up the economic ladder. She may even decide to run away for a while to take one last fling at freedom or, if unmarried, she may decide to have a first child. If she had found previous gratification through child-bearing, she may choose to have another even though her other children are almost grown.

Interestingly, Florine Livson suggests that marriage itself, for some women, serves as a transitional stage in adult development between childhood and full individuation of self. It may have important functions in early adulthood but inhibits further development in middle life.[17] The husband, according to this thesis, serves as a bridge between parental attachment and adult autonomy. If, in this type of marriage, partners cannot move beyond this transitional stage, they may choose to move out of the marriage itself, particularly when approaching midlife sparks the push for change.

In general, we find little evidence that women undergo the same type of existential soul-searching as men do when they cross the threshold into middle adulthood. We *do* find an increasing need as their children grow into greater self-sufficiency and their housekeeping demands decrease, to find new sources of personal gratification "before it is too late." The case that follows well illustrates this point.

SARAH BROWN (#106)

Sarah Brown, age 40, a neatly dressed, agitated black woman, called for an immediate appointment at the outpatient psychiatry clinic of a large metropolitan health center. She began to talk almost before she sat down about the fierce argument she had had that morning with her oldest daughter, who had asked her the day before to buy a pair of shoes for her and then had spent $70 of her own money on a new permanent. Mrs. Brown became so incensed when she heard about this that she rushed out to her car, drove to work, wrote a resignation notice and put it in her supervisor's box, and returned home immediately without giving further explanation. Appalled when she realized what she had done, she panicked and called the clinic.

Mrs. Brown gave brief background information. She had been divorced seventeen years ago and had worked all these years to support her family as an eligibility aide at the county welfare department. Her three children—Janice, 24; Luann, 20; and Percy, 14—lived with her. The two girls worked but contributed virtually nothing to the upkeep of the home, which she had scrimped and saved to buy and maintain. The argument with Janice this morning had been the last straw in a long series of stressful events that started last April when Luann moved back home unexpectedly after her marriage broke up. Two months later, Janice walked in without warning, announcing that she had decided to return to school full-time and didn't want to pay rent on her own apartment. Mrs. Brown felt both shocked and imposed upon by her daughters' return, yet did not see how she could refuse them shelter or deny them the clothes and small loans they kept asking for.

Shortly after this, she passed her fortieth birthday, a crucial milestone for her. She had been awaiting the event with considerable trepidation and had planned to make it a starting point for a whole series of changes in her personal life, including going back to school to get her high school diploma and joining the choir at church. Now she felt forced to put aside her own plans in order to keep up with her daughters' demands. She had grown increasingly depressed, although she tried to deal with the situation by taking on a second job evenings and going straight to her bedroom when she came home to take several tranquilizers and wait until she felt calm enough to emerge. After this last argument, however, she felt herself "falling apart."

Mrs. Brown and the worker agreed that the most immediate problems were the loss of her job and her daughters' refusal to share the support of the household. A third area proposed by the worker, although Mrs. Brown was reluctant to accept it, was her own lack of personal gratification. A set of short-term goals was set up: (1) to help Mrs. Brown regain her job and clarify the behavior that led to her impulsive resignation; (2) to get the girls to take on some of the financial burden and to help her cope more realistically with their demands; and (3) to find ways for her to gain more satisfaction in her personal life.

With her permission, the worker phoned Mrs. Brown's office to explain the circumstances leading up to the submission of her resignation. The supervisor, who had been dumbfounded by Mrs. Brown's note, readily agreed to rescind the resignation and suggested that she take two weeks' vacation from her accumulated overtime to "rest and relax." Mrs. Brown was so relieved to hear this that she began to cry; this was the first time she could recall anyone's telling *her* to take things easy. She had always prided herself on being self-sufficient; ever since Percy's father had left her ten years ago, she had been determined to support her family herself. She felt ashamed at having lost control that morning, but admitted she had reached the end of her rope.

Once her immediate anxiety was reduced, Mrs. Brown began to express her anger at her daughters for not realizing the pressures they placed on her and the way their demands drained her. Somewhat doubtfully, she agreed to invite them in for a family session.

The next day the worker, with Mrs. Brown sitting next to her, told Janice and Luann, both well-groomed, attactive young women, what had happened the day before. They were shocked; their mother had said nothing to them about the incident. They had not realized what tensions were caused by their returning home and were unaware that they had broken up their mother's personal plans. The situation at home was reviewed in considerable detail. The daughters brought up Mrs. Brown's long-standing pattern of encouraging her children to remain dependent on her and trying to keep everying "perfect" at home. Mrs. Brown began to talk freely to them for the first time about how she involved herself totally in her children because they were all she had. Raising them properly was her duty, drilled into her as a child by her strict parents. But for her it was also her way of showing them love, though she admitted it also protected her from becoming involved with a man (and being hurt again).

As the session progressed, the daughters realized for the first time that their mother was a woman who needed male companionship as much as they did. They decided that they didn't have to stay at home; since they were both working, they would rent an apartment together, and Janice could continue at school on a part-time basis. Mrs. Brown agreed that it would be better for all of them to have Janice and Luann try to make it on their own. (Although they had moved away before, the girls admitted they had never felt they had left home.)

For the third session, Percy, a tall, gangling adolescent, joined the rest of the family. The girls reported that they had already lined up a place to live and their mother was helping them sew curtains and bedspreads to brighten it up. Last evening Janice had helped Mrs. Brown experiment with new hairstyles, and this coming weekend Luann planned to take her to a shopping center to help her choose a new fall outfit. Even Percy volunteered shyly that he had lined up an afterschool delivery job with the neighborhood florist "to put money of his own in his jeans."

In a final individual session, Mrs. Brown reported that she had given up her evening job and joined a bowling league with her co-workers at the welfare department—her first social activity, outside of attending church, in the last ten years. She had also started looking into adult-education courses at the nearby community center "just for the fun of it"; maybe next year she would start to study seriously for her diploma. As she rose to leave, she said with a half-smile that maybe for her life really was beginning at forty.[18]

Transition to Post-Parenthood

Transition to post-parenthood is a complex process for both men and women that can loosely be assigned to the age range of forty-five to fifty-four-years, although the limits may be stretched out at each end. It can be considered to be made up of two independent yet interwoven processes which have reverberating effects on each other: the biophysical changes and their psychological equivalents tied to the loss of fertility and reproductive ability; and the individual and family role changes associated with the departure of children from the home (the empty nest syndrome). Since women tend to be affected more extensively and explicitly during this passage, we shall start by discussing the effect of the processes on them and then compare this with the effect on men.

WOMEN'S REACTIONS

THE CLIMACTERIC AND MENOPAUSE.   Although these two terms tend to be used interchangeably, more precisely the term "climacteric" or "climacterium" (from the Greek, meaning "rung of the ladder") refers to the entire transitional period, which may last as long as fifteen years. In women, it starts when the level of estrogen, one of the two ovarian hormones, begins to decrease enough to inhibit ovulation and lasts until estrogen ceases to be produced (which may not be until age sixty). It can be considered the reverse or counterpart of puberty and involves a number of physical and physiological changes. One of these changes is the *menopause*, the actual cessation of the menses or menstrual flow, which takes place at an average age of fifty. The flow may have become less regular and scantier for some months and even years before it ceases completely.[19]

Additional symptoms of the climacteric include "hot flashes," characterized by sensations of warmth over the neck face, and upper body, with a blushing sensation and often excessive sweating; numbness and tingling of the hands and feet; heart palpitations; headaches; dizziness; and faintness. Body hair may become somewhat thinner, and some women report a slight increase in facial-hair growth. Breasts may feel somewhat less elastic and lose some of their fullness, and some women report a tendency to gain weight—or at least more difficulty in losing it. Migraines and insomnia may occur but often can be attributed to increased tension and anxiety rather than to actual hormonal change. Many of these symptoms, it should be stressed, are gradual in onset and scarcely noticed by the majority of healthy women, who tend to pass through the period with relatively little physical distress.

The physical changes of the menopause become complicated by the psychological components of the process, which are usually associated with loss of youth and appeal. In modern Western society, women particularly have had reason to fear the passing of youth:

> Her most socially valued qualities, her ability to provide sex and attractive companionship and to have children and nurture them, are expressed in the context of youth which is endowed with physical beauty and fertility. As she ages, she becomes less physically attractive and desirable and her reproductive and nurturant functions are no longer relevant. Since traditionally women have not been encouraged to develop those qualities which often improve with age, such as intellectual competence and the ability to apply mature wisdom to the solution of problems, it is hardly surprising that depression and feelings of uselessness are identified so frequently in the literature on older women.[20]

The menopause has been described as a *rite de passage.* Coming as it does at a time when the woman is also experiencing other signs of aging and role modification, it is aptly called "the change of life," since it embodies all the various transitions she is going through. Initially, many women are unaware of, or block out, this process of change. Lynn Caine describes her own reactions:

> I was so busy that it did not dawn on me for three months that I had missed three [menstrual] periods. I paid no attention, thought it was because I was working hard. My periods started again, then stopped again, were very irregular, did not last as long. And then, finally one day I realized that this must be the menopause.
>
> I don't know why it took me so long to admit it. I was terribly depressed; I had never believed that that would happen to me; for some reason I had assumed that the laws of nature would be suspended for me. But then, I had never expected to be middle-aged either. . . . I certainly did not want any more children. Nevertheless, it was a sign of age and it bothered me, so I put it out of my mind.[21]

Other women respond psychologically with a range of emotions. Benedek notes that normal, healthy women, freed from the demands of bearing and rearing children, can summon a surge of new energy directed to new aims, such as learning or employment. She views the climacteric as a developmental phase, a "challenge for the reorganization of the personality."[22] Although Helene Deutsch, presenting the traditional psychoanalytical interpretation, saw the psychological reactions to menopause as among the most trying experiences of a woman's life, during which she mourns the loss of her reproductive capacity,[23] more recent investigators have challenged this position.

Neugarten and her colleagues, reporting on reactions of women to menopause, found great variations. Women in their twenties and thirties seemed to view what lay ahead more negatively, while women in their forties and fifties who were going through the process or had completed it seemed to be far less worried about the presence or absence of the menstrual cycle than they were about such concerns as widowhood, children leaving home, cancer, and the aging process itself. Three-quarters of the midlife women said that the elimination of the fear of pregnancy and the bother of menstruation were among the most positive aspects of menopause. Others mentioned better relations, including sex, with their husbands and increases in energy and feelings of well-being.[24]

Of the 10 to 15 percent of women in the menopausal years who do have physical and/or emotional difficulties serious enough to cause them to seek professional help, the most frequent psychological problem cited is depression, characterized psychiatrically by apathy, loss of interest in daily activities, loss of energy and appetite, feelings of worthlessness and guilt, and—in serious cases—the conviction that life is no longer worthwhile.[25] However, since such a depression occurs concurrently with significant role losses, it is hard, as has been mentioned, to isolate the contributions of the menopause to this reaction.

(In this connection, an interesting question can be raised, which does not yet appear to have been investigated. If we consider the climacteric to be a transitional process, what is the effect of its occurring before its appointed time? When a surgical menopause—as a hysterectomy is discreetly described in medical terms—occurs, estrogen is frequently prescribed to counter the physical aftereffects, which are usually more severe than those that occur normally over a period of years. But what about the psychological concomitants? What of the woman's possible loss of self-esteem and self-image when she feels she has been prematurely and suddenly robbed of her fertility and sense of femininity? As one thirty-seven-year-old woman said weepingly, "It's not that I want to have more children; I'd just like to feel that I could if I would!"[26])

Emptying and Restructuring the Nest.   In psychosocial terms, the transition to post-parenthood is concerned with shifts in two primary role networks. With the departure of the last child from the home, the parent-child network—particularly the mother-child tie—must go through a phase of readjustment until it gains a new balance. At the same time and subsequently, the husband-wife relationship undergoes a transformation to achieve a new balance, akin to, yet different from, the bond between them before they had children.

The Mother-Child Role Network.   Duvall, long an exponent of the empty-nest stage in family development, defines the post-parental middle years as starting with the departure of the last child from home.[27] She sees the children's leaving as a turning point for the family, a crisis in that each member, as well as the family as a whole, enters a period in which former habits must be abandoned and new patterns established. She agrees with Neugarten, however, that when the empty-nest stage comes at the expected time, it represents not so much an actual crisis as a phase of adjustment, a normal adaptation to the sequence and rhythm of the life cycle. The primary task is to let go, so that the parent-child tie can continue in a new, more autonomous way.

For some years, researchers have been trying to determine the extent to which the empty-nest transition represents a negative, conflictual situation. Lowenthal and Chiriboga, investigating entry into the empty-nest stage as part of their larger study on transitions, found little evidence that the prospects of the departure of the youngest child would be in any way threatening. On the contrary, respondents said they anticipated establishing a less complex life-style and relaxing or reorienting their child-rearing goals.[28]

Donald Spence and Thomas Lonner, using the same data, noted that the women were at points along the life-course when it was expected that a reorganization of role relationships and life-style would occur. Some women, having anticipated this, appeared to feel little stress and to have few adjustment problems, adapting to changing circumstances and expectations gradually and almost imperceptibly. Others seemed to require a total reorganization of their previous life-style to meet the press of current cultural expectations, encompassing changes in behavior, attitudes, and relationships.[29]

> When some children finally grow up and away, some women discover that they themselves have not grown up and away in any comparable manner. Their interests and involvements outside the home are not of strong commitment or of equal force to the role of mother.... Not having pursued other goals progressively throughout their years of child-rearing, they find themselves at a loss for something to do. They express unclear concerns over helping their husbands to retire and over desires to travel, to do volunteer work, to renew long-ignored artistic interests and talents, and to see their grandchildren. [p. 374]

Moreover, the women studied seemed to have considerably varying ideas as to what constitutes "leaving home"; although in some cases children physically left the house, their mothers anticipated that they would be actively involved in their lives well past the time that they got married and had children of their own.

An interesting expansion on this theme is offered by Hanna Shavit, who investigated the empty-nest syndrome among middle-class women in Israel whose last child* had just left home to enter the army for his compulsory service.[30] Two-thirds of the thirty mothers studied did not perceive this event as either a crisis or the beginning of the empty-nest phase; rather they saw it as a "moratorium" enabling them to become socialized to the departure of their children from home. Despite their youngest child's physical absence, the mothers still participated actively in his new experience (baking cookies, washing his laundry, preparing for his weekend visits, and attending functions in his camp).

The third of the sample who did perceive their child's leaving home as a crisis were those who had been born in central or eastern Europe and who came to Israel at the end of World War II, after experiencing the Holocaust firsthand. Departure of their last child reawakened earlier reactions of loss and emptiness. The physical distance from their last child was perceived as emotional distance, for which they sought compensation by increasing their closeness to their older children.

In an effort to pin down the concept of the empty nest more definitively, Elizabeth Harkins compared three groups of mothers: those whose last child was still in high school (pre–empty nest), those who had experienced the event within the last six to eighteen months (empty-nest transition), and those whose children were over two and a half years past the event (post–empty nest).[31] She found that the effects on mothers of their last child's graduation from high school did not appear to be great; this event was not seen symbolically as the empty nest. Going away to school, moving to a separate residence, and getting married all rated higher as indicators of the child's leaving home. Moreover, the empty-nest transition had only a slight and transitory effect on the psychological well-being and essentially no effect on the physical well-being of mothers. No significant effects of either age or menopausal status upon either psychological or physical well-being were found. This led to the conclusion that the empty nest is *not* a particularly stressful period in most women's lives and that the only threat to well-being may be in having a child who does *not* become successfully independent when he is expected to.

Other data, however, seem to indicate that the empty nest does induce depression in those women who have invested all their energies in their maternal role. According to Sophie Loewenstein, when a child becomes a narcissistic extension of his mother, the departure may leave her with great emotional emptiness. Geographic distance alone is not enough to effect emotional separation. It is an act of dramatic maturational impact on mothers and children alike, and one of the most liberating aspects of middle life, when a woman becomes able to differentiate herself from her child(ren) by

---

*To rule out differences in type and length of service between young men and women, only mothers whose last child was a son were selected for the sample.

releasing her anxious control, letting the child make his own decisions and mistakes and bear his own pain.[32]

Rubin, analyzing in-depth interviews with 160 middle-aged women, sharply challenges the assumption that loss of the mothering role produces feelings of sadness and despair.[33] She insists that the cultural stereotype of the depressed mother which dominates our image of women at midlife comes largely from research on hospitalized patients and is not compatible with the women she interviewed. She found that almost all of her subjects responded to the departure of their children, whether actual or impending, with a decided sense of relief, mixed as it was with some pain. Even those most committed to the traditional homemaker's role, who had never worked outside the home in the past, expressed this viewpoint. Women who had seen one child leave were usually ready to have the next one go.

Sometimes the leave-taking becomes more problematic for working-class mothers than for middle-class ones. In middle-class families, the parents usually anticipate that the child will leave for college at eighteen, and thus they have time to prepare for it. In working-class families, college attendance is not taken for granted and children are expected to live at home until they marry, which makes the time of departure indefinite and preparation for separation more difficult.

Rubin concludes that those who suffer most are women who are disappointed in their children, whose relationships with them are unsatisfactory, and whose disapproval of their life-style makes their interaction with the children difficult and tenuous. Much of the mother's disappointment may be tied up with her own self-blame, as well as the blame laid on her by external sources. Furthermore, many women feel that they have aborted their own hopes and dreams, their own career plans, to invest themselves in their children, and this makes their disappointment all the more poignant.

The Husband-Wife Network. Relatively little exploration has been made of the further phases in the transition, once the children leave the home, when husband and wife return to couplehood. Irwin Deutscher was one of the first to investigate this aspect of post-parental life. He found that the majority of his forty-nine respondents considered this phase as a time of freedom from financial responsibilities, geographic immobility, and housework and other chores. They felt able to be themselves for the first time since the children came along and to "let their hair down" now that they no longer had to be role models. Women seemed to view the post-parental period as part of their passing through a generally critical time of life. Deutscher concluded that the wife felt the loss of the children and the parental role more keenly, that the husband's showdown would come with retirement.[34]

In the San Francisco Transition Study, when asked how they expected their marriage to change after their children left home, both men and women expressed the hope that there would be greater closeness between them. Roughly four-fifths of the middle-aged group described their spouses primarily in positive terms, although the women proved dramatically more outspoken than the men. The men tended to be appreciative of their wives' virtues and readily admitted that they themselves did not meet their wives' expectations; the women, on the other hand, tended to be more critical of their husbands and more confident of their own role performance.[35]

Other studies concur that less marital role tension exists once children are gone. Couples tend to complain less about each other's personality traits and to recognize, if not accept, them as part of the predictable aspects of marriage. For working-class couples, the two added factors of kin contacts and more disposable income appear to ease the transition to the post-parental period. The working-class women studied seemed happier when they saw their children and other relatives often; in contrast, middle-class women were less happy when they had many such contacts, feeling them as impositions. Working-class couples, particularly the men, more often perceived the post-parental period as satisfactory when compared with earlier periods than did middle-class couples, since the relatively greater financial resources available now that the pressure of child-rearing was over allowed them to satisfy their own needs more adequately.

What about sexual relations between husbands and wives in the post-parental period? Masters and Johnson note that the absence of children from the home, usually coinciding with menopause, removes exhausting physical and mental responsibilities from women.[36] Now their energies can be devoted to increased, tension-free sexual activities that provide greater marital satisfaction, particularly when couples enjoy financial security and have a good overall relationship. Many a woman develops a renewed interest in her husband and in the physical maintenance of her person when she experiences a "second honeymoon" during the early fifties. However, for those women who reported earlier frigidity or lack of recurrent or psychosexually satisfactory activity during the active reproductive years, the advent of menopause and post-menopause provides an excuse to avoid the criticism of inadequate sexual performance or the frustrations of unresolved sexual tensions by "closing off" or reducing such activities with their spouses.

A study of extramarital sexual relations during the middle years found that men in the post-parental years seemed to be more open to extramarital involvement than those whose children were about to leave home or than women either before or after the children left home. Husbands having affairs also had lower marital-adjustment scores and received less sexual satisfaction in their marriages than husbands who did not. Wives taking lovers were not clearly differentiated from other wives on either of these factors.[37]

In general, according to Aldous, for wives, who presumably feel more jeopardized by the loss of children than husbands, the entry into post-parenthood can be a good period: menopausal problems are usually taken in stride and sexual relations are even better than in the past. Children continue to be a source of pride and interest but are no longer in need of physical care and socialization. On the whole, marital satisfaction increases at this time. Spouses communicate with each other better (in the middle class, at least) and have greater empathy for each other's beliefs. Spouses develop companionship based on shared expectations and values with respect to marital roles, and agree, to a large extent, on what is important in life, how to interpret events, and how one should behave in everyday situations.[38]

The suggestion has been made that women tend to resolve their feelings of emptiness when children leave home by beginning new careers as "retooled" students or as novices in the work world. My own sense of timing says that, realistically, this phase may be too late to start, since the opposing pressures of age bias plus lack of prior experience would tend to put them at a disadvantage. It is probably more likely that women who have trained for careers early in adulthood may now go back to update their knowledge and skills. Similarly, women who have previously worked may decide to take a part-time job to test their rusted abilities, or, if they have continued to work while their children were growing up, may now look for full-time, more challenging employment. Another area they can and do enter productively is that of voluntary work in the community, a large and many-faceted world.

MEN'S REACTIONS

While men's reactions to the post-parenthood transition generally do not appear to be as severe or as complex as women's, we have come to realize that they, too, experience both biophysical and psychosocial changes during the mid-forties which may last well into the fifties.

THE MALE CLIMACTERIC. Recent investigation has made it clear that while there is no male equivalent to the female's menopause, changes in hormonal levels occur which have an effect on the physical status and well-being of the man. Beginning at about thirty and continuing through the rest of adulthood, a gradual decline in the secretion of testosterone and androgen, male hormones which affect sexual activity as well as physical strength and loss of hair and teeth, takes place. The process of hormonal change is as yet incompletely studied, but biomedical changes at this time tend to affect health and physical appearance, family relationships, attitudes toward work, self-concept, and personality.[39] As with the female, a reversal of the process which occurs during adolescence takes place, bringing about an overall decline in physical strength and stamina, reduced ambition, and in some cases a general state of despondency.

Changes related to sexual functioning include a diminishing in the size and firmness of the testicles, an enlargement of the prostate gland, a weakening in the force of ejaculation, and a lessening in the amount of seminal fluid.

Erectile responsiveness also slows down, and a shift from the specific genital sensations of youth to more diffuse sensations throughout the body has been reported.[40]

Sheehy lists some of the symptoms which have been loosely categorized as associated with the male climacteric[41]:

Physiological: morning fatigue, lassitude, vague body pains.

Psychological: nervousness, irritability, depressive phases, crying spells, insomnia, memory lapses, apprehensiveness, frustration, instability.

Sexual: diminished potency and loss of self-confidence.

Circulatory: dizzy spells, hot flashes, chills, sweating, headaches, numbness and tingling, cold hands and feet, increased pulse rate, heart palpitations.

Unfortunately, because of the vagueness and fluctuating quality of some of these symptoms and because the notion of a male climacteric tends to run counter to the masculine self-image, men often are reluctant to turn to medical sources for relief. Helmut Ruebsaat and Raymond Hull find that spells of bad temper, which are a common characteristic of the climacteric, often cause problems at work and with the man's friends, leading to quarrels, fights, and even murders.[42]

The number of middle-aged men who commit suicide successfully, make suicide attempts but are thwarted, or mask suicide attempts as accidents is hard to determine. However, in their monumental study of suicides, Edwin Shneidman, Norman Farberow, and Robert Litman give a profile of a group of hospitalized suicidal patients whose description sounds familiar:[43]

This group of patients . . . was made up of older men who were reacting with strong emotional disturbances to a threat to their psychological integrity. The threat centered primarily around industrial or occupational failures and the fear of losing economic independence. Other "threats" included sudden illnesses or failing health (resulting in severe limitations to occupational or social activities), and recent changes in the marital or family relationship, such as the loss of sex drive, impotence, frigidity in the spouse, or the loss of children through marriage or death. Characteristically, these men had previously achieved a satisfactory social adjustment, had been productive persons, and had only rarely been physically ill. . . . They had been "successful" husbands and workers for many years in adult life.

Staffs of crisis centers and mental health clinics are trained to be alert to the middle-aged businessman who signifies suicidal intentions or who has made a suicide attempt. Experience has shown, in many cases, that they make their plans carefully and have a high rate of carry-through.

Martin Strickler found that climacteric crises in midlife men were often triggered by such events as disappointments and frustrations in job and career pursuits, the separation process of the late adolescent child, awareness of some decline in sexual potency, and the appearance of symptoms of physical ill-health associated with the aging process.* He notes that the most frequent maladaptive result of a poorly resolved climacteric crisis is involutional or agitated depression.[45]

Probably the most common of men's life goals concerns success in the work area. Unlike the earlier transition into mid-adulthood, when men feel existential despair but are still capable of changing direction or putting forth new spurts of energy to "make it," the climacteric man often realizes that time has run out. He perceives new job requirements or expectations as a threat to his customary ways of coping. His way up the ladder may be blocked; he may be on a plateau and feel that the path ahead can only lead downhill, that there is little point in striving further. Or he may experience an upsurge of adolescent, competitive fantasies associated with the climacteric, so that even if he is doing well vocationally, he may have new, unconscious feelings of fear and guilt about his success.

The central task for the climacteric man, says Strickler, is to accept the reality that he is middle-aged, to appreciate the good things in his life as well as his past accomplishments, to give up some of his unrealistic goals, and to recognize that he has unrealized potential that he can work on for the rest of his life.[46]

EMPTYING AND RESTRUCTURING THE NEST.   Although men do not seem to be as intimately and actively concerned with their children's leaving home as women, recent studies indicate that they feel the loss keenly. Rubin observes that contrary to popular belief, her interviews showed that fathers more often than mothers wanted to hold back the clock, to keep the children at home for just a little longer. Unlike the mother, who had been involved in the daily details of the children's developmental process since birth, the father often worked outside and did not share in this process firsthand. Suddenly, he found his children grown and gone from the home, and, bewildered, he asked, "How did it all happen so fast?"[47]

The Father-Child Role Network.   When children grow up and start separating from the family, the nature of a father's relationship with them undergoes a qualitative change. He no longer feels the same close ties and instead experiences a sense of loss. As he tries to work it out, earlier unresolved conflicts from his own adolescence emerge. In addition, the reshuffling

---

*The entire issue of the rise in physical illnesses among men during their forties and fifties assumes particular significance because of their dual reactions: on the one hand, they tend to become obsessed with their body's functioning, and on the other, they use defenses of denial and rationalization to justify ignoring medical advice. In recent years medical sources have documented a sharp rise in the number of patients with heart attacks, strokes, cancer, and other degenerative diseases. American men are reported to have one of the highest rates of cardiac disease in the world, much of it directly linked to such prevalent factors as stress and tension, smoking, drinking, drugs, poor diet, obesity, and lack of exercise—all conditions current among midlife men. Yet many of these men stubbornly refuse to take their physicians' or psychologists' advice and resist giving up unhealthful life-styles, feeling that they have earned the right to indulge themselves.[44]

of practical roles takes place once the children leave, so that family tasks previously relegated to them (washing the car, running errands) must now be returned to the parents, notably the father.[48]

In a study of the father's role during the post-parental transition, it was reported that although the majority of the fathers felt either neutral or somewhat happy about their last child's leaving, nearly one-fourth expressed unhappiness over it. This reaction was experienced by the same fathers who felt most neglected by their wives, received the least amount of understanding from them, were the most lonely, were least enthusiastic about their wives' companionship, and saw themselves as having the last empathic partners. In short, the fathers who reported the most unhappiness over the emptying of the family nest had the most to lose. They tended to be older, saw themselves as nurturing and caring persons who mourned the diminution of their full-time father's role, and felt unable to look forward to compensatory satisfaction in their marital network since the marriage itself was unsatisfactory.[49]

The Husband-Wife Network.   Men's need to compensate for their children's leaving home appear to be less pressing than women's, since, as has been mentioned, they have been less involved in the daily demands of child-raising and are still absorbed in their primary role as worker and breadwinner. While the house may be quieter and the financial pressures less, actually their role as husband is not as dramatically affected as is their wife's.

Many couples take opportunities at this time to improve the quality of their physical living arrangements. They may decide to redecorate or remodel the family home, refurnishing it in accordance with their own needs rather than the children's. A common tendency is to give up large, suburban homes with extensive lawns and play arrangements and to return to more centrally located, serviced apartments, with emphasis on increased comfort and convenience and less need for physical and financial upkeep. By this time, most major financial outlays are over and the couple can indulge their long-deferred desires for individual gratification by engaging in hobbies, travel, and enjoyment of personal luxuries.

As couples approach the end of the transition to post-parenthood, they have usually worked out the complementarity between them in a mutually satisfactory way. On the other hand, with the removal of the children from the scene, many points of contention which have been deferred "until the children grow up" or have been obscured by parental concerns over the needs of the family are now bared. As one woman said ruefully, "There's no place to hide any more!"

Simmering dissatisfactions between husband and wife frequently emerge at this stage as problems in sexual performance. The following ongoing case from a counselor's notebook in a family agency illustrates this pattern: sexual complaints become the wedge to deal with a wide range of changes in role performances.

BRIAN AND VERA PETERS (#130)

Brian and Vera Peters are each approaching 50 years of age. They have been married almost half their lives and have raised three sons and a daughter; their youngest boy is now 17 years old. The older two sons are married and each has a child; their daughter teaches school in another state. In their initial interview they said they had not had sex with each other or with anyone else for the past seventeen years. Brian, a short but muscular man, asked, "Is it normal for a man and wife to live together like brother and sister?" Vera, small, thin, and fairly good-looking, responded, "I just don't feel like it; I don't feel anything."

In the past, Brian had a drinking problem, but last year, when threatened with the loss of his job and his family, he joined a group for alcoholics at the factory where he works; since then, he has been "on the wagon." During counseling, his group suggested a number of options for his troubles with Vera: to leave her, to have an affair, to go to a prostitute, or to get her to come in with him for counseling. He chose the last, and six months ago the two of them were seen twice by a male counselor. Vera then withdrew, stating that she knew it was her fault but she felt unable to change.

Sometime later, Brian called the agency asking for a female counselor for his wife, who was very upset. The precipitating event occurred when their third son moved out of the house to go to live with his girlfriend. A few weeks before, Vera had, for the first time since their marriage, taken a job outside the home as a clerk in a small office. Although she was timid about her job skills and had not socialized beyond the boundaries of the family for twenty years, she began tentatively to test the water in the world of work.

When asked what they wanted, Brian said he wanted a normal life, which to him meant sex with his wife; Vera replied that she just wanted peaceful companionship without arguments. I told them that they seemed to be going through a normal transitional period, now that their children were leaving home and they were beginning once again to look at each other. I agreed to help guide them through this time of upset, although I wondered how much change they were prepared to make and whether they could take advantage of this "new ball game."

Over the next few months, the couple experienced several crises. Vera's grandfather, to whom she was very close, died; their youngest son joined the army. In addition, Vera visited a gynecologist for the first time in seventeen years and learned that there was no physical basis for her inability or unwillingness to respond to Brian sexually (she had been sure she was irreparably damaged when she last gave birth and was "all dried up down there"). Other changes also took place: Brian applied for a daytime job after having worked nights for the past twenty years; Vera reestablished ties with her church, which she had broken off at the time of her marriage; and she bought a new car for herself with her own earnings. Each of these events represented "stuck points," which brought the two of them into closer harmony as they shared each other's experiences openly.

When Vera discovered that she was physically intact and able to have intercourse, she had a brief hysterical episode. Brian, who had comforted her through her griev-ing over her grandfather's death, was able to be sensitive enough in a detached way not to force himself on her or badger her with recriminations over the lost years. I saw Vera alone for a few sessions and gave her some basic sexual information. We also examined her inability to be sexually responsive, even now when Brian was being so different from what he had been in the past, and dealt with her own ambivalence and self-blame. I suggested a program of graduated sexual activity and we discussed this further in a joint session.

One of the chief issues which arose during these months was changing the couple's communication patterns. Throughout their marriage, when Brian would become angry Vera would grow frightened, since she did not know how to fight back. She would also interpose herself between him and the children in order to avoid direct conflict. Brian would then become caustic and begin to swear in sexual terms, which he knew would upset her. For years she had feared that he would drive the children away from the house with his angry outbursts.

As treatment continued, Vera and Brian began dating anew. They set aside a specific time during the week for themselves only, and the children were told not to come to the house or call them during these periods. They began to learn how to fight with each other and to enjoy it. As Brian's use of sexual expletives diminished, Vera's ability to tolerate them increased. She also learned to say "No" to him on issues other than sex. At the present time they are talking about "when" (rather than "if") they will be ready to deal with each other in an overt sexual way.

Vera has watched with amazement Brian's new management of his own relations with their children. With a smile, she has pointed out how he teases them and does not provoke them as he used to. She is now beginning to flirt openly with him and the whole tone of their interaction has lightened and become more positive. The key aspect of treatment has been to concentrate on the normal aspects of their transitional situation and to educate them to the opportunities available to them at this stage.

RELATIONS WITH AGING PARENTS

Although the matter will also be discussed in Chapters 11 and 12, it should be mentioned at this point that part of the imbalance during the transition to post-parenthood is aggravated by a parallel change taking place in the midlife individual's life: the shift in the person's relations to his or her parents and the parents of the spouse. Whereas people in transition to mid-adulthood are usually able to make the changeover from the young to the mature adult generation fairly comfortably, their ties with their own older generation have also been shifting in focus, until by now they have acquired a new set of dependents—their aging father and/or mother. At this point middle-aged individuals may need (or be compelled) to take responsi-bility for their parents' care.

Eda LeShan points out how pervasive the problem is:[50]

I found as I talked to many of my contemporaries that relationships with elderly parents seemed strong on frustration and weak on gratification. Of the very considerable numbers of people with whom I discussed this problem, only two or three were able to say that their parents were having a good or happy old age, were a pleasure to be with, and had made sensible and adequate plans for continuing to be independent and well cared for until their death.

. . . Almost everyone I spoke to about this subject expressed a feeling of guilt and frustration. Just as our parents were never in any way prepared for the fact of living a long life, so we are in many ways a first generation to have living parents when we are well into middle age ourselves.

In discussing what they call "the *other* generation gap," Stephen Cohen and Bruce Gans point out that more and more middle-aged persons find themselves unprepared for the real and often destructive feelings of anxiety, confusion, and guilt that they experience because of their parents' difficulties.[51] Cohen and Gans see both groups, the elderly parents and their middle-aged children, as being in critical stages of their lives, with different physical and emotional needs that must be met. Both sides need help in making decisions and learning to cope with altered, deteriorating situations on a pragmatic day-to-day basis, without the ethical soul-searching around the questions, "How much do I owe my parents?" or "How much do my children owe me?"

9

Separation, Divorce, and Remarriage

IN THIS CHAPTER and the next, the two main transitional processes by which marriages are terminated will be considered. They have been placed, largely for convenience, within the boundaries of mid-adulthood, although they can—and do—occur during all stages of the adult life cycle once marriage has taken place.

Actually a marriage may be dissolved in five ways: by death (see Chapters 10 and 12); by annulment, which is the legal erasure of a marriage as a result of force, fraud, bigamy, insanity, falsified age, or gross misrepresentation by either party; by desertion, which usually implies that one spouse simply abandons the other and runs away so that no legal steps can be taken to terminate the marriage contract; by separation, which means that the couple has agreed to part, either formally or informally, although the marriage still holds; and by divorce, which is the formal dissolution of the marital contract.[1] Because of its growing prevalence, we shall examine divorce as the form of termination.

Divorce has emerged as a prime area of interest for molders of social policy, researchers, and clinicians. For a number of intrinsic and extrinsic reasons, such as the rising divorce rate, changing social and cultural mores, new divorce legislation, and shifts in the traditional roles of adults, the subject has become the focus for professional and academic conferences,[2] therapy seminars and workshops,[3] and special-interest groups.[4] A number of self-help books have been published on different aspects of the situation.[5] In view of our overall framework, this discussion will concentrate on one facet of the complex divorce picture: its transitional nature and what this implies in terms of understanding the individual's maturational process and his/her adaptation to this basic life change.

Different writers frame the divorce transition in different ways. Bohannan sees it as a complex social and personal phenomenon made up of six overlapping and interacting "stations": (1) the *emotional divorce*, which centers around the problems of the deteriorating marriage and the chain of events and feelings leading to the breakup; (2) the *legal divorce*, which revolves around the judicial procedures for formalizing dissolution of the marriage and provision of the legal basis for remarriage; (3) the *economic divorce*, which deals with the division of money and property and the separation of joint assets; (4) the *co-parental divorce*, which considers custodial arrangements for the children and visitation rights; (5) the *community divorce*, which includes relations with mutual friends and problems of living alone; and (6) the *psychic divorce*, which concentrates on the need to regain (or achieve) individual autonomy.[6]

Reva Wiseman, a divorce therapist, examines the process from the clinical viewpoint, of the person being divorced. She divides it, in keeping with crisis theory, into five phases: (1) denial; (2) loss and depression; (3) anger and ambivalence; (4) reorientation of life-style and identity; and (5) acceptance and achievement of new levels of functioning.[7] Similarly, Samuel Chiancola discusses the separation process in terms of (1) building up emotional distance; (2) reactions to actual separation; and (3) refocusing on the person himself.[8]

We find it useful to consider the divorce process in terms of three stages: (1) the *estrangement and separation stage*, leading up to the actual decision to part; (2) the *formalization stage*, including the legal procedures and adjustment to living without one's partner; and (3) the *building of new life-styles and relationships*, including remarriage.

Stage One: Estrangement and Separation

Marital separation is a particularly upsetting psychosocial transition because it usually demands multiple, drastic changes in the individual's life space: loss of a significant other (or others, if children are involved), probable economic loss, often a change in the routines of living in one's home, loss of the role of wife or husband, loss of status in the community, sometimes a loss of close friends. Thus a person's entire life-style becomes undermined.[9]

The decision to divorce is rarely a sudden, unheralded act; it usually comes as the final step in a process of growing estrangement which may have stretched out over a number of years, during which a series of small acts (discussions, arguments, retaliations) have occurred to cool off the relationship. Nevertheless, husband and wife are usually not at the same point of "divorce readiness" at the same time, nor do they proceed along the path to dissolution of the marital bond at the same tempo or with equal degrees of investment. In the discussion that follows, it becomes apparent that while the request on the part of one partner for a divorce can scarcely come as a total surprise to the spouse, the process is often resisted and blocked by the other so that "stuck points" are frequent. The convoluted steps in the separation process can be viewed from several perspectives.

THE SOCIAL PSYCHOLOGICAL APPROACH

Since intimate relationships are not easily broken, says George Levinger, when the break actually occurs, it usually means that the ties have declined to the point where one or both partners find an alternative state more attractive.[10] *Attractions* that help to cement a marriage derive from the partners' satisfaction of each other's needs for physical subsistence and safety; for psychological security, love, and respect; and for self-actualization or fulfillment. *Barriers* against a breakup are often tied to each partner's personal feelings of obligation toward the other, toward the children, and toward other members in the family's social network, as well as to adherence to abstract values ("Divorce is against God's teaching") and external normative pressures ("Nice people don't divorce"). Levinger sees a process of balancing rewards and costs taking place.

ATTRACTIONS IN MARRIAGE.   Three significant types of rewards serve to keep the marriage intact: *material rewards,* such as sufficient (but not too high) family income and joint ownership of property; *symbolic rewards,* consisting of the couple's social status derived from the husband's educational position or occupational rank; and *affectional rewards,* including satisfaction with each other's companionship, mutual esteem, and sexual enjoyment. These sources of affinity are likely to shift at different stages in the marriage; an early physical attraction may be enhanced by growing mutual interests and, in time, a whole new set of joint concerns. Conversely, minor differences in the early phase of marriage may come to be blown up over the years into major sources of irritation and stress.

On the other side of the scale, three types of costs may serve to impede the cessation of the marriage. In terms of *material costs,* both separation and divorce are expensive, since two establishments have to be maintained. Fixed costs such as legal fees and filing of applications tend to affect the poor more than the rich, while sliding costs such as separate maintenance of wife and children affect the rich more than the poor. *Symbolic costs* related to one's place in a culture and kinship network have shifted over the years, although a feeling of obligation to continue the marriage may be tied to the length of time the couple knew each other before marriage, the duration of the marriage, and the spouses' mutual obligations. Intrafaith marriages seem to hold together better than interfaith marriages, with some variations. While connected kinship and friendship networks serve to stabilize a relationship, the more that close kin or friends disapprove of the marriage, the greater will be the likelihood of divorce. Community pressures also work to hold a couple together—or push them apart if they oppose the group norms. As for *affectional costs*, whereas a childless couple's decision to divorce is largely considered their own affair, dependent children can serve as psychological restraints, since parents often stay together "for the sake of the kids." This seems to hold true even though couples with children have been found to have lower levels of marital satisfaction, greater financial burdens, and more interpersonal stress than childless couples.[11]

ALTERNATIVES.   Levinger contends that a relationship will not be terminated, despite low internal attractions and few barriers, unless sufficient material, symbolic, or affectional alternative attractions exist. Living separately may be more expensive, but the wife can choose to increase her income by going out to work or applying for Aid to Families with Dependent Children. Although the status of being divorced has often been a source of stigma in the past (and may continue to be in some circles), it can also symbolize freedom and new opportunity. As feminist writers have pointed out, despite the distress involved, divorce has its positive aspects; separated women can gain greater control over their lives than they can as married women.[12] Affectional rewards might include finding a more satisfying mate or sex partner or stronger affiliations with one's own kin who had opposed the marriage.

THE CLINICAL APPROACH

Much of the work on marital ties and divorce comes from the projects on loss, bereavement, and separation carried out at the Harvard Laboratory of Community Psychiatry in the early 1970s. Robert Weiss, from material gleaned in his Seminars for the Separated, finds that most marriages begin with the two partners believing that they love one another.[13] Their feelings of positive regard are composed of *idealization* (projection onto the other of aspects of one's own wishes for oneself), *trust* (unquestioning belief in the other's commitment), *identification* (the sense that one's essential self is associated with the other), the sense of *complementarity* (the other's having capacities missing in oneself), and *attachment* (a bonding to the other that gives rise to feelings of at-homeness and ease when the other is present or felt to be accessible). When a marriage begins to go bad, almost every component of the couple's initial love may come under attack. Yet this last element, the sense of bonding to the spouse, seems to persist long after other elements have faded and even after the marriage itself ends formally.[14]

LOSS OF ATTACHMENT.   The nature of the attachment bond as concep-
tualized by John Bowlby in his work with children separated from a parent[15]
has been found to hold equally for the reactions of at least one partner as the
marriage deteriorates. One of the predominant responses is that of *separation distress*, marked by a focusing of attention on the lost spouse and intense
discomfort because that person is inaccessible. In addition, emotions of unhappiness, apprehension, anxiety, or panic are experienced as expressions of
the person's vulnerability. These in turn may give rise to feelings of tension
and vigilance, which may lead to sleep difficulties as well as to appetite loss,
irritability, and susceptibility to sudden anger or tears. Smoking or drinking
may increase. The individual may feel unable to concentrate, even on matters unrelated to the separation. His driving may become erratic, with even
an increase in accidents (often complicated by an increase in drinking). He
may want to hear about the absent partner, to learn how the person is doing,
and to seek the spouse out. He may seek reassurance that the spouse is
potentially available, even visiting or telephoning, ostensibly for other purposes. He may also feel periods of deep sadness, regret, and severe depression coupled with feelings of worthlessness, rejection, and self-blame, which
may even increase to suicidal fantasies.[16]

Sometimes, instead of—or in addition to—separation distress, the opposite reaction, *euphoria*, is felt. Individuals report, not a lessening in self-
confidence and self-esteem, but an actual increase. They may insist that the
separation is for the best, that a new world has opened for them, that their
lives have become adventurous and exciting. However, this "high" is usually
fragile and temporary; even a small reversal can cause it to give way to the
underlying depression. Still, this response serves to manage the first period
of separation effectively by reorganizing attachment feelings so that they are
directed to the self instead of the other. In this way, the person bonds
himself to a more trustworthy figure—himself—resulting in *narcissistic attachment*.

In time, these reactions give way to loneliness, which differs from the
earlier separation distress in that it is more generalized, without focus on a
specific object. Weiss distinguishes between the loneliness of *emotional
isolation* and that of *social isolation*. The first, like separation distress, gives
rise to symptoms of anxiety, tension, vigilance, sleep difficulties, and appetite loss. The world seems desolate, barren, silent, dead; the individual feels
hollow and depleted. Childhood emotions of abandonment may be reactivated, and a central sense of pervasive apprehension—a "nameless fear"—is
experienced.[17]

Loneliness stemming from social isolation produces different symptoms,
primarily feelings of exclusion or rejection. Because there is no one to share
one's concerns, daily tasks tend to lose their meaning and become burden-
some rituals. The individual experiences leaden, almost intolerable boredom
or aimlessness. Restlessness and difficulty in concentration keep him from

reading or watching television; he may feel impelled to leave the house to move among people, to engage in activities in a network that is willing to accept him.

Loss of attachment may also give rise to *anger*, usually directed at the spouse, even though the person himself may have initiated the separation.[18] While some of the anger rises out of genuine conflicts of interest in relation to such issues as property division, support payments, child custody, and visitation rights, it may rise to disproportionate heights and even turn into hate and murderous fantasies. Nevertheless, even when an individual seems most enraged with his partner, the suppression of positive feelings is not total; expressions of hostility are used at times as a way of maintaining proximity to the lost object.

It should be noted that anger can also serve a therapeutic function, since it often "clears the air" of ambivalence and propels the individual forward during periods of being stuck, helpless, and depressed. Anger, on the other hand, often turns into ambivalence, in which the desires for re-union are alternated with, or marred by, eruptions of rage. At times the partners manage these opposite feelings by compartmentalizing them so that they battle each other through their lawyers or in court yet continue to see each other evenings as friends or lovers. Such contrariness may exasperate lawyers, who say that these clients "don't seem to know their own minds."

Many professionals feel that the key to understanding marital separation is to treat it, like bereavement, as an experience of loss—not only of the spouse but of the marital relationship and the youthful hopes, dreams, and fantasies embodied in it.[19] As in the mourning process (to be discussed in Chapter 10), the person goes through a series of phases: numbness, which usually lasts from a few hours to a week; then an interval of yearning and searching for the lost figure, which may last for months and often for years; next a period of disorganization and despair; and finally a phase of reorganization to a greater or lesser degree.[20]

Although this view of divorce as bereavement is widely held by prac-titioners and certainly is consonant with many of the experiences disclosed clinically, others vigorously dispute the parallel, pointing out that divorce merely terminates a customary social relationship, while death terminates a *life*. Susan Gettleman and Jane Markowitz maintain that the deathlike ele-ments in the marital situation usually appear long before actual separation. They see the emotional divorce as characterized by a long-drawn-out process of alienation in which couples gradually sever their ties and cease to feel a deep, positive attachment to each other. They use this time to prepare mentally for the impending change, to muse over or even try out alternative arrangements. Unlike death among young married people, which is usually precipitous and shocking, the final decision to divorce may also bring exhil-aration and relief.[21]

These dual views of the separation process are born out by the research carried out by David Chiriboga and Loraine Cutler.[22] They found that the period immediately before the decision to divorce emerged as a point of major trauma. Yet a substantial portion of their subjects reported that after the divorce they felt better than they had in a long time and were functioning better. No significant differences were found between older and younger persons in the occurrence and timing of both the traumas and the relief experienced, although men were seen as more vulnerable to the emotional stresses of separation than women.

Regardless of the individual motivation and stresses of a particular situation, and whether we view it from the eyes of the divorcing or being-divorced spouse (if the decision is not a mutual one), the first stage of the divorce process is essentially a leave-taking process during which two people, who have been closely bound in the special intimacy of the marriage situation struggle to sever their ties. The following case, seen by an experienced divorce therapist, illustrates this issue.

SUZY (#189)—PART ONE

Suzy, a 21-year-old secretary, became extremely depressed when the divorce which she herself had initiated was in process. She cried constantly, could not sleep, and was unable to make plans to move out of her apartment. Although she gave a long list of reasons for the divorce, she obviously felt ambivalent about leaving the relationship and asked for help in dealing with her reactions and ending the marriage.

Suzy had married Rod, now 22, three years ago. They had dated each other exclusively for four years throughout high school, then waited another year until they felt they both had good jobs and could afford to get married. Although her job was successful, and she had been promoted twice, Rod's turned out to be a "dead end" and left him feeling disappointed and inadequate.

After a year of marriage, he suggested to Suzy that they "switch partners" with other couples. When she refused, he started to date other women and to describe to her his experiences in great detail. He also began to spend extravagantly and soon they were deeply in debt for an expensive car and elaborate stereo equipment. Suzy felt obligated to meet all their debts and took over management of their joint checking account, which infuriated Rod. Their arguments grew worse and sometimes were physically violent. She finally filed for divorce but, instead of easing the situation, this made Rod even more angry and threatening. On her part, she felt unable to stop seeing him or even to move out of the apartment they still shared.

Assessment of the Situation.   Rod's heightened sense of failure and his attempt to compensate for it with sex, spending, and "macho" behavior toward Suzy created an atmosphere she could no longer cope with. Reluctantly she accepted the idea that since he refused to come in for counseling alone or with her, she would have to help herself. She seemed to be struggling simultaneously with two issues: (1) her fear that Rod might become violent if she left him and might damage either her or himself; and (2) her own deep attachment to Rod, whom she had known since she was six and in whom she had invested all her dreams and plans for the future. Underlying this attachment was her own concept of herself as a woman, homemaker, and potential mother. Prior to coming, she had been cycling through grief, anger, self-assertion, and back to grief again, rather than dealing with her own personal needs.

The First Phase of Treatment. We began to work on the grief process. I helped Suzy evaluate her experiences with losses in the past and assured her that her current feelings were normal and necessary. She responded with considerable relief but still wondered why she should still feel so upset. As we worked, she became increasingly able to detach herself from Rod, even though he kept threatening and manipulating her. She continued to take responsibility for his bills but at least was able to put them at the bottom of the pile and pay her own debts first. At the same time, she began to work directly on her fears of abandonment and their origins in her own early turbulent life experiences. This led her to reevaluate her intense relationship with Rod in the context of her search for secure parental relationships. As this was dealt with, she was able to move out of the apartment with Rod and into her parents' home. She continued to meet with Rod for tearful scenes in which she would plead for a reconciliation. Gradually, these encounters became less frequent.

(The second half of this case will be presented later in this chapter.)

SEPARATION FOR MIDLIFE ADULTS

A particular area for consideration is the effect of a marital break on midlife couples. As an extension of the discussion on post-parenthood in Chapter 8 we can ask what happens when the pair are unable to bridge successfully the transition from being parents to living together as a couple again and when the separation from the children leads to a breakup of the marriage itself. Sidney Wasserman points out this neglected aspect of many empty-nest cases:[23]

> We need to gain a clearer assessment of the marriage itself: its past, its present, its potential for further growth, and how the middle-age separation crisis [of parent/child] is being dealt with. . . . The weaker the basis of the marriage, the looser the ties, the greater the ambivalence, and the more difficult it is for the partners to cope with this time of life. . . . If the children succeed at least in some form of physical emancipation, a number of unrewarding marriages then collapse. Significantly, the youngster going off to a university, or into the armed services, or getting married, or moving into his (or her) own living quarters (particularly, the last child leaving home) often brings the crisis to a head. [pp. 40–41]

For such partners, the emptiness of their marital relationship becomes too much to bear and the purpose of having lived together all these years is dissipated. And when the situation becomes further complicated by other social, economic, and cultural stresses which have become exacerbated over the years, the marriage itself is threatened and at times collapses. The following case, also seen by a private practitioner, illustrates this point. Although the formal divorce had already occurred, the client had become stuck at the separation stage and emotionally could not move past it:

CLARA DOUGLAS (#174)

Clara Douglas, age 50, was referred by her family doctor because of nervousness and depression. She described her problem as, "I have been divorced six months and I can't seem to get it together. I want to get on with my life but I am too filled with anger and resentment." She had been married for thirty years and has three children. She believed her marriage to be solid and stable and had no idea that her husband was considering a separation. About a year ago, he suddenly asked her for a divorce, stating that he wanted to be free. Since he was insistent, they became divorced and less than two months later he married a business associate whom he had known for many years.

Mrs. Douglas described her life with her husband as one long deception. As a couple, they were socially active and had many friends. Mr. Douglas was described as a handsome, friendly, flirtatious man, an all-around extrovert. In public he treated her "like a queen." In private, however, their life was totally different. He was unable to handle problems and crises of any kind and she always had to take over. He became a heavy drinker who turned viciously angry when he drank too much; on several occasions he had beaten her, although she never confided this to anyone. She tried to hide this part of their marriage from the children and became absorbed in raising them; the two girls were both now successfully married and living in distant communities, and a year ago their youngest child, a son, had gone east to attend graduate school. She felt she had done everything to maintain her family and marriage and now everyone had abandoned and rejected her.

In treatment, Mrs. Douglas kept ruminating about her past. She could not sort out her feelings; she knew what she should do but could not mobilize her energies to do anything. Instead, her bitterness and anger, as well as a mild depression, left her weak and depleted, unable to work out a satisfactory solution for the crisis created by her divorce.

As we talked she acknowledged the parallel between her marriage and her parents'. Her father had been a tyrant and her mother, a slave to him all her life. She saw now that her mother had acted just as she did; for twenty years she had been mistreated and demeaned by her husband, yet had gone along with it. Mrs. Douglas viewed her whole marriage as a hypocritical act in which she played the role of the good, faithful, loving wife while suffering constantly inside. She said she had suppressed her true feelings because she believed that her husband truly loved her, and that despite all the negative aspects, they had a good family and marital relationship. Now she realized she had taken on a martyr role, just like her own mother.

Mrs. Douglas also recognized that she was like her husband's mother in some ways: she was very hard-working, overconcerned with right and wrong, and somewhat rigid in her attitudes. Her husband had asked her for a divorce almost immediately after his mother's death. Although he had treated both her and his mother with apparent deference and respect, she now saw that he resented both of them, for the same reasons. In contrast, the woman whom her husband had chosen for his second wife was a very relaxed, fun-loving type.

Over a period of four interviews and two telephone calls, Mrs. Douglas was able to make enormous progress in her assessment of her situation and apparently resolved the crisis which had immobilized her. She started going out with friends, began to date, and planned a vacation trip. She also became more interested in her job as a dress saleswoman and began to think of asking for a transfer to a new location. She had shifted her gears to think of the future, and at closing, described herself as feeling easier in her mind, more optimistic, and better able to get her life "back on the track."

Stage Two: Formalization

Once divorce procedures are actually started, the spouses usually enter the second stage of the transition, which is carried out on two levels. On one, the legal, economic, and co-parental aspects of the process take precedence. In contrast to the first stage, when emotional considerations were primary and focus was placed on the psychosocial tasks to be carried out in order to arrive at a decision, the second stage is largely concerned with the material-arrangemental tasks to be dealt with in order to dissolve the marriage formally. On the second level, each spouse struggles to adjust to the mechanics of living alone or as a single parent with the children. (The prizewinning film *Kramer vs. Kramer* addressed itself to this issue, primarily from the man's viewpoint.)

LEGAL ASPECTS

Since marriage involves a legal procedure, one of the first formal steps in terminating the contract requires knowing exactly what the legal process is. Each state enacts and enforces its own divorce laws, and one of the most necessary tasks for each partner is to consult a knowledgeable and experienced divorce lawyer. Actually, says Weiss, four basic legal services are offered by lawyers:[24]

1. They can draw on their knowledge of the law to inform and advise.
2. They can manage negotiations with the spouse or with the spouse's lawyer.
3. They can pilot through the courts a petition for divorce or legal separation or for a particular level of financial support or visitation.
4. They can serve as an advocate for their client before the judge.

In addition, they perform such extralegal services as providing support and opportunities for ventilation of grievances, considering alternatives, and sharing their experiences with other clients in similar situations.

Despite the easing of punitive legal restrictions and the increase in "no fault" divorce laws, divorce is still largely an adversary procedure in civil court, with one party suing the other for breach of contract. This means that a good deal of allocation of blame and battling out of gains and losses results. The intricacies of the procedure have been spelled out in great detail in recent years by the women's movement, including the kind of legal help available, the costs involved, legal definitions of statuses, separation and child-support agreements, alimony conditions, property settlements, specific grounds for divorce, contested actions, custody and visitation arrangements, courtroom procedures, means of appeal, and special modifications.[25]

An almost inevitable byproduct of the legal aspects, once the complaints are filed and the two (or more) opposing lawyers begin the action, is the erosion of many of the positive attitudes which the spouses may have retained toward each other during the separation stage and the transformation of denial and distress over the breakup into anger, blame, and open conflict. If both spouses consent to the divorce, particularly if they have financial means to establish residence in a state where the procedure is relatively painless or where no-fault divorce laws are in force, the legal steps may be carried out with a minimum of recrimination. Where the divorce is contested by either party, where the grounds upon which the decree is granted are excessive or restrictive, or where aspects of property settlement, child custody, or support arrangements are opposed, the procedures can be drawn out, fought over, and end by turning the marital bonds into dragging anchors of hate and mutual recriminations. Gettleman and Markowitz describe the outcome:

> As adversaries in divorce proceedings, plaintiff and defendant accuse and sue each other back and forth, effectively making divorce complicated, costly, and ugly. The spirit of each partner can be broken thoroughly before there is even a divorce decree, since husband and wife try to amass evidence of each other's lying, immoral, or vicious conduct. Couples in conflict are at the mercy of their lawyers and the judges who happen to hear their case.[26]

An interesting suggestion for remedying this adversary type of action is to develop *family mediation procedures* by which spouses can settle issues of termination through arbitration by a neutral third party, on the basis of conflict-resolution principles and transactional-analysis techniques.[27]

ECONOMIC ASPECTS

Two primary economic issues arise during the second stage of the divorce transition. The first deals with severing, or rather rearranging, the economic ties between former husband and wife, and the second is learning to manage financially on one's own once the divorce takes effect.

Financial arrangements in the divorce process usually consist of three types. Since most husbands and wives accumulate a certain amount of joint assets in the course of their marital career, (1) these assets must be divided on an equitable basis; (2) financial support must be given to the wife (if she is not in a position to support herself); and (3) the dependent children of the marriage must be provided for. Sometimes the *property settlement* becomes a matter of recognizing the contribution of each spouse to the accumulation of the joint wealth. A man may hold all of the accumulated assets of his career in his own name, while his wife, who assisted in the growth of his business, career, property, and/or income, may find that her contribution to the partnership is legally unrecognized upon breakup of the marriage. Conversely, a husband may have put most of his assets in his wife's name to avoid taxes or other liabilities, only to find that she claims full title to them when they divorce.[28]

Frequently, property division is arranged directly between husband and wife through agreements worked out between the two lawyers, without their becoming part of the legal record. While regulations may differ in different states, the wife usually receives from one-third to one-half of the common property. Since the value of many of the assets may be hard to assess and are enhanced by their connotative value to one or both of the spouses ("the first picture I ever owned!"), it becomes a matter of negotiation and judgment to equate, say, possession of the family car with the husband's stereo set, the silver tray Aunt Fanny gave as a wedding present, and the family dog.

The issue becomes even more complex when former partners channel their anger and outrage into retaliation by demanding a disproportionate amount ("I'll take that bastard for everything he has!"), or when they express their hurt at the spouse's rejection by voluntarily giving up their rights to property held in common ("If he leaves me, I won't take a single penny from him!"). Sometimes the desire to "get out of the trap" is exploited to the other's advantage, as seen in this excerpt from a case reported elsewhere.[29]

> The same week, Helen asked her husband for a divorce. Although this came as no surprise to him, his main concern was what he stood to lose in terms of the family business and their common property. His chief weapon was passivity: she would ask him to carry out some action in the divorce process and he would delay. As the price of his compliance, she had to make considerable concessions in terms of financial arrangements, property division, and visitation rights. . . . She suffered acutely as their own house, into which she had poured so much effort, was sold and their household effects were divided up.

Alimony payments, rooted in the tradition that the husband as head of the family is responsible for the support of his former wife and children, are granted by court order and are based on the husband's (and, to an increasing extent, the wife's) current income, the length of the marriage, and such special factors as the amount of blame the judge attaches to the guilty party. The concept of alimony is generally considered archaic and punitive, and it has been increasingly challenged in recent years from a number of sources such as bar associations and men's rights groups. While theoretically spouses may petition later on to change alimony arrangements to meet changed financial conditions, even the original amount allocated has generally been found to be insufficient and hard to collect and alimony is granted in less than

10 percent of all divorce cases.[30] Yet for the older woman, untrained and often too old to obtain a job, it often may be her only source of support.

Far less controversial is the awarding of *child-support payments*, which are usually set by the court on the basis of the education, health, and earning power of the husband and wife, the length of the marriage, and the ages and special requirements of the children. The underlying principle is that the father is responsible for support of his children. The amount may be negotiated by the spouses or their lawyers but has to be ratified by the court. While fathers who do not keep up support payments are legally in contempt of court, sanctions are rarely applied. Sometimes payments from the father are routed through state and local welfare agencies and balanced against Aid to Families with Dependent Children (AFDC) allotments.

Against this background of financial bickering and frequent recriminations, the family breaks up as an economic unit, with the children under fourteen usually going to live with the wife. Husbands have been found to be less affected financially by the move. True, they have to continue to support their former family, and in the event of their remarriage may need to provide for two households, but their earning power is rarely affected and may even be enhanced by their increased mobility. In one study, only one of the twenty-two men interviewed reported major economic problems caused by the divorce. Most of the men had held full-time jobs before the separation and either continued in them or obtained better ones. The large majority considered themselves at least as well off as before.[31]

Women, on the other hand, often suffer a sharp drop in their economic standard of living when they divorce. Not only is their income reduced, but they frequently have to leave their previous home and move into smaller, less adequate quarters in poorer sections of town. If they look to augment their income by going out to work, they may find that because they have been out of the labor market for a long time or have never been in it they have no currently marketable skills. If they finally find a job or continue in their previous one (if they had been working prior to the divorce), they now find they have to bear the additional financial burden of baby-sitting or childcare services.

In a study carried out in the Boston area, it was found that the incomes of recently divorced women were more than halved by the event.[32] Moreover, only half of the former husbands were providing any financial support to their families, and less than one-third supplied as much as 50 percent of the family's income. Since women's wages were lower on the whole than men's, over half of the women were unable to "make it" and turned to AFDC either immediately or within a year of the divorce. As a result of their reliance on former husbands or welfare services to supplement or provide their basic income, these women reported multiple constraints and "strings" on their activities and choices.

The following extract portrays the grim circumstances faced by many divorced women living on marginal incomes—circumstances aggravated in this instance by the social problems of poverty, violence, and ethnicity. The case is reported by a public welfare worker:

JOAN (#187)

Joan Barker, age 22, is a young black woman in her eighth month of pregnancy, living in a midwestern town. She was referred by the police to the Welfare Department two months ago for immediate help, after a fire destroyed the shack in which she had been living with her mother and three children, ages 7 years, 4 years, and 16 months.

Background Information.   Joan is the third of four children whose parents were divorced when she was 12. Her mother supported the family by doing housework; her father drifted out of town and has not been heard from since. When Joan was 15, she became pregnant and dropped out of high school. She brought her child home to her mother, and at age 16 married Jim, the baby's father, then age 20. He was employed by the county as a laborer and was a chronic drinker with a violent temper and a penchant for wifebeating and child abuse. When Jim would begin to hit her, Joan would defend herself by throwing household objects such as flowerpots and kitchen knives at him. Police were frequently called, and the couple repeatedly appeared in court on charges of battery, assault, and disturbance of the peace.

After two years Joan and Jim separated, and a year later they were divorced with the encouragement of the court. Jim moved out of the house and supposedly out of town, although he periodically reappears to physically assault and abuse her. He also fathered her third child and the one she is expecting next month. Since the divorce, he has never contributed to the support of the family.

While the divorce saved Joan, to some extent, from the ongoing battles with her husband, it also deprived her of the financial security, limited as it was, that she had had when Jim worked steadily and brought home his pay. From the time they separated, when she was 18, she has lived hand-to-mouth on ADC payments and food stamps, struggling to avoid evictions and utility cutoffs. Eleven months ago, with the help of a special projects rehabilitation worker, she found her first "good" job, as a merchandise checker at a local warehouse. Although the hours were difficult, from 4:00 P.M. to 12:30 A.M., this was by far the best job available to someone with only a tenth-grade education, and she realized this.

For the first time, Joan began to feel the joys of independence; she bought new beds for the children, a secondhand refrigerator for her mother, and a pair of knee-high white leather boots for herself. Working steadily over the summer, she was able to "get off of welfare" and reported that things were beginning to look up for the first time. Her only worry was dodging Jim when he would return to town on one of his periodic binges and come looking for her.

In October, tragedy struck when her mother, whose hands had become crippled with arthritis, upset the kerosene stove on which she was cooking supper. The tarpaper shack ignited immediately, and despite the early arrival of the Fire Department, the house went up in flames so quickly that the firemen were unable to save any of the family's possessions. The grandmother and children were taken to the

YMCA hostel and Joan, who was working at the time, was called to survey the damage. She reported, "I felt as if the whole bottom had fallen out of my life again . . . back to Square One!"

Since then, the Welfare Department has lodged the family temporarily in a trailer, although it is obvious that when Joan's fourth child is born they will have to move into larger quarters. Because of the impending birth, Joan is now worried that she won't be able to hold on to her job for much longer, and because of her mother's deteriorating health, she doesn't know if she'll be able to go back after the baby is born. Her sisters have their own troubles and she feels she cannot turn to them for help. With the family's past history of repeated crises, few private agencies in town are willing to assist her on even an emergency basis; she has used up all of her "eligibility" with them. Although the Welfare Office has been helping her meet her immediate needs by replacing her housing, clothing, and basic furniture, and although we have arranged to reinstate her ADC payments, she sees the future as looking very bleak.

CO-PARENTAL ASPECTS

We cannot, within the overall framework of adult transitional states, enter into the extremely important topic of the effect of divorce on children, although a considerable body of significant research and clinical findings has been amassed in this area within the last decade.[33] Rather, we turn to the effect on the parents of custodial arrangements, visitation rights, and managing a single-parent household.

At various points in the divorce process, the question is raised, "What will happen to the children?" Not only does it concern the parents—with all their own attachments to particular offspring, their recollections of their own childhood experiences (good and bad), and their qualms about their spouse's and their own ability to raise the children—but lawyers spend a good deal of their time working out the issue of custody before the judge makes final adjudication. Weiss points out in his comprehensive review of the history of custody arrangements that most divorcing parents decide on child custody out of court; less than 10 percent fail to reach agreement before the divorce hearing.[34]

Patterns of custody arrangements tend to be, generally, of three kinds. Most commonly, one parent has both *legal custody* (the right to make decisions about the children's life-style, education, religious upbringing, etc.) and *physical custody* (the right to have the child live with him/her); sometimes one parent has legal custody and the other physical custody; and sometimes, *joint custody* is awarded, with both parents sharing custodial rights and responsibilities.[35] The issue becomes even more complicated when various types of visitation rights are granted to the noncustodial parent: some by mutual agreement, some worked out by the lawyers, and some granted after bitter controversy in the courtroom over the issue of parental fitness.

What this means, when translated into the practicality of daily living, is that parents and children shuttle around in a complex pattern of fathers coming to get the children and mothers trying to schedule their and the children's activities to fit into a shifting schedule of weekend, afternoon, and summer vacation visits with Daddy. And when, as frequently happens, the picture becomes further complicated by having to mesh timetables into the programs of father's second family and mother's steady boyfriend, it is no wonder that children become confused and disorientated at times as to who their parents are and where home is. The *Children of Divorce* project carried out by Judith Wallerstein and Joan Kelly amply illustrates the variations of disorientation and dysfunction brought about by the uncertainties and changes in life patterns. They conclude:[36]

> Divorce is a disorganizing and reorganizing process in a family with children. The process extends over time, often several years. Although it has, like most life events and crises, the potential for growth and new integrations, the road is often rocky and torturous, and many people underestimate the vicissitudes and difficulties of the transition.

Wallerstein and Kelly found that events over the *entire* post-separation period—including the pre-divorce interval, the divorce events themselves, and the post-divorce functioning of the custodial parent—are central determinants in the young child's well-being, even after a year of separation. Moreover, the older child's or adolescent's capacity to maintain his/her developmental stride appeared to be inversely related to the parent's need to lean heavily on the children for emotional and social sustenance and to involve them in continuing battles and recriminations with the divorced mate. Many decisions made during the divorce in regard to the subsequent structuring of relationships, including custody and visitation arrangements, have long-term consequences for the future of the parent-child bond. (*Kramer vs. Kramer* deals with this issue.)

Many parents find that the post-divorce period offers a second chance, a growth period for themselves and their children to effect potentially helpful change and to make major decisions regarding their mutual relationships. Unlike death, the continued availability of the departed parent enables the children to work out their conflicts over loss and longings for reconciliation. Even more, it allows both children and adults to achieve new and complex changes in their self-concepts and their intimate relationships, to engage in mourning over the loss of the pre-divorce family, to accept the circumscribed ties with the noncustodial parent, and to adjust to the revised relationship with the custodial parent.[37]

SOCIAL ASPECTS

Over and above the specific aspects of legal, economic, and co-parental changes taking place, the immediate post-divorce period involves a complex transformation in social role activities and relationships. While it is extremely difficult to differentiate between emotional reactions during the estrangement and separation stage and during the formalization stage, since feelings of loneliness and loss tend to persist, I see the formalization period, once the break has been finalized, as one requiring change in *behavioral patterns* as well.

For men, since they tend to continue their work roles, as mentioned above, the primary change is often in their role as fathers. Harry Keshet and Kristine Rosenthal examined in great detail the fathering role after marital separation.[38] They found that the period immediately after a marital breakup was one of severe stress during which the men they studied experienced depression, sadness, anger, loneliness, anxiety, and severe and frequent mood changes. They perceived life as meaningless and lacking in coherence and felt guilty and inadequate as parents. In this last area, however, they had to make concrete changes in their coping patterns, since they had to pick up and care for their children without their former wife to coach and back them up:

> Being the sole parent responsible even temporarily for the welfare of their children is a new experience for most men and is perceived by them as inappropriate, strange, and even frightening. . . . Nevertheless, learning to cope with single parenting has its positive aspects. . . . [They] found joy in meeting their responsibilities to their children and were surprised at feeling good about their own nurturing abilities. The feeling of accomplishment derived from overcoming initial difficulties supports and reinforces the individual's efforts to build a new parenting role. [p. 12]

Concrete activities involved such actions as setting up childcare schedules, helping to decide who would be with whom for holidays and birthdays, transporting children and their belongings back and forth, working out arrangements to fit into work and other responsibilities, developing priorities for parenting, and dealing with the children's emotional needs and the *quality* of the father-child relationship.

For women, the changes occur in different areas. As mothers, they continue to cope with the children's daily needs. The divorce may perpetuate mother–child behavioral patterns started much earlier when the marriage began to "go sour." Now, however, the mothers have to change their overall style of living as well, including the merging of their parental role with those of primary provider and decision maker:

> As a single parent, [the mother] must spread her time to cover all of the family demands. Both schools and work places have inflexible hours and these hours do not coincide. For the employed single mother, getting the children to school, being at work on time, and arranging for after-school pickup and care are the parameters of [a] weekday. . . . One mother described her day, "Everything is a tradeoff, a continuing conflict. There is no

one else to do anything—shopping, dentists, chores, everything has to be done in evenings and weekends, I need the job, so I can't tell the boss to go to hell and take time off."[39]

Adequate childcare arrangements assume particular importance, since without them the working mother cannot function. Housework, repairs, and maintenance must somehow be fitted into the woman's schedule, with many women learning to fix appliances and plaster walls themselves because they have no one to call upon and cannot afford professional repair services. Even more difficult to handle are the changed, stigmatizing attitudes of the people in their social world:

> Elementary school personnel, physicians, bill collectors, gas station atten-dants, repairmen, and married friends seemed free to berate, accuse, bully, refuse service, or advise in a way they never had before. Perhaps this is because of an air of helpless confusion and hopeless incompetence these women exude post-divorce. But a larger component is contributed, I believe, by society's changed perception of a women when she is alone. She is ab-ruptly perceived as a second-class citizen and treated with a condescension, brevity, and arbitrariness reserved for those who probably won't buy or can't pay.[40]

One of the most significant areas affected is the divorced person's rela-tions with his/her own family. Families' various attitudes toward divorce tend to prevent the separating couple from informing the family of their decision until after the fact since it may reawaken—in both the parents and in themselves—earlier developmental issues which have never been dealt with completely. Some of the families of origin may be immediately solici-tous and anxious to help; others are gently or harshly condemning; still others are angry and in the position to say, "I told you so!" Some simply refuse to become involved. Nevertheless, after the divorce, many women have no choice but to turn to their parents.

A concrete form of help which parents can offer a child whose marriage has ended is the refuge of their home. While both a son and daughter may be invited to return, the offer seems to be made more frequently to a daughter, partly because of the parents' guilt over having permitted her to make the unsuccessful marriage, partly to expiate their own past failures, and partly to provide the grandchildren with a more "normal" home.

The return to her parental home may offer the woman a brief moratorium from responsibility, a breathing space during which she can begin to reinte-grate her forces. It can also give her full-time help with the children, reduce her financial burdens, and fill the void of her empty evenings. On the other hand, the cost she may have to pay is often one of reduced autonomy, since her parents may intervene in her social life and in management of the children, and they will rarely hesitate to pass judgment on her past and present behavior. Weiss found that parents can rarely share their home with their separated (or divorced) daughter for more than a few weeks without conflict. A more feasible arrangement seems to be for the woman to make her home in her parents' neighborhood so that she can enjoy her own autonomy while profiting from their available help on an "as needed" basis.[41]

Since many formerly married persons find themselves quite marginal to their previous networks of friends, who have had to choose between being "his" or "hers," they often need to develop a new network of friends with similar interests to combat the core problem of loneliness and role loss. This network may consist of one or two good friends who are in a similar position to the divorced person; it may consist of special-interest or activity-centered groups that allow the person to lose self-consciousness by, say, identifying birds, campaigning for a political candidate, or taking up macramé. Or it may be one of the specially organized groups of divorced, separated, and widowed individuals that have arisen to meet this need, such as Parents Without Partners or Fifth Wheelers. The Women in Transition movement has some down-to-earth advice to offer women in this respect:[42]

> It is probably most important to realize that friends can probably never be a substitute for the intimacy you had with your ex-husband, and that to expect them to replace that will put impossible demands on them. Make some new friends. Try to find other women who are going through similar situations and sit down and talk. Try not to depend too much on friendships that may have been somewhat shaky to begin with. But certainly take advantage of any support you can get from sympathetic sources.

Sooner or later, divorced persons will have to deal with the issue of the sexual aspect of their identity, which most frequently needs reworking at this time, since the divorce may have shaken their confidence in themselves as a desirable and adequate sexual partner. According to Wiseman, the need to experiment sexually at this time is of vital importance to many divorcing persons who seek a variety of sexual experiences with a series of partners to whom they feel little emotional commitment and with whom they feel there is little potential for a long-term relationship. Reasons for this "candy store" type of behavior often lie in people's need to rebuild their damaged self-concept by seeing themselves as sexually desirable; their desire to avoid a serious emotional commitment; and the real need to compensate for previous limited extramarital sexual experience.[43]

In continuing the case of Suzy, started earlier in this chapter, we can see how she dealt with the issue of her social and sexual needs:

SUZY (#189)—PART TWO

A few months before her divorce became final, Suzy began to date Sam, an older man, whom she used as a transitional object to minimize her fears of being alone. Eventually she began to recognize that she was depending on him to "fill the emptiness." Her relationship with Sam served several purposes, however, besides being a buffer against her loneliness. By spending weekends with him while living with her parents, she was placed in the position of presenting herself to her parents as a mature, sexual adult rather than as an acting-out adolescent. She paid room and board, she was over 21, and—after some struggle with the issue—she forced them to see her in this new light. In addition, Sam, as a graduate student, also provided Suzy with intellectual stimulation which she could accept, since it was shared with him. She began to examine her own concept of herself as a woman and to broaden her personal options. While she continued to talk of wanting to be married again, she now added that first she wanted to "live a little."

The Suzy–Sam involvement was tenuous from the beginning, largely because of his lack of commitment. This prevented her from moving too quickly from one dependent relationship to another and pushed her to look at her own dependency and the problems this caused for her. When Sam decided to move to New York for further training, Suzy agreed to go with him, even though she recognized that she was using her tie with him to make a break from Rod and from her parents. She felt that leaving the community and her roots here was not something she could do alone.

Termination took place at Suzy's instigation as she began to taper off her visits and prepare to move to New York. Eventually, before she left, she and Sam had a talk to "clear the air" and agreed that their relationship would be "uncommitted." She continued to see him but not exclusively. Suzy made arrangements for a job and apartment of her own before leaving for New York. A final crisis occurred the day before she was supposed to leave, when, after she had sent Rod the remainder of his unpaid bills, he called her and threatened to kill himself. She was able to accept my instructions as to how to deal with him so that he got help quickly and eventually accepted a referral for psychotherapy.

Meanwhile Suzy and Sam traveled to New York together, but, once there, she established her own life pattern. Her last letter indicated that she was working at a university, taking some courses, and thinking about the future. She admitted having "low days," but she felt quite separated from Rod and avoided seeing him when she returned to visit her family. My evaluation was that she had been dealing with two transitions at the same time: bridging the gap from being married to being single again and moving from late adolescence to early adulthood. Although she still had some way to go on both issues, she had made sufficient progress to move on in her life course.

Stage Three: Building a New Life-Style

Gradually the divorced person's focus and interests change; his life, previously completely disrupted and disoriented, begins to assume a new coherence. This stage, roughly equivalent to Bohannan's "psychic divorce," has the issue of *autonomy* as its chief concern. It involves a distancing in time and sometimes in space so that the person can look back in reflection and not only ask "Why did I marry my former spouse?" but gain some self-awareness and emotional growth as he works out the answer.

Although frequently the period of one year is taken as the length of the *active* transition, full recovery may take much longer. The first few months are generally a time of disorganization, depression, restlessness, and chaotic searching for escape from distress. Later on, the individual begins to make a determined effort to regain his footing, to start to function again, and to restore order to his life.

THE RECOVERY PERIOD

This is followed by a period of *recovery*, in which the individual begins to establish a coherent pattern of life, although he may not have integrated it firmly enough so that it can withstand new stress. Mood swings and depression gradually decrease and the person takes on the deceptive appearance of being well-organized and assured, even though inner self-doubt and renewed stress may still revive, at times, earlier emotional disorganization:[44]

> As time goes on, the integration of separated individuals becomes more resilient. By three or four years after their separation, although they may have become different people from the people they were when married, they should again feel comfortable with themselves and be as stable as their nature permits. This is not to say that at this point they will have achieved happiness, but rather that their troubles will no longer be traceable to the separation and its aftermath. [pp. 240–241]

Gradually, almost imperceptibly, there is a move from casual and transitory social relationships to those which involve one other person for a longer period of time and with a deeper degree of emotional commitment. As the person's self-concept begins to improve and his/her feelings of anger toward the former spouse begin to abate, he/she begins to accept the former partner and the terminated marriage as they really are. This acceptance enables the divorced person to establish new forms of relationships with the former spouse and with in-laws. Relations of the two parents with their children have been worked out, with some of the old social and family relations retained or reestablished and others discarded as outmoded and inappropriate.[45] New educational experiences, new jobs, new friends, and even new communities combine to create new patterns of living in which the person feels increasingly comfortable.

The following brief case summary illustrates this reintegration process:

MARGE (#101)

Marge, age 28, had been married for six years and had a five-year-old daughter, Cathy. The marriage had been under tremendous tension for some time, but when she walked out on her husband she experienced intense feelings of failure as a wife and mother. Deeply fearful of living alone for the first time in her life, she felt dependent, childlike, and sexually inadequate as a woman—altogether, she had very low self-esteem. She became extremely depressed and contemplated suicide at times, although she never attempted it. It was evident that Marge was mourning not only the loss of her husband but the loss of her role as wife. Her own family kept urging her to go back to her husband; they repeatedly asked her what went wrong and prodded her to apologize and ask him to take her back. Since he refused to send her child support, she reluctantly applied for an AFDC grant.

As we started to work together, her view of herself changed rapidly. She began to see herself in broader terms, as adequate, independent, appealing, competent, and "marketable." Concurrently, she began to expand her social world in several directions. She began to make new friends, she started to work part-time, and she volunteered to help mornings at Cathy's school. She also began to make independent decisions about herself and Cathy without first having to ask her parents or her former husband.

By the end of the first year, Marge's situation had changed considerably. Whereas a year before she had been unemployed and on welfare, she now was part-owner of a small but growing plant nursery. From feeling socially isolated and inadequate, she now had a strong supportive network of friends that grew out of a group for single parents she had attended, including a "special friend" she was beginning to date regularly. She had been able to use individual counseling to improve her self-image and used the therapeutic relationship to take risks in order to bring about change in herself, in her relations to Cathy, and in her ties with her parents.

NEW ATTACHMENTS

Some divorced persons prefer to remain single and unattached. On the other hand, when they do work out lasting relationships, the new structures can take several forms. Basically three types of committed attachments can be found: "going together," living together, and remarriage. The difference lies in the underlying assumptions regarding the bond between the two. In going together, the only obligation each has to the other is accessibility. In living together, the pair also agree to intermesh their living routines and to assume the financial and arrangemental obligations of cohabitation. In remarriage, the two assume, in addition to the previous conditions, the special obligations implicit in the formal marriage contract and in becoming one another's "next of kin."[46] Since of the almost one million persons in the United States who divorce each year, 80 percent will eventually remarry,[47] we shall concentrate on that particular pathway of the transitional process.

Re-formed or reconstituted families have become a topic of interest for practitioners only within the last few years, as the number of families asking for help has increased and greater awareness has developed of the difficulties built into the situation. Whereas in the past the death of a spouse was the main reason stepfamilies were formed, today the primary causes are the high divorce rate, the increasing number of children affected by divorce, and the large number of divorced persons who remarry.[48]

Unlike a first marriage, a remarriage made up of one or two divorced parents with at least one child from a former marriage starts out with a set of legal encumbrances. Predictably, these encumbrances usually deal with custody of the children, visiting rights, and support payments.[49] Many formerly married persons, who supposedly marry again to start a new life, enter a field cluttered with unresolved issues left over from the previous marriage(s) and with new issues arising out of the effort to deal with the spouses' conflicting hopes, expectations, and hangups.

If several sets of children live under the same roof, the household can become divided into hostile camps. Even weekend-visiting stepchildren can place a great burden on a new marriage, since they often come as delegates from an angry first spouse and visit with the mission of driving a wedge between the new partners. The stepparent, despite initial good will, can grow highly resentful of the constant difficulties and chaos created by the children, while the natural parent becomes hypersensitive to possible signs of the stepparent's rejection and guilty over having imposed a "package deal" on the new spouse.[50]

Bohannan has traced the complex patterns of "divorce chains" in remarried families, the "pseudo-kinship" groups formed on the basis of links between the new spouses, ex-spouses, and groups of children bound to the adults in various patterns of relationship.[51] Social workers are familiar with the constellation of "your children, my children, our children" which often forms the basis of contention in stepfamilies, as well as with the complexities of the various extended families who jealously protect their special interests in the total scene.

The stages in formation of the reconstituted family are different from those of the first family (see Chapter 6). This process can be divided into three sequential but overlapping phases: recovery from loss, planning the new marriage, and reconstituting the family.[52]

PHASE 1: RECOVERY FROM LOSS.   The first task for persons who will later comprise part of a reconstituted family is to mourn the loss of the pre-divorce family. This may have started at the separation stage of the divorce transition, or, as often is the case, it may be delayed until or reopened when the divorced spouse begins to contemplate remarrying. Both parent and children experience feelings of anger, guilt, sadness, and anxiety over losing the former family, and their final relinquishment can be accomplished only over a period of time with appropriate grieving. If the two persons who plan to remarry are at different stages in overcoming their loss, if only one has been married before, or if they do not discuss this openly, it can complicate their later relationship.

The second task is to give up the fantasy that "someday" the former family will be reunited. Because of their past history as a failed family, both parent and children may be wary or distrustful of setting up new relationships. On the adult's part this may spring from lack of self-confidence or low self-esteem, or from guilt or worry over withdrawing investment in the children in order to seek satisfaction for himself. On the children's part, it may come from resistance to seeing their mother or father engaging in a new adult-to-adult relationship that cuts them out; from fear of abandonment by their remaining parent; or from jealousy or fear of displacement by the children of the prospective stepmother or stepfather. The children will continue to yearn for the reuniting of their original family long after one or both parents have remarried.

PHASE 2: PLANNING THE NEW MARRIAGE.   The first task of the partners in planning the marriage is to come to terms with (1) their own lack of confidence (and that of the other) regarding the ability to sustain close, lasting bonds and (2) their fear of repeating the mistakes and unhappiness of the past. This may include distrust of promises or fear of physical or emotional injury, if this was their former experience. They may feel conflicted over the children's ability to accept a stepparent, particularly in view of the centuries-old fairy tales about the "wicked stepmother" or the "overbearing stepfather."* They may also doubt their own capacity to fulfill a parenting role toward the partner's children, especially when the children demonstrate their anger and fears by unlikable or outrageous behavior.

The second task is to invest in the new family members as primary sources of emotional gratification. The previous exclusive relationship between single parent and child, born out of their loneliness and mutual need during the separation and divorce periods, may be an obstacle to the development of a close bond between the new spouses. On the other hand, one of the partners may choose to guard against being hurt again by framing the proposed mate's role as a "new father for the children," as a provider of material needs, or as a housekeeper or nursemaid. The child may feel distrustful of being rejected by the new mother or father and worried about being forced to give up his emotional attachment to his own other parent or to choose between them. (This may be particularly true when the child is an adolescent and is testing the bonds between himself and his biological parents.) Acknowledgment that the stepparent–stepchild relationship will be a new type of bond, not a replacement for the lost parent or child, is a prime requisite for future success of the new family.

PHASE 3: RECONSTITUTING THE FAMILY.   When a new "combination family" starts its life together, the primary task is to restructure the family roles. Discipline and nurturance are usually the two basic areas in which the second family must redefine its roles. It is crucial for both parent and child to acknowledge the stepparent's right to function in these realms: to comfort or

---

*In one case incident, a divorced father told about his mystification as to his young children's antagonism to his second wife until he learned that, two days before his remarriage, their mother took them to see the Disney film, *Cinderella*.

scold (or spank) the child when it is appropriate. Children of both spouses must also work out their new relations toward each other and find their particular place in the family network. This task also implies rebuilding generational boundaries between parents and children, often weakened and crossed during the divorce process, and separating out appropriate feelings and behavior between parents and children, husband and wife, and sibling and sibling. It also implies defining and building new roles for the extended families on all sides.

The final task is to delineate the appropriate relationship with the divorced biological parent. When the former spouse continues to take the children for visits or shares custody of the children, all members of the reconstituted family must sort out their feelings of loyalty, anger, jealousy, abandonment, guilt, and envy in order to accept the former spouse's role in relation to them, individually and as a unit. Some time may elapse before a viable arrangement of visits, shared responsibilities, and financial commitments can be worked out satisfactorily. The new family may have to come to terms with the fact that there will always be interference, neglect, or retaliation on the part of the former spouse who still retains parental rights.

Jacobson points out that adjustment of the stepfamily is often affected by two myths. The "myth of instant adjustment" or "instant love" fantasies that some magic will occur and that all aspects of the complex situation will fall into place immediately; while the "myth of the recreated nuclear family" supposes that, after the remarriage takes place, stepparents and stepchildren will form a family unit similar to the biological family, whether they live together or whether the children just visit periodically. The reality is often that regardless of their wishes or fears, the previous spouse of one or both marital partners is alive, well, and often living nearby.[53] It may take a long time to develop a workable arrangement; sometimes it may be necessary to settle for a "least worst" arrangement.

The following private case illustrates the effect that the transition to becoming a reconstituted family has on the adolescent child of one of the parents:

MELISSA (#224)

Melissa, age 12, was presented by her father and prospective stepmother when she began to have severe physical symptoms in school—headaches, blurred vision, dizziness, and stomachache—without any apparent physical basis. Each of the adults had been divorced and had custody of the only child of the previous marriage, and each considered him or herself the injured party in the divorce; both seemed to have the problems of being "too nice" and tending to avoid unpleasant realities. After living together for several months on a trial basis, they now had decided to marry and were involved in planning the wedding, an event which the future Mrs. Perry felt was upsetting Melissa.

The acute situational crisis developed a week ago after Melissa returned from a rare weekend visit to her own mother, who lived at some distance. Her stomachache had started before she left, and she returned ill and acutely upset so that she was unable to return to school all week. Although their pediatrician had assured the couple that nothing was physically wrong, Melissa's illness was causing her prospective stepmother so much lost time from work that she began to express her anger, not at Melissa but at the girl's mother. She reported that Melissa became upset each time she visited or called her mother; they were thinking of ending her contacts because of this.

Background Information. Melissa's parents had divorced when she was seven, and her mother had left her in her father's custody while she continued her education. They lived in the same city and visits had been regular, although not very satisfying according to Mr. Perry, who saw his former wife as self-centered and neglectful of both Melissa's needs and his own. After her mother went to New York to take a new position, Melissa would look forward to her visits there with great anticipation, although they cost a great deal in airfare and she received little attention once she got there; on the last few occasions, her mother had not even taken time off to be with Melissa but instead took her to her office with her. Mr. Perry was incensed and now expressed the wish that Melissa would stop caring so much for her own mother and instead learn to love her "real" mother now. The future Mrs. Perry agreed and said she looked forward to the formal wedding ceremony, which she felt would help Melissa feel more comfortable in calling her "Mom."

Treatment. The treatment plan was aimed at helping Melissa, her father, and her about-to-be stepmother recognize their divergent concepts of their reconstituted family. The couple saw their goal as becoming "one happy family" as quickly as possible. Melissa, on the other hand, was "stuck" at the point of dealing with her grief over separation from her natural mother. The prospective wedding had opened up many unresolved feelings over her loss during the divorce, which she had been too young to handle at the time.

When I saw Melissa alone, I found her to be somewhat sedate and mature for her 12 years, very pretty in a winning way. She told me the whole situation in the first few minutes. Her stomachaches in school had begun six months ago when she returned from a visit to her mother. She then began to cry, saying, "I miss my mother!" We began to talk about her mother's inconsistent behavior toward her and her apparent lack of affection. Melissa summed it up well: "I'm stuck with taking what I can get."

Shortly after this interview, Melissa visited her mother again and returned feeling ill and "shaky." For the next four interviews we talked about her feelings about her mother's abandonment of her, though the word itself was never used. During this time I also saw Mr. Perry and his future wife to help them understand Melissa's reactions to the loss of her mother. Since the girl's stomachaches and headaches were beginning to diminish, they began to understand that Melissa felt very differently toward her own mother than they did, and that despite what she did or did not receive from her, Melissa would probably always retain her attachment. They also began to recognize that their "happy family" expectations were unrealistic. They were able to express their fear that Melissa would turn out to be like her mother and would want to live with her. Mr. Perry even admitted that his former wife had been an outstanding mother to Melissa up to two years before the divorce, when she lost a child at birth. The marriage had begun to deteriorate after this.

The Perrys realized that they were in a tug-of-war with Melissa's mother for the child's loyalty and affection and agreed to reduce their pressure. We developed a plan to send Melissa to her mother's at more frequent intervals. Her mother was asked to share the expense and agreed, and Melissa was encouraged to write and phone her frequently.

On her part, Melissa's concerns had shifted to her fear that her new stepmother would be angry at her for her continued loyalty to her own mother. She talked about the coming wedding; she liked her stepmother a lot now, but would she change once she married her father? She was even able to voice her competitive feelings, wishing that her stepmother would go away and leave her alone with her father. She was reassured that it was not fair to ask her to compete with grown women for Daddy. Slowly she began to integrate the loose ends and to move toward accepting the marriage.

Another visit to her mother a week after the Perrys' wedding, which went off smoothly, produced another bout of illness. This time the new Mrs. Perry was instructed by phone to tell the school to keep Melissa comfortable until the end of the school day and have her return to class once she felt well enough, with no secondary gains to be granted for the illness. Melissa was seen three times after this visit. The first time when she was still feeling ill, she was very resistant, but after a long silence she asked, "Do other kids feel this way when their parents divorce?" It was apparent that the reality of the divorce was sinking in at last. In the following session she still did not feel entirely well but said proudly that she was managing and had attended school every day that week. She was trying not to think too much about how her own mother treated her, but she had to when she would visit her; next month her mother was coming to visit her and maybe she would tell her about seeing me. She said that lots of kids in her school had divorced parents and she thought it would help for them to talk together about it.

Although the children's group never materialized and her mother was not able to visit her, Melissa announced in her last interview that she almost broke the appointment because she felt quite comfortable. She had had no more bad dreams or illnesses, and although she knew she would begin to feel sick and even "weird" next month when she would visit her mother again, she agreed to talk about it with her stepmother. Since then I have received several notes from Melissa's stepmother indicating that the whole family is doing extremely well, that she and Melissa have a good relationship, and that Melissa is asymptomatic.

In discussing how to work with stepparents and stepchildren, Emily and John Visher point out that even though stepfamilies tend to be more stressful than intact families, many adults and children find special satisfaction in this arrangement. Adults often mention their awareness of the deep meaning of their interpersonal relationship, and because of the earlier disruptions in their lives, are conscious that such bonds are precious and not to be taken for granted. They feel that the complexity of the stepfamily can forge an emotional commitment as the couple works together to solve problems that arise and thus gains great personal satisfaction from this opportunity for individual growth and human involvement.[54]

10

Untimely Widowhood:
Grief and Bereavement

Why?
Why did it happen to him?
Why is it happening to me?

THESE QUESTIONS, asked endlessly throughout the night, night after night, reflect the bewilderment and despair of newly widowed persons as they pass through the transition of final separation from their mate. For some it marks the culmination of weeks or months of heartbreaking waiting while the husband or wife battles against a debilitating illness or body injury. For others the end comes suddenly, without warning, in a fatal accident, an immediate collapse, an act of war or criminal violence. Whatever the contributing factors, the time arrives when the struggle ends and the widowed spouse is left alone to ask, numbly, "Why?"

During the late adulthood stage, one spouse's death before the other is considered a predictable and inevitable part of the winding down of the adult life cycle. But when this occurs before its time, it initiates a bridging period for the surviving partner which has two separate, although interwoven, aspects: the intrapsychic process of engaging in grief work and the psychosocial process of separating oneself from one's mate, adjusting to living without that person, and building a new life in a new pattern. In considering

169

the transition of widowhood, we shall try to separate these two facets, even though in essence they are two sides of the same coin.

Grief and Mourning

Although we make no attempt to discuss this area as comprehensively as Bertha Simos does in her recent book,[1] we shall start out by borrowing several of her definitions in order to anchor the discussion:

> *Loss* is the state of being deprived of or being without something one has had and valued. Four major categories of loss are: loss of a significant love or valued person, loss of part of the self, loss of external objects, and developmental loss. Death of a loved one is considered the ultimate loss. [p. 10–11]

> *Bereavement* is the *act* of separation or loss that results in the experience of grief. As such, it becomes a precipitating event that starts off the grief process. A different view considers bereavement to be the *response* that follows the loss, and sees it as being made up of two components, grief and mourning. [p. 28]

> *Grief* is the intense emotional suffering caused by loss, disaster, or misfortune. It can be *anticipatory grief*, deep sadness expressed in advance of a loss when the loss is perceived as inevitable, or *acute grief*, the intense sadness which immediately follows a loss. *Chronic grief* is sorrow maintained over a considerable period of time. [p. 29]

> *Mourning* is the process following loss of which grief is a part, but extending beyond the first reactions into the period of reorganization of the new identity and reattachment to new interests and people. It is behavior prescribed by the customs and mores of a given society, which determines how a person should conduct himself after the death of another. [p. 29]

Reactions to grief tend to be intrapersonal, combining both physiological and psychological reactions, while those of mourning are cultural and social, dictated by what is considered accepted and normal in that particular system to which the individual belongs. Both grief and mourning can occur simultaneously in situations where feelings are supported by social customs such as funeral ceremonies, but mourning can also take place where little or no grief is felt. On the other hand, grief can be deep and intensive but the person may lack the mourning rituals by which to express it. As mentioned elsewhere, one of the difficulties experienced in Israel by kibbutz widows during the Yom Kippur War was the lack of meaningful mourning rites through which to channelize their grief.[2]

Widowhood, the loss of a mate, is one particular instance of bereavement. In contrast to separation or divorce, which may have been brewing for some time, and to which the spouse is usually available to react and interact during and after the transition, or in contrast to other types of loss, in which the lost object can be replaced or compensated for, the death of a spouse has specific characteristics: (1) It is stark finality, in that it is irreversible. One cannot turn back the clock or replace the loss; one can only adjust to it. (2) It is a relatively rare occurrence in our lives, so that most of us have little intimate experience with the death of people close to us until comparatively late in our life span, and thus we have no learned coping repertoire with which to handle the loss. (3) It involves giving up a primary relationship tied closely to one's own self-image and self-esteem.

GRIEVING BEFORE THE DEATH

Some years ago, Elisabeth Kübler-Ross worked out a sequence of preparatory grief stages that the terminally ill person passes through before his death: denial and isolation, anger, bargaining, depression, and finally, acceptance.[3] Kübler-Ross feels that in those situations where family members are aware of the approaching death, they go through similar stages of adjustment. At first they cannot believe it is true, and they deny its existence or shop around from doctor to doctor in order to hear that this was a wrong diagnosis. They may expend considerable money, energy, and time until they finally face up to the reality. Then, depending on the patient's attitude, awareness, and ability to communicate, the family has to be able to share with him their common concerns, as well as their genuine emotions, so that they can take care of important matters early and settle issues between them. If, however, each tries to keep the impending death a secret from the other, they set up an artificial barrier between them that makes any preparatory grief difficult.[4]

In the following passages taken from a diary kept by a thirty-year-old wife whose husband was discovered to have a terminal illness, we see the heartbreak in the masked truths and semi-truths, the rising hopes and severe letdowns which marked their last months together:

EDNA STONE (#203)

One day when I went to visit Bob in the hospital, I felt there had been a change in his attitude. He seemed scared. He tried to act and talk naturally but suddenly he burst into tears. "I'm dying," he said. "I overheard one of the doctors telling his students. They came in and examined me, and then went out to the hall. I heard the doctor say, 'That was a typical case... Hodgkin's disease... no known cure... better for the patient to be at home.'"

What a horrible way for him to have found out, I thought, and the fact that we had kept it from him made it that much worse! Now he wondered what else we were hiding. It took a great deal of talking on the part of both of our families, his doctors, and myself to convince him that they were not sending him home to die. For that matter, they were not even sending him home.

When I saw how weak and unhappy Bob was, my heart broke. My mind knew that my love should be strong enough to wish him the best possible way out. I knew I should ask God to take Bob quickly and painlessly if He did not mean for Bob to get well. I couldn't do it. I just couldn't. Instead I kept praying, "Please don't take Bob from me. I need him so much. I'm not brave enough or strong enough to say, 'Thy will be done.' Please, dear God, let Bob live. I need him so terribly."

April 27 was Bob's thirty-fifth birthday. The doctor allowed him to come home for four hours. His family and mine came to help celebrate. I very carefully counted the candles and placed thirty-six on the birthday cake. It's funny how human beings are. We had been told by the doctor that Bob would probably never see his thirty-sixth birthday, and yet, when he blew out all the candles, both he and I burst into tears from utter relief. I was so sure that this was a sign that a "miracle" would happen.

At home, the situation was becoming more difficult. Bob was considerably weaker and this was obvious to our six-year-old, Gail. She began having stomachaches, which we had checked several times by the pediatrician. I suspected the pains were psychosomatic, but Bob was very concerned, so we made an appointment for a gastrointestinal series. The night before she was to go to the hospital, she broke down and cried bitterly. She said she had been asking God to make her stomachaches go away and make Daddy better. She had also been asking God not to take Daddy to live with Him because she wanted Daddy to live with her. My father tried to assure her that her Daddy would be all right but she shook her head. She knew he would not be all right because, if he was going to get well, why had he been so sick for such a long time?

The baby, of course, was much too young to know what was going on. She called him "Dada" and her face would light up whenever he came home from a stay in the hospital, but I guess she thought all daddies came and went like that.

On Friday the doctor examined Bob and said he would have to be admitted again to the hospital immediately to be given more blood. He also wanted to do some more tests and start treatments again, regardless of the risk involved. That afternoon I called every doctor I knew, asking for their opinions. They all agreed that, difficult as it might be, we must steel ourselves to further treatments. As long as there was a slim chance, we should take it. Bob agreed, saying he was doing this for me. He wanted to be a normal husband, to be able to work and take vacations and love his wife. My reaction, I'm afraid, was a selfish one; I felt I'd rather have him as he was than not have him at all, even though I was told the end could not be more than a few weeks away.

I had gone home to do some grocery shopping and received a message that I better come back to the hospital right away. I called Bob's family, grabbed a skirt and blouse, putting them on as I left the house. I probably broke every speed law getting back to the hospital. My mother was already there and his parents came down a few hours later from New Hampshire. Everyone sat in the lounge waiting, but I went down to Bob's room. I went over to the bed and Bob asked me to take off the mask and gown, saying he wanted to see me as I really was. Something about the way he said it scared me. He took my hand, told me that I was beautiful, and said he wanted to apologize; he was sorry for nagging me about my weight and asked me to forgive him. He said to tell the children that he loved them very much and to kiss them for him. He kissed me, really kissed me as he had been too weak to do in months, and said, "That ought to keep you for a while."

Then he put something in my hand. I looked down and saw it was his wedding ring. "You put this on my finger seven years ago and I never once took it off until now," he said, "but I'm giving it back to you." I insisted that he take it back. I even put it on his finger again. "Do you want me to go with it on?" he asked.

By 2:45 Bob had gone into a state of shock. He was trembling from head to foot. He had lost his power of speech but kept making horrible sounds. I continued talking to him, saying I loved him. I put my arms around him and held him. I said every prayer I could think of, but mostly the Twenty-third Psalm, "Yea, though I walk through the valley of the shadow of death, I shall fear no evil. . . ." Bob stopped shaking, and I like to think he knew I was there and was not afraid anymore. About 3:15 he had no blood pressure or pulse and began turning blue—his forehead, his fingers, then his whole face, his arms—but still he breathed. About 3:30 I noticed he was skipping breaths. We called for a doctor. At 3:40 in the afternoon, Bob was officially dead.

For the rest of the afternoon I felt as if I were someone else. I went home to tell Gail. All I said was that I wanted to talk to her, when she started to cry. She said she knew what I was going to tell her, I was going to say that Daddy would die. I told her he had already died. She began to cry hysterically and could not understand why Daddy would rather live with God than with her. I told her he wanted to, but it hurt so much he had to go to God.

Then I got on the phone and began to make the funeral arrangements, but it wasn't me doing all this and it wasn't for Bob that it was being done. The next day at the funeral it all seemed very unreal. I was fine until the last moment at the cemetery; it suddenly seemed so final. I just could not walk away and leave him there.

The past ten months were the hardest months any of us will probably have to face. I feel sorry for Gail. She had her sixth birthday a week later with no Daddy. Linda was 14 months on the day her father died. She'll never remember him. And I? I must be a wife to no husband, a mother to two fatherless babies. I must learn self-sufficiency and independence—but how? And how do I fill the empty void that stretches as far as I can see?

GRIEVING AFTER THE DEATH

Even though a person may know that his spouse is expected to die, and even if he or she engages in anticipatory mourning before the event, the death of the mate comes as a cataclysmic blow. One husband described his initial reactions:[5]

The first devastating pangs of intolerable loneliness filled my entire being. My children and I had known that this call would come. Still, after a hundred, maybe a thousand fantasied acts, I was unprepared. I remember telling our children, "I'm sorry," while tears streamed down the faces of all. Then for the first time of many more, I felt pangs of guilt; I should have been there. Then anger. I hit the cupboard as hard as I could.

What is the nature and process of the adjustment to such a significant loss? Although Freud discussed the mourning process incidentally in one of his papers and even coined the phrase "grief work,"[6] grief was never developed into a major theme in psychodynamic theory until World War II. Much of our understanding of how individuals respond to the death of their loved ones is rooted in the first major observations in this area, analyzed by Erich Lindemann almost forty years ago following the disastrous fire at the Coconut Grove nightclub in Boston.[7]

Lindemann was the first to catalogue the symptoms of normal grief and categorize them into five areas: somatic distress, preoccupation with the image of the deceased, guilt, hostile reactions, and loss of patterns of conduct. He also found that the duration of a grief reaction seemed to depend on the success with which the person did his grief work, which he defined as *achieving emancipation from the bondage to the deceased, readjustment to the environment in which the deceased is missing*, and *formation of new relationships*. Much of the time-limited aspect in recent crisis theory is predicated on his belief that within eight to ten interviews over a period of four to six weeks, it is possible to settle an "uncomplicated and undistorted" grief reaction.

Since then, considerable investigation has been carried out both in the United States and in England on the related topics of grief, mourning, and bereavement. Starting from Bowlby's earlier work on children's mourning[8] and Parkes's research on widows in London,[9] a profile was developed to delineate the four phases in the grieving process in adult life:[10]

1. Phase of numbness, usually lasting from a few hours to a week. This may be interrupted by outbursts of intense distress and/or anger.
2. Phase of yearning and searching for the lost figure, lasting from several months to several years.
3. Phase of disorganization and despair.
4. Phase of greater or lesser reorganization.

Although others have used other terms and have broken up the transition into different intervals,[11] we shall use these four steps to examine the process. Needless to say, the phases are overlapping and may even change sequentially within the overall progression. (Since much of the process is nonconscious and internalized, it seems artificial to speak of "tasks" in this connection. We shall therefore note the changes that occur over time, whether brought about by time, the influence of others, or conscious volition on the part of the widow or widower.)

PHASE 1: NUMBNESS.   The initial reaction to the death of the spouse is usually one of incredulity, of feeling stunned and unable to "take in" the news. When the event is entirely unexpected, the element of shock and numbing enters, as the person's response mechanisms fail to react. Parkes notes that many widows in his study said the news completely failed to register at first. Others reported that they felt as though they were having a bad dream or "walking on the edge of a black pit." Along with this numbness came outbursts of extreme behavior, in which tearfulness, aggressive outbursts, and even states of elation occurred. Attacks of panic were alternated with periods of restless "busyness" and other efforts to avoid cognizance of the loss. Occasionally, feelings of anger toward the deceased surfaced momentarily.[12]

It should be noted that this phase encompasses the first week or two, during which the funeral and other after-death rites take place. The sense of unreality is often heightened by the tranquilizers and other medication pressed onto the bereaved by well-meaning relatives, friends, and medical personnel. (This will be discussed further in the next section on psychosocial reactions.)

PHASE 2: YEARNING AND SEARCHING FOR THE LOST FIGURE.   Within a short time the numbness begins to wear away and the bereaved starts to register the reality of the death. Restlessness increases, along with pining and preoccupation with thoughts of the deceased partner, directing attention to places and objects in the environment associated with the lost person, developing a perceptual "set" for the person—a tendency to perceive and to pay attention to any stimuli which suggest his or her presence and to ignore those not relevant to this aim—and crying for the person to come back. Insomnia and sleep disturbances are common, together with appetite and weight loss.

The predominant features of this period are weeping and anger. Anger is frequently directed not only against the deceased ("How could he leave me?") but against doctors and hospital staff, clergy, officials, relatives, and even employers, with the implication that they were in some part responsible for, or negligent about, the death. God, too, is blamed for having allowed the death to occur. ("You're supposed to watch over us; how could you let him die?") Some of the anger, mixed with guilt and self-reproach, is self-directed—for real or imagined wrongs done the deceased, for death wishes, for secret relief, and for the fact that the survivor is still alive.[13] Guilt often is centered on some small act of omission or commission connected with the death ("Why didn't I go with him that night?") to which the spouse's thoughts return again and again. Spouses may blame themselves for having failed their partner in some way during the last illness, for events leading up to the death, or for the way they behaved following the death.

The concept of searching for the lost person is grounded in Bowlby's theory of attachment, directed in this case toward the spouse. With this person irretrievably gone, the surviving mate feels intense separation anxiety as the natural and inevitable response.[14] This may even lead to panic attacks as the reality of the loss is brought home, again and again, in the first months after the death.

PHASE 3: DISORGANIZATION AND DESPAIR.   During the latter part of the first year, phase two imperceptibly merges into phase three, during which we find a deepening and prolongation of the sorrow and despair aspects of the mourning process. The acuteness of the loss has passed as the person struggles repeatedly to face the reality of living without the deceased partner. As friends and relatives resume their other activities, the widow or widower is left to deal with the loss in his or her own way. Some continue their pre-occupation with thoughts of the loss, feeling the compulsion to talk about the dead mate and to try to retrieve the lost relationship. They may feel disorganized, confused, unable to initiate any activity, as though life could never be worthwhile again.

Some identify with the traits, values, and even physical symptoms of the lost person. Others regress to earlier feelings and behaviors connected with previous losses. Some develop psychosomatic symptoms, and sometimes there is an actual deterioration in physical health. Symptoms of serious depression may also be evident at this time. Feelings of apathy and aimlessness are common.

During this period, the bereaved may experience such contrary, irrational feelings that they begin to worry whether they are going crazy. They may feel intense ambivalence toward the lost spouse, debating with themselves over their previous interactions with their mate. Sometimes they block out the "bad" parts and idealize the harmony between them. Again and again they recall the past, sometimes with such vivid intensity that some report actually feeling the physical presence of the lost one. Others carry on an ongoing dialogue with the spouse, which they rationalize by saying they are "checking" to see whether they are doing things as the departed would have wanted them to do or as a continuation of his ways. Intermingled with this are deep feelings of loneliness, of inability to communicate with others in the real "everyday" world.

Gradually the pangs of grief become more intermittent and are followed by periods of relative calm, Parkes found that the widows in his study developed their own patterns of mitigation, which included a blocking out or denial of affect, partial disbelief in the reality of external events, inhibition of painful thoughts by selective forgetting and idealization, and evocation of pleasant or neutral thoughts in order to deliberately occupy the mind. Sometimes, patterns of identification were developed in which the widow tended to behave or think even more like the spouse than she had when he was alive.[15]

Marris notes that at first a widow cannot separate her own purposes and understanding from those of her husband, who figures so centrally in them; she has to revive the relationship and continue it by symbols and make-believe in order to feel alive. As time goes on, however, she makes the gradual transition from talking to him "as if he were sitting in the chair beside me" to thinking of what he would have said and done, and from there to what he would have wished her to do, until finally the wishes become her own.[16]

PHASE 4: REORGANIZATION. The length of time that the grieving process takes varies widely. Simos generalizes that the initial phase of shock can last from a few hours or days to a week or more, merging gradually into the next phase of denial and acute grief, which reaches a peak of intensity between the second and fifth weeks of bereavement. Experts tend to agree that for most people, it takes from six to twelve weeks for the pain of intense grief to begin to diminish.

The third phase may continue well past the first anniversary of the death, which becomes a critical time during which the sense of loss is revived. Sometime between the first and second year, however, the bereaved spouse begins to return to some semblance of normalcy. Gradually, weeping grows less and the need to talk compulsively and indiscriminately about the deceased diminishes. Sleep and appetite patterns are gradually restored. The bereaved may find that several hours and even a day may pass without thoughts of the deceased. Life is no longer marked by anxiety and restlessness, and the person experiences a sense of relief.[17] Although widowed persons agree that one never "gets over" the death of a spouse, they recognize that, in time, one learns to live with the loss.

Simos concludes that if the outcome is favorable, the bereaved person will accept the reality of the death with restored self-esteem. He or she will be able to focus on the present and future, enjoy life again, and become aware of having grown through the experience. The loss is remembered with poignancy and caring instead of with pain. Thus the widower quoted earlier can say:

> The love I had for her and the life we had together is over. Only memories remain. They are but the path behind me. In retrospect, the beginning steps of that life were light, fanciful, and hurried. They slowed in maturity and stopped in death.[18]

On the other hand, if the outcome is unfavorable, the loss is associated with a continued sense of depression, physical aches and pains, diminished sense of self-esteem, constriction of personality and involvement, and increased vulnerability to new separations and losses. Both Lindemann and Krupp have discussed pathological responses to death of a mate, which result in prolongation of grieving and maladaptation over time.

As in the case of a "successful" divorce, grieving over a lost mate can even become an opportunity to progress further along the road to personal growth and maturity. Since the death revives earlier losses and developmental deficits, the person can use the grief process to rework not only the current loss of the spouse but earlier losses and separations which are symbolically attached to it. Martin Greene points out that in situations where dependence upon parents had shifted to dependence upon the mate, the person may be experiencing not only real grief over the present loss but depression in response to earlier lacks and losses in early childhood and adolescence. The chance is offered now to dissolve these earlier ties and gain a more advanced level of separation-individuation.[19]

In the following case example from a family agency, we see how death of a husband has aroused previous unresolved losses which add to the wife's difficulties in passing through the grieving process:

RITA RODRIGUEZ (#147)

Mrs. Rodriguez, age 39, was referred for help with her depression over the sudden loss of her husband, Juan, age 45, two weeks ago. When seen, she was crying uncontrollably. She felt extremely angry at the doctor who released him prematurely from the hospital, and was sure she was going crazy because the events leading up to his death kept being "replayed in her head." She described in great detail how he had been recovering well from a kidney operation when the young resident on duty released him because of a shortage of beds in the ward. She brought him home in a cab, but he had to climb three flights of stairs to get to their apartment. That night he slept very fitfully, and in the middle of the night his remaining kidney evidently stopped functioning; by the time the ambulance came, he had already lapsed into a coma. He died on the way to the hospital without even saying good-bye. Although the attending physician, after examining Juan, assured her that everything had been done to save him and that the collapse of the second kidney was a predictable risk, she felt bitterly that the hospital had been negligent in releasing him too soon. She was sure this couldn't have happened if he had been in a private hospital instead of at County General.

Since then, the neighbors had been very kind and had taken care of their four children so that she could rest. But she was unable to sleep or even stay in bed; instead she kept wandering from the livingroom to the bedroom to the kitchen all night, thinking endlessly of what had happened and how she should have "stood up" to the resident and insisted that the head doctor examine Juan before he was released. She had thought of killing herself, but what would happen then to their babies?

Mrs. Rodriguez described what a wonderful man her husband was and how happy their nine years of marriage had been. Both she and Juan had been born in Puerto Rico but hadn't met until she came to this midwestern city ten years ago after her first marriage had broken up. Her first husband, Pablo, had been very wild and had gotten into serious trouble a number of times; they lived in New York and finally he was sent to prison for ten years for armed robbery. She knew no one in New York, so she divorced him and came here to stay with an aunt. She had been unable to have children with Pablo, although she had had two miscarriages. She was thankful that her parents had lived to see her married again to such a good man as Juan and to know that she finally had a live baby. Both of them were killed in a plane crash, coming to visit her for the first time after the baby was born; they never even got to meet her husband.

For the next several interviews, Mrs. Rodriguez kept repeating these events over and over again, ventilating her anger and her grief. In contrast to her first husband, Juan was a quiet, steady man who was very respected at the machine shop where he worked. He didn't drink and always brought his pay home. On Sundays after church they would take their four children to the park or the zoo and then would have a picnic under the trees. Even in the winter, when it was too cold to go out, he would play with the children and tell jokes. Sometimes she couldn't believe her good fortune.

Several months ago he began to complain of pains in his side but refused to see a doctor. Then, one night, she saw that he was urinating blood. She insisted that he go to the county clinic, and the head doctor immediately put him into the hospital and ordered a long series of tests. Finally they were told that his right kidney had ceased to function and would have to be removed. By this time she felt numb with worry, but they agreed to the operation when the doctor assured them he could live to be 100 with only one kidney. And now he was dead and she was left alone with the four little ones.

I pointed out to Mrs. Rodriguez that her husband's death was the last in a long series of losses she had experienced: the breakdown of her first marriage, the two miscarriages, the death of her parents, the fact that her aunt, who was her only relative in this country, had moved back to Puerto Rico two years ago. Each time she experienced a loss, she would "swallow" the pain and avoid talking about her feelings by turning to someone else who would help her pick up the pieces. This time, when Juan died, there was no one left to turn to and the hurt was very great. For the first time, she began to listen to what I was saying and admitted she had never thought of her life in that way. She had never talked much about her suffering, even to Juan.

Together we reviewed the events of her past life. She told how she had run away from home when she was just 16 and come to New York, where she worked in a factory until she met her first husband. They had a lot of fun in the beginning, until he and his friends began stealing cars. He'd come home drunk or "hopped up" and would beat her; she guessed that was why she lost the babies. Finally, after he was sent up, the priest insisted she come here to stay with her aunt; he even arranged for the divorce. She also talked about her parents back in Puerto Rico, recalling how she used to rebel against her father. He had been very angry when she ran away and refused to have anything to do with her. Finally, after she had married Juan, her aunt wrote to tell her father how much she had changed. Her parents were coming to visit her here when they were killed; she never go the chance to tell her father how sorry she was for the trouble she had caused him.

By the sixth session, Mrs. Rodriguez's depression had begun to lift. She was talking more coherently, was less "stuck" on what the doctors had done, no longer talked about dying, and had begun to grieve appropriately for both her husband and her parents. At home she was starting to take care of her children and was able to get them dressed and the older two ready for school on time. She also joined a widows' group at the church near her home and was beginning to get ideas from the other women about how to handle the children's reaction to their father's death. Her husband's boss had come to visit her, and she would be getting part of his pension as well as Social Security payments. Gradually she appeared to be starting the reintegration process, although she still felt the loss of her husband very deeply.

Surviving and Rebuilding

Even as the widow or widower struggles with the grieving aspects of the transitional process brought about by the death of the spouse, she or he is expected to act, react, and interact in certain ways with many facets of the external world. Significant decisions have to be made all along the line and vital role changes have to be carried out. This process can be divided into three phases (not necessarily coincidental with those discussed in the previous section). Although these periods have been labeled in different ways, it seems simplest to describe them as (1) *bridging the past;* (2) *living with the present;* and (3) *finding a path into the future.* In each phase there is a need to carry out both material-arrangemental and psychosocial tasks.[20]

Of course, passing through the transition of widowhood is made easier in societies where mourning procedures are clearly prescribed and rigorously adhered to, where the role of the widow or widower is carefully delineated down to what they should wear, whom they should see, and how they should behave. Similarly, the existence of significant mourning rituals is helpful in keeping the process moving and allowing the bereaved to pass from one stage to another.[21]

BRIDGING THE PAST

Phyllis Silverman, who carried out some of the early significant research on widows and directed the Widow-to-Widow Project of the Community Psychiatry Laboratory at Harvard, points out that widowhood does not just "happen" when a spouse dies; although a woman (or man) may become legally widowed, this does not always coincide with the person's social and emotional acceptance of the role. The survivor first has to learn what the role definitions and dimensions are and how one is expected to act. In the first period after the death, the spouse is in an anomic position: he or she does not know what to do, what it means, and what to anticipate.[22]

One widow, who reflects the confusion and sense of lost purpose brought on by the death of her husband, voices this primary need for direction:

> I knew I needed guidance, a road map for the new world of widowhood. I
> didn't need the slim volumes of inspirational verse or uplifting passages that

well-meaning friends press into the unresisting hands of every widow. I needed practical help and I knew it. There may be some women who are so completely self-reliant and independent that they don't require outside help and advice, but most of us hunger for it. . . . But no one will sit the widow down . . . and tell her, "This is the way it is; this is the way you'll feel; this is what needs doing; these are the problems you'll face; they are the rules which will now govern your life." That's what I needed and I also needed someone to tell me how brave and capable I was, even though I was quivering with fear at the awesome responsibilities confronting me.[23]

During the first few days, even though the bereaved person may be in a state of shock, a number of practical decisions and arrangements have to be made regarding the funeral, burial, financial payments, and so on. Despite his grief, the widower is expected to continue to take primary responsibility for such matters.[24] The widow, on the other hand, may choose to leave the decisions in the hands of competent relatives and friends, or a physician, clergyman, or funeral director. Even when she does "take hold" by herself, she often still acts as if she were her husband's wife and carries out arrangements as she thinks (or as he has indicated) he would have wanted them to be. She has not yet begun to think of herself as a widow.

In other areas, however, the widow may have to continue her previous roles for lack of choice: feeding the children, preparing meals, signing checks, buying groceries, and carrying out all the other daily tasks which cannot be deferred. Widows report moving through the days after their husband's death as if they were automatons, unable to absorb fully what has happened and is happening. Parkes feels this is the time when family, friends, and others should "rally round" to give the widow the chance to get over the initial shock.[25] Their primary task would be to help out with practical matters such as preparing meals and caring for children until the widow is able to rouse herself. Caplan, too, has indicated the importance of the primary and extended kinship system in offering practical and emotional support at this critical time.[26]

The primary psychosocial task in the first phase is to loosen the ties with the deceased and to accept the fact that he or she is dead. To do this, the widowed person must learn to break the thousands of strands of shared experiences which make up the marriage bond and to internalize them as memories. This may include such overt acts as learning to use the past tense in talking about the spouse, and beginning to say "I" instead of "we."

Condolence visits serve the function of providing a benign, permissive atmosphere that encourages the overt expression of grief and loss. As mentioned above, prescribed rites such as the Jewish *shi'va*—the week of ritual mourning following the funeral, during which relatives, friends, and even casual acquaintances come to visit the immediate family—add significantly to the process. This ceremony not only builds a common tie as the male mourners say the twice-daily prayers for the dead, but visitors and family members join in bringing up memories of the deceased, telling stories—both funny and serious—about childhood experiences, and helping the survivor see the spouse in a broader perspective. This sense of shared community is very important in giving the bereaved a measure of comfort and the feeling of continuity.[27]

The task of acceptance may be made either easier or harder by the need to tell the children about their parent's death. Most widows in the Silverman study said they did not remember how they told their children that their father was dead, since the first period was a blur to many of them.[28] Although one of the first family tasks is to give permission for the grief process to proceed, the parent may frequently refrain from crying or showing unhappiness so as not to frighten the children. On their part, children may react with expressions of disbelief and denial, even physical violence or uncharacteristic behavior. One mother reported her fifteen-year-old daughter's reaction:

> Her room had been plastered with pictures of the Beatles. The day her father died she went up and took them down. She said, "I'm not a baby anymore, Mom." I tried to explain to her that she was still a child, even if her father had died. But I guess when you go through something like that you never feel the same. The pictures never went up. [p. 66]

Although some parents become upset over the children's lack of reaction or apparent unconcern, Temes points out that while most adults begin the first stage of mourning immediately, it may take several weeks or even months for children to absorb the significance of what has occurred. They may postpone mourning until they are assured that their survival needs, their physical and psychological security, will be taken care of. Sometimes the parent is unable to carry out this task of telling the child or children of the death and delegates it to another child, a relative, or a close friend.

Sometimes the reading of the will becomes a testament to the dead person's concern for his family and for the spouse in particular. One young woman told of her father's anticipatory guidance:[29]

> My father was a lawyer and became very worried, when he learned he had only a few months to live, that my mother would not be able to manage after he died. He spent hours, despite his pain, putting everything into top shape. After he was gone, when we opened his safety deposit box, we found everything arranged in meticulous order, in separate envelopes, each with explicit, detailed instructions for every contingency. My mother was so touched—it was so characteristic of him—that she burst into tears. She said it was as if he had reached out and took her in his arms.

LIVING WITH THE PRESENT

Once the funeral and first round of condolence visits are over and the fog begins to lift, the bereaved spouse passes (or is pushed) into the second phase, in which attention is turned to the reality of the present. One of the first tasks is to close the family circle and to reapportion roles within its boundaries.[30] Some of the role tasks are at the instrumental level: to provide financial support, to cook and clean the house, to take care of the children, to supply transportation for family members, to do the shopping, to arrange dental appointments, and so forth. Other role tasks are more expressive: to comfort the children when they cry for the absent parent, to cuddle them before bedtime, to share the joy of the good moments and the pain of the sad ones, and to provide them with the sense of support and security so badly shaken by the recent death of the other parent.

Many bereaved parents feel the need to be both mother and father to the children and wear themselves out trying to fill all of the spouse's vacated roles. Both widowed persons who have passed through the transition and professionals tend to agree that this task is virtually impossible and advise settling for being a *better* mother or a *better* father rather than trying to make up for the lack of the other parent. Sometimes outside persons such as an uncle, a grandparent, a favorite teacher, or a club leader may be enlisted to fill the vacant slot on at least a temporary basis.

As in the divorce process, much of the activity at this stage is geared to working out practical living arrangements. While a man does not usually suffer significant loss of income when his wife dies (except for the loss of her salary if she also worked), the woman may be forced to go to work if her life-insurance payments and other survivors' benefits prove inadequate to meet the family's needs. If she worked before, she may have to increase her hours or change her job to a full-time or better-paying one. If she stopped working when she was married or had her first child, she may now have to be retrained to meet changing labor demands. If she never worked, she may have to enter the labor market for the first time. In general, women report that during this period their jobs are a source of comfort and role continuity, apart from their being widows.[31] Not only do they have to get up in the morning, dress, wash their face and put on lipstick, and venture forth into the outside world, but the work itself allows them to forget for a few hours the changed reality awaiting them at home.

In addition, the widow may have to grapple with such unfamiliar matters as mortgage payments, inheritance taxes, investment amortization, and bank overdrafts. She may find herself trying to salvage her husband's faltering business, suing for dissolution of a partnership, or trying to settle his debts and liquidate his assets. While some women may see this as a challenge and zestfully enter the business world, others may rely on poor advice or follow their own untutored judgment and may make serious financial mistakes at this time.

One of the key concerns in this period is centered on housing arrangements. Because the family home is filled with haunting memories of the deceased, surviving spouses will often make, or be forced into, a hasty decision to sell or move away—only to regret it later when they realize the need for familiar surroundings for themselves and the children. A rule of thumb many counselors use at this stage is to urge the widowed person to refrain, if possible, from making significant, lasting changes until some months have passed following the mate's death.

Another basic issue is that of loneliness, of lack of companionship quite apart from the sense of loss of the spouse. Once family members return to their own homes and well-meaning friends become impatient with the frequent references to the departed and bored with repeated tales of how things used to be, widowed persons find themselves increasingly alone and unable to reenter either the world of the "singles" or that of the "marrieds." Yet they also find it difficult to take part in social events and feel themselves "fifth wheels" at parties and gatherings of friends, somehow carrying the stigma of having had the bad grace to lose their mate. Widows see their friends embarrassed when they try to participate in joint activities with them and their husbands, and annoyed when their husbands offer social (and at times sexual) solace to the discomfitted widow. One woman described such an incident:

> I met my friends for lunch. They came to visit during the day as before. Then someone suggested going with the men to the theatre. It was awful; I felt so alone. My husband's name came up because he would have enjoyed this play. They got embarrassed. Imagine, *I* had to comfort them. When we left, there was some discussion about taking me home. I had wanted to drive myself, even though I had never gone out alone at night. Then they got into this kind of nonsense. I'll never agree to do that again and I'm not sure they want me anymore either.[32]

Since often the only persons they feel comfortable with during this stage are others like themselves, many widowed persons join bereavement support groups: programs like the Widow-to-Widow Project in Boston already mentioned, or religiously sponsored organizations such as the Naim Conference in Chicago or Post-Cana in Washington, D.C. Still others join social groups for the formerly married, like Parents Without Partners. Some find an outlet in entering special-interest organizations—such as PTA programs, conservation groups, or little-theatre projects—in which mateless status is not the focus.

In Israel, the use of small social groups of war widows, led jointly by a social worker and a widow who had already passed successfully through the mourning process, was found to be very helpful for about a year following the death of the women's husbands. During this time they comforted each other, shared practical advice on how to manage the children, and swapped stories of in-laws' interference.

Other widows became much more family-centered. They spent this period crystalizing the memory of their husbands by preparing an album of snapshots of their lives together, splicing films and tapes of trips taken over the years, and collecting letters, poems, and essays to be published privately. A common practice was to set up "memory corners" in the living-room filled with pictures and mementoes of soldier husbands and fathers who had fallen in the various wars.[33]

In general, this second phase is a time of advances and retreats, of giving up old habits formed in the marriage and trying to work out new ones appropriate for single heads-of-families. Often widowed persons report that ties with children become stronger as they are drawn closer together and learn to communicate more openly about their common loss. In the same way, relations with their own family and/or that of the spouse may be renewed and strengthened through the bond of the joint bereavement. On the other hand, sometimes the reverse takes place: relatives begin to argue over the deceased's legacy, over property owned jointly, or over how the children should be raised.

Progress through this phase is often marked by turning points, events associated with a major revision in feelings, attitudes, and behavior. Such points may occur, for example, when the widowed person goes shopping alone for the first time, goes out on a first date, takes a first job, redecorates the house. These steps reflect both the giving up of old patterns and the development of new ones. Some of these turning points may coincide with holidays or anniversaries connected with the death of the spouse: the end of the year of mourning, the first New Year's Eve alone, the first wedding anniversary after the death. Parkes finds that a memorial service, or a visit to the cemetery, at such times can have the significance of a rite of passage, setting the bereaved person free and allowing him to undertake fresh commitments.[34]

FINDING A PATH INTO THE FUTURE

Gradually a change takes place. Usually, between the first and the second year, the widowed enter the third phase of the transition, during which they find some measure of stability in functioning and begin to reorganize their lives without their former spouse. By now, they have mastered such mysteries as keeping house, tending the family car's needs, or dealing with income-tax forms. They and their children have established a new family circle in which each carries out his allocated roles and tasks. They have developed a bank of experiences in operating independently and making their own decisions.

For some, the path to readjustment is bittersweet. In the following report of a single interview carried out by the intake worker in a mental health center connected with a medical health insurance program, we see how an older widow struggles to come to terms with the direction her life has taken.

BILHA HARARI (#225)

Mrs. Harari, age 50, was referred by her family physician because of insomnia, periods of depression, and frequent headaches for which no physiological basis could be found. She is a plump, matronly looking woman, dressed conservatively in dark gray, with a pale, unsmiling face and dark shadows under her eyes. She described her situation frankly. She is a widow; her husband died a year and a half ago of a heart attack and she now lives alone.

The Hararis were married when they were fairly young and had a full life together for twenty-four years. She described her husband as a warm, intelligent, outgoing person with many interests which they shared together. They had had four daughters, all married now, and fourteen grandchildren. (At this point she brought out a folder of snapshots, which she pridefully displayed.) They owned their own home, so her husband didn't have to work so hard anymore; and they were just beginning to enjoy the fruits of all those difficult years they had put in together when he was taken. She began to cry quietly, and I waited in silence until she wiped her eyes and neatly put away her handkerchief.

She then said, thoughtfully, that this wasn't the only loss that had happened to her at that time. Just before this their youngest daughter had left home to be married; her wedding was the last social event the Harari family had celebrated. His heart attack occurred just a week later. With a deep sigh, she said that at least he had lived to see all of their girls married to good husbands. But now she was left alone, without another living person for her to worry and fuss over. She used to be so busy with the children; all the noise and bother of the four girls running in and out of the house were part of her life. These days the house seems so quiet, so empty. She finds her patience wearing thin; she is unable to remain at home alone, particularly in the evenings. The long nights are very hard for her and she finds herself tossing and turning, unable to sleep. In the morning she gets up unrefreshed, with a splitting headache.

Mrs. Harari said her family tries to help her and worries about her spending so much time at home alone. Two of her daughters who live in the neighborhood frequently ask her to sleep over. But she knows that this gives only temporary relief; in the end, she will have to face up to being alone. Several months ago she tried to help one of her nieces, an adolescent who was having trouble with her parents, by bringing her home to live with her. But the girl was very difficult to handle. Mrs. Harari found she didn't have the patience to cope with her problems, so she sent her back home. Now she works for two mornings a week as a volunteer in a neighborhood child nursery, but that doesn't fill up her days either.

Finally she rose and said, with another sigh, that at least it was good to talk to someone who understood what she was going through. She thought if she could just get through this winter, things might get better in the spring. She doesn't expect miracles and she knows she'll have to find the strength to bear the situation. She realizes she has no alternative.

By this time many widows and widowers start to chafe at the limitations imposed by their role of bereaved person and begin to seek restitution for the loss of their ties with their former spouse by developing new core relationships. These relationships can take various forms: (1) remarriage; (2)

intimate relationships with a partner outside of marriage; (3) close relationships with relatives such as a brother, sister, or parent; or (4) close relationships with children to the exclusion of other ties.[35]

Setting aside older widowed persons who marry in their later years to
find companionship and to pool resources, remarriage usually appeals most
to, and is most viable as an option for, younger persons. In general, however, widowed persons, unlike the divorced, usually do not remarry in order
to replace the dead spouse, but rather to refocus their lives, to find another
parent figure for their children, to reengage themselves in a long-term intimate relationship which will give them comfort and closeness, and/or to ease
the economic and social strains of living without a spouse.

An honest comment is given by the widower quoted previously:

> When I finally decided that the woman I was dating was the one with whom I
> would like to spend the rest of my life, questions still arose in my mind:
> wasn't my first love unique, a once-in-a-lifetime experience? My first mar-
> riage was so perfect, could anything else replace it? I put aside these
> thoughts. I realized that Beth wasn't the only woman I was capable of loving.
> This didn't mean that I loved her less because I had found someone new to
> love and to spend the rest of my life with. . . . Why did I remarry? Because I
> was in love and this answer is the only true and wonderful reason.[36]

Widowed persons who remarry generally find it difficult to compare their
first and second marriages, since they have become, as Lynn Caine puts it,
different persons.[37] Those who do remarry pass through an additional transitional phase, that of reconstituting a new life as a married person.

Since many of the issues in remarriage and rebuilding of second families
have been discussed in the previous chapter, they need not be repeated
here. It should be pointed out, however, that complications arise when the
first stage in the transitional process has not been completed and the emotional separation from the deceased spouse has not taken place. Unlike the
divorced person, who can bring about closure through the healthy cathartic
effect of anger ("I'll show that bastard!") or become mellow through the
simple distancing of time and place ("We don't have much in common but
we stay in touch because of the children"), the widowed person may en-
shrine the memory of the dead mate even after marrying again. At such a
time, the deified dead may cast a shadow over the second marriage. As one
harassed second husband said, "How can you compete with a glorified
ghost?"

Moreover, where soldier-husbands are memorialized publicly as heroes,
as they often are in Israel, the wife's remarriage may be looked upon by her
social networks as disloyalty to the first husband's memory. (It should be
recalled that a similar public reaction occurred when John F. Kennedy's
widow remarried.) Frequently, families of the dead spouse raise complications concerning the custody of the children of the first marriage or property
that was left jointly to the widow and children.

The issue of divided loyalties does not take on the same dimensions for the children in blended families where one or both parents have been widowed as it does in divorced families, where the second parent often uses the children to rekindle past arguments. Nevertheless, matters of the step-parent's rights to discipline or to reorder priorities often arise. Another question that may bring about complications is that of adopting the children legally, which may mean the erasure of the first father's name—often a significant legacy in the minds of the children and their grandparents.

TYPES OF WIDOWS

Some widowed persons, particularly women, prefer to retain this role identification for many, if not the rest of their adult years; others, particularly those who have several children or who are in their middle years, have no choice. In her far-reaching study on widows in the metropolitan Chicago area, Helena Lopata was able to identify a number of types of women who carried out their widowhood roles in different ways.[38]

At one extreme were women, generally fairly well educated and middle-class, who had been strongly involved in the wifely role while their husbands were alive and who had built their other roles around his presence as a person, a father, a partner in leisure-time activities, a member of couples groups, a coresident in the household, and a member of two kinship groups. These women's lives were completely disrupted by their husbands' death.

At the other extreme were the women who had lived in a sex-segregated world, relatively independent of their husbands, who had solved their problems without his involvement, and whose activities clustered around roles in which he was not the important member. This type of widow, immersed in her family relations, her neighborhood, her job, or her voluntary activities, reported that she felt lonely for her husband but that her identities and life-style had not changed much.

Lopata identifies seven types of life-styles among widows:

1. The "liberated woman," able to lead a truly urban and multidimensional life as an individual with a well-rounded identity.
2. The "merry widow," involved in a round of social activity, dating, and utilizing the resources of the city in pleasurable interaction with friends.
3. The working woman who, though widowed, operates on the job to which she is committed individualistically. She is likely to have been trained early in life, or after an educational interruption, in skills guaranteeing an interesting job with satisfactory economic returns and increasing self-confidence.
4. A second type of working woman, who withdrew from the labor market upon marriage or first pregnancy. She has no marketable skills and

has haphazardly taken any job that happens to be available, with minimal economic rewards. Still, she likes her job since it helps her leave the empty house, interact with others, and be out in the world.

5. The "widow's widow," who joins the "society of widows" and engages in a round of activities out of an independently run home in which she is the only resident. She enjoys the company of other widows, not just during the grieving period, because of the similarities in their life-style.

6. The traditional widow, who remains immersed in her family roles and relationships, devoting herself to her children and grandchildren, sometimes interacting with her own siblings. She tends to live with one of her children, usually a daughter, and limits her financial, service, social, and emotional interactions to her relatives.

7. The "grieving wife," who cannot enter new social relations or complete her grief work and becomes socially isolated and bitter, unable to start the series of steps heeded for social reengagement. Hampered by lack of mobility, finances, or bad health, she tends to withdraw, rarely leaving her home and unwilling or unable to initiate new contacts with other persons or groups.

Much of Lopata's recent work on support systems[39] is focused on determining which types of supports are used by each of these widowed types. It provides important background in determining what kinds of help the widowed person needs and can use.

11

The Late Adult Years: Coming to Terms with Limitations

How old is old?

If we continue to use the same approach to the last stages of the life cycle that Levinson used for early and mid-adulthood, we can place the stage of late adulthood as starting at around age sixty-five, the figure most commonly given. The five years before would be considered the transition to late adulthood.*

In this chapter and the next, we shall consider specific aspects of late adulthood rather than the overall aging process—although, in a general sense, the entire period can be viewed as one of continuous change and adaptation to decreasing physical and psychological abilities and to the giving up of vital social roles. A large and multidimensional body of theoretical and research literature and practice experience has accrued, particularly in the past twenty years, in the field of aging, under the interdisciplinary title, "gerontology." Our discussion will focus on several transitions which stand out during the aging process.

This chapter will deal with the vertical transition linking middle and late adulthood and with the closely associated psychosocial transition of retirement. It applies largely to Neugarten's well-functioning "young old," whose

---

*Once again it is suggested that chronological age alone is a weak indicator of change. Readers are reminded of Neugarten's admonishment that age norms and expectations must be viewed within social-class and cultural contexts.[1]

age limits she sets at fifty-five to seventy-five years. Chapter 12 will examine the final years and the adjustment processes in dealing with health impairment, increasing inability to manage in one's own home, the search to find alternative living arrangements, and finally, learning to survive alone after the death of one's spouse. These most often pertain to the "old old," aged seventy-five and over, although, of course, the age boundaries are fluid.

Transition to Late Adulthood

As the individual moves through his fifties and enters his early sixties, he becomes increasingly aware that he is approaching the final stage of his adult life. Actually, the person views the coming years with mixed feelings. On the one hand, numerous cues point to the inroads of time: new lines appear on the forehead; the hairline recedes and the strands become brittle and sparse. Climbing a flight of stairs brings on shortness of breath; other people's voices no longer sound as clear or as loud as they once did; recall of names and faces grows erratic. Generally, the individual finds it increasingly difficult to respond to the pressures of work or the demands of the family with his former vim and vigor. On the other hand, he may feel insulted or threatened at the suggestion that he is "slowing down," "marking time," or "waiting out the years." Most individuals, even though they may have learned to moderate their activities to a slower, more deliberate pace, tend to feel that they still have a great deal to impart and anticipate a number of productive years ahead of them.

The vertical bridging period from mid-adulthood to late adulthood may occur so imperceptibly as to be virtually unnoticeable. A spritely widow in one case study reported:

> I was going along, doing "my own thing," with each day filled with activities—working at the hospital, taking part in fund-raising drives, helping my daughter in her shop when she had too much to do, playing golf with my friends. Then one day I received a letter from my insurance company and I checked with my desk calendar. And I said to myself, "My God, in three months I'll be sixty-five! I'll be an old woman soon and I don't even feel it!"

As in other types of inter-stage transitions, the interval between the two stages can be conceived of as three overlapping phases: *leaving mid-adulthood, crossing the line,* and *entering late adulthood.* Since, except for retirement and possibly registering for Social Security and Medicare, few rites of passage mark the transition, we find a wide range of individual reactions.

It has been found that older people are far more heterogeneous than younger ones. Not only do they bring their own unique personalities into the aging phase, but they have a higher degree of differentiation as the outcome of their longer lives and more varied experiences. Thus the way in which they deal with marker events and changes related to old age (retirement, grandparenthood, illness, death) becomes, to a large extent, a function of their own personalities and their longstanding life-styles.[2]

LEAVING MID-ADULTHOOD

Although we suggested at the beginning of this chapter that the years from sixty to sixty-five might be considered the period of transition to late adulthood, actually the "lead-in time" might start considerably before this. Stanley Cath feels that meeting the aging "crisis" requires a preparatory process that lasts for many years, probably from the mid-thirties on. Over this time the individual has encountered life traumas such as having parents, friends, sisters and/or brothers become seriously ill or impaired or even die. His life-style has been built up by his emerging capacity to relate to significant others, to become intimate and bound to them, to tolerate and grieve for the loss of them, and then to repair the loss by restitution.[3]

At some point during mid-adulthood, individuals begin to become aware that they have lived more years than they expect to live in the future. This realization stimulates a process of self-assessment through which the goals and ideals of childhood, adolescence, and adulthood are reviewed and progress toward them evaluated. By this time, tangible evidence of their successes and failures in the major tasks of adulthood such as marriage, bearing and rearing children, and work have accumulated. They can begin to measure what they have done with their lives and to deal with their feelings of failure, crisis, or disappointment without becoming overwhelmed, and they can also take pride in their accomplishments even when the outcomes have fallen short of expectation.[4]

Mary Parent suggests that three developmental tasks must be successfully mastered in order to leave mid-adulthood and enter late adulthood: (1) *completion of one's life goals;* (2) *evaluation of one's life performance and the resolution of conflict about one's failures and disappointments,* and (3) *preparation for decline.*[5] In relation to the first, she points out that in the past many tasks of the generative period as delineated by Erikson continued well into old age. Families were large and children were spaced throughout the childbearing period. Thus child-launching occurred much later in the life span. At present, with couples having fewer children spaced closer together, they usually launch their offspring and relinquish their childbearing role by their late forties and early fifties, thus accomplishing a set of major goals and at the same time incurring a major role loss.

Loss of the parental role, however, is just the first in a series of major identity-threatening losses which take place during middle age. (See the discussion on loss in Chapter 8.) Others are the loss of parents and/or spouses, as well as the departure of friends, relatives, or neighbors as the outcome of moving away, separation, or changing jobs. While these last decrements may not be as traumatic as the loss of family members, they still require readjustment and reorganization of social networks and points of orientation. Now, at the close of mid-adulthood, they may surface again to become part of the life review that frequently takes place as part of the second task of assessing one's successes and failures.

According to Cath, carrying out this second task often results in the person's seeking restitution—that is, attempting to restore what has been depleted and to make amends for past failures, mistakes, and inadequacies. He does this by turning to religion or philosophy, becoming involved in civic or philanthropic works, or engaging in new creative activities.

The third task, that of preparing for decline, can be carried out on two levels. On the practical plane, the person can prepare for old age by simplifying his life-style, preparing for future financial security, and arranging for future physical care. Many plan in advance by taking out retirement insurance, joining pension plans, and putting aside part of their earnings in the form of savings. Others sell their large, family-oriented homes in the suburbs and rent utility apartments in the central city, close to shopping and recreation facilities. Some may consider investing in condominiums or in "retirement communities" in Florida or Arizona. Sometimes persons with low income and little family will plan to move in with siblings or others* to help their future income stretch.

At the emotional level, the individual also begins to appraise the road ahead, becoming consciously aware of the fact that someday he will die. This awareness, says Parent, lies somewhere between intellectual knowledge of the fact and emotional reaction to imminent threat. It permits reflective consideration of what it means to die and thus what it means to have lived. Out of this reflection, the integrity designated by Erikson as the central issue to be resolved in old age will in time evolve.[6]

The following case example illustrates what happens when the long-term balance in an aging family is upset—in this case by the husband's unemployment. Beyond his discomfort over the inability to express his authority over his son lies the shadow of approaching old age and the worry of what will happen if he can no longer "pay his way."

GEORGE PETERSON (#145)

Mr. Peterson, age 60, asked for help with a family problem. He was a thin, stooped, sallow-faced man with sparse gray hair and a habit of blinking nervously. He said he needed advice about his 25-year-old son, who was still "tied to his mother's apron strings." The son, Jim, still lived at home although he had a good job and could afford to be on his own. He refused to obey his father or do any of the household

*The phenomenon of older men and women moving in together without marriage is an interesting example of how practical reality—in this case, the fact that they receive more in Social Security benefits as singles—often changes group norms.

chores, and his mother "backed him up all the way." The incident which precipitated the call had occurred the day before, when Mr. Peterson asked Jim to clean out the garage. He refused, and Mr. Peterson, rather than "create a fuss," cleaned it himself but became very angry. That evening, when his wife came home from work, they had a terrible argument and he had to restrain himself from walking out.

Background Information. The Petersons' marriage had been a rocky one almost from the start, thirty-three years ago. They had been married near the end of World War II, when he was stationed at the naval base nearby. After the war he switched to the merchant marine and continued as a sailor on the Great Lakes, transferring from ship to ship. His wife, a "very independent type," continued her job, first as a waitress and then as a cook. When he would come home, sometimes after a week's absence and sometimes after several months, they had little to say to each other, except to bicker over money and his beer drinking.

After eight years they finally had one son, but the doctors warned Mrs. Peterson that this would probably be her only child because of "something wrong inside." Since then she had pampered and protected the boy, and Mr. Peterson had felt increasingly shoved aside. She refused to let him have any say in rearing the child, and as Jim grew older mother and son would form a "common front" against him. His way of dealing with this was to clam up and either retreat to his workshop down in the basement, which he had fixed up with an old couch and a TV set, or to spend the evening at the corner tavern.

Twelve years ago he had hurt his back lifting some cargo on the ship and had been transferred to the company repair yard sixty miles away as a supply-room clerk. Since then he would come home only twice a month. He said that he and his wife still had very little in common; she was mostly interested in looking after Jim and "yakking" with her sisters on the phone. He felt that his only contribution to the family life was in providing money for expenses.

Five months ago the company for which he worked had been bought out by a competitor and the repair yard had been closed. He had returned to the city, and since then has been unemployed. Although still covered by unemployment insurance, he feels increasingly uncomfortable and "touchy." He and his wife have been arguing almost every night, sometimes about his way of running the house but even more about Jim's extravagance, his open contempt for his father, and his refusal to cooperate in helping about the house. Looking back over his life generally, Mr. Peterson sees it as futile and meaningless. He has expressed concern that something may be wrong with him for putting up with such a situation for so long.

Treatment. Although Mr. Peterson clung to his request for help in changing Jim, I told him I was powerless to do so. We explored his own discomfort in taking a firm stand with his family and the change in the family equilibrium created when he returned home full-time and became unable to contribute financially to the family's support. Mr. Peterson decided to stop giving his wife and son free access to the family charge accounts and checkbook and to tell Jim openly that *he* was head of the house; if he didn't like it, he could leave home.

From his report, there was an initial uproar during which Mrs. Peterson refused to cook, do his laundry, or even speak to him. His son, however, immediately began to spend more time away from the house and to act more like a responsible adult. After several weeks, Mrs. Peterson calmed down and seemed to acknowledge her husband's authority somewhat more. Mr. Peterson reported, "Things are working out much better. I realized that I needed to take some action; words didn't work." He said he should have taken these steps years ago. His wife and he have begun to talk to each other at meals, something they haven't done for years. They even went to play bingo together last week.

In the process of asserting himself, Mr. Peterson found himself a job in a local plant as a packer; even though it doesn't pay too much, he feels he is holding his end up. He also has begun to involve himself at the Boys' Club nearby, teaching kids how to carve and rig old-time sailing ships, a secret hobby of his for years.

CROSSING THE LINE

The major rite of passage in the transition to late adulthood is the retirement process, to be discussed separately below. For many persons, a related ritual is that of applying for Social Security and medical-insurance benefits. For some, this is an eagerly awaited milestone, for which they have assembled the necessary documents long in advance. Those with limited or marginal incomes, who have been "waiting out their time" in low-paying or unsatisfactory jobs, or even getting along marginally on income from property, savings, or family supplements, find that receiving old-age benefits, whether based on deductions from previous earnings or as part of other assistance programs, can mean the difference between continuing to live with dignity and self-sufficiency or subsisting as often-debased dependents. Medicare and Medicaid benefits remove from many older persons the major fear that haunts them, that they will be unable to pay for their health care as they continue to age. Frances Feldman points out that Old Age, Survivors, Disability, and Health Insurance benefits (OASDI) and other forms of transfer payments have many positive values. They represent security on both the external and psychological levels, and in some socioeconomic groups keep aging persons from becoming dependent on scarce community resources.[7]

For others, filing for Social Security benefits is viewed with ambivalence. While earlier objections to "getting relief" have long since been overcome because of the designation of the program as prepaid insurance. ("You paid for it; it's coming to you"), present-day hesitation may often be less tangible and tied to the person's feelings about *identifying* himself as having entered the stage of late adulthood, with what this implies in terms of no longer being fully productive and independent. (Recent amendments in Social Security regulations address themselves to this issue by raising the levels of earned income allowed.)

Often this ambivalence is carried over to other, similar marker events, such as identifying oneself as being eligible for "golden age" benefits. One youthful-appearing man of seventy declared indignantly that he refused to pay reduced rates on buses or at civic events in his community because he didn't want to be "bunched with all those old folks."

ENTERING LATE ADULTHOOD

The core psychosocial issue in late adulthood, according to Erikson, is the development of a sense of *ego integrity* (integration) as opposed to *despair*. This has been interpreted in a number of ways.[8] Peck sees it as representing the culmination of all the psychological crises in the second half of life (see Chapter 8). He lists three developmental tasks as characteristic of old age: *ego differentiation vs. work-role preoccupation; body transcendence vs. body preoccupation;* and *ego transcendence vs. ego preoccupation.*[9]

1. *Ego differentiation vs. work-role preoccupation.* This issue, created by the effect of retirement, implies a shift in the person's value system so that he can reappraise his worth in terms of a broader range of role activities than just his work role. Peck paraphrases this into the question "Am I a worthwhile person only insofar as I can do a full-time job or can I be worthwhile in other, different roles and because of the kind of person I am?" The ability to find a sense of self-worth through a variety of activities seems to make the most difference between maintaining a continued vital interest in living or losing it in despair.

Since retirement brings a sharp reduction in income and a consequent reduction in living standards, ego differentiation requires finding meaningful satisfaction in non-status-type activities and in the development of different, non-money-based attributes of personality and interpersonal relationships.

2. *Body transcendence vs. body preoccupation.* Later adulthood brings a marked decline in resistance to illness and in recuperative power. Persons who are concerned with their physical well-being may find this a serious, mortal type of insult and become increasingly preoccupied with the state of their bodies and their health. Others, who suffer just as much physical discomfort, may enjoy life greatly because they have learned to define happiness and comfort in terms of satisfying human relationships or creative mental activities which can transcend physical discomfort.

3. *Ego transcendence vs. ego preoccupation.* A positive adaptation to the eventuality of one's own death would mean that one can live so generously and unselfishly that even the prospect of personal death becomes less important than the secure knowledge that one has built for a broader, longer future through one's children, through contributions to the culture, and through friendships as a way of self-perpetuation. This would require, not passive resignation or ego denial, but engaging in a deep, active effort to make life more secure, meaningful, or happier for those who go on after one dies.

On a more practical, activity-oriented level, Duvall sees the married couple who enter into later adulthood as having to carry out a series of joint developmental tasks: making satisfying living arrangements; adjusting to retirement income; establishing comfortable routines; safeguarding physical and mental health; maintaining love, sex, and marital relations; remaining in touch with other family members; keeping active and involved; and finding meaning in life.[10]

While most of these activities make up the substance of living throughout late adulthood, several of them require shifts in role activities and interactions that carry different weights at different phases in the years to come. Since many of the initial changes are made in relationship to retirement, we shall delay discussion of these tasks until the retirement transition is examined.

Retirement as a Bridge

The act of retirement can be viewed in two ways: as a bridging interval in the individual's work role and as a rite of passage in the overall transition into old age. "Retirement" in its narrow sense refers to the cessation of work and work-related activities and has been defined as the "institutionalized separation of an individual from his occupational position.[11] In its broader frame of reference it implies withdrawal from the mainstream of social and communal activities and from active responsibility for many productive work-based roles (e.g., manager of the company baseball team).

Many gerontologists feel that retirement is probably the most crucial life change to which older persons must adjust. Not only must they fill a sizeable time void in their former working day, but they are faced with a series of other work-connected role changes as well. This holds true equally for men and women who have held active work positions in which they have invested a good deal of their efforts and energies over time. Where only one of the spouses has been employed and now retires, the act of retirement has a secondary, reactive effect on the mate and on the relationship which will be discussed later on in this chapter.

As with other transitions, we shall not enter into the broader implications of social policies concerning retirement.[12] Instead our focus will be on retirement as a transitional process. As such, it can be viewed as being made up of three phases: *leaving the work world, the act of formal separation*, and *adjustment to post-retirement*, each of which has its own concerns and developmental tasks.

LEAVING THE WORK WORLD

For retirement to take place smoothly, preparation should be started long before the actual event gets underway. Three developmental tasks are involved: to recognize it as a future possibility and begin to shape one's future with that in mind; to begin to take active steps to arrange for it; and to make the formal decision to retire at a particular time, in a particular way.

RECOGNITION OF THE POSSIBILITY.   Atchley sees retirement as a gradual withdrawal which begins when the individual first recognizes that someday he will end his work career. In general, most younger adults look on retirement in a vaguely favorable way, but they know little about it and prefer not to think about it as pertaining to themselves. As workers grow older, however, they are more likely to view it in terms of themselves and to dread the possibility.

Attitudes toward retirement tend to be closely tied to one's financial situation. Research studies have shown that the higher the expected retirement income, the more favorable the attitude. Persons at lower occupational levels, who earn less and consequently can expect less financial security during retirement, do not favor retirement because they see their income as being drastically reduced. Persons at middle occupational levels have been found to have the most positive orientation toward retirement, since they anticipate sufficient retirement income to be comfortable and usually have no lasting commitment to their jobs. At the upper occupational levels, the picture is mixed: while the size of the future income is not seen as a problem, the individuals find their jobs interesting and have a high work commitment. Theoretically they favor retirement; in actual practice, they tend not to retire easily or at the expected time.

In a study of factors which go into preparation for future retirement, Abraham Monk found that both administrative and professional men, between the ages of fifty and fifty-nine, were reluctant to anticipate, much less prepare for, retirement.[13] Neither group seemed to have any consistent pattern of discussing or reviewing their own retirement plans, of making advance financial preparations, or of joining other retirement programs to supplement their Social Security and employer's pension plans. Discussion of future retirement was confined largely to their own family group, particularly their wives. Administrators tended to ask for retirement advice and orientation from colleagues on a private, informal basis, while professionals either approached personnel officials or private investment or insurance counselors. Reading up on retirement was chance and incidental. Advance financial preparations were viewed from a savings and investment orientation rather than as deliberate preparation.

When asked why they were so hesitant to plan ahead, respondents tended to rationalize on the basis of the inflationary state of the economy, their anticipation that they might not live long enough to retire, or their determination to remain active all their lives without retiring.

GETTING READY FOR RETIREMENT.   As the time to leave their work world draws closer, few people make advance plans, even though the changeover involves socialization to a new position in the sense of learning new attitudes, values, beliefs, knowledge, and skills in order to take on a new social role. Atchley found that counseling programs on retirement, either mounted by companies themselves or offered by community resources, tend to be of two kinds. *Limited programs* are directly related to imparting factual information. They explain pension plans, retirement benefits, options in the timing of application for Social Security and Medicare, and other possibilities for supplementing retirement income. *Comprehensive programs,* which are far less common, go beyond financial planning and deal with the broader aspects of retirement such as physical and mental care, housing, leisure-time activities, and legal complications which may arise.

However, preparation for retirement involves far more than planning for the future. It also means dealing with one's past and one's present in the work scene. It involves beginning the slow process of detaching oneself both from the work role and from the physical and relational ties in one's workplace—from the desk and the files and the servers in the cafeteria. It implies thinking of, searching for, and taking on a successor to be trained for one's own job (to the extent that the person has control and responsibility for it), to whom one can impart all of the specific ways one has of doing the job, all of the secret little shortcuts developed over time to finish the work faster and better, all of the wisdom accrued over the years, which becomes, in a very real sense, one's work legacy. This has deep emotional implications because it can mean, at one level, the "passing on of the torch," and on another, the admission that one is not indispensable and that one needs to start cutting out a significant part of one's life. It also means envisaging oneself as continuing without this vital aspect of one's identity, the work role.

Although there seems to be general recognition that it is often difficult to leave one's job, with all of the affectional and social ties that are bound up with most long-held positions, the need to begin the process well in advance is not always comprehended. In this sense, preparation for retirement takes on many of the aspects of anticipatory grieving, which has been discussed in other contexts.

THE DECISION TO RETIRE.   At some point along the line, the actual decision to retire has to be made. Then one has to inform one's superior, one's fellow workers, and the various other persons with whom one comes in contact (clients, customers, professional colleagues, and so forth). It means taking the formal steps to implement the decision by beginning the severance process, including filling out forms, calculating vacation time coming, returning company property, and completing work commitments at hand.

All of this is predicated on the assumption that the company has a mandatory retirement-age policy, which is being applied in this instance. Actually, many organizations have retirement policies based on other criteria— on years of service, for example. This policy, which is used in federal civil service and some state and local governmental offices, as well as in the armed forces, can result in complications of the retirement process, since it may mean retiring "out of sync," before the person is ready to retire from other work-related roles or before his family is ready to reorient itself.[14] Others may encourage early retirement, either as part of an overall union contract or company policy or for special considerations such as a changeover to new technology, merger with another company, or move to a new location, or because it is felt that the worker in question is no longer able to carry on his job.

Many workers leave the work world voluntarily and take early retirement in order to experience some years of leisure while they are "still young enough to enjoy it." Others find themselves retiring suddenly, without advance preparation or a calculated decision, as a result of health problems (illness or injury), family difficulties (divorce), business failures, personnel cuts, or because they have left one job and are unable to find another one at their age. Companies tend to discriminate against hiring older workers, largely on the unsubstantiated claim that they cannot meet the physical or skill requirements for the job. In some instances, their refusal to hire older applicants is tied to employment policies which imply the need to "get one's money's worth" out of an employee before permitting him to share in retirement and other employee benefits.

One recent comprehensive study compared persons who had retired voluntarily with those for whom the decision was nonvoluntary—either for reasons of poor health, mandatory age, or pressure from superiors—to see the effect on post-retirement satisfaction.[15] They found that 52 percent of their 1,486 respondents had retired voluntarily, giving such reasons as wanting to enjoy retired life (82 percent), having enough money to afford it (66 percent), and being tired of working and having earned the right to retire (45 percent). The 48 percent in the nonvoluntary group emphasized that they wanted to keep on working but were asked to retire (62 percent) or had reached the mandatory retirement age (61 percent).

The voluntary group felt that they were more in control of the decision to retire, and almost two-thirds had retired early, as compared with less than one-quarter of the nonvoluntary group. Some 72 percent of the voluntaries had made advance plans for retirement, as compared to only 40 percent of the nonvoluntaries. Only 4 percent of the voluntaries retired unexpectedly, as against almost half the nonvoluntaries.

Income and occupation were factors clearly related to the decision to retire voluntarily. The three top categories were executives (70 percent), managers (53 percent), and clerical workers (51 percent). Voluntary retirees also earned higher incomes before retirement than the nonvoluntary ones. Eighty-six percent of the voluntary group said they were in good or excellent health at time of retirement, as compared to 77 percent of the nonvoluntary group. The voluntaries reported that their families gave them more encouragement to retire; they had planned more for post-retirement financial arrangements and activities; and were almost twice as likely to have positive feelings about retiring.

A different type of study was reported by Majda Thurnher as part of the overall project on transitions carried out at the University of California, San Francisco.[16] A group of sixty men and women facing the retirement of at least one of the spouses were asked about their goals, value orientations, and life appraisals. Most of the group said that they had considered and had made decisions as to their future activities and life-styles, with about three-quarters of them actively engaged in arranging to implement their plans. About two-fifths referred to material and economic goals and about the same percentage spoke of engaging in travel and touring. About one-fourth planned to relocate in rural areas, retirement communities, or trailer parks, and one-fifth looked forward to leisure-type activities such as gardening, carpentry, golf, and camping (for the men) and handicrafts and cultural pursuits (for the women).

The pre-retirement men showed a decline in instrumental/material values and an increase in ease/contentment and hedonistic values, while the pre-retirement women showed a decline in interpersonal/expressive values (those centering on marriage and the family), as well as a rise in ease/contentment values.

In considering whether life transitions trigger a review of one's past life, Thurnher felt that the major transition for women that involves such a review occurs at the time of the completion of the family cycle (empty-nest period), while for men it occurs at the time of retirement. Many of the men indicated that they had abandoned previous work goals (such as advancement within their chosen occupations or moving into a closely related field that would have been more lucrative, prestigious, or of greater intrinsic interest to them) but did not regret their choice. Women tended to be less philosophical than the men over having abandoned earlier goals; the choices for many had been between career and marriage, and they were open in revealing their disappointments and renunciations. Responsibility for their own lack of achievement was frequently attributed to the attitudes or demands of significant others.

RETIREMENT AS A FORMAL EVENT

As the actual date for retirement approaches, most persons look upon the event with mixed feelings, as this wry quotation from one person reflects:

> I was a young man once. Now I'm not. Now I'm an old man. Leastwise, the company I work for tells me I'm old. I'm almost sixty-five. In a couple of months they're going to retire me. Put me out to pasture.
> What's old? Folks sixty-five don't think sixty-five's old. It's the young people who think sixty-five's creaking age. Once I thought anybody sixty-five

was ready for the grim reaper. Now? Well, now I'm hoping I've got a few years left, anyways. I find that life doesn't become less precious as you get older. . . .

Now, though, I'm going to get retired. . . . That's what my company says. They hold a little party. Not much. I'm not a big shot. All the young ones, they say, "Boy, are you lucky. No more getting up early to rush to work. Play golf, work at hobbies. Don't do nothing if you don't want to." They laugh and clap me on the back. They sort of look at me. Yeah. It would be nice to have some time off, all right. But they sure wouldn't want to be old. What can you do when you're old? Striving's gone, ambition's gone. Competition's gone. Challenge's gone. This old man here, his road's all downhill now. Down and out.[17]

The final departure from the world of work, with the implication that the separation is intended to be permanent, is an event of considerable social and personal significance in our society. The retirement ceremony itself becomes a rite of passage, usually an informal one, that bridges the gap between productive maturity and nonproductive old age. For some employees, particularly those with long years of service for one employer and typically in the middle and upper status ranges, the transition may be marked by a public ceremony and the presentation of some memento like a gold watch, an embossed plaque, or a silver platter.[18] Such ceremonies, says Atchley, have little of the rite-of-passage significance that other transitional rituals do. The ceremony usually stresses the person's past successes and contributions but seldom deals with the event itself in terms of the meaning of separation from work or the strictures posed by retirement, a status that society prefers not to dwell on.

The majority of departing employees may not even rate such a ceremony; a final check with a note from management, a quick clearing out of one's desk or locker, a final luncheon with "the girls" or a beer with "the boys," and the bonds with one's place of work, which has occupied such a predominant place in one's adult thoughts and activities for so many years, are severed. A particularly pathetic figure, familiar to many large organizations, is the former "dedicated" employee, male or female, whose whole life was wrapped up in his or her work. After retirement, such individuals may come back for a visit, "just to talk" and to observe how the place is getting along without them. Almost invariably, after the first greetings and small talk, a sense of embarrassment sends the other workers back to their desks or benches. The retiree soon finds himself or herself alone, roleless, arrested in a frozen moment of time—the last day on the job. After this first visit, the person rarely returns.

Other individuals, who have not been so heavily invested in their work roles, whose occupation was not so satisfying, or who worked where the social aspects of the job were not so gratifying, may have waited a long time for the last day of "servitude." As they figuratively wipe their feet on the doormat on the way out, they may reflect, gratefully, "Thank goodness, that aspect of my life is over!" and willingly move on.

ADJUSTMENT TO POST-RETIREMENT

EXPECTATIONS OF RETIREES.   When a worker gives up his work role, voluntarily or not, he takes on the new role of "retiree" or "retired person." Considerable disagreement exists as to what are the cultural expectations of this role. As a worker, the person had a definite role prescription. He was expected to appear at a certain place at a certain time to perform certain functions for which he was paid a certain sum. He also was expected to belong to various job-related networks: his union, his professional association, his credit union, his Friday-night bowling team. He had circles of friends made through his job and he was expected to relate to them in prescribed ways.

Now, as a retiree, it is anticipated that he will drop not only his work role but all these other work-affiliated roles as well. No new set of role specifications have been given for the retiree. Instead, a vague series of broad do's and dont's are offered. For example, the retired person is expected to spend more time at home with his spouse or with his family (if they are available). He is expected to increase the amount of time spent in leisure pursuits, to take up new sports such as golf which he may never have had time for before, and to develop new hobbies or expand old ones. He is expected to give up working for pay (if he can afford it) and to get by on less income. He is expected to spend more time with his old non-work friends or find some new ones. He is expected to increase his involvement in non-work-related organizations, such as voluntary or civic groups. And, indeed, Atchley finds that most retired persons do conform to these expectations fairly well.[19] Gradually, the narrow interpretation of retirement as cessation of work merges into the broader view of retirement as a way of living during the final stage of the life cycle.

An interesting question is how such a major life reorganization affects the individual's concept of himself. One study found that the higher the occupational status a person had, the less likely he was to miss his job. Another study concluded that the overriding effect of retirement seemed to be the feeling of loss of involvement; without the job around which their lives had been built for some forty to fifty-nine years, retirees felt less useful, less effective, and less busy than men who were still employed. Nevertheless, this did not affect their overall morale.

Atchley reports that despite popular stereotypes, retired people appear to be as healthy after stopping work as they were before, or even healthier, although "poor health" was given as one of the major causes of retirement. Furthermore, retirement was not found to have a direct effect on mortality.

Little evidence was found that retirement per se had any relationship to social or psychological problems among individual older people, except those caused indirectly by the sharp drop in income and associated changes in life-style. In general, the negative effects of retirement earlier reported were found to have been largely overestimated. However, the central point remains: the retiree must shift his point of reference regarding his own behavior in such matters as style of dress or how to spend his vacation from his former occupational framework to that of his retired peers. His family and friendship networks now become his central orbit of activity.

In a later investigation, Atchley attempted to verify his contention that adjustment is the outcome of the interaction between *internal compromise* and *interpersonal negotiations*.[20] He found that less than one-third of the retired population experience difficulty in adjusting to retirement. Of those that do, the most common difficulty appears to be adjusting to reduced income (40 percent). Another 22 percent miss their previous job. The remaining 38 percent have problems related to the death of their spouse or declining health, part of the overall aging process.

Adjustment to the loss of job can be viewed in terms of the individual's hierarchy of personal goals, says Atchley. If the job is high on this hierarchy, the individual can be expected to seek another one. If he cannot find a new job, he will then have to reorganize his hierarchy, either by searching for alternate roles or by lowering the place of work on his list of priorities. Of course, if the job was not high to begin with, no serious change in personal goals is needed.

Who are the men who continue to work after age sixty-five? It has been found that they tend to come from the extremes of the occupational ladder: either those at the lower end who are impelled to work by financial necessity or those in high occupational statuses who work for a combination of personal and psychosocial reasons. Among the male faculty members of universities, for example, one study showed that nearly all of those in the physical sciences and about half of those in the social sciences worked for pay at some time after retiring; very few of those in the humanities did.[21]

PERSONALITY TYPES.   In research carried out some years ago, five distinct types of retired men were identified, falling into two groups:[22]

A. *Well-adjusted types*
    1. The "mature" men moved easily into old age, felt relatively free of neurotic conflict, were able to accept themselves realistically and to find genuine satisfaction in activities and personal relationships. They took old age for granted and made the best of it.
    2. The "rocking-chair" men were generally passive, welcomed the opportunity to be free of responsibility. Old age brought satisfactions that compensated for its disadvantages.

    3. The "armored" men were unable to face passivity or helplessness in old age. They warded off their dread of physical decline by a strong defense of keeping active, which protected them from the fear of growing old.

B. *Poorly adjusted types*

    4. The "angry" men were bitter over having failed to achieve their earlier goals and blamed others for their disappointments. They were unable to reconcile themselves to growing old.

    5. The "self-haters" looked back on their past with a sense of disappointment and failure, turning their resentment inward and blaming themselves for their misfortunes. They tended to be depressed, feeling inadequate and worthless as they grew old.

Both sets of the poorly adjusted seemed to have had lifelong personality problems, while the personalities of the rocking-chair and armored groups also seemed to have changed very little throughout their lives. Only the mature men appeared to have overcome earlier difficulties in personal adjustment and become better adjusted as they grew older.

The behavior patterns of the three well-adjusted types reflected both the activity and disengagement theories of aging.[23] Both the mature and the armored functioned equally well at work and were actively engaged in hobbies, social activities, and organizations—for different reasons. Now, after retirement, the mature men continued to participate actively because they enjoyed what they were doing, while the armored remained active because of their compulsive need to keep busy as a defense against aging. The rocking-chair men, on the other hand, used disengagement as a satisfactory way to adjust—they withdrew gracefully.

ACTIVITIES OF RETIREES.   When a person retires, he can engage in several types of activities. Generally these can be divided into (1) *work-substitute activities* (unpaid activities similar to work, such as volunteering); (2) *leisure activities* which are engaged in solely for personal pleasure; or (3) *doing nothing*—that is, not engaging in any activity, remaining withdrawn.[24]

Enjoyment of leisure activities becomes very important, since this is considered the acme of retirement. It becomes the focus for many retirement programs in community centers and retirement communities, and also for many individual plans. Atchley differentiates between *leisure activities*, which are pursued purely as ends in themselves, unplanned and unrequired, and generally directed toward self-development, and *recreational activities* such as sports, games, and hobbies which aim to renew the mind and body by relieving them of tension and delivering them from boredom.

Retired people usually expand their leisure activities gradually and in moderation. During the week their most frequent activity tends to be watching television; on the weekends they entertain or visit friends. A relatively small proportion engage in crafts, hobbies, or artistic activities. The only outside activities that increase with age are gardening and walking. Vacation and travel are generally limited to the comparatively few who can afford the expense on retirement income. In recent years educational programs, both credit and noncredit, have grown in popularity.[25]

Visiting friends, watching TV, performing odd jobs at home, traveling and touring, and reading have been reported as the most popular activities for retirees. A strong relationship was found between the number of activities in which the person engaged and his life satisfaction score. Eight of the top ten most popular activities were carried out without companions.[26]

RELOCATION DURING RETIREMENT.   A popular fantasy nourished by many persons preparing to retire or already in retirement is that, after "putting in their time," they can rid themselves of previous commitments and involvements by moving to a warm, sunny place of perpetual enjoyment. Retirement communities have sprung up throughout the country, largely in areas like southern Florida and California. They are geared to virtually all levels of income and range in facilities from squalid, crowded trailer parks to rows of neat little surburban bungalows to luxurious high-rise condominiums set in self-contained complexes providing action-packed leisure activities to suit every taste. Many of these retirement communities are very successful, although participation in them depends, to a large extent, on the expectations of the persons themselves and their ability to adjust to the new style of life. Since this move involves a double transition, both to retirement and to a new geographic location, the changeover can be difficult.

In a candid, down-to-earth book addressed to older persons facing or experiencing retirement, Ruth Turk, who lives in a retirement complex in Florida, quotes a letter from one of the readers of her newspaper column which expresses the ambivalence and difficulties in adaptation felt by many recent retirees:[27]

> Dear Ruth:
>   My wife persuaded me to sell my business and retire to Florida even though I felt I was not ready for retirement. She said we would make up for the many years of hard work and unpleasant conditions of living in a large, crowded city. She painted such a beautiful picture of leisure living that I finally agreed, even though I had always imagined that only very sick or old people are forced to retire.
>   Now after almost two years, I find that my worst fears are being realized. This life is boring and pointless because I haven't anything worthwhile to do. When I ran my business, I was "on the go" from morning to night.
>   Now the hours and days drag by and every day is like Sunday, so I haven't anything to look forward to. Eating, sleeping, playing cards, taking long walks, or sitting around the pool is not my "cup of tea." I am ready to return

to the Big Town, but my wife begs me to give it more time. Will six months or
a year make any difference if my environment remains the same?

Not Ready

RETIREMENT FOR WOMEN

Despite the assumption frequently made that retirement is a particular
problem for men, investigators have found that retired women report a
sharper increase in feelings of uselessness than do their male counterparts.
Retired men, in addition, often have strong social support systems at home.
Women in general tend to live longer than men; moreover, if they are
married, they usually marry men older than themselves. Consequently, in
late adulthood, they are likely to outlive their husbands and many of the
couple's mutual friends.[28]

For the married working woman, retirement—either her own or her
husband's—poses a range of economic and psychosocial problems in various
combinations. Many of her difficulties during this transitional period are
similar to those faced by the retiring man. In addition, however, she faces
further complications.

First, if she continues to work after her husband retires, she may find
that he resents the shift in their marital balance because he has already
ended his work role. He may express this by depression or by refusal to take
responsibility for household tasks while she is at work. He may also object to
taking financial responsibility for paying household bills, since now *she* is the
money earner.[29]

If both husband and wife retire from work at the same time, they may
find it difficult to realign their household management responsibilities,
which now become the center of their activities, without expressing criticism
of or anger at each other. The long hours of continuous contact, after so many
years of spending only evenings and weekends together, require a basic
reorganization of their areas of responsibilities as well as their ways of relating and communicating with each other. Feldman feels that the wife may
find the transition easier, since she probably still retains many of the
homemaking functions that she performed throughout her working years.
Many couples find that it takes considerable time and goodwill to reestablish
their balance in functioning once they both spend the major part of their
time at home together.

One of the big issues which often face them at this point is the reduction
in their joint income as they shift from two salaries to pooled retirement
income. Since this last usually amounts to considerably less than their former
joint working income, their anxiety is understandable. In such a work-
oriented household, even though their current expenses may be reduced, it

becomes both frightening and upsetting to realize that money spent cannot be replaced by more earnings.

If the wife has retired before the husband, or if she has never worked or worked only intermittently or part-time, the adjustment is probably easier, although it is risky to generalize. Traditional women frequently mention the difficulties in having their spouses underfoot all the time once they retire. While the wife retains her daily pattern of activity, the change in meal schedules, the complications of the husband's mere presence ("He always wants to watch TV when I want to vacuum the living room!"), and even his well-meaning interference in what she regards as her domain ("He keeps telling me how inefficiently I run my own kitchen!") may cause considerable friction until they work out new patterns of functioning.

Fortunately, most couples in the retirement stage have had long years of experience in living together behind them and have established patterns of mutual cooperation as well as ways of negotiating differences that now stand them in good stead until a new balance is achieved. Wives are usually grateful to have their husbands take over some of their heavier household chores while, within their new time frame, they can now carry out such tasks as shopping and seasonal housecleaning together in the spirit of companionship that most frequently marks living together during retirement.

When marital adjustment in the post-retirement years was investigated by Morris Medley, he found that the onset of retirement is likely to bring a couple "face to face" in a way they have not experienced since the initial years of marriage.[30] While in the pre-retirement stage couples could avoid the intimate nature of the marital relationship by focusing on child-rearing and occupational duties, during the post-retirement years such escape mechanisms are no longer available.

Three patterns of marital behavior were identified. The *husband–wife* type of relationship characterizes couples who stress the intimate and shared nature of their life together and focus on their husband–wife roles. In the *parent–child* type, one spouse assumes the role of parent, acting in a nurturant, protective, and dominant fashion. The other tasks on the child role, behaving in a dependent, submissive manner. (This type is most apt to develop—although not necessarily so—if one of the spouses has become incapacitated.) The *associates* type of relationship refers to those couples who act toward each other largely as friends; although they appreciate each other's company, their most rewarding ties lie outside of the intimacy of the husband–wife relationship (with their children or grandchildren, for example, or even their chess partners).

RETIREMENT FOR SINGLES

For many unmarried persons, retirement brings both advantages and difficulties in adjustment. The older single person, whether male or female, tends to be a relatively independent type of person who has made his or her adjustment to living alone long before reaching old age.

Some retirees maintain that being single in old age is a "kind of premium." In a study of aged singles carried out by Jaber Gubrium, their self-reports tended to be more positive than those of divorced or widowed old people. Since their daily routines appeared to have been developed over a lifetime of relative isolation, they insisted that now, in old age, they were not especially lonely. Never having had, for the most part, a long-term intimate relationship bond, they also had not suffered the desolating effects of loss and bereavement following the death of a spouse. They were found to value highly the independence of being single, which they felt eliminated the burden of dependent relatives, even though some claimed that their reason for never having married was that they had been responsible for aging and ailing parents.[31]

Many older single persons use their work network as their chief source of interest and social interaction. Thus, when they retire, they often lose the one interactional system that provides them with a basis for self-validation. For those who have worked out patterns of leisure-time activities, such as going fishing, watching TV, or reading newspapers in the library, the transition to retirement can be taken in stride. For others, who have immersed themselves in their work, retirement or the anticipation of retirement can be particularly threatening.

The following case, adapted from the casebook of Seema Allen, psychiatric social worker in a crisis clinic for many years, illustrates this issue very poignantly, although actual retirement is only implied:

FRANCES SMITH (#113)

Miss Smith, long-boned and thin at age 61, had gray hair severely drawn into a bun. Her straight features and sober expression immediately reminded me of the woman in Grant Wood's *American Gothic*. She began to talk in a quiet, dragging voice, saying she had felt so low on Saturday she called the psychiatric ward and talked to a nurse. On Sunday she felt worse and stayed in bed all day. She called the nurse again and told her she was thinking about killing herself. The nurse told her to come to the crisis clinic.

"But today I got up and went to work. It's such a habit. I'm always mobilized when I get to the job. I called the minute I reached the office." When asked what had happened, she began to cry. Soon she wiped her tears away and continued in her slow, dulled voice.

"I don't know. I just got to thinking, 'What's the use?' It all seems so purposeless, so meaningless. I've been interested in my job and I've got a wonderful boss. He just returned on Friday from a buying trip abroad and told me they are planning to transfer him to Philadelphia. . . . He didn't say so, but I'm sure that he thinks I'm too old for them to transfer me there when he gets moved."

After a few moments, crying silently, she continued, describing in meager words her meager life. "That's the way it's always been. Just work. I got out of high school in two years, graduated on a Friday night and started work on Monday morning. I've always worked. I'm not lazy, I really love my job. But there's so little else. There's always been so little else. And soon there won't even be that."

She described her childhood, always earning her way at home by being useful. She had taken care of her parents till they died, coming home from high school to fix their lunch. She always got jobs in the neighborhood so she could take care of them as they grew increasingly helpless. After they finally died, she took care of her sister's child, moving in with her sister "temporarily" and staying five years. Then, when she left her sister's, she became attached to three different families with children. In one place, she lived in the maid's quarters of a suburban home for three years, taking care of children in the evening while their young parents went out on the town. One day she abruptly quit.

She then joined the army and stayed four years. She was promoted and given inducements to reenlist but felt she didn't belong with the younger girls around her and left. Lasting rewards always came from the work itself. She tried, however, to keep to a familiar structure with people she knew.

Her present job was in a large department store, where she had started as a secretary. Her boss valued her enough to take her with him as an assistant when he became buyer for a large department. He fought the administration when they wanted someone else for the job and not only kept her but got her a raise. She now has an office and a part-time secretary. Once, when they tried to bring in a good-looking young girl, she blew up and told her boss, "Either she goes or I!" He decided her proven dependability was worth more than the other's young looks and things settled down. Then rumors began that the store was being taken over by an eastern firm. She began to get worried, since she was getting to the age where it would be hard to find another job, particularly one as good as this.

She began to develop stomach trouble for which the doctor could find no cause and began to call in sick. Last year, for the first time, she had received a bad rating and her boss had said he couldn't recommend her for a raise. This threw her into a panic and for a while she was treated for "depression." She thought things were better until last week, when her boss came back with the news.

"All my life's gone by with nothing to show for it. What is there for me?" She sat with two fists pressed into her eyes, crying silently. Suddenly, she reached into her purse and brought out a small satin box. Inside, on a bed of white velvet, lay a pin with small glittering blue stones encased in a ring of gold.

"Isn't it beautiful? My boss brought it to me from Hong Kong. He gave it to me on Friday, but I couldn't put it on. It only seems to prove I'm given things because I'm a good worker, not because I'm me. . . . I know he appreciates me. But I'm not important to his life, only to his job. Nobody needs me just for myself."

Although she felt better for having relived her story, Miss Smith was exhausted. She agreed to come back on Friday so we could make some plans. When she came in, she was wearing a smart blue suit with a pink blouse. On her lapel was the glittering blue pin. She said she had put it on after she left and had been wearing it ever since. In general, she felt better and had even picked up the knitting she hadn't touched for months. She said knitting was her way of expressing herself; she could sit for hours, making up new patterns and working out the design and colors. Collecting beautiful yarns had been a hobby of hers for years. But she had never done anything with her knitting or showed it to anyone.

She said she didn't have many friends, just some of the woman at work, but lately they had drifted away. When I asked whether she'd like to teach others how to knit, she said she had never thought of it. I suggested she visit the Volunteer Bureau of the hospital and ask about starting a knitting class. She agreed and left without making another appointment.

A week later she stopped in to say that Mrs. Nielson at the Bureau was already inquiring, not only at the hospital, but at several nearby community centers. Meanwhile she was setting down plans for a series of classes and collecting yarns and patterns.

When she left she was almost smiling and her cheeks were pink with excitement. She looked as if she had already embarked on a new career, a new job to replace the one that was leaving her.

One part of the comprehensive, long-term research program on aging women that was started in 1977 at the University of Wisconsin-Madison focuses on older single women, including an examination of how they differ from married women in making and implementing retirement plans.[32] From preliminary observations, the investigators conclude that single women may be able to cope more efficiently with being alone if they have a sense of mastery over their lives and environment. They note that psychologists feel that the critical variable is *ego strength* or *emotional autonomy*, while sociologists tend to believe that *social connectedness* or *ties to a network of social relationships* are most likely to help. For some women, the two factors may be mutually reinforcing; for others, one set may serve as the substitute for the other.

Once the first transitional period is over, the aging but still competent person settles down into late adulthood. Whether alone or as part of a couple, working or in retirement, living in his hometown or having moved to a retirement community, he starts the final stage of his life span dealing with the issue of integrity vs. despair. The extent to which he is able to consolidate his gains and losses and integrate them into a meaningful whole that he can pass on to succeeding generations will be determined by the way in which he lives out these next years.

12

The Final Years

Every morning I wake up in pain. I wiggle my toes. Good. They still obey. I open my eyes. Good. I can see. Everything hurts but I get dressed. I walk down to the ocean. Good. It's still there. Now my day can start. About tomorrow I never know. After all, I'm 89. I can't live forever.

THIS GALLANT COMMENT, by one of Barbara Myerhoff's "old ladies" in her anthropological study of growing old in a southern California community, expresses the concerns of the aged as they live out their numbered days.[1]

As the individual moves toward advanced old age, we find a clustering and dynamic interaction of age-related stresses which include decrements in physical and mental capacities; chronic and/or catastrophic illnesses; interpersonal losses such as death or severe illness of the spouse, other relatives, peers, and even adult children; diminished income; cessation of productive work; and loss of social roles and status.[2] A typical profile gives an idea of the multiplicity of issues with which a person in this age bracket may be dealing at the same time:

The 85-year-old is not newly widowed but may in fact have spent as much as one-third of her life in this status. She has been a grandmother for more than one-third of her life; her grandchildren may now be parents. She is one of a million who are older than almost everyone around and is one of the last survivors of her family and her generation. Few people remember her as a bride; fewer still remember her as a child. She is faced with the tasks of developing relationships of great dependence with her children and other younger family members, of coping with increasing physical disabilities, of conserving her remaining physical, emotional, and financial resources. She may also be struggling with a decision about a move from independent living to institutional care.[3]

In short, she is a survivor and has learned to cope with her shrinking world with tenacity and fortitude. She has also learned to use her inner strengths and resources.

In this chapter, we will attempt to examine three of the most significant transitions in this last stage of the adult life cycle; *health impairment, the path to institutionalization*, and *death of the spouse and survival of the mate*. Without giving the impression that each cannot take place independently and at an earlier phase, we shall focus on their occurrence during the final years, when their complicated interactional nature makes it difficult to separate cause and effect. In many situations these changes can be viewed as different aspects of the overarching transition of decline in functioning and role decrement in late life.

Health Impairment: Physical and Mental Restraints

Life expectancy in the United States had increased from about 47 years in 1900 to 71.9 years in 1974, 75.9 for females and 68.2 for males.[4] As a result, more old people are growing frailer and sicker than they used to be. Because of medical and social advances, they tend to live longer, and in doing so have more debilitating things happen to them which, while not severe enough to kill them, change the nature of the way they live out their final years. Such enfeebling conditions fall into two categories which profoundly affect each other: physical and psychological. Let us examine their effects on the aging individual.

PHYSICAL AND PHYSIOLOGICAL CONDITIONS

Interestingly, older people seem to be affected less by *acute* illness than younger individuals are.[5] A greater degree of immunity to common pathogens, a diminished level of awareness of symptoms, and a lessened concern regarding the less acknowledged illnesses are among the possible reasons. When acute illnesses do occur, however, to a group of older persons with varying kinds of chronic conditions, these often result in greater disability and more restricted activity than for other age groups.

Prevalence of *chronic* disease, however, increases markedly with age, with 85 percent of individuals sixty-five years or older and living outside of institutions reporting at least one chronic illness and about 50 percent acknowledging some limitation of their normal activities related to chronic health conditions.[6] Heart disease is the chronic impairment experienced most frequently, with over half of the persons over age sixty-five suffering from various forms of it. Arthritis is almost as prevalent, with such other disorders as diabetes, asthma, obesity, hernias, cataracts, varicose veins, hemorrhoids, hypertension, and prostate disease also common. One source reports that about 30 percent of those over age sixty-five consider themselves to be limited by illness in activities such as moving about, feeding themselves, and climbing stairs. About two-thirds can still function without aid, although three-fourths may require help in traveling in public conveyances.[7]

In addition, other forms of physical limitations and reduced functioning also occur. Eyes, ears, and teeth may need mechanical assistance in the form of glasses, hearing aids, and dentures. Impairments of speech, extremities, and back also rise sharply with advancing age. The aged tend to be hospitalized three times as often as younger patients and their average hospital stay is twice as long. The number of physician's visits increases with age, as do the number of days spent in bed and the total personal health care expenditures.[8]

The aged are also more prone to accidents, partly because their hands tend to shake, their feet are less steady, and their attention wanders so that they do not watch out for icy pavements and extra bottom steps or may not hear the horn of an approaching car or see that a traffic light has changed. Once they fall, their injuries tend to be more serious because their bones have grown brittle with advancing age and their resistance to complications is lowered. When hospitalized, such patients often deteriorate rapidly and are unable to return to the preaccident level of functioning.

Debilitating accidents often occur after some sudden change in the person's psychosocial situation has precipitated a crisis. Joan Lipner and Etta Sherman found that hip fractures in the elderly are frequently tied to real or imagined losses such as the death of a spouse, retirement, illness, and changes in financial situation or living conditions.[9]

MENTAL AND EMOTIONAL DISTURBANCES

Physical and mental health in older persons tend to be closely related. Some 10 to 12 percent of those over sixty-five suffer from mental impairment. While neurotic disorders and symptoms may not increase with age, the elderly show a sharp rise in psychotic illnesses and in symptoms experienced as physical illnesses.[10] One of the main reasons for this increase is the rise in organic disorders associated with old age, such as chronic brain syndromes of cerebral arteriosclerosis and senile brain disease, marked by relatively permanent deficits in intellectual functioning and symptoms such as confusion and difficulties in orientation, memory and perception, knowledge, and judgment. Such persons are also likely to have various forms of physical illnesses at the same time.

FUNCTIONAL DIFFICULTIES.   Eric Pfeiffer points out that psychopathology in later life can be the result not only of impaired brain functioning but of failures in adaptation despite intact brain functioning.[11] The most frequent functional disorders seen are the *depressions,* ranging from fleeting episodes of saddened affect, loss of energy, and short-lived interest to serious and prolonged depressive reactions. Psychological characteristics of depression include abject and painful sadness, withdrawal of interest and inhibition of activity, and a pervasive pessimism with diminished self-esteem and a gloomy evaluation of the present and future. Depressed persons often experience difficulty in making decisions, and their thought processes, speech, and movements are significantly slowed down. Physical symptoms include loss of appetite, weight loss, severe fatigue, sleeplessness, constipation, and/or diarrhea. In addition, a considerable rise in tension and anxiety often occurs. Tremulousness or even agitation may be present. Strong self-accusations and feelings of guilt regarding past transgressions may be felt. Weeping may be evident, although severely depressed persons often say they are unable to cry, even though they feel like it.

As a variation, the "depressive equivalents" occur with individuals complaining of severe pains, usually in the back, head, or neck. These pains may start off gradually or fairly suddenly and often are self-treated with aspirin or other analgesics or with alcohol for prolonged periods before medical help is sought. Patients tend to deny feeling sad or depressed and usually want help only for their physical pain.

Often, thoughts of suicide accompany severe depressions; they range from relatively passive death wishes to active suicide plans. According to Pfeiffer, suicide among the elderly occurs at more than three times the rate in the general population. He points out that suicide attempts among the elderly, unlike the suicidal gestures of younger people, are almost always serious and the person fully intends to die. Rescue is often accidental and due to poor planning on his part.

Paranoid reactions are probably, after depressions, the next most common psychiatric disturbance in old age. Paranoid patients are suspicious of persons and events around them and often construct faulty or unrealistic explanations of events that happen to them. However, these reactions are less serious in terms of their implications and often much more down to earth than the ideation of younger paranoidal patients. Pfeiffer sees such reactions primarily as an effort to "fill in the blank spaces" in the aging individual's cognitive maps of his environment. Thus they are substantially more common in persons with various kinds of sensory deficits, particularly hearing losses, decreased vision, and lowered intellectual capacity:

> Typically, such an elderly person might misplace her glasses or her wallet, or some other valued or needed possession and then accuse those around her of stealing them. Or a woman might notice that she has been receiving less and

less mail. Rather than coming up with the explanation that she was simply writing fewer letters and was involved in fewer business transactions, she comes to the conclusion that the postman is stealing the mail from her. . . . Another accusation might be that someone is trying to poison the person. Changes in taste perception occur in old age and do contribute to making foods taste different now then they did earlier in life. If some hostility has occurred recently between the older person and the provider of food, then a "logical" conclusion might be that someone is in fact trying to poison the person. [p. 656]

Unfortunately, such accusations tend to alienate other people, particularly care-providers. Thus a live-in companion or nurse will quit after her patient accuses her of stealing. Since paranoids are suspicious of many things, they are also suspicious of medication given to them. Pfeiffer warns that perhaps 60 percent of drugs given in pill form may never be taken.

Hypochondriasis is the third most prevalent functional psychiatric disorder. It occurs more frequently in women than in men and increases with advancing age. It is characterized by excessive preoccupation with bodily functioning, a symptom which tends to interfere with interpersonal reactions within the family and with outsiders. Persons with this disorder have found the outside world unrewarding and hostile and have turned instead toward their own bodies. The result is a long list of physical symptoms and complaints. Such patients are resistant to and resentful of any attempt to interpret their symptoms and even to discuss psychological factors and prefer to dwell on their physical condition. The basic message such a patient is sending, according to Pfeiffer, is that he is sick and in need of medical care, since physical illness rather than emotional disturbance is considered a highly acceptable excuse for nonperformance in Western society.

In response to adverse circumstances or traumatic events, such as the death of a loved one or an unforeseen change in living arrangements, some older persons may experience *transient or lasting adjustment reactions*. The most prominent manifestation is anxiety, with all of its psychological and physiological components. Fear, sometimes to the point of panic, perplexity, emotional lability, tearfulness, and feelings of helplessness predominate among the psychological symptoms, while tremulousness, muscular tension, rapid heart rate, subjective feelings of shortness of breath, epigastric discomfort, and disturbed sleep characterize the physical side of this syndrome. Considerable pressure of speech, with a need to repeat the story of the disturbing events over and over, occurs, punctuated by weeping and moaning.

Many elderly persons complain of a variety of *sleep disturbances*, including difficulties in falling asleep, insufficient total sleep, restless sleep, and early awakening. Changes in sleep patterns are sometimes a part of normal aging and at other times manifestations of emotional or psychiatric disturbances. Patterns of more frequent awakening, less deep sleep, and the need for several naps during the daytime are considered normal for aging persons and do not require the use of sleeping medication. On the other hand, pronounced sleep difficulties, characteristic of depression and transient situational reactions, may be helped by the temporary use of medication.

ORGANIC DISORDERS. Approximately half of all persons sixty-five years and older with significant mental deficits have *organic brain syndromes* due to brain-cell damage or malfunction. Characteristic functions affected are the ability to remain oriented to the environment; short- and long-term memory; visual-motor coordination; and the abilities to learn and retain spatial arrangements, to abstract, to change sets, to assimilate new information, and to carry out sequential tasks.

When the onset is gradual and the defect mild, only the highest intellectual functions may be impaired, such as the ability to abstract and absorb new information. Sometimes the first symptoms may be vague emotional or behavioral changes such as depression, loss of interest, fatigue, restlessness, or agitation as well as irritability, withdrawal, emotional outbursts, irregular work attendance, and changes in behavioral standards. Pfeiffer notes that such changes may be present for months or even years before any clearcut memory deficit, confusion, or disorientation is noticed.

As the deficit increases, however, gross disorientation for time and place, loss of names and telephone numbers, and general memory gaps begin to appear. The person may seem confused, bewildered, perplexed. He may begin to lose his way, at first in new surroundings and then in familiar settings as well. Memories for time sequences and for highly learned material from earlier life also begin to disappear. He may no longer be able to recall the names of his own children, his previous occupation, place of residence, birthday, or even his age. In extremely advanced cases, speech may become garbled and repetitive so that he becomes difficult to understand. Motor control is impaired and the person may no longer be able to feed or dress himself or go to the toilet in time. Eventually, the person may reach the stage of no longer knowing his own name or responding to it. (At this point he usually can no longer function independently and must be cared for by others.) Finally he lapses into a coma, loses sphincter control, or becomes bedridden, subject to bedsores and local or systemic infections.

Some 10 to 20 percent of the elderly persons with organic brain syndromes have a reversible form, due to temporary malfunctioning of cortical cells as a result of metabolic disturbances or drug intoxication; these can respond to treatment. Irreversible organic brain syndromes, on the other hand, are untreatable—the result of the permanent death of brain cells which cannot be regenerated.

Arteriosclerotic brain disease is due to the localized death of brain tissue related to occlusive arterial or arteriolar disease with subsequent blocking of brain tissue ("stroke"). In the typical case, a sudden onset of both intellectual impairment and peripheral neurological deficit, including weakness and paralysis or decreased sensation in the face or limbs on one side of the body, is found. Gradually both cognitive and neurological losses improve, although one episode may be followed by others in other areas of the brain, with cumulative and even lasting damage.

In summing up the deteriorating health picture commonly presented by elderly patients, Charles Gaitz finds that symptoms generally fall into three overlapping spheres:[12]

Cognitive: shortened attention span, slowed thought processes, unusual thought content, reduced mental acuity, thinking disturbances, poor concentration, disorientation, hallucinations, forgetfulness, confusion.
Emotional: emotional lability, uncooperativeness, . . . unsociability, irritability, loneliness, depression, hostility, agitation, anxiety.
Somatic: joint pain or stiffness, diminished locomotion, urinary incontinence, sensory deficits, muscle cramps, constipation, chest pain, dizziness, anorexia, insomnia.

Gaitz also finds that such conditions are caused by multiple stresses and strains which tend to accumulate and mutually reinforce each other. These stresses, both internally and externally generated, also fall into three clusters:[13]

Psychological: impaired cognitive functions, loss of authority/self-esteem, depression/agitation.
Physiological: brain deterioration, greater risk of injury, acute medical disorders, normal catabolic changes, chronic physical diseases, impaired homeostatic mechanisms, spontaneous degenerative processes.
Socio-environmental: inflation, substandard housing, loss of job/work role, communication breakdowns, inadequate transportation, social isolation/rejection, loss of loved ones/associates, increased dependence on others, insufficient retirement benefits.

DEALING WITH HEALTH LIMITATIONS

Since declining health in late adulthood is a central condition that cuts across all social, political, and economic lines, Atchley suggests viewing it along a continuum ranging from good to poor health:[14]

Good Health						Poor Health
Absence of disease or impairment	Presence of a condition	Seeks treatment	Restricted activity	Restricted in major activity	Institu-tionalized	Illness, death

An aged person's health "trajectory" may move slowly and irregularly downward or descend precipitously. At first the condition may simply not be noticed. The next step may be to recognize that it exists but to ignore it as much as possible or possibly treat it oneself with such home remedies as aspirins, hot baths, mustard plasters, and massage. When these do not help, the person may reluctantly pay a visit to the family physician. By this time movement usually has become somewhat restricted, although the individual may still continue to carry out customary activities.

The next step may be for the person's major activity to become restricted so that he is unable to engage in his usual work or housework functions. At this point he is usually considered disabled. Following this his condition may become so serious or medically demanding that he can no longer care for himself and may require institutionalization in some type of facility. Finally, his situation deteriorates to the point where his ability to withstand the ravages of illness or injury are overrun and death results.

This does not imply that all illnesses or injuries are necessarily fatal for the older person. As already mentioned, most aging persons continue to function for many years with at least one or more chronic conditions, some quite serious in nature.* With increasing age, the duration of any health condition tends to be prolonged as a result of the person's declining recuperative powers. Moreover, clustered disabilities and ailments may interact to mask or exacerbate each other so that the condition is often assumed to be age-related and untreatable.[15]

When health impairment is first noticed, the older individual, usually living alone or with a spouse, may attempt to deal with it, as noted above, first by ignoring it and then by using a variety of home remedies, based on past personal experience, old wives' tales, or "sure-fire" cures reported by friends and neighbors. After a time, when the pain and discomfort can no longer be ignored, either by the individual or by others, he may seek medical assistance. Here the problem becomes complicated by limited financial means, by restrictive Medicare and Medicaid benefits which emphasize acute care and neglect long-term needs, and by the fluctuating levels of medical treatment available in a community. Gaitz points out that medical treatment for the aged, when given, is often limited and fragmentary.[16]

Professionals working with the aged agree that the ability to deal with health impairment depends to a large extent on the individual's determination to remain active in order to retain his functioning and on the availability of medical and social service resources in the community that can support this level of functioning. The following case illustrates how an eighty-four-year-old woman doggedly resisted attempts to place her in a protected environment and struggled to maintain herself in the community. She was seen

*Once, in visiting a home for the aged and commenting on the air of well-being among the residents, I was told that not one of them had fewer than *five* debilitating illnesses or conditions.

by a social worker in the community services division of a county welfare office, on referral from a city public health nurse:

ETHEL KOWALSKI (#162)

Mrs. Kowalski, age 84, referred by the city health nurse for supportive services, was living alone in a small rented cottage and had numerous health problems. At the time of first assessment it was learned she suffered from diabetes, arthritis, glaucoma, and chronic heart disease. In addition she had fractured her hip three years earlier and it had never healed properly. Because keeping house was becoming difficult for her, I arranged to provide once-a-week housekeeping service and visited her periodically to check on her functioning and to "keep in touch."

Background Information. Mrs. Kowalski was born in a small upstate town and lived there most of her life. She was first married at age 20, and she and her husband had three children. After six years he died suddenly, and two years later she remarried, this time to a farmer. They had six children and lived a full life together until he died after forty-four years of marriage. In addition to raising her family, Mrs. Kowalski helped her husband on the farm; in her spare time she made patchwork quilts and did other needlework, which she sold for "side money." After her husband died twelve years ago, she moved to the city to be near her oldest daughter and two of her sons. She had always prided herself on her independence and self-sufficiency, but by now had few friends still alive. One neighbor brought in her mail daily and stopped to chat with her, but since she also had health problems, Mrs. Kowalski didn't like to rely on her too much.

Mrs. Kowalski's daughter, Joanne, was the one on whom she depended for shopping and other services. However, she worked during the week and had teenage children, so that she could not come over every evening as her mother would wish. One of the sons who lived in town was crippled; he tried to visit or call daily but was not able to help much. The other son had separated himself from the situation, feeling he had his hands full with his own family situation. The other six children were scattered throughout the United States and not available except at holidays.

Precipitating Crisis. In March, Mrs. Kowalski's daughter called to say she had found her mother lying helpless on the floor when she came to visit her the evening before. She evidently had had a small stroke early that morning and had been lying on the floor all day, unable to call out or attract anyone's attention. She was taken to the local hospital. When I visited her a few days later, her acute condition had improved, although she was still not able to stand or walk alone. She was receiving physical therapy three times a day.

We discussed the possibility of a temporary nursing home placement until she was "stronger on her feet," but she had had an unfortunate experience in such a home after she broke her hip three years ago and didn't want to enter one now. However, it was evident that she no longer could remain in her present cottage, since her landlord had recently raised the rent and she could no longer make ends meet on her limited income. She was struggling at this time with revising her own image of herself as a capable, independent person able to care for herself and her own needs. I agreed to arrange to provide supportive service in the form of a housekeeper five days a week and to mobilize other community resources in an effort to help her remain on her own, although she would undoubtedly have to move to a smaller place.

Two weeks later Mrs. Kowalski went home, moving about with the aid of a walker, although she was in extreme pain and very unsteady on her feet. A few days later she began to have so much trouble with her left leg that she was forced to return to the hospital. After three weeks on the rehabilitation ward, during which an exhaustive series of tests on her leg and knee was carried out, she was again ready for discharge.

The medical staff reported that they had found irreversible nerve damage and that nothing more could be done for her leg pains. They suggested nursing home placement, but I convinced them that Mrs. Kowalski preferred to try living independently. We would support this plan by providing full home help five days a week. On weekends, her family agreed to take responsibility for her needs.

Current Situation. At the time of recording, Mrs. Kowalski has been living at home for a month, beginning to adjust to her limited physical capabilities and to accept the fact that she will never recover fully. I have been supporting her in her determination to "take each day as it comes." In addition, I have been coordinating all services for her and remain in continuous contact with her doctor and home-care nursing service. Mrs. Kowalski has been working hard to maintain her independent living arrangement and to become more adjusted to her physical restrictions. She says she knows she cannot stop getting old but is going to fight as hard as she can to remain on her own as long as possible.

Starting the Path to Institutionalization

INABILITY TO MANAGE ON ONE'S OWN

As a person grows older, one of his basic needs is for a reasonably stable, benign environment in which he can feel secure and whose patterns are familiar enough so that he can continue to function at an optimal level. Being able to manage on his own or together with his spouse depends very much on the interaction between several key factors: the state of his physical and mental health, which we have already discussed; where and with whom he lives; what backup systems he has at his disposal; what his financial resources are; and what viable roles he is still carrying. All of these change over time and all play a vital part in where and how the person lives.

LIVING INDEPENDENTLY.   Couples in late adulthood usually attempt to retain their own living quarters as long as possible. Environmental factors affecting the older person's capacity to function are proximity to and accessibility of relatives and friends; closeness to needed health, recreational, shopping, and occupational facilities; availability of appropriate transportation; condition of the person's dwelling and availability of adequate funds for rent and repairs; and safety from physical or personal hazards. Because of their interpersonal, economic, social, and functional losses, the elderly tend to become increasingly vulnerable to environmental pressures.[17]

If at this stage an individual lives alone, he or she must take on all the tasks of daily living. The mechanics become very complex, as when the eighty-nine-year-old woman whose quotation begins this chapter deals with her daily life structure:

> Basha wants to remain independent above all. Her life at the beach depends on her ability to perform a minimum number of basic tasks. She must shop and cook, dress herself, care for her body and her one-room apartment, walk, take the bus to the market and the doctor, be able to make a telephone call in case of emergency. Her arthritic hands have a difficult time with the buttons on her dress. Some days her fingers ache and swell so that she cannot fit them into the holes of the telephone dial. Her hands shake as she puts in her eyedrops for glaucoma. . . . She must take the bus to shop. The bus steps are very high and sometimes the driver objects when she tries to bring her little wheeled cart aboard. A small boy whom she has befriended and occasionally pays often waits for her at the bus stop to help her up. When she cannot bring her cart onto the bus or isn't helped up the steps, she must walk to the market. Then shopping takes the better part of the day and exhausts her. Her feet, thank God, give her less trouble since she figured out how to cut and sew a pair of cloth shoes so as to leave room for her callouses and bunions. . . .
>
> Managing means three things: taking care of herself, stretching her monthly pension of $320 to cover expenses, and filling her time in ways that have meaning for her. The first two are increasingly hard and she knows that they are battles she will eventually lose. But her free time does not weigh on her. She is never bored and rarely depressed.[18]

The task becomes both easier and harder if the couple is still intact and they can help each other manage. Even when illness or disability impairs one partner's functioning, the other will try to nurse the spouse or at least assist in carrying out his or her daily needs. At first, they may both believe that the impairing condition is temporary. In time, however, they come to realize that the ill spouse will not recover, and will in fact grow steadily worse. Sometimes the pace of the illness is very rapid; at other times it may stretch out for years, during which one mate gradually takes over the responsibilities of the other, makes decisions that formerly the other made or both of them made together, and nurses the other as he or she grows weaker and less competent.

Care of a chronically ill husband, particularly if a wife has her own health problems, is one of the most difficult tasks the wife has to face. However, when *she* becomes ill, her husband may have an even more difficult time, since he has to learn a whole new set of role-linked activities. Until now, the wife took care of him and provided for both his and her needs; now he has to care for both her and himself. He has to learn to shop for and cook an edible meal, make the beds and empty the bedpan, administer medication, and keep the house reasonably neat and clean. Traditionally oriented men, who previously had never shared household tasks, often feel uncomfortable and inept in taking on these functions. Other men, who have learned, often after retirement, to take on daily housekeeping chores, find it easier to enlarge their role repertoire at this time to include the care of an invalid wife.

Much of this giving and taking of care hinges on the couple's living arrangements and housing conditions. Since many older couples live on very limited budgets and find that their financial assets become depleted by time and inflationary pressures, they may find themselves tied to homes or apartments bought at an earlier stage in life. Even though these living quarters become too large and too old-fashioned and the neighborhood changes in composition and deteriorates in condition, they may be forced to remain where they are, since the house represents their only tangible asset and security hedge. In addition, they may be attached to it and to the neighborhood by many bonds of association and familiarity. Despite the inconvenience, loneliness, and even dangers, they may prefer to stay on in their old surroundings. If they have not made the physical move in an earlier stage, either when their last child left home or at the time of retirement, the chances are that they will now try to remain where they are until forced to make the change for health or external reasons.

Community planners recognize that the older poor tend to remain in the inner city long after the more affluent and mobile elements have abandoned it. They are apt to live in rented apartments in older, more dilapidated buildings, often partitioned off within older homes. They tend to become "block bound" and must rely on the other inhabitants of the area to support their needs. Services and facilities grow less accessible and may even cease to exist for the older resident. Minority elders, such as Asian-Americans, Latin-Americans, and blacks, live in even more inadequate housing than do other elements in the community, since their housing problems become compounded by racial discrimination and poverty.[19]

SEARCHING FOR ALTERNATIVES.   Although the large majority of older people may start late adulthood living in their own households, as their age and impairment increase, more and more are forced to leave their homes for alternate arrangements. Despite health facilities, social services, and other sources offered within the community, the increased loneliness, the decreased ability to move about freely and to care for themselves, and the threat of muggings and break-ins become powerful pressures that finally add up, in time, to the conclusion that a change is necessary. Sometimes a major life disruption such as a prolonged illness, a severe economic setback, or the death of a spouse signals an abrupt drop in a person's level of independence and thus becomes the precipitating event to bring about the change.[20]

At this point, the individual or couple may decide unilaterally to move, or may be urged into it by their children, sisters or brothers, or other family members. They may discuss the proposed change with friends, neighbors, clergymen, physicians, or even lawyers. Family service agencies; family or aged departments of public welfare offices; and social service departments of medical, psychiatric, and geriatric facilities are frequently called in at this point. If the elderly person is unable or unwilling to make the decision, others may have to decide for him. Often the family becomes the crucial element in this decision-making process.[21]

To digress briefly, at this point in the family life cycle (if not before) the relationship between elderly parents and their adult, middle-aged children shifts its balance. At one time this was described (and still is, to a certain extent) as "role reversal" and "parenting one's parents." Margaret Blenkner finds this to be a physical and psychological impossibility and offers instead the concept of "filial maturity" as a developmental task that takes place when the individual is in his forties or fifties and the "parents can no longer be looked to as a rock of support in times of emotional trouble or economic stress but may themselves need their offspring's comfort and support."[22]
Ideally, the shift in the balance of the filial-parental bond should be resolved as a normal developmental task rather than in the crucible of an acute crisis. On the other hand, it may take the pressures of a crisis-linked disequilibrium for children to be able to deal openly with their needs, rights, and responsibilities. Such an event may also provide them with the opportunity to settle unfinished accounts among themselves in terms of past givings and takings, parental favoritism, and earlier coalitions that were part of the family history. Charlotte Kirschner points out that communication processes and patterns that helped maintain family equilibrium in the past become dysfunctional at this time. When aging parent(s) need help, the adult children are drawn back again into the family constellation. Previous accomodations, such as distancing, that were worked out over the years, now become threatened by the pressures of the family crisis.[23]

MAKING THE CHANGE

As with other transitions, the need to make a change in living arrangements calls for a chain of decision-making steps, during which various alternatives need to be weighed[24] and a series of material-arrangemental and psychosocial tasks carried out. (Much of this process is a special variation of the transitional process of moving discussed in Chapter 7):

1. *Making the Decision* as to whether the elderly person can continue to remain in, or return to, his current living situation. As already discussed, this can be a very difficult step for the aging person to make, since so many of his memories and associations of the "good old days" are tied up in the physical attributes of *his* home, *his* garden, *his* street, and *his* neighborhood. Even isolated individuals who have withdrawn from active involvement with neighbors and friends still cling to peripheral contacts like the

postman, the newsboy, and the janitor who cleans the stairs. Thus the first question to be asked is: must this move be made?

Sometimes it is possible for the elderly person to remain in his home if appropriate support systems can be built into the situation, as in the case of Mrs. Kowalski reported above. For example, a younger relative or friend might be invited in to share the dwelling. A housekeeper can be provided who could double as nurse if need be. Neighbors may be asked to take on some of the household chores and/or provide daily contact. If none of these informal arrangements are possible or sufficient, community-based services offered by medical and social agencies may be utilized. These range from such services as "Meals on Wheels" or occasional home help to periodic visits by a medical team and intensive crisis intervention when needed.[25]

If this type of arrangement maintains the situation, even for a limited period of time, then no further action is called for.[26] However, if for some reason such an arrangement is not functional, then the search for alternatives continues.

2. *Investigating Other Living Arrangements.* Here the need is first to list and then to examine all possible options. These may include (a) *moving in with one of the elderly person's children and that child's family,* either into the home itself or into some type of semi-detached arrangement such as an added extra room, a finished-off upper story, or a lower-floor playroom made over into a small apartment which would permit some privacy for both parties while providing direct contact. Even renting a room or apartment in close proximity to children or other family members permits ongoing interaction. Shanas points out that even when parents and adult children do not share the same household, they remain in close, direct touch, with the majority of old people living either with a child or within a half-hour of him.[27]

Although the role of grandparent is not a new one to the elderly person, it takes on new significance at this stage when he or she comes to live within or near the family. While the elderly person can probably no longer take an active role in household management or take care of the grandchildren or great-grandchildren, he can provide them with a sense of continuity and historicity that becomes very important, particularly for the youngest generation.[28] The reminiscences or "old wives' tales" that children have grown tired of over the years take on a new sharpness when grandchildren ask their aging grandparent, "What was it like when you were young?" Not only does this give the youngsters a developmental perspective and a sense of roots, but it offers the elderly person the opportunity to review his life's accomplishments and begin the task of ego integration that becomes vital in the final life stage.[29]

If living with family is not feasible, the next option (b) is to investigate *living with nonrelated persons in a private type of arrangement.* Options might range from renting a room with a private family to living in a regular rooming house to banding together with friends in some joint living arrangement.[30] It would have to be weighed, however, whether such a plan, which might be possible for the "young old," would still be practicable for the person in the "old old" stage, when physical and psychological impairments limit adaptability.

A third alternative would be (c) to consider *various types of institutions*. In contrast to other forms of living arrangements for the elderly, the institution stands outside of the general patterns of social life in a community. Although its residents are physically located there, they are not usually part of it. Jordan Kosberg points out that institutions for the aging may range from *residences* (homes for the aged), *nursing homes*, and *convalescent homes* to *geriatric hospitals* and *psychiatric facilities*.[31] They vary widely in the level of care offered, physical facilities, and professional services available. Enforcement of minimal standards, even after the advent of medical reimbursement programs which call for some supervision, may also differ considerably.[32]

Shanas finds that old people in the United States seem generally opposed to institutional living and continue to associate it with the poorhouse, senility, and physical decline. (Periodic exposés on TV of institutional abuse of the aged reinforce this image.) Whether the person is well or ill, the *idea* of institutionalization usually is disliked and rejected by the elderly, and at best tolerated by their children. Thus it often becomes the "least worst solution," chosen as a last resort when other alternatives can no longer work.[33] Similarly, the decision to hospitalize in a psychiatric facility is often used to solve problems of maintenance rather than to carry out treatment measures.[34]

Within the last few years, however, the image of the institution is changing, with the advent of a new type of sophisticated facility for the aged which offers a broad continuum of services from hotel-like units for healthy older individuals and couples through graduated levels of nursing care and services up to hospital-like arrangements for the extensively impaired and terminally ill. Often these develop into extensive complexes, financed and operated by benevolent or religious organizations, by private investors or insurance firms, or as a part of social services or medical programs.[35]

3. *Making a Choice and Carrying It Through.*   The decision to make the change involves the weighing of alternatives, the arriving at a conclusion, and then the implementation. This may entail agreement by the aged person, the family, and the other parties concerned. (Or, in the case of a deteriorated or senile individual, it may require taking legal action.) The process itself may be stretched out over some years as one type of living arrangement after another is tried and monitored. It may include, in the case of institutional placement, the filling out of complicated forms, being interviewed by social workers and medical personnel, making a series of visits, and waiting until one's turn on a waiting list is reached.

It also means a period of preparing to make the move, including the sorting out of cherished possessions in order to decide which to take along and which to discard.[36] To many this becomes part of the mourning ritual, the grieving over giving up one's home, and is a vital step in the transitional process. Leafing through an old picture album or sorting out a trunk of old-fashioned clothes becomes a review of significant milestones in one's past life. The transition also involves visiting neighborhood landmarks and saying good-bye to old friends and neighbors, who probably will not be seen again.

4. *Becoming Inducted into the New Setting.*   If the move is from one's own home to one's children's, this may involve no more than moving in one's belongings and unpacking one's luggage. With other types of arrangements, much more may be required: learning where one's room is in connection with the rest of the building, getting to know staff members and other residents, learning the customs and rules of the setting, and establishing a rapport with other residents in such matters as what television programs are listened to and who sits where in the dining room.

In the case of some aged persons who have never lived outside of their own homes, this disruption in their life pattern may call for a large number of adjustments. For example, one couple who moved into a residential home for the aged became extremely upset upon learning that the main meal was served at noon rather than in the evening, when they were accustomed to having it. For others, the lack of privacy or the timing of bath arrangements may become the crucial issue. Caroline Ford reports that the elderly person feels a certain degree of stigma or loss of status when he enters even the best of group residences. Despite the most considerate and thoughtful arrangements in group living, the person experiences a loss of privacy and freedom and resents the necessity to conform to institutional rules. Other initial signs of stress are fear and anxiety, confusion and immobility, hostility and intense rage.[37]

5. *Going Through a Period of Adjustment and Habituation.*   This is the final phase in the transition and lasts until the person becomes fully integrated into the new setting and no longer feels strange in it. The extent and rapidity of this adjustment are, of course, very much a function of the person's age, health condition, degree of activity or disengagement, and long-term personality patterns. Individuals living in group residences for the aged tend to develop a variety of defense mechanisms to deal with their being there.[38] A frequent one is that of *denial* ("I don't see what I'm doing here with these old people"), particularly of their impaired physical stamina. At this stage in life, Ford sees this defense as protective and supportive, revealing a quality of undaunted strength that commands respect.

Sometimes the person may use *regression* to an infantile level of dependency, making excessive demands for help despite lack of evidence of the incapacities he claims to have. He may ask to be fed or bathed or helped in walking; he may insist on a wheelchair, become incontinent, or cling to anyone who is nearby. Others resort to *physical flight*, trying to cope with their painful situation by running away. This may come out as an unplanned impulse in plain view of others, or be planned and executed at a time when staff members are elsewhere. The runaway may wear adequate outdoor clothing and have a specific objective in mind, such as his former home, or he may just wander out aimlessly in his nightclothes, without any particular objective or desire to escape from the home.

Still another device is *withdrawal* from others. The person may simply retreat from the social life about him, appear listless and passive, and display reduced emotional energy in all of his relationships. He may remain quiet and undemanding, staying in his room most of the day and interacting only minimally with the rest of the residents. Or he may engage in excessive sleeping or resting in bed as a form of withdrawal. Ford sees such instances as essentially ego-protective, since the individual is able to make a fair adaptation and to maintain some degree of self-esteem without any evident rise in anxiety.

Sometimes a resident uses *manipulation* to help him adjust and to gain his ends. He may cry, threaten, sulk, or pout. His sinking spells, fainting, agitated telephone calls to his family, or frantic ringing for the nurses can be viewed as a means of attempting to influence and change the facility's rules or the staff's behavior toward him. His goal becomes to increase his control over his own life and, as such, his behavior becomes a relatively healthy defense mechanism, despite the disturbance and anger it causes others.

Finally, some residents see the aging process as a challenge which they approach with vigor and even enthusiasm. To them, the best defense is a good offense and they rally their forces by *integration* and *sublimation*. They channel their energies into activities and accomplishments, showing great determination to overcome physical handicaps and find new kinds of satisfactions within the realistic restrictions of their new environment. Not only do they accept their own handicaps, but they sublimate their anxieties by reaching out to others with warmth, support, and humor.

In the case example summarized below we see how an aging couple dealt with the increasing mental deterioration of the wife, which threatened to force placement, and the various steps in the decision regarding placement. It is reported by a social worker in the psychiatric unit of a large general hospital:

FRANK AND LENA KRAUS (#173)

Mrs. Kraus, age 78, was admitted to the psychiatric ward of St. Mark's Hospital after she had been brought to the Emergency Room by her 75-year-old husband the night before. When I saw them the next morning, he told me that she had been growing increasingly confused and tended to wander off by herself and then be unable to find her way back. Last week she had walked into a neighbor's house and insisted it was her own. Mr. Kraus was afraid to leave her at home alone. (He still works full-time at the nearby airfield as an airplane mechanic.) He is a tall, spare, vigorous man, looking much younger than his age. Mrs. Kraus appeared quite dazed and frightened as she sat next to him, clinging to his hand. However, when I asked if she knew where she was, she straightened up and said haughtily that of course she knew; this was the County General Hospital and she was a surgical nurse who worked here. She identified Mr. Kraus as her father and said that she herself was 54 years old.

Background Information. Mr. Kraus said they have lived here for the past forty years. They met at a USO party when he served on the technical crew at the air force base. She had been a registered nurse at the base hospital and continued to work throughout their married life, since they had no children. She served as chief nursing supervisor at one of the other city hospitals for over twenty years, and was highly respected and successful in her professional life. Even after she retired, fifteen years ago, she continued to take on private-duty cases on occasion.

For about the last five years, she had tended to withdraw more and more, spending most of her time puttering about the house and watching TV. During the past year her memory began to fail, and at times she would become disorientated both as to time and place. She would call her husband by her father's name, and some evenings would insist she'd have to go to work on the night shift at the hospital. Mr. Kraus felt that the process was accelerating; she was no longer able to do many household tasks and could not operate the washing machine or vacuum cleaner. She no longer remembered her favorite recipes and at times would start cooking and then forget; twice he came home to find food burning on the stove and the kitchen filled with smoke.

Mr. Kraus saw himself faced with the choice of resigning from his job at the airfield—from which he derives much satisfaction—in order to stay at home to take care of his wife or arranging to place her in a nursing home or other facility.

Treatment Plan. At the staffing held on Mrs. Kraus, it was agreed that she was showing the beginning of a senility process with possibly some organic damage. She would be placed on medication and referred to an activities and occupational therapy program. Meanwhile I would work with her and her husband on developing a plan for future living under some type of supervision.

Treatment. I saw Mrs. Kraus six times individually on the ward over the next ten days. Her episodes of confusion and slipping back into the past did not occur at all during our sessions together. She spent much of the time reminiscing coherently about the past and her professional life as a nurse. Several times, she cried because she and her husband had not been able to have children; she felt that would have added to their married life. I also saw the Krauses together twice, and they talked about their life and how they had cared for each other over the years. Much of the time was spent recalling past events, but during the second interview they began to look at what they still had and could enjoy together. She acknowledged that she felt a burden to him since his functioning was not as hampered by the effects of old age as hers had become.

Mrs. Kraus responded well to the total team effort. The medication prescribed reduced her confusion and brought her more in contact with the world around her. Occupational therapy reawakened her interest in handicrafts, at which she had always been skilled, and she took pride in several of her "projects" that were put on display.

Meanwhile, Mr. Kraus and I were investigating other choices open to them as an alternative to placing her in a nursing home, such as his reducing his working hours and using community resources to provide his wife with some activities and to supervise management of the household. We also considered their extended family, and Mr. Kraus reported that both his widowed sister in town and another who lived in an adjoining state would be willing to spend time at home with Mrs. Kraus.

A plan was put together by which her sisters-in-law would either come to stay with her or would check in with her daily. Arrangements were made for a visiting nurse to provide supportive supervision of her medication and general health condition twice a week. The Coalition for the Aging, a community-based service organization, agreed to arrange for daily phone contacts and regular visits by the volunteer outreach workers. They would also try to involve Mr. and Mrs. Kraus in a social group for senior citizens at a nearby community center. Meanwhile, Dr. Cole, the hospital psychiatrist, would continue to follow her progress and prescribe medication as needed. As the social worker on the case, I would be available to both Mr. and Mrs. Kraus if they requested it or if some change occurred in the ongoing situation.

After ten days, Mrs. Kraus's confusion had cleared up and she seemed quite reality-oriented. The treatment team agreed that she had derived maximum benefits from her hospital stay, and she was discharged from the psychiatric unit. Although the consensus of the group was that an organic process of increasing deterioration was involved and that her remission would not continue indefinitely, it was felt that under the proposed plan she could continue to remain in the community for some time. The Krauses felt that their immediate problems had been resolved and returned home, happy to be together once more.

Death of a Spouse and Survival of the Mate

The topic of death and dying has been written about so extensively and discussed so frequently in conferences and workshops over the past fifteen years that it seems anticlimatic to raise the issue here.[39] However, we are concerned at this point with one particular aspect of the multifaceted question: that of death as the final stage of life, as the last of the developmental transitions which the individual or his spouse undergoes in the life cycle. The stance taken by Elisabeth Kübler-Ross, probably the person who has made the greatest contribution in recent years to the open discussion of death as a vital life issue, exemplifies this approach.[40]

The death of an aged person is similar in many aspects to death at any age. However, there are also important differences. The process will be examined here from the dual perspective of the elderly person who is about to die and that of his spouse who witnesses the dying. Although in this section I shall use the term "spouse" or "mate," it should be understood that this could equally apply to a cherished friend, a sibling, or adult children. What is important is understanding that dying is a significant transition of leave-taking, not only for the person involved but for those who are close to him and are part of the process. Once more we can differentiate three phases: *the anticipatory period, the dying process itself,* and *death and its aftermath.*

THE ANTICIPATORY PERIOD

THE INDIVIDUAL.   An individual begins to become aware of death early in his life span and may have even, in the course of his years, been brushed unexpectedly by death or by the experience of having someone close to him die. Still, the issue probably does not assume practical significance until he recognizes, or has been told, that he himself will soon die.

As mentioned earlier, the aging person approaching the end of his life span has developed a number of chronic illnesses and conditions, which, he recognizes, may eventually result in his own death. Indeed, his pain and discomfort may be so great that at times he wishes for an end to his torment. In addition, since he has already experienced the loss of many relatives, friends, and possibly his spouse, he may be feeling the desolation of loneliness and even be waiting to join them in afterlife.

The difficulty of telling terminal patients, particularly those who are very old, that they are approaching death or that death is inevitable is a many-pronged issue that has been discussed extensively.[41] Often the physician who is responsible for imparting the information has a "let him die in peace" attitude and not only refuses to tell a patient his terminal diagnosis but prohibits other staff members from doing so.* Nevertheless, most patients probably have suspected their condition for some time and have picked up a number of direct and indirect clues from the responses of their family and the medical staff. These sources may include direct statements from the physician or other personnel; overheard comments by staff or hospital workers; remarks by family, friends, clergy, and lawyers; changes in the behavior of others toward the patient; changes in the medical-care procedures or medication; changes in physical location; signals from the person's own body and changes in physical status; and altered responses by others when the subject of the future comes up.[42]

Kübler-Ross has found that in general, terminally ill persons, when told of their impending death, usually experience an initial shock and numbness. They then tend to pass through the five discernable stages which have already been mentioned in Chapter 10: denial, anger, bargaining, depression, and acceptance. However, in the case of the elderly, it is doubtful that they experience the same reactions to the same extent or in the same order.

---

*I prefer to dodge, at this point, the broad issue of "who tells whom what and when" about the impending death, since I see this primarily as a professional-ethical question not directly relevant to this discussion.

It has been stressed that there probably is as wide a variation in death-style as there is in life-style.

In one study of elderly, noninstitutionalized persons, it was found that they expressed less angry protest or rage at the thought of dying and exhibited less fear of death itself than did younger persons. Most viewed death as preferable to continued illness or chronic disability and even looked forward to it as timely and welcome. Many adapted to the news of their approaching death by utilizing coping patterns that they had developed at previous times of change and crisis in their lives. Some turned backward to review their past achievements and shared their reminiscences with children and grandchildren. For others, their belief in life after death and their religious faith served as a shield against the fear of death. Still others, on a more practical note, began to make detailed arrangements for their funerals, paid up past bills, made wills, and signed property over to their children.[43]

Defense mechanisms tended to be used in clusters. *Denial,* for example, was difficult for the aged to maintain in the face of their own decreasing capacities. Some, however, did block out for a time the signs of the approaching end by utilizing the defenses of *suppression, rationalization,* and *externalization* to exclude the information from their awareness.

Others tended to retreat from the source of anxiety by using *regression, withdrawal, disengagement,* or even *surrender* through suicide, both actual or attempted. (A relatively frequent phenomenon in old age has been called *occult* or *slow suicide,* during which the person becomes clinically depressed, loses his appetite, and experiences lowered vitality, sometimes even literally willing himself to death, as has been noted in hospitals and homes for the aged.) Others in the study escaped through the use of alcohol or drugs, or withdrew into hypochondriacal preoccupation with their bodies.

A third cluster of reactions emphasized attempts at mastery and resolution. These included defenses such as *intellectualization, counterphobic mechanisms, hyperactivity, sublimation,* and *acceptance.* In this connection, some used the opportunity to engage in an abbreviated *life review,* during which they recalled some of the major events and relationships in their past life.[44] Such a review is part of the way in which the aged utilize the final stage of living to work through the Eriksonian issue of integrity (integration) versus despair.

THE SPOUSE.   The spouse and adult children may have been living with the elderly person's failing health for some time. Finally, when ominous symptoms accumulate or when a sudden collapse precipitates hospitalization, they join in waiting for the diagnosis and prognosis with mixed emotions. Physicians will often discuss the diagnosis of approaching death with family members prior to (or instead of) telling the dying person himself and often decide together whether the person should be told. The doctor may also enlist the family's help in working out an appropriate medical regimen.

In addition to dealing with the patient's situation, the spouse has to begin his or her own process of anticipatory grieving. As already has been mentioned in the discussion on widowhood, Kübler-Ross finds that family members pass through stages of adjustment similar to those which patients pass through.[45] At first, many of them refuse to believe the diagnosis. ("But I was the sick one all these years. Why should he be the first to go?") They may go through the phase of anger—both at the previous doctor, who did not discover the illness, and the present doctor, who has confronted them with the sad reality. They may project their resentment onto hospital or nursing home personnel for not caring enough or not treating the patient properly, as well as express their own guilt for not having done enough. Finally, when anger, depression, and guilt have been worked through, the family gradually comes face to face with the reality of the impending separation.

The lingering death of the very old can often be particularly tragic from the family's point of view. Many elderly persons become physically and emotionally disabled and require large sums of money simply to be maintained at the level of dignity and comfort their family desires for them. This often means mobilizing all available funds, including loans, savings, and retirement funds, to pay for final care even though the end result, says Kübler-Ross, is still only maintenance at a minimal level. Should complications occur, expenses tend to skyrocket. The pressure faced by the family is compounded by their guilt and the wish they dare not express—that the person die quickly and painlessly.

THE PROCESS OF DYING

THE INDIVIDUAL.   The onset of the terminal phase of "living-dying," E. Mansell Pattison points out, is not precise, although it can be said to start when the dying person begins to withdraw into himself in response to internal body signals that tell him he must now conserve his energies.[46] He loses interest in food, activities, and friends and expresses the desire just to be left alone in peace and quiet.

As he grows weaker, the person may want to see his relatives for one last time to say good-bye; then his children, to give them the last of his most valued keepsakes and his verbal "legacy"; and finally he may ask to be left with his spouse to await the inevitable. He also may be paid a last visit by his religious preceptor (priest, rabbi, minister), although he may be too ill to respond to the words of comfort.

Most older persons, if conscious at the time of death, tend to accept the passage from life to death with relief and even with anticipation. If they have completed their leave-takings and have come to terms with the inevitability of their own demise, they may express the feeling that they are glad to go.

THE SPOUSE.   Once family members have, each in their own way, managed to communicate openly with the dying person, and once they have all finished their transactions together, they can approach the terminal phase with sorrowful resignation.[47] The last days and hours can become a very meaningful experience, particularly for the elderly spouse who sees this as the end to the dying person's suffering. If the husband and wife are bound by a common religious faith, they can express their confidence that they will rejoin each other soon.

Death of a mate in the final years of late adulthood tends to be less painful and spouses seem more resigned than when death occurs at an earlier stage of development. Kosberg finds that the death of a geriatric patient may not, in many cases, be disruptive to the family.[48] Instead, it can be considered a relief, since the heavy financial burden of institutional care is ended, guilt over placing the elderly person becomes resolved, and the trouble caused by periodic visits or the guilt over not having visited enough is assuaged. Nonetheless, grief is real and genuine and may be too often dismissed as nonexistent.

Much of the discussion on the terminal care of dying older persons has centered around the "how to die with dignity" issue. Recent developments in the care of the dying patient have produced such programs as the SHANTI Project, which provides psychosocial support to the patient and the families who face life-threatening illnesses,[49] and the hospice movement, imported from England, where St. Christopher's Hospice has become world-famous for its palliative care of the dying patient.[50] While the structure of service and auspices may vary, these programs share the common goal of keeping the patient pain-free, comfortable, and fully alert during the final phases of the dying process. In the hospice program, professionals and volunteers combine to help the patient deal with his terminal *physical pain*, through the optimal use of analgesics; with his *psychological pain*, by helping to alleviate the overall upset, depression, and anxiety which are seen as normal reactions to approaching dying and death; with this *social pain*, by aiding him in coping with the level and intensity of his interpersonal relations; and with his *spiritual pain*, in terms of his specific religious, racial, or cultural background and belief systems. Variations of these programs have sprung up in the last ten years throughout the United States and Canada and are spreading rapidly to other countries, many of them located as units within or attached to general or geriatric hospitals.

DEATH AND ITS AFTERMATH

THE INDIVIDUAL.   With the spreading use of sophisticated machines designed to support physical survival, the point of actual death is being increasingly debated. Without entering into the controversy as to when, how, and for how long such machinery should be employed, we should differentiate among the four basic kinds of death:[51]

1. *Sociological death.* Withdrawal and separation from the patient by others may occur days or weeks before actual death; the person is treated as

if he or she were already dead. Some families desert the aged in nursing homes where they may continue to linger on for some time. For such families, the patient no longer is considered part of the family.

2. *Psychic death.* The person accepts his death and regresses into himself in the final pre-death phase. Ordinarily this is accompanied by the physical manifestations of dying, although in some instances he may withdraw, "turn his face to the wall," and simply refuse to go on living before his body is ready to stop functioning. This is sometimes seen in the first period after institutionalization.

3. *Biological death.* The organism as a human entity no longer exists. There is neither consciousness nor awareness, as in the case of irreversible coma. Heart and lungs may continue to function with artificial support, but the biological organism as a self-sustaining mind–body is dead.

4. *Physiological death.* At this point, vital organs such as lungs, heart, and brain no longer function and the person is considered clinically dead. The "bleeps" on the monitor attached to the machines have flattened out and no longer show signs of organ-functioning.

Pattison points out that when these four types of death do not coincide, ethical and personal confusion results. As noted above, a person might be sociologically dead long before his vital signs have stopped. On the other hand, when he suddenly deteriorates and dies before his expected time, biological and physiological death occur before social and emotional preparation for death has a chance to take place. Finally, if both psychic and biological death have occurred but the patient is kept alive artificially, this may become a source of agony and even legal controversy for the family.

THE SPOUSE.   Since the bereavement process has already been discussed in Chapter 10, we shall not repeat this aspect of the death-and-survival transition here. At this stage, since both the aged dead person and the surviving mate had already given up many of their social roles over the previous years, post-death adjustment may not be as difficult as at an earlier stage. The critical issue for many elderly widowed persons is loneliness, despite family and friends' efforts to provide support and companionship.[52]

Women who have lost their husbands in their later years are likely to find a large community of other widows in the same situation, so that they can, in time, find friends and neighbors with whom to relate. Others immerse themselves in their children's and grandchildren's lives, not always to their family's appreciation. While those in the young old-age bracket can adapt to the death of a spouse with relatively little difficulty,[53] and even remarry,[54] as they pass through their own final years their sense of detachment and growing physical incapacity leads to gradual disengagement as they withdraw into their own private world of memories and associations of their former life with their mate.

The following brief case vignette illustrates how an elderly couple dealt with the final illness of the wife. The wife went from a hospital back to their own home and then into a geriatric facility, where she died. The case was reported by the social worker in a family agency which does intake and screening for a sectarian home for the aged:

BESSIE AND BERT ADLER (#177)

Bessie Adler, 85 years old, was seen at the Bay Hospital on the geriatric ward. Her husband, Bert, age 87, their son Richard, age 58, and their daughter Helen, age 61, had requested help sometime previously in evaluating and managing the parents' difficult situation, but it was not until this hospitalization that they decided that Mrs. Adler could no longer receive adequate care and requested her admission to the Jewish Home for the Aged.

Background Information. The Adlers were a very close couple who had owned and operated a small grocery store for over fifty years. Upon retirement, they spent their time together, living in their modest apartment and sharing their hobbies and interests. They had been fiercely proud of their ability to manage independently, never asking for financial or other help from their five children or anyone else.

Ten years previously, Mrs. Adler had undergone a colostomy. She had managed fairly well at home, however, until a year previously, when her health began to deteriorate rapidly, resulting in frequent hospitalizations for weakness, fainting spells, and malnutrition. Most recently her arms and legs had begun to swell considerably. As she grew weaker, her husband took over most of the household management tasks as well as caring for his bedridden wife, despite his own physical limitation of having an implanted pacemaker. Several months ago, the agency introduced a home health aide to relieve Mr. Adler of some of the nursing and cleaning chores.

Since Mrs. Adler seemed depressed and was reported not to be eating regularly, it was decided to investigate nursing-care facilities. The two children living in town, as well as the three living in other parts of the country, had suggested at various times that their parents come to live with them. The oldest daughter offered to convert the second floor of her large home into a self-contained apartment for the parents, since her own married children were living out of town. In view of Mrs. Adler's serious deterioration in health, this did not appear to be an appropriate plan, and it was agreed that they would apply for her admission to the Home.

Attempt was made to involve Mrs. Adler in the discussion, but she tended to deny the seriousness of her health condition and the amount of attention she needed. She was resigned to the fact that she "might" need nursing-home care but was quite unrealistic in admitting the amount of skilled nursing required. Instead she felt angry with her husband for suggesting that he "leave her," although even this was not expressed directly.

Mr. Adler, on the other hand, had come to realize that he was no longer physically able to care for his wife at home, despite the difficult separation anxiety that this evoked in him. As for himself, he said he would like to remain as long as possible in their own apartment, which was an easy bus ride from the Home. We agreed to continue to provide a home health aide twice a week to help him maintain himself there.

The Adlers's children, who appeared to be devoted and concerned about their parents' situation, initially expressed considerable guilt over not having insisted that they move into one of their homes earlier. At the same time, they felt proud of their parents' determination to remain independent as long as possible. The application forms were filled out in due time and sent, with the agency's report and recommendation, to the Home. Although the wait for admission often lasted for a year or more, Mrs. Adler was able to enter the facility within two months after the application.

During the waiting interval, the Adlers spent much of their time sitting on their back porch, enjoying the view of the park below and the lake in the distance. Mrs. Adler seemed to be deteriorating rapidly, and, when admitted, was taken directly to the intensive-care floor. Two months later, her husband informed us that she had died quietly in her sleep after having lapsed into a coma a week earlier.

Dr. Kübler-Ross tells of becoming very concerned over the implications of her teachings when she heard two nurses express their worry that a dying patient in their charge was going so fast he "wouldn't have time to go through all the stages before he died." In the same spirit of concern, we can only hope that practitioners do not see the material in Part II as literal prescriptions for the way transitions have to go. The point is made once more that each person's transitions are unique unto himself and are part of his total life pattern. We have merely tried here to indicate some of the common threads which become woven into these bridging periods. The extent to which they apply in a particular instance is a matter of individual assessment.

At this point we turn to the application of this approach in professional practice.

PART III

Intervention at Times of Transition

It is time to draw the strands of our discussion together. Initially we spoke of the need to help people caught in transitional situations. Then we defined our terms and presented some of the theories and conceptualizations in this area. Next we presented a series of developmental and psychosocial bridging intervals in the adult life cycle and tried to sketch out the various phases in each process which must be passed through in order to return to stable functioning, as well as the tasks which must be carried out in order to effect such change. What remains is to try to define at which point intervention is called for, what forms such intervention can take, and what the purpose, goals, and tasks of intervention would be.

When we speak of "intervention" or "treatment" at times of transition, we bring up a paradox. If we are referring to the "normal problems of normal people," the expectable concomitants of change in human living experienced by many, if not most, of us, why should professional help be needed? The answer has to do with the timing, with the echoing effects of change during transitions, and with the acute nature of the crises which sometimes punctuate the process.

As indicated in Chapter 1, a major part of the social service activities in such settings as family agencies, marriage and family counseling centers, physical and mental health clinics and hospitals, and private practice deal with persons passing through transitional phases of their lives. Some of the changes may be anticipated, but the individuals and families are still unable to carry them out without support and guidance. In other instances, the difficulties encountered trigger off acute, unanticipated crisis situations which demand immediate intervention. And sometimes, individuals make changes which turn out to be inappropriate, debilitating, or maladaptive; only later do they come to the attention of the professional community as disturbed, deviant, or seriously malfunctioning persons.

In this section we shall look at this interventive process during periods of transition. In Chapter 13 we shall consider the sources and forms of help which people need and seek. Then, in Chapter 14, we shall consider the nature of the problems which may arise, the appropriate goals toward which intervention can be directed, and strategies by which these goals can be met.

Because of the preliminary state of conceptualization in this area, no definitive treatment model can be offered; instead we shall simply suggest some guidelines which, on the basis of practice reported, seem to lead to constructive forms of intervention.

13

Sources and Forms of Help During Transitions

THE POINT HAS BEEN MADE several times that not every transitional state is, by definition, problematic.[1] Most individuals can pass through these periods of change with enough inner strength and/or outer support to weather uncertainty or disruption. Parkes, whose views are discussed in Chapter 2, reminds us that our life space is constantly changing. Some of these changes fulfill our expectations and require little or no change in our assumptive world; others necessitate a major restructuring in our feelings, thoughts, and behavior, including the abandonment of one set of assumptions and the development of a new set to enable us to cope with our new, altered life situations.[2]

A series of key questions can act as indicators to determine whether difficulties have arisen or will arise in the predictable future. Was the transition expected or unexpected? Was sufficient time allowed to prepare for and anticipate the changes which occur? How much change is needed and in what areas? Does the person possess the competence to carry out the changes on his own? At what point in the bridging period did his coping ability falter or break down? And—most important—what happens to the transitional process at this point: is it still continuing at a reduced pace, is it foundering, or has it stopped completely?

Both Neugarten and Parkes, it should be recalled, emphasize that if change takes place gradually, the chances are that the transitional process will be carried out without perceptible disruption. On the other hand, if the

241

transition is unexpected and abrupt, with no time or opportunity for advance preparation, it is more likely to bring about a major upheaval in personal and family living.

The time may come when the changes which have occurred or are occurring can no longer be ignored or denied; when the need to effect change, both internally and in relation to other persons and situations in the person's life space, demands urgent attention. To whom does the adult turn to for help? Since only a certain proportion of such situations come to the attention of professionals, a good starting point might be to look at the entire continuum of potential sources of help from the perspective of the "helpee," the person in trouble.

Over twenty years ago, when Gerald Gurin, Joseph Veroff, and Sheila Feld carried out their monumental study of mental health needs in the United States, one of their most interesting findings was that most people tended to rely upon their own inner resources to face their problems. When they did ask for help, it was usually informal, expedient, and temporary.[3] These observations, confirmed in several in-depth studies of how services for emotionally distressed persons were being offered in various communities, led to the suggestion that more needs to be learned about the makeup and ways of giving and taking help.

Since then, a number of researchers have attempted to plot the sources of help available to a person in need or in distress.[4] The following continuum is an amalgam of several versions of these compilations of resources:[5]

Self	Natural Help System: family, friends, neighbors	Mutual Help System: informal and formal	Nonprofessional Support System: voluntary organizations, community caregivers, paraprofessionals	Professional* Help System

*The use of the term "professional" is ambiguous. It is not intended to imply any hierarchy of values or to denigrate the level of preparation or skills of other helping occupations. Rather it is used here simply to identify those persons whose special training and discipline designate them as qualified to help troubled individuals and families with their psychological and/or social problems in living. These persons are given community or institutional sanction to practice in this area through licensing, certification, or other means. The term "mental health practitioner" is, to my mind, too limiting, while "human services worker" is too encompassing.

In examining these sources to see what each can offer to pressured persons during times of transitional change, we should note at the outset that rarely just one form of help is used. What we usually find is a weaving back and forth, an intricate combination of asking for and getting aid that merges into a pattern of multiple needs (or multiple aspects of the same need) attended to by various sources within a community.

The Self

The "use of self" is a standard social work term, yet professionals tend to pay insufficient attention to the natural processes by which a person faced with a problem analyzes the situation, examines what needs to be done to change it, and then calls upon his own resources to accomplish the task. Since much of this type of coping behavior is learned at an early age, it becomes in time habitual, and only when complications develop or when changes in life events call for a change in adaptation is the use of self brought to conscious awareness. (The discussion on adaptation, mastery, and coping in Chapter 2 is relevant at this point.)

Of course, this form of help is the basis for the problem-solving process. Perlman made the point almost twenty-five years ago when she stressed that only the exercise of a person's own powers in problem solving develops self-direction and self-dependence.[6] Somewhat later, Genevieve Oxley emphasized the part that successful action or "active experience" plays in the normal development of the individual's self-esteem and self-worth.[7] Most recently, Anthony Maluccio has recognized that the natural life histories of human beings reflect their varied and creative efforts to develop competence in dealing with environmental challenges.[8]

The use of self as helper during transitions receives ample verification in the numerous self-help and autobiographical accounts written from this viewpoint.[9] The fortitude and initiative that emanate from records of how individuals have learned to cope with the tangled balls of old and new problems that emerge during these bridging periods is impressive. Caine, for example, offers a "survival kit" for widowed mothers struggling alone to deal with their growing children's inevitable problems.[10]

Several years ago, when carrying out a pilot study on how young Israeli couples passed through the transition of getting married, we were struck by the fact that 43 percent of the time they said they tended to rely on themselves to solve their problems. A frequent answer to our question was, "Sure, we had problems [in a particular area], but we sat down and talked it over and decided we could handle it between us."[11]

The Natural Help System

But what if people can't help themselves? The next step, probably, would be to turn to what Caplan has called the *kith and kin system*, which includes not only the immediate and extended family but friends, acquaintances, and neighbors; and to the *informal caregivers*, the "generalists" known in the neighborhood for their overall wisdom and knowledge of the system, and the "specialists" who have suffered misfortunes in the past and have worked out ways to adjust successfully.[12] I would suspect this to be the foremost source to which persons in transitional difficulties turn. Sitting at a kitchen table over ten o'clock cups of coffee and exchanging experiences while waiting in a supermarket checkout line are prevalent, easily accessible, and nonstigmatizing means of giving and taking help.

FAMILY

The family itself probably ranks first among natural support systems. Alice Collins and Diane Pancoast point out that people see relatives as a primary source of help during crises.[13] Even if they don't live close by, calls for help can be relayed by telephone to distant points in minutes, while airplanes can convey sisters and maiden aunts across the country in less than a day, should the need arise.

Caplan finds that the family carries out its help-giving function in a number of ways: it acts as a collector and disseminator of information about the world, provides a feedback and guidance system through reporting and monitoring, and instills beliefs, values, and codes of behavior to give the person a cognitive map and a compass to find his way.[14] During acute and transitional crises, the family offers concrete guidance, not only telling the person how to find external sources of assistance but actually helping him make arrangements and even accompanying him as he does so. Over the years, most families develop a list of dependable community professional and nonprofessional caregivers and build up a network to whom they can turn when a family member is in need.

Living as part of a family helps individuals to expect and accept a series of inevitable personal role changes, while the family group actively helps its members to deal with their cognitive and emotional upsets during periods of role transition. It also provides practical services and concrete aid during these times, when the individual is preoccupied with his predicament and has little personal energy to deal with the ordinary demands of life. Discussing his observations during the Yom Kippur War in Israel, Caplan notes:

> I was impressed by the acute need of many families of wounded or fallen soldiers for help in shopping, doing household chores, getting lifts to a distant hospital, and taking care of young children or elderly relatives. The timely mobilization of the family network . . . enables those most centrally affected to devote all their energies to visiting the wounded or mourning the dead. . . .
> In addition to the benefit of the concrete help, the fact that it was immediately available as needed, usually without having to be asked for, was a source of great strength. . . . When a person knows that he is receiving what he needs as his right and not at the price of having to ask or beg for it, his pride in his own autonomy and his self-respect are likely to be maintained, even though he is actually a dependent recipient.[15]

Caplan points out that when an individual is grappling with crisis, the confusion and frustration of the situation, together with his pressures to

master his emotions and to cope with tl
bly to fatigue and exhaustion. The fam
and by temporarily taking over essen
caring for a sick child or parent, legi
relieving the person of his feelings of

Moreover, Caplan notes that indi
crises and role shifts to become va;
Since a person in a period of life tra
on the messages he receives from
identity, the family (and other signi
role by reminding him of abilities
which he may be temporarily in (

The family can help its members cai,
work" by counteracting feelings of dispair and heipic...
pressions of love and comfort, and by providing transitional objects oi ru-
in the family circle until such items as the struggling individuals can rebuild
their lives once more.

The role of family members in providing help during transitions shifts
with age, family role, and the nature of the ties between different parts of the
family. Reuben Hill points out that each generation turns to relatives for
help from time to time: the grandparents to parents, when help is needed
during illness and with household management; the parents to children, for
emotional gratification; and the married children to parents, for material aid
and childcare assistance. Hill sees a vast network of interaction between
generations developed to ask for and to provide help during illnesses, financial binds, household problems, and emotional stress.[16]

Some of the strictures on this give-and-take have been raised by Marjorie
Lowenthal and Betsy Robinson, who point out that current norms do not
sanction older people making demands on the young except in matters of
illness or other dire necessity.[17] Hope Leichter and William Mitchell, in
their comprehensive study of kinship relationships among casework clients,
found that most clients had a strong sense of responsibility toward their aged
parents but felt that financial assistance should ideally go from parents to
children, rather than from children to parents. Obligations to parents are
met by giving, in turn, to one's own children.[18]

In examining the contribution of family networks to the support of
widows in the Chicago area, Lopata found that, contrary to expectation, only
children were active in providing help. Other kin not directly in the
parent–child line were not found to be important contributors to the widows'
support systems.[19] In other contexts, however, larger kinship units, such as
family circles and cousins' clubs, were considered to provide a supportive
function during periods of social change:[20]

> Cousins' clubs serve as a way of uniting the younger generation and maintain-
> ing their kinship solidarity. . . . This organized bond . . . may help it as a group

he ways of life of the older generation, who are generally
rticipate. . . . Individuals, too, may be assisted in making a
new set of values. Cousins' clubs may also offer a collective
or trying out new types of social activity, often things that the
ily would not do alone.

ga of immigration to the United States has been founded upon the
help developed by established settlers, who found place for distant
ns on their diningroom "davenport" and in their family businesses until
newcomers were sufficiently acclimatized to make it on their own. Even
oday, Collins and Pancoast remind us that this help pattern continues:[21]

> People do not enter the city as individuals. Often friends and relatives have
> induced them to migrate. . . . The executive who is transferred to another
> town has the corporate structure in the new town to help him integrate into
> the community. When people announce their intention to move, friends and
> relatives frequently supply them with names and addresses of persons to
> contact in the new place.

FRIENDS AND NEIGHBORS

In addition to blood-related networks, an uncounted number of informally bound friends and neighbors form the nuclei for active help networks
during times of need. Some of these become part of the ongoing life structure of some individuals, as in the "tavern culture of homeless men" described by Matthew Dumont. Often these revolve around the key figure
whom Caplan would call a generalist:

> Peter, who was also the proprietor of a boarding house for single men, had a
> central position in the network. Men frequented the bar only when he was
> there, asked him to handle their welfare checks, borrowed money from him
> when they were broke, and accepted his regulation of their drinking and their
> "pesty" manners. Peter differentiated his role as bartender from his roles as
> friend and landlord, but he was sensitive to the men and willing to invest
> time and effort in meeting them.[22]

In another instance, the tenant network of single-room-occupancy buildings in a slum neighborhood was led by three persons, each of whom served
the tenants as a self-appointed specialist for one aspect of home care (physical
health needs, welfare benefits, psychiatric medication).[23] Similar instances
can be found in many communities, such as the beauty-shop operator who
acts as a clearinghouse for information on baby-sitting and housecleaning
services for her customers, the rural route mailman who keeps isolated farm
housewives posted as to their neighbors' ailments and delivers their special
homemade remedies to cure undiagnosed illnesses, and the *rabbanit* (rabbi's wife) who acts as succorer, confidante, and oracle to religiously orthodox
housewives in her Jerusalem neighborhood.

Quite a different type of informal caregivers are the specialists who are known in a community to have suffered some misfortune or trying experience themselves, and to have worked out ways to achieve a good level of adjustment and adaptation. When other persons find themselves in similar situations, they begin to seek out these persons who have successfully weathered the same stressful event to ask them for advice and guidance. In time these specialists may develop a widespread reputation as help-givers during periods of crisis and transition.[24]

The Mutual Help System*

Over the past decade, mutual-aid groups have proliferated rapidly throughout the country until now an extensive network of them can be found in virtually every community.[25] In many areas they are organized and cross-indexed into local chapters, regional councils, and national clearinghouses. Periodic newsletters are published to inform others of their activities, areas of interest, and particular methods of operation.[26] Their form may range from the indigenous helping networks that abound in a community—a group of mothers of preschool children who provide baby-sitting services so that some of them can go out to work or engage in needed errands, or the aging residents in a central city apartment block who band together to help each other shop and care for their health needs—to the formal, structured services that have been developed to meet the special needs of a defined population or to spread a particular philosophy of mutual assistance.

Despite their diversity and multiple roots, mutual-aid groups tend to share a common belief in the efficacy of peer help and are focused on the the core problem area which binds them together: the participants are all widowed, all parents of retarded children, all former mastectomy patients, etc. Their starting point may vary in that some are formed spontaneously as, say, when a group of mothers of children with learning disabilities meet to discuss common difficulties with the local school system. Others are formally organized as local chapters of national or regional organizations, such as Parents Without Partners, Alcoholics Anonymous, or Recovery Inc. They may differ as to their specific purpose: started primarily either to offer support and exchange of information or to act as a pressure group on the local or national political scene. They may also vary in the type of leadership offered: that of a peer member and/or a trained professional. Silverman finds that in general they can be grouped into four main types according to their primary activities: fund raising, political action, consumer advocacy, and personal help.[27]

---

*Although the terms "mutual help system" and "self-help system" tend to be used interchangeably, I prefer the former in order to differentiate between this type of help and the use of self as helper, discussed earlier in this chapter.

In the area of transitions, numerous mutual-support groups have been formed, such as the *Womem Helping Women* group for divorced women, *Candlelighters* for parents of children with cancer, and *Choice* for persons struggling with midlife transitions.[28] Silverman has expanded her initial interest in mutual help for the widowed to cover a broad range of groups which have developed to help persons in transitional states.[29] She finds that help often combines individual counseling with group meetings. Groups are usually led by persons who themselves have either successfully passed through the transition, if it is temporary, or have learned to accommodate themselves to their changed situation, if it is irreversible. When a professional is involved, it is often as coleader or as consultant behind the scenes.

Silverman outlines three kinds of phase-linked activity which must take place from the viewpoint of the person receiving help in passing through a transition:

1. During the initial *impact* phase, which starts when the critical (marker) event occurs, and when his major affect is usually numbness and disbelief, the person must be helped to establish a common bond with the helper who has "made it." Gradually he begins to give up his use of denial of the marker event and to take on his new role (as widow, as paraplegic, as retiree). As he starts to recognize part of himself in the helper who is functioning well, he finds concrete evidence and the beginning of hope that life can continue.

2. In the *recoil* phase, when the numbness lifts and he must face the reality of his altered situation, the person's despair, loneliness, and pain emerge. He must now grasp the reality that he can no longer return to the life-that-was. He needs help in dissolving those old roles (and assumptions) that are no longer functional and in concentrating on obtaining specific information and learning the practical details of how to carry out his new roles and develop new skills. He also needs help in understanding that his present feelings and reactions are typical and normal under the circumstances—that "this, too, shall pass."

3. In the final *accommodation* phase, the individual needs help in accepting the fact that both his inner and outer worlds have changed in the course of the transition and that he is becoming a different person. He practices his new behavior patterns, and gradually, with group support, begins to integrate the past with the present and even plan for the future. At this point, he may change his status as a member of the group and either become a helper himself or leave the group to continue on his own life course.

The critical aspect of the mutual help process, according to Silverman, is to learn how someone else has dealt with the problem and to identify with the person who provides a role model, hope, and the information needed to live successfully as a member of a new social category. Frequently mutual-help groups shade off into educational, structured workshops and seminars led by professionals (discussed in the final section). In some instances, it is the professionals who recognize a specific need and organize a mutual-aid program around that need.[30]

In general, natural support systems, mutual help networks, and the professional caregiving system may relate to each other in three ways: they may actively compete for clients, members, or converts; they may collaborate in an active exchange of resources including information, people, and material or financial support; or they may influence each other indirectly through the effects they have upon individuals in the community in need of care and support.[31] In some instances, the most fruitful kind of collaboration takes the form of having the professional act as consultant, either to key figures within the mutual support system or to the entire network.[32]

The Nonprofessional Support System

VOLUNTARY SERVICE ORGANIZATIONS

In progressing along the help continuum, we note that many of the large fraternal and voluntary organizations often take on special projects to help individuals and families pass through particular transitions, such as newcomers moving into a community ("Welcome Wagons") or offenders leaving prison after serving time. The Junior League and the Lions Club are examples of membership organizations with required service components. In addition, many private service organizations and institutions such as hospitals and clinics have women's auxiliaries which, in addition to raising funds to support specific programs, provide members to staff such projects.

Volunteers from such groups are often recruited as "big brothers" or as substitute parent figures for children following the loss of a parent through separation, divorce, or death. Untold hours and efforts are spent in helping families bridge the transitional interval by taking on some of the lost person's role within the family on a temporary basis or by having the fragmented family join a volunteer's intact one for such activities as picnics, holiday celebrations, and trips to the circus.[33] To a large extent these organizations plan their own programs and develop their own networks of contact with persons in need quite outside of the formal help-giving system, although they are frequently used as resources to provide specific help to persons at risk.

COMMUNITY CAREGIVERS

Because of the widespread nature of developmental and psychosocial transitions, a large number of "first line" community caregivers come in contact with persons stuck at various points in the process during the course of their regular professional duties. Lee Ann Hoff observes that teachers, pastors, youth directors, guidance and residence counselors, and school nurses are in powerful positions to help young people during such periods.[34] To this list we might add such workers as policemen, firemen, athletic coaches, lawyers, physicians, and nursing home operators, who frequently provide significant assistance to persons in transition whom they encounter.

The divorce lawyer, for example, can perform an important function in addition to his legal counseling by giving practical advice based on the experience of previous clients, offering emotional support at a time when the divorcing individual is particularly vulnerable and upset, and providing practical guidance about the best ways to deal with angry, confused children and vindictive, noncooperative spouses.[35]

Similarly, the family physician or internist may spend a considerable part of his office hours listening to patients discuss their spouses' infidelities or their parents' excessive demands while he is taking their medical histories and measuring their blood pressure. Frequently he is the first to become aware that an impending or current family transition has reached crisis proportions.[36] Rabbis, priests, and ministers center a good deal of their pastoral counseling on issues arising out of individual and family disruption during periods of role transition following the loss of a family member.[37]

The relationship between community caregivers and professional helpers is usually a close and ongoing one.[38] The former often are quick to spot troubled situations or potential difficulties and to refer persons for professional help. On the other hand, agencies and therapists frequently find that these community "first liners" can become pivotal figures in providing support and guidance, and the former often make full use of the latter's specialized expertise and positions of influence.

PARAPROFESSIONALS

Within institutional frameworks such as public welfare departments, family agencies, social service departments of hospitals, community mental health centers, and children's service agencies, increasing use has been made in recent years of volunteers, indigenous workers, case aides, and "counselors" of various types—often grouped together under the blanket term "paraprofessionals." They often are assigned responsibility for major activities and tasks in cases where transitional difficulties arise.

A good deal of gifted, appropriate help is offered at this level—for example, in crisis clinics, where the need is for relatively concrete, immediate intervention to carry out specific, defined activities aimed at restoring the person's equilibrium. Similarly, much of the work in dealing with individuals during late adulthood is geared to providing both tangible services ("Meals on Wheels," telephone services, supervision of homemakers, etc.) and continuing support and attention. Without further exploring the issue of the use of paraprofessionals vs. professionals and the relationship between them[39], we note that their importance during periods of role change and adaptation to new conditions has been amply demonstrated.

The Professional Help System

The professional system lies at the far end of the continuum, often chosen when all else fails. Help during transitional states can be provided by members of any of the disciplines usually offering this type of service: psychiatrists, social workers, psychologists, marriage and educational counselors, psychiatric nurses, and so on, each with his or her particular area of competence and modes of intervention.

As already mentioned, individuals who need help passing through transitions rarely come to a professional person for that declared purpose, since the implication usually is that one should be able to deal with such situations by oneself. (The outstanding exception is probably divorce, which, like its counterpart, marriage, has been recognized in recent years as a situation for which intervention may legitimately be asked.) The precipitating factor which brings the situation to the attention of the practitioner is often a critical event, an exacerbation of an unsettled situation which has ballooned out into a full-blown acute situational crisis: a young man wrecks a tavern after his girlfriend refuses to marry him; a middle-aged accountant makes a suicide attempt when he is passed up for promotion; an aging widow is found incapacitated with a broken hip, having fallen while trying to shovel the snow from her front walk.

Sometimes the acute crisis erupts as part of the underlying transitional process and is the culmination of a series of attempts to grapple with the changing life situation; sometimes it is coincidental with but accentuated by the fact that the person or family is already upset by the need to adjust to the transition. Events which in calmer periods might have been taken in stride now become turning points which bring about disequilibrium.

Professional intervention may take a number of forms. The following review of current practice will deal with (1) direct work with individuals; (2) family treatment; (3) group services; and (4) structured educational programs. Often several modalities are employed at the same time or in sequence.

DIRECT WORK WITH INDIVIDUALS

Much of the direct work of helping people pass through transitions that is carried out within primary and secondary settings is so imbedded in customary forms of practice that it is difficult to "tease out" the treatment aspects unique to this type of situation. From the case examples reported in Part II, as well as from other case examples studied and from previous experience and discussion, it is apparent that practitioners tend to use a wide variety of interventive strategies and techniques, depending on the problem, the setting, and their own practice orientation.

Professionals are accustomed to working with individuals and families in the process of developmental or psychosocial change, either as direct clients or as persons reacting to changes in significant others or in important parts of their assumptive world. While it is becoming fashionable to label certain types of cases as "transitional," the work of identifying the unique techniques and strategies appropriate to such situations has only just begun. Nevertheless, we do find certain commonalities:

1. The emphasis in treatment is often on the interactional aspects of the situation: the person in his interplay with other persons and elements in his social environment.
2. The time frame is usually the present, with some attempt to project into the near future.[40] When elements of past relationships and events are brought in, an effort is made to compare them to or differentiate them from the current situation and to return the focus to the present.
3. Stress is placed on specific problems in role adjustment: difficulties in taking on new roles; differences in interpreting roles in new settings; role ambiguities; and value clashes. Here educational and interpretive techniques play a large part in worker–client activities, including the development of new ways to cope.[41]
4. Treatment is frequently carried out according to the planned short-term model, with major focus on explicit client-centered tasks to be accomplished, often within a definite period of time or number of interviews.[42] At the same time, it is flexible enough to accommodate to changes in the client's life situation.
5. When acute crisis elements are the precipitating factor, first priority is given to dealing with these. However, some effort is made to tie them into the ongoing transitional process.[43]
6. Some emphasis is placed on the preventive aspects of the situation: on how to limit future disruptions and enhance adaptation.[44]

As an example of this type of practice, during a period of terminal illness one of the designated areas for intervention is helping the family (or one of its members) to face the prospect of the patient's death before it occurs and to deal with it during and after the event.[45] Two separate fields of operation can be designated: one concerning the person's or family's relations to the dying patient and the second concerning their needs to cope with the disruptions in their own lives.[46]

The practitioner takes on specific tasks to expedite a family member's transitional process: she* helps him develop competence in visiting the patient by offering her own physical presence to facilitate the visit; she discusses the stages of dying to help him understand the importance of allowing the patient to express his anger and disbelief; she teaches him how to listen and to interpret the patient's coping patterns and helps him to recognize the patient's need for help yet difficulty in asking for it. In addition, she shows him how to communicate with the patient and how to open up discussion on such practical matters as family finances, childcare, and funeral plans. She acts as intermediary with the hospital system and teaches him advocacy skills so that he may obtain adequate medical services and comforts for the patient.

Throughout this period, the worker supports the family member's own sense of competence by helping him talk about his other key relationships and roles. She aids him in mobilizing others within his social network in order to reduce the pressures during this difficult time. She may identify and mobilize formal service networks and sources of assistance of which he may not be aware. She tries to improve communication between him and the medical staff and clarifies technical information given about the patient's condition and prognosis. And she helps him consider realistic plans for the future both before and after the patient's death.

After the death, the practitioner has to change the direction and focus of her activity in order to carry out grief therapy with the (now) bereaved person—if he is still available. She has to become a listener who can bear to hear repetitively the family member's reactions to and reminiscences about the deceased person and the nature of their relationship. She has to support the expression of feelings, offer reassurance as to the normality of emotions and behavior (when warranted), remain serene as the family member becomes dependent until this phase has run its course, and empathetically tolerate the person's pain without prematurely cutting off its expression.[47] This post-death intervention may be short-term or long-term, depending on what underlying issues are opened up, but the worker must be able to tailor the course of treatment to the specific demands of the situation.

FAMILY TREATMENT

In developmental and transitional situations, the division between work with the individual and with the family often becomes obliterated, since role change (which by definition must be reciprocal) and interaction with significant others are prime foci of intervention at such times.[48] The emphasis in treatment is usually on the interactional system as such, whether it be the marital couple or the family as a whole.[49] Virginia Satir's approach of having each family member take responsibility for becoming an agent of change to

*For the sake of convenience, "she" is used here for the worker, "he" for the client.

improve communication within the family is particularly relevant during periods of transition.[50]

Thus Oxley, in doing short-term therapy with student couples, sees their main relational difficulties as revolving around the repetitive themes of communication difficulties, inability to express negative feelings, sexual problems, role confusion, inability to handle differences, and problems with intimacy and alienation (all, by implication, difficulties in the transition to couplehood).[51]

Similarly, among family therapists, John Weakland et al. see normal transitional steps in family living as the most common and important "everyday difficulties" leading to problems that call for intervention:[52]

> These transitions include: the change from the voluntary relationship of courtship to the commitment of marriage, and from this to the less reversible commitment when the first child is born; the sharing of influence with other authorities when a child enters school and with the child himself and his peers in the adolescent period; the shift from a child-oriented marital relationship back to a two-party system when the children leave the home, and its intensification at retirement; and return to single life at the death of one spouse. [pp. 147–148]

They believe that each of these stages requires major changes in personal relationships that can be dealt with by their "focused problem resolution" form of brief therapy, in which difficulties are dealt with primarily through the substitution of behavior patterns that can interrupt vicious positive feedback loops.

Although several approaches to family therapy have been based on a developmental framework,[53] a recent clear conceptualization makes use of Duvall's stages in the family life cycle.[54] Four overlapping areas of possible difficulties are identified: *physical needs, social needs, interpersonal needs,* and *intrapsychic needs.* Developmental tasks which are performed within a given family life stage are viewed as problems which require first-order change, while those of moving from one stage to another require second-order change.[55] In the first instance, change occurs within the family system, which itself remains unchanged; in the second, the system itself requires changing. In order to bring about substantive change, the therapist first joins the system through the process of *accommodation,* by which he gains knowledge of the family transaction patterns, and then uses the technique of *restructuring,* by which specific changes in the family system are carried out.[56]

A different framework for family intervention emphasizes the acute situational crisis aspects of the situation rather than the developmental issues and starts at the individual level with the person initiating the contact. This then is expanded to include the interactional and intrafamilial aspects of the immediate problem.[57] The most common themes in this type of family crisis-intervention cases include shifts in family structure such as divorce, remarriage, introduction of stepchildren, and other additions or losses of family members, as well as anniversary reactions and minor events that stir up unresolved feelings about estranged spouses or parents. Other disruptions are developmental changes such as school entry or confrontations with adolescents that threaten separation between children and parents due to normal growth processes.

In Bonnefil and Jacobson's structured, six-session form of intervention, the goal of treatment becomes, not resolution of the crisis per se, but finding the most adaptive resolution possible, given the inner and outer resources available to the individual. Three main categories of techniques are used: (1) *environmental*—the external hazard is removed; (2) *generic*—without regard to individual differences, a particular kind of crisis, such as bereavement, is identified and anticipatory guidance is used to encourage the most generally adaptive kind of coping; and (3) *individual*—attention is paid to the dynamics of the individual situation. In the last approach, particular heed is given to why the caller contacted the clinic at that particular time and what event happened just before the call to precipitate a feeling of crisis.

Among the various frameworks for divorce counseling and therapy, the form advocated by Wallerstein and Kelly at the Community Mental Health Center of Marin County, California, is probably the most developed conceptually.[58] They found that families with children were affected by at least five related stages or situations in the divorce process: the nature of the predivorce family; the disruptive process of the divorce itself; the changed social, economic, and psychological realities of being reared in a post-divorce family; the alterations in the parent–child relationship after the marital breakup; and (sometimes) the remarriage of one or both parents, often to a partner with children. Almost all of the children and many of the adolescents seen in the Children of Divorce project experienced divorce as painful and disruptive.

This five-year program of experimental intervention resulted in several significant conclusions:[59]

1. Divorce is a disorganizing and reorganizing process in a family with children that extends over several years of disequilibrium before job, social, and sexual relationships become stabilized enough to provide comfort and a renewed sense of continuity.

2. The entire post-separation period, rather than simply the pre-divorce period or the divorce events themselves and the functioning of the custodial parent, are the central determinants in the young child's well-being at the end of the first year of separation.

3. The older child's and adolescent's capacity to maintain his developmental stride is related inversely to the parent's need to lean heavily on him for emotional and social sustenance and to involve him in continuous battles with the divorced spouse. Some emotional distance may be needed to protect the offspring's integrity of development.

4. The period immediately following separation seems particularly useful for interventive efforts, since relationships are shaking loose, considerable anxiety is generated, and the chances for effecting change are greatly enhanced. The divorce represents a nodal point of change in the parent–child relationship, for both the custodial and the noncustodial parent.

5. Like death, divorce has the psychic and developmental hazard that loss in the external world will not be fully assimilated within the individual's inner world. However, unlike death, divorce presents for the child the continued availability of the departed parent as a live object for the intense living out of conflict and longing. Both child and adult must achieve new and complex changes in their intimate relationships and self-concepts, and complete their mourning over the loss of the pre-divorce family.

Interventions carried out during the Children of Divorce project were primarily child-centered, relationship-centered, or adult-centered. They also ranged along a continuum from being predominantly educational to being predominantly clinical in approach. In the first instance, the parents were taught to observe, make psychological connections, and employ particular techniques to change behavior or alleviate distress. On the other hand, efforts to encourage psychological change within the parents in order to increase their parenting capacities fell more closely within a clearly psychotherapeutic approach. Interventions dealing primarily with the parent–child relationship lay in between.

Treatment relationships, according to Wallerstein and Kelly, significantly reflected the overarching divorce experience, with displacements becoming evident almost at once:

> While it is no surprise that direct work with people in crisis is difficult and depleting of physical and psychic energy, the full impact was somewhat greater than expected. The narcissistic blows that so many of these people had sustained made for irritability, defensiveness, and combativeness. Also, the sense of having been injured and wronged led to their needing to invoke us to confirm their moral correctness or to restore their lessened self-esteem. [p. 19].

The staff used a style of counseling that was, from the start, open, direct, personal, and more advice-giving and directive than the usual clinical practice. They expressed their personal concerns over a particular situation within a family and used advocacy on behalf of both the child and the parents as they tried to meet the parents' legitimate expectations that they could reach out in an ongoing crisis to find competent advice, guidance, and support. Implicit in the relationship were the assumptions that the parents were capable of more mature functioning, that reasonably conflict-free spheres of parenting did exist, and that their incapacity, helplessness, and regression were temporary. By being helped to perform their parenting roles, they were addressed as adults, and this increased their confidence and self-esteem.

Brief, focused intervention was the treatment of choice. As part of the interventive strategies, support systems for the children took on particular significance.[60] Such supports included the current parent–child relationship, siblings, the extended family on both sides, the school system, and peer groups. These support networks, when combined with the developmental and divorce-specific assessment, provided the base for the several treatment models used.

Looking at divorce therapy from a far different conceptual framework, Kenneth Kressel and Morton Deutsch analyzed the activities of twenty-one experienced therapists and found that their intervention during the transition focused on two distinct periods; helping the client (or clients, if both adults were involved) decide whether or not to divorce and assisting in the negotiation of the final divorce or separation agreement.[61]

Three main groups of interventive tactics were used. Reflexive interventions which enabled the therapist to orient himself to the marital conflict, included such strategies as building trust and confidence, diagnosing the marital situation, and maintaining impartiality. Contextual interventions, which helped the therapist affect the climate of the dispute, included efforts to reduce the level of emotional tension through behavioral tactics (such as clarifying the real source of the anger, shifting the focus from the partner to the self, relabeling an accusation, encouraging positive interaction, and reducing anxiety) and structural tactics such as modifying the format by introducing a cotherapist, enforcing physical separation, regulating contacts with lawyers, and mediating between client and lawyer. Substantive interventions, which enabled the therapist to take an active and direct hand in promoting specific agreement on substantive issues, included arguing in favor of divorce, disrupting negative assertions about the self, enforcing physical separation, increasing "marketability," enlisting the support of family and friends, making suggestions for compromise, and protecting the welfare of the children.

GROUP SERVICES

The use of the group format in dealing with life transitions has expanded tremendously over the past few years, not only in the mutual-aid or self-help framework but in professional settings as well. Some programs are provided within established agencies as part of ongoing services offered to special elements within the client population; others are set up as updated versions of family life education programs. Some community-based groups are designed to appeal to that segment of the public-at-large which happens to be interested in a particular transition, and participants are recruited through public announcements and newspaper ads; other services are largely educative and directed to the general public in the form of classes.

Marc Schwartz, of the Transition Center in New Haven, Connecticut, reports that regardless of the particular format, such "situation/transition groups" usually have certain common, essential features: they are primarily oriented toward helping members cope more effectively with some shared external event; they have the characteristics of small groups and meet regularly over a period of weeks or months for a specific number of meetings; they offer social support, factual information about the shared life stress, and an opportunity for emotional interaction with others that is focused on the stress in question; and they do not encourage or require members to espouse a particular moral or behavioral value system.[62]

Some of the help has a *suppressive* function in that group members find a relatively safe haven, a place where they can give each other comfort, support, and acceptance and look up to the leader as a parental figure; an *expressive* function in that timely and appropriate verbalization and mutual ventilation of feelings enable participants to reduce tension and make affect more manageable; and a *neutral* function in that information is shared and factual presentations are made with the aim of providing assistance and augmenting self-confidence.

Sometimes group services are set up for particular age divisions which seem to be in particular need of this approach. Irving Miller and Renée Solomon point out that among groups set up to serve the elderly, formal and informal educational groups attempt to help them develop or maintain their mastery and competence in areas of common interest. In addition, life-task or problem-solving groups aim to work with people who share similar feelings of being alone and helpless, particularly during periods of life crises. The emphasis here is on working out developmental tasks for such persons as recent retirees, recent widows and widowers, disabled persons, those living in foster care or adult home settings, and those contemplating or in the process of moving from independent to institutional living.[63]

The following examples show the range of group programs that have been reported within the past few years. Some groups are offered as part of ongoing counseling services in family agencies. At the Catholic Family Service of Saginaw, Michigan, three couples are placed in a conjoint treatment group to work with two cotherapists on their marital problems.[64] The Family and Children's Service of Greater St. Louis offers an eight-session discussion group to help married couples enhance the intimacy of their relationship on a preventive and educational level,[65] as well as a series of six weekly discussion-group sessions for retirees and their spouses, led by professional leaders who emphasize the developmental aspects of retirement.[66] The Child and Family Service of Washtenaw County, Michigan, combines didactic and therapeutic goals in two-generational groups to provide older parents and their adult children with basic information on aging and to help them discuss their own intergenerational situations,[67] while the Child and Family Services of Newport County, Rhode Island, offers a six-session group for couples called "Choosing Parenthood: The Pros and Cons of Having Children."[68]

Sometimes the groups are set up outside of established agency structures and become closer in format to the mutual-help groups described earlier. Thus a six-session neighborhood workshop led by a social worker and recreational therapist met in a local library in suburban New York with a group of women who were expecting to move to a new community and were apprehensive about the changes this would bring.[69] A support group to help pregnant women and new mothers to deal with their pregnancy and parenting experiences was established by a psychiatric nurse in the Boston area.[70] A group for widowed parents and their children was led by a social worker in New Jersey, combining monthly social and discussion sessions with direct visits to newly bereaved families to provide support and comfort,[71] while another support group was started in Orange County, California, for parents whose children had recently died.[72]

EDUCATIONAL PROGRAMS

At times the programs are offered as structured educational workshops and seminars. Thus the Expectant Parent Program of Bedford County, Pennsylvania, was developed by mental health professionals as a six-session community course on medical and psychological aspects of parenting.[73] The University of Utah offers a "Three to Get Ready" class, developed and conducted by a social worker, to provide an informational and supportive climate in which middle-aged women can prepare to move into the job market or onto the campus to obtain an academic education.[74] The University of Kansas Adult Life Resource Center offers a continuous program of workshops and seminars on changes in the adult life cycle.[75]

In one of the most carefully spelled out of these programs, a group of family theorists, researchers, and therapists from the University of Minnesota's Family Study Center, in cooperation with five Midwest family service agencies, developed a six-session course, the Minnesota Couple Communications Program, which uses an educational-developmental approach to help young engaged and married couples improve their communications skills.[76]

The transition of divorce has inspired a rapid proliferation of various types of educational programs.[77] One of the earliest and most successful is Seminars for the Separated, organized by Robert Weiss at the Harvard Laboratory of Community Psychiatry.[78] These seminars have a structured format, meeting once a week for eight sessions. Some of the meetings start with a formal lecture and then break down into discussion groups; others are more informal demonstrations. Topics include the emotional impact of separation; the ambivalent relationship between former spouses; the impact of the separation upon friends, kin, in-laws, and others in the social milieu; the impact on children; the development of new relationships; and sources for individual help.

Participants reported that the most immediate benefit from the seminars appeared to be the reassurance that the emotional distress following separation was a normal and even universal reaction; this perception resulted in a dramatic reduction in their own anxiety. Membership in the supportive discussion groups was also considered an important aspect of participation in the program. From his experience, Weiss feels that a good transition program should include three kinds of helpers: the *expert*, who has studied the problems of a particular type of transition and can speak with authority; the *veteran*, who has been through the transition and is able to draw upon his own past experiences; and the *fellow participant*, who can offer the immediate understanding that comes from being in the same boat.

In some settings, such as the Valley Adult Counseling Center of South Grafton, Massachusetts, groups are set up, in coordination with individual treatment, to help clients deal with the personal and social-network losses accompanying separation and divorce.[79] Similarly, professional counselors in the Chicago suburbs lead eight-to-ten-week groups for persons in various stages of the divorce process, who are struggling with such issues as the need to make a decision, the changes divorce has brought to their lives, their concern over their children, religious repercussions, and social sanctions.[80] Divorce groups at the San Luis Valley Comprehensive Community Mental Health Center in Alamosa, Colorado, help persons suffering from adjustment reactions to share their common concerns and facilitate interaction between participants.[81] A program in Toronto, Canada, which developed groups to prepare divorced families for remarriage considers such questions as relations with the children of the opposite partner, the ties linking the second marriage with the first, and the quality of parenting that can be offered to stepchildren.[82]

Out of all this welter of different sources and forms of help, a picture of a complex, interacting system of help services during periods of transition, offered at various levels and with different groups, begins to emerge. How this can be shaped into a usable and viable program of intervention will be discussed in the next chapter.

14

Guidelines for Intervention During Transitions

FROM WHAT HAS GONE BEFORE, what generalizations can we make about practice during transitional periods? One of the important ingredients is adoption of a basic stance towards working with normal people with normal troubles during critical times in their life span.

Approaches to Practice

One of the basic premises on which this book rests is that adults pass through periods of transition in their life cycle during which they have to make a number of adjustments—to changing conditions within themselves, to evolving situations in their surrounding physical and social environments, or to shifting interactions between these inner and outer worlds. A second premise is that at various times and for various reasons, individuals become stuck at points during these intervals of passage when their customary coping mechanisms are not sufficient and they need help in changing their feeling, thinking, and behaving to adapt to their altered state. A third premise is that practitioners from various helping disciplines who devote a sizeable share of their activities to working with clients in the process of transitional change can have a key influence in shaping both the immediate and long-range course of their lives.

TIES TO THE PSYCHODYNAMIC APPROACH

It should be stressed at the outset that this approach is based upon, and consonant with, the psychological, ego-oriented interpretation of the development of the individual personality.[1] This basic personality structure has been shaped during infancy and early childhood and honed during later childhood and adolescence. It involves the emergence of basic patterns of object relations, defense mechanisms, cognitive processes, and coping styles as an outcome of intrapersonal and interpersonal reactions and interactions with significant others during the formative years.

However, superimposed upon this basic personality structure is the individual's continued growth, change, and adaptation as he interacts with other persons, situations, and networks, particularly during periods of transition in the adult life cycle. During these crucial intervals he reacts not only retrospectively in terms of his past experiences but prospectively in terms of the demands of the current situation and what he anticipates (or fears) will be the outcome, immediately and in the future. Nevertheless, the practitioner working with clients engaged in a transitional process must have a firm grasp of the developmental issues of the individual and/or the family—"where they are at" dynamically. Only then can he plan appropriate intervention.

TIES TO THE ECOLOGICAL PERSPECTIVE

In terms of its approach to current life situations, this view is consonant with that offered by the ecological approach, which emphasizes the importance of general systems theory for practice and the humanistic push by individuals and groups toward gaining active control over their own lives. Carel Germain, in discussing this perspective,[2] offers a life model which underlines the role of the environment as a means of helping and the individual's capacity for adaptive activity and decision making. This model stresses Erikson's view of ego development through phase-specific task resolution in interaction with the physical, social, cultural, and institutional environments:

> The approach is patterned after the behavior of well-adapted or socially competent people of varying life-styles in solving problems, dealing with discomfort, stress, or crisis, and managing symptomatology without decompensation or regression. The model recognizes that the ego has many kinds of skills, not only for coping, but for enjoying the world, achieving goals, and modifying the environment. Some of these skills can be translated into helping procedures. . . . Successful action results in ego growth and does not necessarily require the development of self-understanding. [p. 327]

Becoming even more specific, Alex Gitterman and Germain list three types of problems in living faced by individuals, families, and groups: (1) problems and needs associated with tasks involved in life transitions; (2) problems and needs associated with tasks in using and influencing elements

home - loss/job, nursing
loss help nursing
wife - separation

of the environment; and (3) problems and needs associated with the inter-personal obstacles that impede the work of a family or a group as it deals with the transitional and/or environmental tasks.[3] Transitional problems are de-fined as difficulties in dealing with developmental tasks, the status and role changes that occur over the life span, and the expectable and exceptional crisis events—the threats and natural losses that come to everyone over time as well as the catastrophic threats and losses that occur too early, too "un-fairly," or too profoundly to be considered expectable.

TIES TO THE PROBLEM-SOLVING MODEL

In terms of intervention, this view of practice during transitions is very much a product of the problem-solving model, which sees the casework process as consisting of calculated action on the helper's part in three areas:[4]

1. To release, energize, and give direction to the client's *motivation* to change.
2. To release and then repeatedly exercise the client's mental, emo-tional, and action *capacities* for coping with the problem or with himself in relation to it.   *Client's strengths*
3. To make accessible to the client the *opportunities and resources* necessary to the solution or mitigation of the problem.

Diagnosis, according to Perlman, is aimed at identifying and explaining the nature of the person's problem, appraising it within the framework of specific intentions and goals, and using that appraisal as the guide for further action. As treatment progresses, the bits of evidence gathered from the client shape the caseworker's judgment of how fast to move, what supports and services seem called for, and what parts of the applicant's problems need priority consideration. Therapeutic techniques vary according to the person worked with, his particular problem, his conception of what he wants, and the caseworker's treatment style.

The crux of the problem-solving process is to offer the help-seeker a sustaining relationship with a caring and competent helper; a clarified per-ception and grasp of his problem and of his own part in it; repeated exercise of his drives and capacities to cope with greater competence and satisfaction; provision of access to material means or enriched opportunities; and the strengthening or modifying of the linkages and transactions between the client and others in his social network.

TIES TO CRISIS INTERVENTION

This viewpoint also has direct links to the crisis intervention approach, from which it has recently become differentiated as an area of practice.[5] As mentioned throughout this volume, many parallels and similarities exist between practice in crisis situations and practice dealing with transitional states. First, the professional is often called in only when some acute situational hazard or emergency, either natural or man-made, brings about a severe stress situation or accelerates it into a state of disequilibrium. This may become the starting point for working on the transitional process of identity transformation and role change that continues long after the initial acute phase of disorganization is overcome—as in the case of untimely widowhood. On the other hand, the practitioner may be called in relatively late in the transitional process, when the person's or family's coping patterns have proved insufficient or too inflexible to adjust to the numerous changes required by the new situation and a crisis develops—as in the case of mistreatment of an infant or a suicide attempt after retirement.

A second link is the need to help the client gain an affective and cognitive "encompassment": he needs to "take in" all aspects of the changed situation and needs help in handling the increased levels of anxiety or depression which are concomitants of the subjective reactions of threat to past security and loss of significant persons, roles, and/or attributes.

A third link is the emphasis on the learning of new and appropriate patterns of behaving and coping in order to deal with the altered life situation and the changed capabilities (for better or worse) of the person in transition. This is closely tied to the emphasis on the building of new support systems and natural helping networks to replace those which have been lost in the transitional process (or before)—part of the "broad push" approach used during crisis situations.

A fourth link is the stress on prevention. In crisis theory, although articulated at an early stage,[6] this aspect often remained more of a pious hope than a reality in actual practice. In transition theory, where future events or the progress of the transitional process can be predicted to some extent, it should be—and often is—possible to anticipate future difficulties and to build safeguards or "cushions" in advance through anticipatory guidance, provision of support systems, and participation in educational programs such as those discussed in the last part of Chapter 13. Whether such activities can, in fact, pave the way for smoother transitions remains to be tested over time.

TIES TO TASK-CENTERED PRACTICE

The task-centered model of short-term treatment is very appropriate for use during transitional periods in certain respects. The basic treatment model lists eight types of acknowledged problems addressed by this system, of which three—difficulty in role performance, decision problems, and reactive emotional distress—can become key issues in transitional situations.[7]

In addition, the focus on specific, client-centered tasks, with its emphasis on developing client competence, is central to promoting passage through the bridging period. (This task aspect will be discussed in greater detail later.) The importance of providing the client with a constructive problem-solving experience which will strengthen his own coping capacities is also a vital component of practice during transitions.

However, a sharp difference occurs when we consider the time-limited aspects of the task-centered model. In transitional work, where the entire linking interval may cover several months or even years, it is difficult to set in advance a specific number of interviews or a definite span of time during which intervention will take place. In teaching the task-focused model, I find myself using the term "segmental treatment" when speaking of situations involving transitions. That is, the nature of the practitioner's activity will vary from engaging in intense, focused treatment during the acute crisis phase, to providing minimal support or "maintaining a watching brief," to use Caplan's term, during periods when the person has become mobilized and can proceed ahead on his own, to offering intensive, insight-oriented psychotherapy when the individual has sufficiently distanced himself from the acute crisis phase to want to understand, retrospectively, "How things got to be that way" or "How I got into this mess."

The Nature of Transitional Problems

At which point in the transitional process can problems be expected to arise? Our preliminary investigations show that most problems encountered during such periods seem to involve one or more of these basic complications:

1. *Inability to separate from the past* or difficulties in sustaining the losses and threats to past role performance and comfort involved in the separation process.
2. *Inability to come to a decision* as to which path to choose, which direction to take, whether or not to assume a proposed new role or to follow a proposed plan of action.
3. *Difficulty in carrying out the decision* through a lack of understanding of what is involved in making the change, a lack of information on the expectations of self and others in the new role(s), or a lack of preparation for carrying out the new role or coping with the new conditions.
4. *Difficulty in weathering the period of adjustment* until the changes are stabilized and the transitional process is completed. This could include lack or resources to implement the changes required.

Implied in this general classification are the various types of problems which arise either from inappropriate decisions previously taken or from the adverse reactions of others to the changes made or about to be made. Also involved are the acute situational crises which emerge either as an exacerbation of the transitional changes or as a coincidental but complicating factor.

Because persons and families can become involved in so many different aspects of transitional difficulties, it is difficult to make precise predictions as to which situations will become problematic. Certainly, innate and learned personality characteristics of the participants, past performance in passing through transitions, unresolved issues left over from earlier transitional and developmental stages, the extent and nature of natural support systems and environmental resources, cultural and ethnic values and standards of performance, and community investment in resolving issues posed by the transition will all play a part in determining both the nature of the problems and the form of their resolution. The distinction between *difficulties*, which imply complications or "bumps in the road" that the person can still overcome unaided, and *problems*, which imply the inability to resolve the situation without some form of help, is important to note, although the boundaries between the two may, in fact, be a matter of happenstance.[8]

The Helping Process

As has already been noted, intervention in situations involving transitions can be carried out using various treatment approaches. Some years ago, in considering how normal individuals could be helped during periods of change, attempt was made to "take apart" the immigration process (see Chapter 7). Somewhat later, the transition of widowhood was also analyzed in this way (see Chapter 10). More recently, several other transitional situations have been or are in the course of being examined. The central feature in these various analyses is the working out of the axes of *material-arrangemental and psychosocial tasks*, which have already been alluded to at various points in this book but which bear repetition, since they form the key to both the assessment and interventive processes.

Assuming that a person comes in or is referred because of an exacerbation of his transitional situation, which may have crisis elements in it, the key to helping him resolve the difficulties—once the initial shock phase is overcome and he has ventilated his feelings of anxiety, upset, guilt, anger, rage, disbelief, sadness, relief, and sorrow—appears to be, first, to help him identify actual and potential problem areas: where, along the continua of tasks-to-be-resolved, he is having difficulties; then to help him carry out and to master the tasks as they arise.

Material-arrangemental tasks (which should be worked out for each problem area and/or role network) entail the seeking out of concrete assistance in the form of money, services, information, and substantive arrangements. These client tasks are usually action-oriented and frequently can be carried out with the help of volunteers and nonprofessionals on the staff of an agency or by community caregivers. To be effective they usually imply an ordered progression of problem-solving steps.

1. To recognize the lack of supplies and services, the insufficiency or inappropriateness of the old situation, the need to "do something about it."
2. To explore available and potential solutions, resources and possible new or changed roles; investigate choices and options; weigh alternatives.
3. To make a choice and implement it by applying formally for the solution or resource, taking on the new role.
4. To begin to use the new solution or resource, function in the new role; explore expectations, limitations, requirements, conditions, etc.
5. To go through a period of adaptation and development of increasing competence until performance rises to acceptable norms and pressures decrease to manageable proportions.

This level of help may be all that many clients need to overcome their feelings of strangeness and "discombobulation" while passing through the transition process or adjusting to it successfully. Many agencies and services offer help through information services and with supportive casework, individually or in groups, which focuses on the reality situation: what is possible, what is available, and—in situations involving loss and irremediable dificit—what is the least-worst alternative under the circumstances.

In addition, because individuals and families tend to react to change in complex, irrational, and unpredictable ways, and often find themselves unable to carry out what they rationally know they ought to do, clients often need help on the cognitive and affective level as well. These *psychosocial tasks* run parallel to and are intermingled with the material-arrangemental ones but usually require the services of a professional versed in intra-personal and interpersonal dynamics and knowledgeable about both developmental and maturational processes and the key epigenetic issues which may underly the person's inability or reluctance to take action. Tasks would follow this hierarchy of phases:

1. To cope with the threat to past security, sense of competence, and feelings of self-esteem; deal with the sense of loss and longing for the past.
2. To deal with anxieties and frustrations in making decisions about new solutions, resources, or roles, and the accompanying pressures, panics, and ambivalences.
3. To handle the pressures generated in applying for the selected solution or resource, in taking on the new role, and in meeting the stress and frustration in implementation.

4. To adjust to the new solution, resource, or role with all of its implications in terms of shifts in position and status, feelings of inferiority or implied criticism from others, and lack of satisfactions and feelings of appreciation.

5. To develop new standards of well-being, agree to lessened gratification, diminished satisfaction, and changed self-image until the level of functioning or way of operating rises to acceptable norms and the person feels comfortable in the new situation or role; to come to terms with the new, different reality and begin to look for new ways of gratification and sources of enjoyment.

These general overall tasks are really, it should be recognized, *interim or short-term goals*. The term "task" as used in the Reid–Epstein model of practice describes the specific actions which the client or practitioner agree to undertake.[9] To qualify as a task, the action to be undertaken by the client would have to be (1) planned and agreed upon with the practitioner; and (2) capable of being worked on outside of the treatment session.

Several years ago, while participating in a field test of the Reid–Epstein model of task-centered practice, we worked out a triad for planning treatment strategies with clients.[10]

A. The *target problem*, the "felt difficulty" in specific behaviors or circumstances for which the client asks for help and on which he expresses his willingness to work.

B. The *target goal*, the projected situation in which the client would feel he no longer needs help, the stage at which he might continue on his own—that is, when he feels competent to manage his life.

C. The *task*, the means of going from Point A to Point B. General tasks become broken down into operational tasks and subtasks, the specific stepping-stones along the path.

Thus the deceptively simple description of tasks as "the means of going from Point A to Point B" becomes the crux of intervention during transitional periods. By taking full advantage of Havighurst's "teachable moment," practitioner and client map out together the specific tasks which the client will carry out, which the worker will do on his behalf, which they can work on together, and which can be delegated to others to do. The significant factor is that the *client* becomes the prime mover, the one who acts to improve his coping competence by performing a series of planned moves to draw closer to becoming autonomous. Even in the acute phase of a stressful situation, when the person has become numbed by severe shock or exhausted by the batterings of a series of debilitating events and the situation forces the worker to become extremely active, the latter aims as quickly as possible to decrease his own level of activity and to increase that of the client by encouraging him to carry out a series of specific problem-oriented tasks.

Actual techniques for carrying out treatment may vary, depending on the orientation and training of the practitioner. They usually include a combination of reflective consideration of the current situation—both its good and bad aspects; analysis of what can and should be changed; and acknowledgement of what must be endured as part of the changes wrought by the marker event and its consequences. Such treatment involves going back selectively into the past, to lay old ghosts and resolve unfinished conflicts that may have been arrested or frozen before they were resolved. It includes the transforming of previous ties into memories and the airing of regrets and guilt feelings that usually start with the phrases "If only I had known . . . " or "If I could do it over. . . ." It also means some looking ahead to consideration of long-range goals and the weighing of the possible effect of the marker event and its consequent changes on the person's or family's future life course.

Many practitioners prefer to concentrate on examining current relationships and restructuring communication patterns among members of the individual's social network, using Gestalt devices and transactional analyses of problematic behavior. Behavioral procedures and assertive techniques can also prove useful in developing new patterns of action appropriate to the changing situation.

The issue of *time* becomes an important factor in helping clients pass through transitional periods. (See the above discussion on task-centered practice.) Leaving one phase of development or one set of transactional circumstances and passing on to another is often a complex process which may take months and even years of one's life span. Clearly this differs from the sudden eruption of a situational crisis and rarely can be encompassed within the concentrated, time-limited, structured blocks of treatment offered in the crisis model. As already mentioned, help may be asked for at various stages along the process and may be needed at different levels of intensity for varying lengths of time. Some of the introspective reworking of loss situations can take place only after a certain period of time elapses, when the person can bear to look back more clearly and talk more openly about the experience.

Without going into the implications for agency policy and planning of services, it appears clear that effective treatment during periods of transition must be carried out at changing tempos, perhaps alternating intervals of intense, concentrated work with fallow periods during which the person goes off on his own to work on his life situation while maintaining occasional telephone contact with the practitioner. The intermittent periods of intense joint activity may be triggered by incidents such as an anniversary reaction, a reawakened memory, a new proposal of marriage, or a job promotion.

Termination thus becomes somewhat ambiguous. Although a case may be formally closed in an agency's books, the person often continues to keep in touch with the practitioner for years, "checking in" from time to time through telephone calls, postcards, or even drop-in visits. Sometimes periodic followups can be planned together to ensure the carrying through of earlier plans and the retention of gains made. This obviously varies with the client's situation and the type of transition. For example, the transitions of late adulthood might call for continuous followup over a period of years. On the other hand, the transition to marriage would probably require only a quick entry, rapid intervention, and early exit, leaving the young partners to proceed on their own as expeditiously as possible.

The Use of Relationship

In considering the difference between intervention in acute crises and intervention in transitional situations, the outstanding change, to me, occurs in the nature of the helper–helpee relationship. According to Lydia Rapoport, in crisis intervention, as in brief treatment, the client–worker relationship takes a new direction.[11] The worker's authority of competence and expertise is used more powerfully to capitalize on the client's readiness to trust and to relate, particularly during the acute period, when he feels confused, helpless, and anxious. She sees the degree of involvement in the common stress situation rather than attachment as the important component. In another context, she uses the term "limited positive transference" to describe the nature of the practitioner–client bond.

In practice involving transitional situations, I see the relationship returning to the place described by Perlman in her most recent book.[12] She defines a human relationship as

> a feeling or sense of emotional bonding with another. It leaps into being like an electric current or it emerges and develops cautiously when emotion is aroused by and invested in someone or something and that someone or something "connects back" responsively. [p. 23]

Because many of the developmental difficulties that arise over the life span are tied in with inappropriate, non-nourishing, or skewed relationships, it seems evident that one of the most important ingredients that a professional can inject into a treatment experience is the quality of a warm, empathic, concerned, and genuine relationship that really accepts the person as he is, with all of his "bumps and warts." Such a relationship is geared, according to Perlman, to

> resolve or cope in some more effective ways with some identified problem that is currently troubling or undermining [the client's] functioning and/or to enable him to utilize himself and resources to achieve a desired goal. [p. 62]

Persons passing through transitions are engaged in a normal growth experience. Therefore, this type of bonding can have both educational and therapeutic implications quite over and beyond the nature and content of the intervention itself. Even though the intensity of the interchange may vary with the phase of the transitional situation and the nature of the practitioner–client activity, the establishment and continuation of this running thread of mutual commitment to the client's growth and development should continue throughout the case until the transition is completed and the person is able to manage on his own, buttressed by new ties and natural, mainstream relationships.

This, of course, opens up a new issue: is it possible to offer a committed relationship for a limited time and then to retreat?[13] To me, this is the mark of the worker's personal and professional development. In its way, one can even view the therapeutic relationship as a transitional phase in the client's ego growth and, correspondingly, in the worker's. To give openly and freely during a time of need and then to withdraw, saying with a farewell pat (or a kiss or a handshake) "We meant a lot to each other when we worked together, but now you can manage on your own; good-bye and good luck!" implies a depth of personal maturity that should be—and is—an important goal for professional caregivers.

Notes

Chapter 1. Where Transitions Are Met—and Missed

1. Resources are too numerous to enumerate and readers are referred to any standard bibliography on child development. Typical volumes are Sibylle Escalona, *The Roots of Individuality* (Chicago: Aldine, 1968); Alexander Theron, *Children and Adolescents* (New York: Atherton Press, 1969); Irene M. Josselyn, *Psychosocial Development of Children,* 2nd ed. (New York: Family Service Association of America, 1978).

2. For example, Ewald W. Busse and Eric Pfeiffer, eds., *Behavior and Adaptation in Late Life* (Boston: Little, Brown, 1969); Robert H. Binstock and Ethel Shanas, eds., *Handbook of Aging and the Social Sciences* (New York: Van Nostrand Reinhold, 1976); Robert C. Atchley, *The Social Forces in Later Life* (Belmont, Ca.: Wadsworth, 1972).

3. See Paul B. Baltes and K. Warner Schaie, eds., *Life-Span Developmental Psychology: Personality and Socialization* (New York: Academic Press, 1973); Nancy Datan and Leon H. Ginsberg, eds., *Life-Span Developmental Psychology: Normative Life Crises* (New York: Academic Press, 1975); Henry S. Maas and Joseph A. Kuypers, *From Thirty to Seventy* (San Francisco: Jossey-Bass, 1977); Martin Bloom, *Life-Span Development: Bases for Preventive and Interventive Helping* (New York: Macmillan, 1980).

4. Two notable instances which I discovered are the courses taught at the Schools of Social Work at Simmons College (Boston) by Sophie F. Loewenstein and at the University of Kansas (Lawrence) by Eileen Brennan.

5. For example, the Adult Life Resources Center, Division of Continuing Educa-

tion, University of Kansas, runs programs of "Lifelong Learning: The Adult Years" at its home center in Lawrence and throughout the state.

6. Blanca N. Rosenberg, "Planned Short-Term Treatment in Developmental Crises," *Social Casework* 56 (Apr. 1975): 195–204; Susan M. Shilling and Ellen J. Gross, "Stages of Family Therapy: A Developmental Model," *Clinical Social Work Jrnl.* 7, 2 (Summer 1979): 105–114; Jane W. Ransom, Stephen Schlesinger, and Andre P. Derdeyn, "A Stepfamily in Formation," *Amer. Jrnl. Orthopsychiatry* 49, 1 (Jan. 1979): 36–43.

7. Anne Minahan and Allen Pincus, "Conceptual Framework for Social Work Practice," *Social Work* 22, 5 (Sept. 1977): 347–352.

8. Carel B. Germain, "General Systems Theory and Ego Psychology: An Ecological Perspective," *Social Service Review* 52, 4 (Dec. 1978): 543.

9. Helen H. Perlman, *Persona: Social Role and Personality* (Chicago: Univ. of Chicago Press, 1968).

10. Martha W. Chescheir, "Social Role Discrepancies as Clues to Practice," *Social Work* 24, 2 (Mar. 1979): 89–94.

11. Erik H. Erikson, *Identity and the Life Cycle. Psych. Issues* 1, 1 (New York: International Universities Press, 1959): 116–121.

12. Erik H. Erikson, *Identity: Youth and Crisis* (New York: W. W. Norton, 1968): 96.

13. Gerald Caplan, *Principles of Preventive Psychiatry* (New York: Basic Books, 1964): 35.

14. John Cumming and Elaine Cumming, *Ego and Milieu* (New York: Atherton Press, 1966): 53–54.

15. Lydia Rapoport, "Crisis Intervention as a Mode of Brief Treatment," in Robert W. Roberts and Robert H. Nee, eds., *Theories of Social Casework* (Chicago: Univ. of Chicago Press, 1970): 275.

16. Erich Lindemann, "Symptomatology and Management of Acute Grief," *Amer. Jrnl. Psychiatry* 101, 2 (Sept. 1944). Reprinted in Howard J. Parad, ed., *Crisis Intervention: Selected Readings* (New York: Family Service Assn. of America, 1965): 7–21.

17. James S. Tyhurst and Libuse Tyhurst, "Displacement and Migration: A Study in Social Psychiatry," *Amer. Jrnl. Psychiatry* 107 (1951).

18. Rhona Rapoport and Robert Rapoport, "New Light on the Honeymoon," *Human Relations* 17 (1964): 33–56.

19. E. E. LeMasters, "Parenthood as a Crisis," *Marriage and Family Living* 19, 4 (1957). Reprinted in Parad, (1965): 111–117.

20. Stanley H. Cath, "Some Dynamics of the Middle and Later Years," *Smith College Studies in Social Work* 23, 2 (1963). Reprinted in Parad (1965): 174–192.

21. Robert S. Weiss, "Transition States and Other Stressful Situations: Their Nature and Programs for Their Management," in Gerald Caplan and Marie Killilea, eds., *Support Systems and Mutual Help: A Multidisciplinary Exploration* (New York: Grune & Stratton, 1976): 213–232.

22. Naomi Golan, "When Is a Client in Crisis?" *Social Casework* 50, 7 (July 1969): 389–394.

23. Naomi Golan, "The Influence of Developmental and Transitional Crises on Victims of Disaster," in Charles Spielberger and Seymour Sarason, eds., *Stress and Anxiety,* Vol. 8 (Washington, D.C.: Hemisphere Press, 1980).

24. Naomi Golan, "Using Situational Crises to Ease Transitions in the Life Cycle," *Amer. Jrnl. Orthopsychiatry* 50, 3 (July 1980): 542–550.

25. Most recently presented in Erik H. Erikson, ed., *Adulthood* (New York: W. W. Norton, 1976): 25. (See Chapter 3.)

26. Naomi Golan and Ruth Gruschka, "Integrating the New Immigrant: A Model for Social Work Practice in Transitional States," *Social Work* 16, 2 (Apr. 1971): 82–87; Naomi Golan, "Wife to Widow to Woman," *Social Work* 20, 5 (Sept. 1975): 369–374.

27. See Naomi Golan, *Treatment in Crisis Situations* (New York: Free Press, 1978): 149–186.

Chapter 2. The Nature of Transitions and the Change Process

1. I have been unable to trace the original source but this passage from Samuel Butler is quoted in Aaron Antonovsky, "Conceptual and Methodological Problems in the Study of Resistance Resources and Stressful Life Events," in Barbara S. Dohrenwend and Bruce P. Dohrenwend, eds., *Stressful Life Events: Their Nature and Effects* (New York: John Wiley & Sons, 1974): 245.

2. *Random House Dictionary*, unabridged ed. (New York: Random House, 1967): 1505.

3. James S. Tyhurst, "The Role of Transitional States—Including Disasters—in Mental Illness," *Symposium on Preventive and Social Psychiatry* (Washington, D.C.: Walter Reed Army Institution of Research, 1957): 149–169.

4. Rhona Rapoport, "Normal Crises, Family Structure, and Mental Health," *Family Process*, 2, 1 (1963). Reprinted in Parad, *Crisis Intervention* (1965): 75–86.

5. Daniel J. Levinson with Charlotte N. Darrow, Edward B. Klein, Maria H. Levinson, and Braxton McKee, *The Seasons of a Man's Life* (New York: A. A. Knopf, 1978): 49–50.

6. Phyllis R. Silverman, *Mutual Help Groups: A Guide for Mental Health Workers* (Rockville, Md.: National Institute of Mental Health, 1978): 12.

7. See, for example, Peter Marris, *Loss and Change* (New York: Pantheon Books, 1974); Paul Watzlawick, John H. Weakland, and Richard Fisch, *Change: Principles of Problem Formulation and Problem Resolution* (New York: W. W. Norton, 1974); Virginia Satir, James Stachowiak, and Harvey A. Taschman, *Helping Families to Change* (New York: Jason Aronson, 1975); Stephen A. Appelbaum, *The Anatomy of Change* (New York: Plenum Press, 1977).

8. Helen H. Perlman, "Adulthood and Personal Change," in *Persona: Social Role and Personality* (Chicago: Univ. of Chicago Press, 1968): 30–32.

9. Robert J. Havighurst, *Human Development and Education* (London: Longmans, Green, 1953): 5.

10. Howard Spierer, *Major Transitions in the Human Life Cycle* (Academy for Educational Development, 1977): 10–18.

11. Bernice L. Neugarten, "Adult Personality: Toward a Psychology of the Life Cycle," in Neugarten, ed., *Middle Age and Aging* (Chicago: Univ. of Chicago Press, 1968): 137–147.

12. Orville G. Brim, Jr., "Adult Socialization," in John A. Clausen, ed., *Socialization and Society* (Boston: Little, Brown, 1968): 184–193.
13. Howard S. Becker, "Personal Change in Adult Life," in Neugarten (1968): 148–158.
14. Cornelis B. Bakker, "Why People Don't Change," *Psychotherapy: Theory, Research, and Practice* 12, 2 (Summer 1975): 164–172.
15. Marris (1974): 5–22.
16. C. Murray Parkes, "Psycho-Social Transitions," *Social Science and Medicine* 5 (1971): 101–115.
17. Robert W. White, "Strategies of Adaptation: An Attempt at Systematic Description," in George V. Coelho, David A. Hamburg, and John E. Adams, eds., *Coping and Adaptation* (New York: Basic Books, 1974): 47–68.
18. David A. Hamburg and John E. Adams, "A Perspective on Coping Behavior: Seeking and Utilizing Information in Major Transitions," *Archives Gen. Psychiatry* 17 (1967): 277–284.
19. John E. Adams and Erich Lindemann, "Coping with Long-Term Disability," in Coelho, Hamburg, and Adams (1974): 127–138.
20. Lois B. Murphy and Alice E. Moriarty, *Vulnerability, Coping, and Growth: From Infancy to Adolescence* (New Haven: Yale Univ. Press, 1976).
21. Lois B. Murphy, "Coping, Vulnerability, and Resilience in Childhood," in Coelho, Hamburg, and Adams (1974): 69–100.
22. Aaron Antonovsky, *Health, Stress, and Coping* (San Francisco: Jossey-Bass, 1979).
23. For its most recent version, see Naomi Golan, "Intervention at Times of Transitions: Sources and Forms of Help," *Social Casework* 61, 5 (May 1980): 259–266.
24. For a somewhat similar but more detailed effort to chart the stages in the response to stress, see David Reiss and Mary Ellen Olivieri, "Family Paradigm and Family Coping: A Proposal for Linking the Family's Intrinsic Adaptive Capacities to Its Response to Stress," *Family Relations* 29, 4 (Oct. 1980): 431–444.

Chapter 3. Change Throughout the Adult Life Cycle

1. Arnold Van Gennep, *Les Rites de Passage* (Paris, 1908). Translated and reprinted as *The Rites of Passage* (Chicago: Univ. of Chicago Press, 1960).
2. Annemarie Malefijt, *Religion and Culture* (New York: Macmillan, 1968): 190–195.
3. Mircea Eliade, *Rites and Symbols of Initiation: The Mysteries of Birth and Rebirth* (New York: Harper & Row, 1958).
4. Paul Bohannan, *Social Anthropology* (New York: Holt, Rinehart & Winston, 1963): 337–339.
5. See Joseph Campbell, ed., *The Portable Jung* (Harmondsworth, Eng.: Penguin, 1971), "The Stages of Life": 3–22; Barbara Hannah, *Jung: His Life and Work* (New York: G. P. Putnam's Sons, 1976); Anthony Storr, "C. G. Jung," *The American Scholar* 31 (1962): 395–403. Also see Levinson's discussion on Jung in *Seasons of a Man's Life* (1978).

6. Charlotte Bühler, "The Developmental Structure of Goal Setting in Group and Individual Studies," in Bühler and Fred Massarik, eds., *The Course of Human Life: A Study of Goals in the Humanistic Perspective* (New York: Springer, 1968): 27–54. Also Bühler, *The Way to Fulfillment: Psychological Techniques* (New York: Hawthorn Books, 1971).

7. Erik H. Erikson, *Childhood and Society* (New York: W. W. Norton, 1950).

8. Erik H. Erikson, *Identity: Youth and Crisis* (New York: W. W. Norton, 1968): 96.

9. Erik H. Erikson, *Insight and Responsibility* (New York: W. W. Norton, 1964): 114.

10. Presented as Keynote Address at opening of Einstein Centennial in Jerusalem, March 1979. Personal communication.

11. Erik H. Erikson, "Reflections on Dr. Borg's Life Cycle," in Erikson, ed., *Adulthood* (New York: W. W. Norton, 1976): 1–31.

12. Robert J. Havighurst, *Human Development and Education* (London: Longmans, Green, 1953): 257–283.

13. Klaus F. Riegel, "Adult Life Crises: A Dialectic Interpretation of Development," in Nancy Datan and Leon H. Ginsberg, eds., *Life-Span Developmental Psychology: Normative Life Crises* (New York: Academic Press, 1975): 123–126.

14. Klaus F. Riegel, "Toward a Dialectical Theory of Development," *Human Development* 18, 1–2 (1975): 50–51.

15. Bernice L. Neugarten, "Continuities and Discontinuities of Psychological Issues into Adult Life," *Human Development* 12 (1969): 121–122. Also, Neugarten and Nancy Datan, "Sociological Perspectives in the Life Cycle," in Baltes and Schaie, *Life-Span Developmental Psychology* (1973): 56–59.

16. Bernice L. Neugarten, "Adaptation and the Life Cycle," *Counseling Psychologist* 6, 1 (1976): 16–20.

17. Mathilda W. Riley and Joan Waring, "Age and Aging," in Robert K. Merton and Robert Nisbet, eds., *Contemporary Social Problems*, 4th ed. (New York: Harcourt Brace Jovanovich, 1976): 379–389.

18. Evelyn Duvall, *Marriage and Family Development*, 5th ed. (Phiadelphia: Lippincott, 1977): 148–153.

19. Duvall (1977): 167–180.

20. Joan Aldous, *Family Careers: Developmental Change in Families* (New York: John Wiley & Sons, 1978): 79, 108.

21. Alice Rossi, "Family Development in a Changing World," *Amer. Jrnl. Psychiatry* 128 (1972): 1058–1059.

22. Frances H. Scherz, "Maturational Crises and Parent–Child Interaction," *Social Casework* 52, 6 (June 1971): 362–369.

23. Sonya L. Rhodes, "A Developmental Approach to the Life Cycle of the Family," *Social Casework* 58, 5 (May 1977): 301–311.

24. Daniel J. Levinson with Charlotte N. Darrow, Edward B. Klein, Maria H. Levinson, and Braxton McKee, *The Seasons of a Man's Life* (New York: A. A. Knopf, 1978). Earlier findings were reported by the same authors in D. F. Ricks, A. Thomas, and M. Roff, eds., *Life History Research in Psychopathology*, vol. 3 (Minneapolis: Univ. of Minnesota Press, 1974): 241–258, and in "Periods in the Adult Development of Men: Ages 18–45," *Counseling Psychologist* 6, 1 (1976): 21–25.

25. Wendy Ann Stewart, "Psychosocial Study of the Formation of the Early Adult Life Structure in Women," Dissertation, School of Arts and Sciences, Columbia University, 1977.

26. Vaillant, George E., *Adaptation to Life: How the Best and Brightest Come of Age* (Boston: Little, Brown, 1977).

27. Roger L. Gould, "The Phases of Adult Life: A Study in Developmental Psychology," *Amer. Jrnl. Psychiatry* 129, 5 (Nov. 1972): 521–531. Also, Gould, "Adult Life Stages: Growth Towards Self-Tolerance," *Psychology Today* 8, 9 (1975): 74–78.

28. Marjorie F. Lowenthal, Majda Thurnher, David Chiriboga, and Associates, *Four Stages of Life: A Comparative Study of Women and Men Facing Transitions* (San Francisco: Jossey-Bass, 1975).

29. Gail Sheehy, *Passages: Predictable Crises of Adult Life* (New York: E. P. Dutton, 1976).

Chapter 4. The Early Adult Years: Laying the Foundations

1. Norman Goodman and Kenneth A. Feldman, "Expectations, Ideals, and Reality: Youth Enters College," in Sigmund E. Dragastin and Glen N. Elder, Jr., eds., *Adolescence in the Life Cycle: Psychological Change and Social Context* (Washington, D. C.: Hemisphere, 1975): 163.

2. Kenneth Kenniston, "Youth, a (New) Stage of Life," *American Scholar* 39 (Autumn 1970): 631.

3. Peter Blos, *The Adolescent Passage* (New York: International Universities Press, 1979): 406–419.

4. Beatrix A. Hamburg, "Early Adolescence: A Specific and Stressful Stage of the Life Cycle," in Coelho, Hamburg, and Adams, *Coping and Adaptation* (1974): 103.

5. Levinson, *Seasons of a Man's Life* (1978): 73–78.

6. Robert H. White, *Lives in Progress*, 3rd ed. (New York: Holt, Rinehart & Winston, 1975): 336–362.

7. Perlman, *Persona* (1968): 74–75.

8. Theodore Lidz, "Occupational Choice," in *The Person: His and Her Development Throughout the Life Cycle*, rev. ed. (New York: Basic Books, 1976): 392–409.

9. Guy J. Manaster, *Adolescent Development and the Life Tasks* (Boston: Allyn & Bacon, 1977): 211–229.

10. See discussion in ibid., 219–220.

11. Barbara M. Newman and Philip R. Newman, *Development Through Life: A Psychosocial Approach* (Homewood, Ill.: Dorsey Press, 1975): 264–267.

12. Levinson (1978): 101–106.

13. Ibid., 141–143.

14. For a fuller discussion of this issue, see Robert S. Weiss, Edwin Harwood, and David Riesman, "The World of Work," in Robert K. Merton and Robert Nisbet, eds., *Contemporary Social Problems*, 4th ed. (New York: Harcourt Brace Jovanovich, 1976): 613–617.

15. Emanuel Kay, "The World of Work: Its Promises, Conflicts, and Reality," in *The Middle Years* (New York: Amer. Medical Assn., 1974): 63–69.

16. Lillian B. Rubin, *Worlds of Pain: Life in the Working Class Family* (New York: Basic Books, 1976): 155–184.

17. Robert J. Havighurst, "Social Roles, Work, Leisure, and Education," in Carl Eisdorfer and M. Powell Lawton, eds., *The Psychology of Adult Development and Aging* (Washington, D.C.: Amer. Psychological Assn., 1973): 601.

18. Rhona Rapoport and Robert N. Rapoport, "Further Considerations on the Dual Career Family," *Human Relations* 24 (1971): 519–533.

19. Carol Ireson, "Girls' Socialization for Work," in Ann Stromberg and Shirley Harkess, eds., *Women Working: Theories and Facts in Perspective* (Palo Alto: Mayfield, 1978): 178–200.

20. Cynthia F. Epstein, *Woman's Place: Options and Limits in a Professional Career* (Berkeley: Univ. of Calif. Press, 1971): 17.

21. Stewart, "Life Structure in Women" (1977).

22. Lucile Duberman, *Gender and Sex in Society* (New York: Praeger, 1975): 86.

23. Myrna Weissman et al., "The Educated Housewife: Mild Depression and the Search for Work," *Amer. Jrnl. Orthopsychiatry* 43, 4 (July 1973): 565–573.

24. Linda Brooks, "Supermoms Shift Gears: Re-Entry Women," *Counseling Psychologist* 6, 2 (1976): 33–37.

Chapter 5. Transition to Marriage/Couplehood

1. Duvall, *Marriage and Family Development* (1977): 185.

2. Lidz, "Marital Choice" and "Marital Adjustment" in *The Person* (1976): 410–433, 434–466.

3. William J. Lederer and Don D. Jackson, *The Mirages of Marriage* (New York: W. W. Norton, 1968): 42–46.

4. Aldous, *Family Careers* (1978): 134–140.

5. Rubin, *Worlds of Pain* (1976): 53–59.

6. Bengt Ankarloo, "Marriage and Family Formation," in Tamara K. Hareven, ed., *Transitions: The Family and the Life Course in Historical Perspective* (New York: Academic Press, 1978): 123.

7. Robert G. Ryder, John S. Kafka, and David H. Olson, "Separating and Joining Influences in Courtship and Early Marriage," *Amer. Jrnl. Orthopsychiatry* 41, 3 (Apr. 1971): 450–464.

8. Rapoport in Parad, *Crisis Intervention* (1965): 79–85.

9. Rhona Rapoport and Robert Rapoport, "New Light on the Honeymoon," *Human Relations* 17 (1964): 33–56.

10. Lidz (1976): 435.

11. Duvall (1977): 194–195.

12. Ryder, Kafka, and Olson (1971): 457–459.

13. Naomi Golan and Shlomo Sharlin, "Using Natural Helping Systems to Intervene," paper presented at Annual meeting of American Orthopsychiatric Association, Atlanta, Ga., Mar. 5, 1976. Mimeo.

14. Lidz (1976): 436–437.

15. Arthur L. Leader, "The Place of In-Laws in Marital Relationships," *Social Casework* 56, 8 (Oct. 1975): 486–491.
16. Peter J. Stein, "Singlehood: An Alternative to Marriage," *Family Coordinator* 24, 4 (Oct. 1975): 489–503.
17. Rosabeth Kanter, Dennis Jaffe, and D. Kelly Weisberg, "Coupling, Parenting, and the Presence of Others: Intimate Relations in Communal Households," *Family Coordinator* 24 (1975): 433–53. Reprinted in Gladys K. Phelan, ed., *Family Relationships* (Minneapolis: Burgess, 1979): 338–357.
18. Wayne L. Cotton, "Social and Sexual Relationships of Lesbians," *Jrnl. Sex Research* 11, 2 (May 1975): 139–148. Reprinted in Arlene S. Skolnick and Jerome H. Skolnick, eds., *Family in Transition*, 2nd. ed. (Boston: Little, Brown, 1977): 537–545.
19. Sandra B. Coleman, "A Developmental Stage Hypothesis for Non-Marital Dyadic Relationships," *Jrnl. Marriage and Family Counseling* 3, 2 (Apr. 1977): 71–76.
20. Ida Davidoff, "Living Together as a Developmental Phase: A Holistic View," *Jrnl. Marriage and Family Counseling* 3, 3 (July 1977): 67–76.
21. Rubin (1976): 69–73.

Chapter 6. Transition to Parenthood

1. E. E. LeMasters, "Parenthood as Crisis," *Marriage and Family Living* 19, 4 (Nov. 1957): 352–355. Reprinted in Parad, *Crisis Intervention* (1965): 111–117.
2. Everett Dyer, "Parenthood as a Crisis: A Restudy," *Marriage and Family Living* 25, 2 (May 1963): 196–201. Reprinted in Parad (1965): 312–323.
3. Daniel F. Hobbs, Jr., "Parenthood as a Crisis: A Third Study," *Jrnl. Marriage and the Family* 27, 3 (Aug. 1965): 367–372.
4. Daniel F. Hobbs, Jr., and Sue P. Cole, "Transition to Parenthood: A Decade Replication," *Jrnl. Marriage and the Family* 38, 4 (Nov. 1976): 723–731.
5. Daniel F. Hobbs, Jr., and Jane M. Wimbish, "Transition to Parenthood by Black Couples," *Jrnl. Marriage and the Family* 39, 4 (Nov. 1977): 677–689.
6. Alice S. Rossi, "Transition to Parenthood," *Jrnl. Marriage and the Family* 30, 1 (Feb. 1968): 26–39. Reprinted in Skolnick and Skolnick, *Family in Transition* (1977): 351–362.
7. Perlman, "Parenthood," in *Persona* (1968): 117.
8. Rossi (1968): 32.
9. Lidz, "Parenthood," in *The Person* (1976): 467–481.
10. Perlman (1968): 117–118.
11. Lucie Jessner, Edith Weigert, and James L. Foy, "Development of Parental Attitudes During Pregnancy," in E. James Anthony and Therese Benedek, eds., *Parenthood: Its Psychology and Psychopathology* (Boston: Little, Brown, 1970): 214–216.
12. Nancy Chodorow, *The Reproduction of Mothering* (Berkeley: Univ. of California Press, 1978): 39.
13. Nancy F. Russo, "The Mothering Mandate," *Jrnl. Social Issues* 32, 3 (1976): 143–153.
14. Miriam D. Mazor, "The Problem of Infertility," in Malkah T. Notman and Carol

C. Nadelson, eds., *The Woman Patient: Medical and Psychological Interfaces*, vol. 1 (New York: Plenum Press, 1978): 137–160.

15. Jessica G. Davis, "Decisions about Reproduction: Genetic Counseling," in Notman and Nadelson (1978): 33–54.

16. For further discussion of this topic, see Lydia Rapoport and Lea Potts, "Abortion of Unwanted Pregnancy as a Potential Life Crisis," in Florence Haselkorn, ed., *Family Planning: A Sourcebook of Readings and Case Materials* (New York: Council of Social Work Education, 1971): 249–266; Leah Potts, "Counseling Women with Unwanted Pregnancies," in Haselkorn (1971): 267–280; Cornelia M. Donovan, "Psychotherapy in Abortion," in Jules Masserman, ed., *Psychiatric Therapies* 15 (1975): 77–83; Betty Russell and Sylvia Schild, "Pregnancy Counseling with College Women," *Social Casework* 57, 5 (May 1976): 324–329; Alice S. Honig, "What We Need to Know to Help the Teenage Parent," *Family Coordinator* 27, 2 (Apr. 1978): 113–119; Nancy H. Horowitz, "Adolescent Mourning Reactions to Infant and Fetal Loss," *Social Casework* 59, 9 (Nov. 1978): 551–559; D. Tracy Magid, Barbara D. Gross, and Bernard J. Shulman, "Preparing Pregnant Teenagers for Parenthood," *Family Coordinator* 28, 3 (July 1979): 359–364; Mary K. Zimmerman, *Passage Through Abortion* (New York: Praeger, 1977).

17. Aldous, *Family Careers* (1978): 158.

18. Therese Benedek, "The Psychobiology of Pregnancy," in Anthony and Benedek (1970): 137–152.

19. See Emanuel A. Freedman, "The Physiological Aspects of Pregnancy," in Notman and Nadelson (1978): 55–71; and Gay Guzinski, "Medical Gynecology: Problems and Patients," also in Notman and Nadelson (1978): 181–202.

20. Jessner, Weigert, and Foy in Anthony and Benedek (1970): 216–225.

21. Perlman (1968): 119–120.

22. Carol C. Nadelson, "Normal and Special Aspects of Pregnancy: A Psychological Approach," in Notman and Nadelson (1978): 73–86.

23. Perlman (1968): 119.

24. Benedek (1970): 148.

25. Aldous (1978): 161.

26. Jessner, Weigert, and Foy (1970): 232–233.

27. Laurence Barnhill, Gerald Rubenstein, and Neil Rocklin, "From Generation to Generation: Fathers-to-Be in Transition," *Family Coordinator* 28, 2 (Apr. 1979): 229–236.

28. Michael E. Lamb. "Fathers: Forgotten Contributors to Child Development," *Human Development* 18 (1975): 245–266.

29. See Sheldon H. Cherry, *From Women of All Ages: A Gynecologist's Guide to Modern Female Health Care* (New York: Macmillan, 1979): 115–147.

30. For the following account of the birth process, I am indebted to Juanita H. Williams, *Psychology of Women: Behavior in a Biosocial Context* (New York: W. W. Norton, 1977): 265–281.

31. Anne M. Seiden, "The Sense of Mastery in the Childbirth Experience," in Notman and Nadelson (1978): 87–106.

32. Arel S. Wente and Susan B. Crockenberg, "Transition to Fatherhood: Lamaze Preparation, Adjustment Difficulty, and the Husband–Wife Relationship," *Family Coordinator* 25, 4 (Oct. 1976): 351–357.

33. Donald W. Winnicott, "The Mother–Infant Experience of Mutuality," in Anthony and Benedek (1970): 245–258.
34. Nadelson, (1978): 78–79.
35. Williams (1977): 281–282.
36. Barnhill, Rubenstein, and Rocklin (1979): 233–234.
37. Rubin, *Worlds of Pain* (1976): 74–83.

Chapter 7. Geographic Moves and Migrations

1. Lee Ann Hoff, *People in Crisis: Understanding and Helping* (Menlo Park, Ca.: Addison-Wesley, 1978): 202–203.
2. Larry H. Long, "Migration and Resettlement Services," in *Encyclopedia of Social Work*, 17th issue, vol. 2 (Washington, D.C.: National Assn. of Social Workers, 1977): 914–919.
3. Brim, "Adult Socialization" (1968): 217–222.
4. Joseph W. Eaton, ed., *Migration and Social Welfare* (New York: National Assn. of Social Workers, 1971): ix–xvi.
5. Robert T. Constable, "Mobile Families and the School," *Social Casework* 59, 7 (July 1978): 421–423.
6. Myrtle R. Reul, "Migration: The Confrontation of Opportunity and Trauma," in Eaton (1971): 6–18.
7. Francine S. Hall and Douglas T. Hall, *The Two-Career Couple* (Reading, Mass.: Addison-Wesley, 1979): 191–213.
8. Reul (1971): 9.
9. Marc Fried, "Grieving for a Lost Home," in Leonard J. Duhl, ed., *The Urban Conditions: People and Policy in the Metropolis* (New York: Basic Books, 1963): 51–117. Reprinted in Alan Monat and Richard S. Lazarus, eds., *Stress and Coping: An Anthology* (New York: Columbia Univ. Press, 1977): 375–388. Also, Marc Fried, Peggy Gleicher, Lorna Ferguson, and John Havens, "Patterns of Migration and Adjustment Among the Black Population of Boston," in Eaton (1971): 117–141.
10. Maxine Gaylord, "Relocation and the Corporate Family: Unexplored Issues," *Social Work* 24, 3 (May 1979): 188.
11. Myrna M. Weissman and Eugene S. Paykel, "Moving and Depression in Women," *Society* 9 (July/Aug. 1972). Reprinted in Robert S. Weiss, ed., *Loneliness: The Experience of Emotional and Social Isolation* (Cambridge: M.I.T. Press, 1973): 154–164.
12. Carlos E. Sluzki, "Migration and Family Conflict," in *In the Family* 3 (Mar. 1978): 1–3. Report of Workshop at Second International Congress of Family Therapy, Jerusalem, July 1977.
13. Reul (1971): 10–15.
14. Judith Shuval, *Immigrants: On the Threshold* (New York: Atherton Press, 1963).
15. Elliott Aronson, "Dissonance Theory: Progress and Problems," in Robert Abelson et al., eds., *Theories of Cognitive Consistency: A Sourcebook* (Chicago: Rand McNally, 1968): 6. Quoted in Reul (1971): 11.
16. Golan and Gruschka, "Integrating the New Immigrant (1971): 82–87.

17. Stella B. Jones, "Geographic Mobility as Seen by the Wife and Mother," *Jrnl. Marriage and the Family* 35, 2 (May 1973): 210–218.

18. Curtis L. Barrett and Helen Noble, "Mothers' Anxieties vs. the Effects of Long-Distance Moves on Children," *Jrnl. Marriage and the Family* 35, 2 (May 1973): 181–188.

19. Constable (1978): 424–426.

20. Sluzki (1978).

21. Ibid.

Chapter 8. The Mid-Adult Years: Adjusting and Changing

1. Dante Alighieri, *The Divine Comedy*, vol. 1. Translated by Charles S. Singleton (Princeton: Princeton Univ. Press, 1975), Canto 1.

2. For a fascinating discussion of this topic see Elliott Jaques, "Death and the Mid-Life Crisis," *Intl. Jrnl. Psychoanalysis* 46 (1965): 502–514. A review of the midlife crisis as it is currently portrayed in popular culture can be found in Stanley D. Rosenberg and Michael P. Farrell, "Identity and Crisis in Middle-Aged Men," *Intl. Jrnl. Aging and Human Development* 7, 2 (1976): 153–170.

3. Among the more recent are: Joel and Lois Davitz, *Making It from 40 to 50* (New York: Random House, 1976); Barbara Fried, *The Middle-Age Crisis*, rev. ed. (New York: Harper & Row, 1976); Estelle Fuchs, *The Second Season: Life, Love and Sex for Women in the Middle Years* (Garden City, N.Y.: Anchor Press/Doubleday, 1978); Eda J. LeShan, *The Wonderful Crisis of Middle Age: Some Personal Reflections* (New York: David McKay, 1973); Nancy Mayer, *The Male Mid-Life Crisis: Fresh Starts After Forty* (New York: Signet, 1978); Lillian Rubin, *Women of a Certain Age: The Midlife Search for Self* (New York: Harper & Row, 1979); Henry Still, *Surviving the Male Mid-Life Crisis* (New York: Crowell, 1977).

4. Richard L. Kerckhoff, "Marriage and Middle Age," *Family Coordinator* 25, 1 (Jan. 1976): 5.

5. Committee on Work and Personality in the Middle Years, Social Science Research Council, Progress Report, June 1, 1974–Oct. 1, 1976. New York. Mimeo.

6. Bernice L. Neugarten. "The Awareness of Middle Age," in Neugarten, *Middle Age and Aging* (1968): 93.

7. Erikson, *Insight and Responsibility* (1964): 131–132.

8. Robert C. Peck, "Psychological Developments in the Second Half of Life," in Neugarten (1968): 88–90.

9. Neugarten (1968): 94–96.

10. Fried (1976): 8–16.

11. The Davitzes did a survey of 100 men's and women's recollections of how they passed through the decade of their forties. See Davitz and Davitz (1976): 21–44, for men's reactions.

12. Jaques (1965).

13. Levinson, *Seasons of a Man's Life* (1978): 191–259.

14. David L. Krantz, *Radical Career Change* (New York: Free Press, 1978).

15. See Davitz and Davitz (1976): 132–165, for women's reactions.

16. Sheehy, *Passages* (1976): 261–268.

17. Florine B. Livson, "Coming Out of the Closet: Marriage and Other Crises of Middle Age," in Lillian E. Troll, Joan Israel, and Kenneth Israel, eds., *Looking Ahead: A Woman's Guide to the Problems and Joys of Growing Older* (Englewood Cliffs, N.J.: Prentice-Hall, 1977): 82–83.

18. This case first appeared in Naomi Golan, "Building Competence in Transitional and Crisis Situations," in Anthony N. Maluccio, *Building Competence in Clients* (New York: Free Press, 1981).

19. Chief source for this material is Cherry, *Women of All Ages* (1979); 193–198.

20. Williams, *Psychology of Women* (1977): 356–357.

21. Lynn Caine, *Lifelines* (New York: Dell, 1977): 173.

22. Therese F. Benedek, "Climacterium: A Developmental Phase," *Psychoanalytic Quarterly* 19, 1 (1950): 1–27.

23. Helene Deutsch, *The Psychology of Women: A Psychoanalytic Interpretation* (New York: Grune & Stratton, 1944): 436.

24. Bernice L. Neugarten, Vivian Wood, Ruth L. Kraines, and Barbara Loomis, "Women's Attitudes Towards the Menopause," in Neugarten (1968): 195–200.

25. N. Shafer, "Helping Women Through the Change of Life," *Sexology* 36 (1970): 54–56.

26. For a stimulating discussion of the surgical and personal implications of hysterectomies, see Fuchs (1978): 193–216.

27. Duvall, *Marriage and Family Development* (1977): 355–356.

28. Marjorie Lowenthal and David Chiriboga, "Transition to the Empty Nest: Crisis, Challenge, or Relief?" *Archives of General Psychiatry* 26 (Jan. 1972): 8–14.

29. Donald L. Spence and Thomas Lonner, "The Empty Nest: A Transition Within Motherhood," *Family Coordinator* 20, 4 (Oct. 1971): 369–375.

30. Hanna Shavit, "The Empty Nest as a Transitional Period for the Mother," M.A. Thesis, University of Haifa School of Social Work, 1979. Mimeo.

31. Elizabeth B. Harkins, "Effects of Empty Nest Transition on Self-Report of Psychological and Physical Well-Being," *Jrnl. Marriage and the Family* 40, 3 (Aug. 1978): 547–556.

32. Sophie F. Loewenstein, "Toward Choice and Differentiation in the Midlife Crisis of Women," Simmons College School of Social Work, 1979. Mimeo.

33. Rubin (1979): 13–30.

34. Irwin Deutscher, "The Quality of Postparental Life," in Neugarten (1968): 263–268.

35. Majda Thurnher, "Midlife Marriage: Sex Differences in Evaluation and Perspectives," *Intl. Jrnl. Aging and Human Development* 7, 2 (1976): 129–135.

36. William H. Masters and Virginia E. Johnson, "Human Sexual Response: The Aging Female and Aging Male," in Neugarten (1968): 269–272.

37. Ralph E. Johnson, "Marital Patterns During the Middle Years." Unpublished doctoral dissertation (Minneapolis: Univ. of Minnesota, 1968). Reported in Aldous, *Family Careers* (1978): 191.

38. Aldous (1978): 193–194.

39. Orville G. Brim, Jr., "Theories of the Male Mid-Life Crisis," *Counseling Psychologist* 6, 1 (1976): 2–9. For a simple but detailed review of the endocrinal changes in men, see Fried (1976): 28–34, or Still (1977): 20–26.

40. Jessica F. Cohen, "Male Roles in Midlife," *Family Coordinator* 28, 4 (Oct. 1979): 466–467.
41. Sheehy (1976): 316.
42. Helmut J. Ruebsaat and Raymond Hull, *The Male Climacteric* (New York: Hawthorn Books, 1975). Quoted in Sheehy (1976): 317.
43. Edwin S. Shneidman, Norman L. Farberow, and Robert E. Litman, *The Psychology of Suicide* (New York: Science House, 1970): 356.
44. Still (1977): 43–57.
45. Martin Strickler, "Crisis Intervention and the Climacteric Man," *Social Casework* 56, 2 (Feb. 1975): 85.
46. Ibid.: 89.
47. Rubin (1979): 30–36.
48. Strickler (1975): 86.
49. Robert A. Lewis, Phillip J. Freneau, and Craig L. Roberts, "Fathers and the Postparental Transition," *Family Coordinator* 28, 4 (Oct. 1979): 514–520.
50. LeShan (1973): 268–269.
51. Stephen Z. Cohen and Bruce M. Gans, *The Other Generation Gap: The Middle-Aged and Their Aging Parents* (Chicago: Follett, 1978): 3–12.

Chapter 9. Separation, Divorce, and Remarriage

1. Duvall, *Marriage and Family Development* (1977): 434–435.
2. See *Divorce and Separation*, special issue of *Jrnl. of Social Issues* 32, 1 (Winter 1976), for a representative collection of papers on this topic.
3. Any current issue of practice journals contains numerous announcements of local, regional, and national workshops sponsored either by special institutes of individual psychotherapy or marriage counseling or by professional organizations. Recently, divorce therapy has become a recognized subspecialization in the clinical field.
4. The volume *Women in Transition: A Feminist Handbook on Separation and Divorce* (New York: Scribner's, 1975), is a prime example of the effort to present divorce from a specific, vested viewpoint.
5. Characteristic of these are June and William Noble, *How to Live with Other People's Children* (New York: Hawthorn Books, 1977); Arlene Richards and Irene Willis, How to Get It Together When Your Parents Are Coming Apart (New York: Bantam Books, 1976); Persia Wooley, *Creative Survival for Single Mothers* (Millbrae, Ca.: Celestial Arts, 1975).
6. Paul Bohannan, "The Six Stations of Divorce," in Bohannan, ed., *Divorce and After* (Garden City, N.Y.: Doubleday Anchor Books, 1971): 33–62. Also see Judith S. Wallerstein and Joan B. Kelly, *Surviving the Breakup: How Children and Parents Cope with Divorce* (New York: Basic Books, 1980): 304–305.
7. Reva S. Wiseman, "Crisis Theory and the Process of Divorce," *Social Casework* 56, 4 (Apr. 1975): 205–212.
8. Samuel P. Chiancola, "The Process of Separation and Divorce: A New Approach," *Social Casework* 59, 8 (Oct. 1978): 494–499.
9. Sophie F. Loewenstein, "Helping Family Members Cope with Divorce," in

Sheldon Eisenberg and Lewis Patterson, eds., *Helping Clients with Special Concerns* (Chicago: Rand McNally, 1979): 195.

10. George Levinger, "A Social Psychological Perspective on Marital Dissolution," in Levinger and Oliver C. Moles, eds., *Divorce and Separation* (New York: Basic Books, 1979): 37–60.

11. A. Campbell, "The American Way of Mating: Marriage, Si, Children, Only Maybe," *Psychology Today* (May 1975): 37–43.

12. See *Women in Transition* (1975): 19–24. Also, Jessie Bernard, *The Future of Marriage* (New York: World, 1972).

13. Robert S. Weiss, *Marital Separation* (New York: Basic Books, 1975): 36–40.

14. Robert S. Weiss, "The Emotional Impact of Marital Separation," in Levinger and Moles (1979): 201–210.

15. John Bowlby, "Affectional Bonds: Their Nature and Origin," in Robert S. Weiss, ed., *Loneliness: The Experience of Emotional and Social Isolation* (Cambridge, Mass.: MIT Press, 1973): 38–52. See also Bowlby, *Separation: Anxiety and Anger* (New York: Basic Books, 1973).

16. Weiss (1975): 47–52.

17. Weiss, "The Study of Loneliness," in Weiss (1973): 20–22.

18. Weiss, in Levinger and Moles (1979): 207–210.

19. Loewenstein, in Eisenberg and Patterson (1979): 196.

20. John Bowlby and C. Murray Parkes, "Separation and Loss Within the Family," in E. James Anthony and Cyrille Koupernik, eds., *The Child in His Family*, vol. 1 (New York: Wiley-Interscience, 1970): 198–199.

21. Susan Gettleman and Jane Markowitz, *The Courage to Divorce* (New York: Ballantine, 1975): 33–41.

22. David Chiriboga and Loraine Cutler, "Stress Responses Among Divorcing Men and Women," *Jrnl. of Divorce* 1, 2 (Winter 1977–78): 95–106.

23. Sidney Wasserman, "The Middle Age Separation Crisis and Ego Supportive Casework," *Clinical Social Work Jrnl.* 1, 3 (Spring 1973): 38–47.

24. Weiss (1975): 261.

25. See *Women in Transition* (1975): 105–253. Also, Gettleman and Markowitz (1975): 157–210.

26. Gettleman and Markowitz (1975): 163.

27. John M. Haynes, "Divorce Mediator: A New Role," *Social Work* 23, 1 (Jan. 1978): 5–9; O. J. Coogler, Ruth Weber, and Patrick C. McKenry, "Divorce Mediation: A Means of Facilitating Divorce and Adjustment," *Family Coordinator* 28, 2 (Apr. 1979): 255–259.

28. Duvall (1977): 445.

29. See "The Case of Helen," in Golan, *Treatment in Crisis Situations* (1978): 180–181.

30. Duvall (1977): 443–444. Also Gettleman and Markowitz (1975): 202–207.

31. Graham B. Spanier and Robert F. Casto, "Adjustment to Separation and Divorce: A Qualitative Analysis," in Levinger and Moles (1979): 221.

32. Janet A. Kohen, Carol A. Brown, and Roslyn Feldberg, "Divorced Mothers: The Costs and Benefits of Female Family Control," in Levinger and Moles (1979): 234–235.

33. See Mary Jo Bane, "Marital Disruption and the Lives of Children," in Levinger and Moles (1979): 276–286; Shirley Jenkins, "Children of Divorce," *Children*

Today 7, 2 (Mar.–Apr. 1978): 16–20, 48; Cynthia Longfellow, "Divorce in Context: Its Impact on Children," in Levinger and Moles (1979): 287–306; Bernard Steinzor, *When Parents Divorce* (New York: Pantheon, 1969); Judith S. Wallerstein and Joan B. Kelly, "The Effects of Parental Divorce: Experiences of the Pre-School Child," *Jrnl. Amer. Academy of Child Psychiatry* 14 (Autumn 1975): 500–616; Kelly and Wallerstein, "The Effects of Parental Divorce: Experiences of the Child in Early Latency," *Amer. Jrnl. Orthopsychiatry* 46, 1 (Jan. 1976): 20–32; Wallerstein and Kelly, "The Effects of Parental Divorce: Experiences of the Child in Later Latency," *Amer. Jrnl. Orthopsychiatry* 46, 2 (Apr. 1976): 256–269; Wallerstein and Kelly, "The Effects of Parental Divorce: The Adolescent Experience," in Anthony and Koupernik, *The Child in His Family: Children at Psychiatric Risk*, vol. 3 (New York: John Wiley & Sons, 1974); Jane D. Woody, "Preventive Intervention for Children of Divorce," *Social Casework* 59, 9 (Nov. 1978): 537–544.

34. Robert S. Weiss, "Issues in the Adjudication of Custody When Parents Separate," in Levinger and Moles (1979): 324.
35. For specific issues related to the last, see Constance R. Ahrons, "The Coparental Divorce: Preliminary Research Findings and Policy Implications," paper presented at Annual Meeting of Natl. Council on Family Relations, Phila., Pa., Oct. 1979. Mimeo.
36. Judith S. Wallerstein and Joan B. Kelly, "Divorce Counseling: A Community Service for Families in the Midst of Divorce," *Amer. Jrnl. Orthopsychiatry* 47, 1 (Jan. 1977): 5. See also Lora H. Tessman, *Children of Parting Parents* (New York: Jason Aronson, 1978).
37. Ibid., 5–7.
38. Harry F. Keshet and Kristine M. Rosenthal, "Fathering After Marital Separation," *Social Work*, 23, 1 (Jan. 1978): 11–18.
39. Carol A. Brown, Roslyn Feldberg, Elizabeth M. Fox, and Janet Kohen, "Divorce: Chance of a New Lifetime," *Jrnl. Social Issues* 32, 1 (1976): 123.
40. Kay Tooley, "Antisocial Behavior and Social Alienation Post Divorce: 'The Man of the House' and His Mother," *Amer. Jrnl. Orthopsychiatry* 46, 1 (Jan. 1976): 37.
41. Weiss (1975): 139–142.
42. *Women in Transition* (1975): 35.
43. Wiseman (1975): 209–210.
44. Weiss (1975): 234–241.
45. Wiseman (1975): 211.
46. Weiss (1975): 294–295.
47. Gillian Dean and Douglas Gurak, "Marital Homogamy the Second Time Around," *Jrnl. Marriage and the Family* 40, 3 (Aug. 1978): 559.
48. Doris S. Jacobson, "Stepfamilies: Myths and Realities," *Social Work* 24, 3 (May 1979): 202.
49. Kenneth N. Walker, Joy Rogers, and Lillian Messinger, "Remarriage After Divorce: A Review," *Social Casework* 58, 5 (May 1977): 277.
50. Loewenstein (1979): 208–209.
51. Paul Bohannan, "Divorce Chains, Households of Remarriage, and Multiple Divorces," in Bohannan (1971): 128–131.
52. Jane W. Ransom, Stephen Schlesinger, and Andre P. Derdeyn, "Stepfamily in

Formation," *Amer. Jrnl. Orthopsychiatry* 49, 1 (Jan. 1979): 37–39. The tasks have been changed somewhat in this version.

53. Jacobson (1979): 203–204.
54. Emily B. Visher and John S. Visher, *Stepfamilies: A Guide to Working with Stepparents and Stepchildren* (New York: Brunner/Mazel, 1979): 258.

Chapter 10. Untimely Widowhood: Grief and Bereavement

1. Bertha G. Simos, *A Time to Grieve: Loss as a Universal Human Experience* (New York: Family Service Association of America, 1979).
2. Naomi Golan, "Wife to Widow to Woman," *Social Work* 20, 5 (Sept. 1975): 372.
3. Elisabeth Kübler-Ross, *On Death and Dying* (New York: Macmillan, 1969): 34–121.
4. Kübler-Ross (1969): 149.
5. Jane B. Kohn and Willard K. Kohn, *The Widower* (Boston: Beacon Press, 1978): 1.
6. Sigmund Freud, "Mourning and Melancholia," in James Strachey, ed., *The Complete Psychological Works of Sigmund Freud* (New York: Macmillan, 1964).
7. Erich Lindemann, "Symptomatology and Management of Acute Grief," *Amer. Jrnl. Psychiatry* 101 (Sept. 1944). Reprinted in Parad, *Crisis Intervention* (1965): 7–21.
8. John Bowlby, "Grief and Mourning in Infancy and Early Childhood," *Psychoanalytic Study of the Child* 15 (1960): 9–52.
9. C. Murray Parkes, *Bereavement: Studies of Grief in Adult Life* (New York: International Universities Press, 1972).
10. John Bowlby and C. Murray Parkes, "Separation and Loss Within the Family," in E. James Anthony and Cyrille Koupernik, eds., *The Child in His Family* (New York: Wiley-Interscience, 1970): 198–199.
11. See Simos (1979): 32–33. Also, Phyllis Silverman, "Background to the Development of the Widow-to-Widow Program," in Silverman, Dorothy MacKenzie, Mary Pettipas, and Elizabeth Wilson, eds., *Helping Each Other in Widowhood* (New York: Health Sciences, 1974): 4–10.
12. C. Murray Parkes, "The First Year of Bereavement," *Psychiatry* 33 (1970): 448–449.
13. George Krupp, "Maladaptive Reactions to the Death of a Family Member," *Social Casework* 53, 7 (July 1972): 426.
14. Bowlby and Parkes (1970): 202–203.
15. Parkes (1970): 457–458.
16. Marris, *Loss and Change* (1974): 34.
17. Roberta Temes, *Living with an Empty Chair: A Guide Through Grief* (Amherst, Me.: Mandala, 1977): 29–30.
18. Kohn and Kohn (1978): 123.
19. Martin Greene, "Loss of Mate—A Third Individuation Process," *Clinical Social Work Jrnl.* 4, 1 (Spring 1976): 44–47.
20. Golan (1975): 370–373.

21. Helena Z. Lopata in *Women as Widows: Support Systems* (New York: Elsevier, 1979): 13–46, offers a comparative perspective on widowhood in various societies. See also Marris (1974): 29–31.
22. Phyllis R. Silverman, "Widowhood and Preventive Intervention," *Family Coordinator* 21, 1 (Jan. 1972): 96–97.
23. Martha Yates, *Coping: A Survival Manual for Women Alone* (Englewood Cliffs, N.J.: Prentice-Hall, 1976): 7.
24. Kohn and Kohn (1978): 24–25.
25. Parkes (1972): 154.
26. Gerald Caplan, "The Family as a Support System," in Caplan and Marie Killilea, eds., *Support Systems and Mutual Help* (New York: Grune & Stratton, 1976): 27–29.
27. Maurice Lamm, *The Jewish Way in Death and Mourning* (New York: Jonathan David Publishers, 1969): 77–144.
28. Phyllis Silverman and Sue Englander, "The Widow's View of Her Dependent Children," *Omega* 6, 1 (1975). Reprinted in Sara Cook, *Children and Dying* (New York: Health Sciences, 1975): 63–66.
29. Taken from case record.
30. Stanley B. Goldberg, "Family Tasks and Reactions in the Crisis of Death," *Social Casework* 54, 7 (July 1973): 378–404.
31. Silverman (1972): 98.
32. Quoted in Silverman (1972): 99.
33. Golan (1975): 373.
34. Parkes (1972): 175–177.
35. Ira O. Glick, Robert S. Weiss, and C. Murray Parkes, *The First Year of Bereavement* (New York: John Wiley & Sons, 1974): 208.
36. Kohn and Kohn (1978): 113.
37. Lynn Caine, *Widow* (New York: William Morrow, 1974): 222.
38. Helena Z. Lopata, "Widowhood: Societal Factors in Life-Span Disruptions and Alternatives," in Datan and Ginsberg, *Life-Span Developmental Psychology* (1975): 229–231.
39. Lopata, *Women as Widows* (1979).

Chapter 11. The Late Adult Years: Coming to Terms with Limitations

1. Bernice L. Neugarten and Gunhild O. Hagestad, "Age and the Life Course," in Robert H. Binstock and Ethel Shanas, eds., *Handbook of Aging and the Social Sciences* (New York: Van Nostrand Reinhold, 1976): 36–46.
2. Elaine Brody, "Aging and Family Personality: A Developmental View," *Family Process* 13, 1 (Mar. 1974): 29.
3. Stanley H. Cath, "The Orchestration of Disengagement," *Intl. Jrnl. Aging and Human Development* 6, 3 (1975): 204.
4. Bernice L. Neugarten, "The Awareness of Middle Age," in Neugarten, *Middle Age and Aging* (1968): 93–98.
5. Mary K. Parent, "The Losses of Middle Age and Related Developmental Tasks,"

in Elizabeth Prichard et al., eds., *Social Work with the Dying Patient and the Family* (New York: Columbia Univ. Press, 1977): 147–150.

6. Ibid., 152–153.

7. Frances L. Feldman, *The Family in Today's Money World*, 2nd ed. (New York: Family Service Association of America, 1976): 132.

8. See Vivian Clayton, "Erikson's Theory of Human Development as It Applies to the Aged: Wisdom as Contradictive Cognition," *Human Development* 18, 1–2 (1975): 119–128.

9. Robert C. Peck, "Psychological Development in the Second Half of Life," in Neugarten (1968): 90–92.

10. Duvall, *Marriage and Family Development* (1977): 390.

11. Robert C. Atchley, *The Social Forces in Later Life: An Introduction to Social Gerontology*, 2nd ed. (Belmont, Ca.: Wadsworth, 1976): 102.

12. For various cross-national views on retirement age, see "Mandatory Retirement: Blessing or Curse?" Proceedings of Symposium presented by International Federation on Aging, Jerusalem, Aug. 25, 1978.

13. Abraham Monk, "Factors in the Preparation for Retirement by Middle-Aged Adults," *Gerontologist* 11, 4 (Winter 1971): 348–351.

14. For special problems entailed, see Alice C. Kilpatrick and Ebb G. Kilpatrick, Jr., "Retirement from the Military: Problems of Adjustment," *Social Casework* 60, 5 (May 1979): 282–288.

15. Douglas C. Kimmel, Karl F. Price, and James W. Walker, "Retirement Choice and Retirement Satisfaction," *Jrnl. Gerontology* 33, 4 (1978): 575–585.

16. Majda Thurnher, "Goals, Values, and Life Evaluations at the Preretirement Stage," *Jrnl. Gerontology* 29, 1 (Jan. 1974): 85–96.

17. James A. McCracken, "The Company Tells Me I'm Too Old," *Saturday Review*, Aug. 7, 1976. Reprinted in Ronald Gross, Beatrice Gross, and Sylvia Seidman, eds., *The New Old: Struggling for Decent Aging* (Garden City, N.Y.: Doubleday Anchor Books, 1978): 317.

18. George L. Maddox, "Retirement as a Social Event in the United States," in Neugarten (1968): 357.

19. Atchley (1976): 167–169.

20. Robert C. Atchley, "Adjustment to Loss of Job at Retirement," *Intl. Jrnl Aging and Human Development* 6, 1 (1975): 26.

21. Gerda Fillenbaum and George L. Maddox, "Work after Retirement: An Investigation into Some Psychologically Relevant Variables," *Gerontologist* 14, 4 (1974): 418–424.

22. Suzanne Richard, Florine Livson, and Paul G. Petersen, "Adjustment to Retirement," in Neugarten (1968): 178–180.

23. In the interest of brevity, it was decided not to review the various theories of aging in this chapter. Readers are referred to any text on gerontology for a discussion of this topic. See, for example, Robert J. Havighurst, Bernice L. Neugarten, and Sheldon L. Tobin, "Disengagement and Patterns of Aging," in Neugarten (1968); Richard A. Kalish and Francis W. Knudtson, "Attachment vs. Disengagement: A Life Span Conceptualization," *Human Development* 19, 3 (1976): 171–181. For the original theory, see Elaine Cumming and William E. Henry, *Growing Old: The Process of Disengagement* (New York: Basic Books, 1961); and its sequel, Cumming, "Engagement with an Old Theory," *Intl. Jrnl.*

Aging and Human Development 6, 3 (1975): 187–191. Atchley (1976) gives an overview of the current theories, pp. 31–36.

24. Robert W. Kleemeier, "Leisure and Disengagement in Retirement," *Gerontologist* 4, 4 (Dec. 1964). Reprinted in William C. Sze, ed. *The Human Life Cycle* (New York: Jason Aronson, 1975): 667–668.

25. Hyman Hirsch, "Higher Education in Retirement: The Institute for Retired Professionals," *Intl. Jrnl. Aging and Human Development* 8, 4 (1977–78): 367–374. Also Evaline P. Carsman, "Education as Recreation" in Troll, Israel, and Israel, *Looking Ahead* (1977): 140–146.

26. L. G. Peppers, "Patterns of Leisure and Adjustment to Retirement," *Gerontologist* 16, 5 (1976): 441–446.

27. Ruth Turk, *You're Getting Older. So What?* (New York: Cornerstone Library, 1976): 19–20.

28. Virginia Wood, "The Older Woman Alone," paper presented at *Forum on Aging: Problems, Patterns, and Prospects*, Calif. State Univ., Fresno, Mar. 22, 1979, mimeo. Also, *Operational Grant Proposal on Multidisciplinary Project on Aging Women*, Faye McBeath Institute on Aging and Adult Life, Univ. of Wisconsin-Madison, 1977, mimeo.

29. Feldman (1976): 131–132.

30. Morris L. Medley, "Marital Adjustment in the Post-Retirement Years," *Family Coordinator* 26, 1 (Jan. 1977): 5–11.

31. Jaber F. Gubrium, "Being Single in Old Age," *Intl. Jrnl. Aging and Human Development* 6, 1 (1975): 31–32.

32. Vivian Wood, Beth Howe, and Mary Wylie, "Growing Old Single," *Summary Report, 1978*, Faye McBeath Institute on Aging and Adult Life, Univ. of Wisconsin-Madison, mimeo.

Chapter 12. The Final Years

1. Barbara Myerhoff, *Number Our Days* (New York: E. P. Dutton, 1978): 1.

2. Elaine M. Brody, "Aging," in *Encyclopedia of Social Work*, 17th Issue, vol. 1 (Washington, D.C.: National Association of Social Workers, 1977): 60.

3. Irving Miller and Renee Solomon, "The Development of Group Services for the Elderly," in Carel B. Germain, ed., *Social Work Practice: People and Environments* (New York: Columbia Univ. Press, 1979): 81–82.

4. Brody (1977): 56.

5. E. Harvey Estes, Jr., "Health Experience in the Elderly," in Ewald Busse and Eric Pfeiffer, eds., *Behavior and Adaptation in Late Life* (Boston: Little, Brown, 1969): 115–117.

6. Ethel Shanas and George L. Maddox, "Aging, Health and the Organization of Health Resources," in Binstock and Shanas, *Handbook of Aging* (1976): 602.

7. Estes (1969): 117–118.

8. Brody (1977): 62–63.

9. Joan Lipner and Etta Sherman, "Hip Fractures in the Elderly—A Psychodynamic Approach," *Social Casework* 56, 2 (Feb. 1975): 97–100.

10. Charles M. Gaitz, "Aged Patients, Their Families and Physicians," in Gene

Usdin and Charles K. Hofling, *Aging: The Process and the People* (New York: Brunner/Mazel, 1978): 209.

11. Eric Pfeiffer, "Psychopathology and Social Pathology," in James E. Birren and K. Warner Schaie, eds. *Handbook of the Psychology of Aging* (New York: Van Nostrand Reinhold, 1977): 653–665.
12. Gaitz in Usdin and Hofling, "Aged Patients" (1978): 212–213.
13. Ibid., 214.
14. Atchley, *Social Forces in Later Life* (1972): 113–115.
15. Brody (1977): 63–64.
16. Gaitz in Usdin and Hofling (1978): 206–207.
17. Brody (1977): 67.
18. Myerhoff (1978): 1–2.
19. Frances Carp, "Housing and Living Environment of Older People," in Binstock and Shanas (1976): 249–253. Also, Pei N. Chen, "A Study of Chinese-American Elderly Residing in Hotel Rooms," *Social Casework* 60, 2 (Feb. 1979): 89–95.
20. L. M. Nelson and M. Winter, "Life Disruptions, Independence, Satisfaction, and Considerations of Moving," *Gerontologist* 15 (1975): 162.
21. We cannot at this point go into the very complex issue of parent–child relations in the later years. Thought-provoking discussions of some of the aspects of this subject can be found in Elaine M. Brody, "Aging and Family Personality: a Developmental View," *Family Process* 13, 1 (Mar. 1974): 23–37; Anne O. Freed, "The Family Agency and the Kinship System of the Elderly," *Social Casework* 56, 10 (Dec. 1975): 579–586; Charlotte Kirschner, "The Aging Family in Crisis: A Problem in Living," *Social Casework* 60, 4 (Apr. 1979): 209–216; Alida G. Silverman, Beatrice H. Kahn, and Gary Anderson, "A Model for Working with Multigenerational Families," *Social Casework* 58, 3 (Mar. 1977): 131–135; Teresa J. Tuzil, "The Agency Role in Helping Children and Their Aging Parents," *Social Casework* 59, 5 (May 1978): 302–305; Wayne C. Seelbach, "Correlates of Aged Parents' Filial Responsibility, Expectations, and Realizations," *Family Coordinator* 27, 4 (Oct. 1978): 341–350; Marvin B. Sussman, "The Family Life of Old People," in Binstock and Shanas (1976): 218–243; and Russell A. Ward, "Limitations of the Family as a Supportive Institution in the Lives of the Aged," *Family Coordinator* 27, 4 (Oct. 1978): 365–373.

    Two volumes speaking directly to children of aging parents on this issue are Stephen Z. Cohen and Bruce M. Gans, *The Older Generation Gap: The Middle-Aged and Their Aging Parents* (Chicago: Follett, 1978), and Arthur N. Schwartz, *Survival Handbook for Children of Aging Parents* (Chicago: Follett, 1977).
22. Margaret Blenker, "Social Work and Family Relations in Later Life with Some Thoughts on Filial Maturity," in Ethel Shanas and Gordon Streib, eds., *Social Structure and the Family: Generational Relations* (Englewood Cliffs, N.J.: Prentice-Hall, 1965). Quoted in Brody (1974): 32–34. Also see Note 21.
23. Kirschner (1979): 209–210.
24. Ethel Shanas discusses this fully in her section, "Living Arrangements of Old People," in Busse and Pfeiffer (1969): 129–138.
25. William G. Bell, "Community Care for the Elderly: An Alternative to Institutionalization," *Gerontologist* 13, 3 (1973): 349–354. Also, Eloise Rathbone-McCuan, "Geriatric Day Care: A Family Perspective," *Gerontologist* 16 (1976): 517–521.

26. See "Home Care Pays Off," Report in *Newsweek*, Mar. 10, 1980: 53.
27. Shanas in Busse and Pfeiffer (1969): 134.
28. Lillian E. Troll, "The Family of Later Life: A Decade Review," *Jrnl. Marriage and the Family* 33 (1971): 279. Also, Joan F. Robertson, "The Significance of Grandparents: Perceptions of Young Adult Grandchildren," *Gerontologist* 16 (1977): 137–140; Newman and Newman, *Development Through Life* (1975): 353–355.
29. Allen Pincus, "Reminiscence in Aging and Its Implications for Social Work Practice," *Social Work* 15, 3 (July 1970): 47–51.
30. Gordon F. Streib, "An Alternative Family Forum for Older Persons: Need and Social Context," *Family Coordinator* 27, 4 (Oct. 1978): 413–420.
31. Jordan T. Kosberg, "The Nursing Home: A Social Work Paradox," *Social Work* 18, 2 (Mar. 1973): 104.
32. For an extensive discussion of the various types of institutions, see Brody (1977): 67–71; Alvin I. Goldfarb, "Institutional Care of the Aged," in Busse and Pfeiffer (1969): 289–312; and Richard A. Kalish, *Late Adulthood: Perspectives on Human Development* (Monterey, Ca.: Brooks/Cole, 1975): 99–102. The social policy of placement is also discussed.
33. See Schwartz (1977): 113–131, for a description of various types of community living facilities and what to look for in choosing each. For a discussion of the social worker's role in placement, see Barbara McNulty, "Home Care for the Terminal Patient and His Family," in Prichard, (1977): 171–179, and Lee H. Suszycki, "Effective Nursing Home Placement for the Elderly Dying Patient," also in Prichard, *Social Work with the Dying Patient* (1977): 185–197.
34. Marjorie F. Lowenthal and Alexander Simon, "Mental Crises and Institutionalization Among the Aged," *Jrnl. Geriatric Psychiatry* (Spring 1971): 173.
35. For such a layout, see Alan Lipman and Robert Slater, "Homes for Old People: Towards a Positive Environment," *Gerontologist* 17, 2 (1977): 146–156.
36. Edmund Sherman and Evelyn S. Newman, "The Meaning of Cherished Personal Possessions for the Elderly," *Int. Jrnl. Aging and Human Development* 8, 2 (1977–78): 181–192.
37. Caroline S. Ford, "Ego-Adaptive Mechanisms of Older People," *Social Casework* 46, 1 (Jan. 1965): 16–21. Reprinted in Sze, *Human Life Cycle* (1975): 600–603.
38. Ibid., 603–608.
39. See, for example, Charles A. Garfield, ed., *Psychosocial Care for the Dying Patient* (New York: McGraw-Hill, 1978); John Hinton, *Dying*, 2nd ed. (Middlesex, Eng.: Penguin Books, 1972); Kübler-Ross, *On Death and Dying* (1969); Robert J. Lifton and Eric Olson, *Living and Dying* (New York: Praeger, 1975); Prichard, *Social Work with the Dying Patient* (1977).
40. Elisabeth Kübler-Ross, *Death: The Final Stage of Growth* (Englewood Cliffs, N.J.: Prentice-Hall, 1975): 5.
41. For many of the issues involved in informing about death, see Garfield (1978).
42. Richard A. Kalish, "The Onset of the Dying Process," *Omega* 1 (1970): 57–69.
43. Frances C. Jeffers and Adriaan Verwoerdt, "How the Old Face Death," in Busse and Pfeiffer (1969): 164–178.
44. Robert N. Butler, "The Life Review: An Interpretation of Reminiscence in the Aged," *Psychiatry* 26, 1 (Feb. 1963). Reprinted in Neugarten, *Middle Age and Aging* (1968): 486–496.

45. Kübler-Ross (1969): 149–152.
46. E. Mansell Pattison, "The Living-Dying Process," in Garfield (1978): 152.
47. Richard A. Kalish, "Death and Dying in a Social Context," in Binstock and Shanas (1976): 500.
48. Jordan I. Kosberg, "Social Work with Geriatric Patients and Their Families," in Prichard (1977): 158.
49. Charles A. Garfield and Rachel O. Clark, "The SHANTI Project: A Community Model of Psychosocial Support for Patients and Families Facing Life-Threatening Illness," in Garfield (1978): 355–364.
50. John Knoble, "Living to the End: The Hospice Experiment," in Gross, Gross, and Seidman, *The New Old* (1978): 369–399; C. Murray Parkes, "Evaluation of Family Care in Terminal Illness," in Prichard (1977): 49–79; Robert Woodson, "Hospice Care in Terminal Illness," in ibid., 365–385.
51. Pattison (1978): 153–154. Also, Kalish (1976): 495–496.
52. Greg Arling, "The Elderly Widow and Her Family, Neighbors, and Friends," *Jrnl. Marriage and the Family* 38, 4 (Nov. 1976): 757–768.
53. Dorothy K. Heyman and Daniel T. Granturco, "Long-Term Adaptation by the Elderly to Bereavement," *Jrnl. Gerontology* 28 (1973): 359–362.
54. Barbara H. Vinick, "Remarriage in Old Age," *Family Coordinator* 27, 4 (Oct. 1978): 359–363.

Chapter 13. Sources and Forms of Help During Transitions

1. An earlier version of this chapter appeared in *Social Casework* 61, 5 (May 1980): 259–266.
2. Parkes, "Psycho-Social Transitions" (1971): 113.
3. Gerald Gurin, Joseph Veroff, and Sheila Feld, *Americans View Their Mental Health* (New York: Basic Books, 1960).
4. David Guttman et al., *Informal and Formal Support Systems and Their Effect on the Lives of the Elderly in Selected Ethnic Groups.* Final Research Report, National Catholic School of Social Service, Catholic Univ. of America, Jan. 1979. This comprehensive study investigates this issue in great detail.
5. Donald Warren, "Neighborhood Structure and Riot Behavior in Detroit: Some Exploratory Findings," *Social Problems* 16 (1969): 464–484; Gerald Caplan, *Support Systems and Community Mental Health* (New York: Behavioral Publications, 1974: 4–32; Bennett S. Gurian and Marjorie H. Cantor, "Mental Health and Community Support Systems for the Elderly," in Usdin and Hofling, *Aging* (1978): 184–205; Lopata, *Women as Widows* (1979).
6. Helen H. Perlman, *Social Casework: A Problem-Solving Process* (Chicago: Univ. of Chicago Press, 1957): 60. Also Perlman, *Persona* (1968): 44–47.
7. Genevieve Oxley, "A Life-Model Approach to Change," *Social Casework* 52, 10 (Dec. 1971): 627–633.
8. Anthony N. Maluccio, "Promoting Competence Through Life Experiences," in Carel B. Germain, ed., *Social Work Practice: People and Environments* (New York: Columbia Univ. Press, 1979): 282–302.
9. Among some of the autobiographical accounts are Caine, *Lifelines* (1977); Yates,

Coping (1976); Turk, *You're Getting Older, So What?* (1976). Equally interesting are the "how-to-do" books offering practical, down-to-earth advice on problems for persons having difficulties, such as Arbie M. Dale, *Change Your Job, Change Your Life* (New York: Playboy Press, 1977); Arlene Richards and Irene Willis, *How to Get It Together When Your Parents Are Coming Apart* (New York: Bantam Press, 1977); Martin Shepherd, *Someone You Love Is Dying: A Guide for Helping and Coping* (New York: Charter, 1975).

10. Caine (1977): 89–98. Also, Hall and Hall, *The Two-Career Couple* (1979), outline a step-by-step method of making decisions in job-transfer situations.

11. Naomi Golan and Shlomo Sharlin, "Utilizing Natural Help Systems to Intervene: How Young Couples in Israel Cope," paper presented at 53rd Annual Meeting of American Orthopsychiatric Assn., Atlanta, Ga., Mar. 5, 1976. Mimeo.

12. Caplan, *Support Systems* (1974): 4–13.

13. Alice H. Collins and Diane L. Pancoast, *Natural Helping Networks: A Strategy for Prevention* (Washington, D.C.: National Association of Social Workers, 1976): 22.

14. Gerald Caplan, "The Family as a Support System," in Caplan and Marie Killilea, eds., *Support Systems and Mutual Help: Interdisciplinary Explorations* (New York: Grune & Stratton, 1976): 19–36.

15. Ibid., 27–28.

16. Reuben Hill, "Interdependence Among the Generations," in Hill et al., *Family Development in Three Generations* (Cambridge, Mass.: Schenkman, 1970). Quoted in Duvall, *Marriage and Family Development* (1977): 153.

17. Marjorie F. Lowenthal and Betsy Robinson, "Social Networks and Isolation," in Binstock and Shanas, *Handbook of Aging* (1976): 436–439.

18. Hope J. Leichter and William E. Mitchell, *Kinship and Casework: Family Networks and Social Intervention*, enlarged ed. (New York: Teachers College Press, Columbia Univ., 1978): 84–85.

19. Helena Z. Lopata, "Contributions of Extended Families to the Support Systems of Metropolitan Area Widows: Limitations of the Modified Kin Network," *Jrnl. Marriage and the Family* 40, 2 (May 1978): 362.

20. Leichter and Mitchell (1978): 157.

21. Collins and Pancoast (1976): 22.

22. Matthew P. Dumont, "Tavern Culture: The Sustenance of Homeless Men," *Amer. Jrnl. Orthopsychiatry* 37 (Oct. 1967): 938–945. Cited in Collins and Pancoast (1976): 47.

23. Joan Shapiro, "Dominant Leaders Among Slum Hotel Residents," *Amer. Jrnl. Orthopsychiatry* 39 (July 1969): 644–650. Cited in Collins and Pancoast (1976): 47.

24. Caplan (1974): 13. Also, Walter N. Leutz, "The Informal Community Caregiver: A Link Between the Health Care System and Local Residents," *Amer. Jrnl. Orthopsychiatry* 46, 4 (Oct. 1976): 678–688.

25. Collins and Pancoast (1976); Alan Gartner and Frank Reissman, *Self-Help in the Human Services* (San Francisco: Jossey-Bass, 1977); Marie Killilea, "Mutual Help Organizations: Interpretations in the Literature," in Caplan and Killilea (1976): 37–93; Phyllis Silverman, *Mutual Help Groups: A Guide for Mental Health Workers* (Rockville, Md.: National Institute of Mental Health, 1978); Matthew Dumont, "Self-Help Treatment Programs," in Caplan and Killilea

(1976): 123–133; Joanne E. Mantell, Esther S. Alexander, and Mark A. Kleiman, "Social Work with Self-Help Groups," *Health and Social Work* 1, 1 (Feb. 1976): 51–60.

26. For example, *The Self-Help Reporter*, published by the National Self-Help Clearing House, under Gartner and Riessman's direction.

27. Phyllis R. Silverman, "Mutual Help: An Alternate Network," in *Women in Midlife—Security and Fulfillment*, Select Committee on Aging, U.S. House of Representatives (Washington, D.C.: U.S. Government Printing Office, 1978): 260–261.

28. A wide range of such groups are described in *Women in Transition* (1975). See also S. Roxanne Hiltz, "Helping Widows: Group Discussions as a Therapeutic Technique," *Family Coordinator* 24, 3 (July 1975): 331–336; Robert S. Weiss, "The Contributions of an Organization of Single Parents to the Well-Being of Its Members," *Family Coordinator* 22, 3 (July 1973): 321–326.

29. Silverman (1978): 11–16.

30. Ruby B. Abrahams, "Mutual Help for the Widowed," *Social Work* 17, 5 (Sept. 1972): 54–61.

31. Frank Baker, "The Interface Between Professional and Natural Support Systems," *Clinical Social Work Jrnl.* 5, 2 (Summer 1977): 146–147.

32. Collins and Pancoast (1976): 105–111. Also, Thomas J. Powell, "The Use of Self-Help Groups as Supportive Reference Communities," *Amer. Jrnl. Orthopsychiatry* 45, 5 (Dec. 1975): 756–764.

33. Gordon F. Streib, "Older Families and Their Troubles: Familial and Social Responses," *Family Coordinator* 21, 1 (Jan. 1972): 17–18.

34. Hoff, *People in Crisis* (1978): 155, 187.

35. Gustave Simons, *Coping with Crisis* (New York: Macmillan, 1972) is a good example of the practical advice offered by an experienced lawyer on transitional issues. See "Marital Infidelity," pp. 26–31; "Divorce Settlements," pp. 217–224.

36. David Schmidt and Edward Messner, "The Role of the Family Physician in the Crisis of Impending Divorce," *Jrnl. Family Practice* 2, 2 (Apr. 1975): 99–102; Alice I. Snyder, "Periodic Marital Separation and Physical Illness, *Amer. Jrnl. Orthopsychiatry* 48, 4 (Oct. 1978): 637–643.

37. See Earl A. Grollman, *Explaining Divorce to Children* (Boston: Beacon Press, 1969); Grollman, *Concerning Death: A Practical Guide for the Living* (Boston: Beacon Press, 1974).

38. Kenneth Kressel, Martin Lopez-Morillas, Janet Weinglass, and Morton Deutsch, "Professional Intervention in Divorce: The Views of Lawyers, Psychotherapists, and Clergy," *Jrnl. of Divorce* 2, 2 (1978): 119–155. Reprinted in Levinger and Moles, *Divorce and Separation* (1979). Also, Nancy L. Weston, and Norman B. Hartstein, "Mental Health Interventions in Divorce Proceedings," *Amer. Jrnl. Orthopsychiatry* 48, 2 (Apr. 1978): 273–283.

39. For a discussion of this issue and the relationship between paraprofessionals and professionals, see Meyer, *Social Work Practice* (1976): 204–211.

40. Grace H. Lebow, "Facilitating Adaptation in Anticipatory Mourning," *Social Casework* 57, 7 (July 1976): 458–465.

41. Helen H. Perlman, "In Quest of Coping," *Social Casework* 56, 4 (Apr. 1975): 213. Also Ruth H. Lebovitz, "Loss, Role Change, and Values," *Clinical Social Work Jrnl.* 7, 4 (Winter 1979): 285–295.

42. Blanca N. Rosenberg, "Planned Short-Term Treatment in Developmental Crises," *Social Casework* 56, 4 (Apr. 1975): 195–204; Elizabeth C. Lemon and Shirley Goldstein, "The Use of Time Limits in Planned Brief Casework," *Social Casework* 59, 10 (Dec. 1978): 588–596; Elin J. Cormican, "Task-Centered Model for Work with the Aged," *Social Casework* 58, 8 (Oct. 1977): 490–494; Wiseman, "Crisis Theory and the Process of Divorce" (1975).
43. David L. Hoffman and Mary L. Remmel, "Uncovering the Precipitant in Crisis Intervention," *Social Casework* 56, 5 (May 1975): 259–267; Strickler and LaSor, "The Concept of Loss" (1970).
44. Woody, "Preventive Intervention for Children of Divorce" (1978): 537–544.
45. Carleton Pilsecker, "Help for the Dying," *Social Work* 20, 3 (May 1975): 190.
46. Marion Wijnberg and Mary C. Schwartz, "Competence or Crisis: The Social Work Role in Maintaining Family Competency During the Dying Period," in Prichard et al., *Social Work with the Dying* (1977): 97–112.
47. Bertha G. Simos, "Grief Therapy to Facilitate Healthy Restitution," *Social Casework* 58, 6 (June 1977): 337–342.
48. Joan Aldous, "The Making of Family Roles and Family Change," *Family Coordinator* 23, 3 (July 1974): 231–235.
49. See Frederick J. Duhl, "Changing Sex Roles—Concepts, Values, and Tasks," *Social Casework* 57, 2 (Feb. 1976): 87–92, for an approach to family treatment set in a matrix of changing roles and capacities to cope.
50. Virginia Satir, "You as a Change Agent" in Satir, Stachowiak, and Taschman, *Helping Families to Change* (1977): 37–62.
51. Genevieve B. Oxley, "Short-Term Therapy with Student Couples," *Social Casework* 54, 4 (Apr. 1973): 216–223.
52. John Weakland, Richard Fisch, Paul Watzlawick, and Arthur M. Bodin, "Brief Therapy: Focused Problem Resolution," *Family Process* 13, 2 (Jan. 1974): 147–153.
53. See Scherz, "Maturational Crises" (1971); Michael A. Solomon, "A Developmental Conceptual Premise for Family Therapy," *Family Process* 12, 2 (1973): 179–188.
54. Sally F. Hughes, Michael Berger, and Larry Wright, "The Family Life Cycle and Clinical Intervention," *Jrnl. Marriage and Family Counseling* 4, 4 (Oct. 1978): 33–41.
55. Watzlawick, Weakland, Fisch (1974).
56. Salvador Minuchin, *Families and Family Therapy* (Cambridge, Mass.: Harvard Univ. Press, 1974): 123–129.
57. Margaret Bonnefil and Gerald F. Jacobson, "Family Crisis Intervention," *Clinical Social Work Jrnl.* 7, 3 (Fall 1979): 204.
58. Judith S. Wallerstein and Joan B. Kelly, "Children and Divorce: A Review," *Social Work* 24, 5 (Nov. 1979): 468–475.
59. Wallerstein and Kelly, "Divorce Counseling" (1977): 5–7.
60. Kelly and Wallerstein, "Brief Interventions with Children" (1977): 27–29.
61. Kenneth Kressel and Morton Deutsch, "Divorce Therapy: An In-Depth Survey of Therapists' Views," *Family Process* 16, 4 (Dec. 1977): 413–443.
62. Schwartz, "Situation/Transition Groups" (1975): 745–747.
63. Irving Miller and Renée Solomon, "The Development of Group Services for the Elderly," in Germain (1979): 87–90.

64. Jacinth I. Baublitz, "Transitional Treatment of Hostile Married Couples," *Social Work* 23, 4 (July 1978): 321–323.

65. Helen Hunnicutt and Barry Schapiro, "Use of Marriage Enrichment Programs in a Family Agency," *Social Casework* 57, 9 (Nov. 1977): 555–561.

66. William Kiefer, "A Preretirement Program in a Family Agency," *Social Casework* 59, 1 (Jan. 1978): 53–54.

67. Alida G. Silverman, Beatrice H. Kohn, and Gary Anderson, "A Model for Working with Multigenerational Families," *Social Casework* 58, 3 (Mar. 1977): 131–135.

68. Janice Prochaska and Jane R. Coyle, "Choosing Parenthood: A Needed Family Life Education Group," *Social Casework* 60, 5 (May 1979): 289–293.

69. Mildred Kaplan and Anne Glenn, "Women and the Stress of Moving: A Self-Help Approach," *Social Casework* 59, 7 (July 1978): 434–436.

70. Maureen F. Turner and Martha H. Izzi, "The COPE Story: A Service to Pregnant and Postpartum Women," in Notman and Nadelson, *The Woman Patient* (1978): 107–122.

71. Lynn Witken, "Group Helps Widowed Parents Deal with Children's Grief," *Practice Digest* 2, 2 (Sept. 1979): 27–28.

72. Lilian B. Macon, "Help for Bereaved Parents," *Social Casework* 60, 9 (Nov. 1979): 558–561.

73. E. Rick Beebe, "Expectant Parent Classes: A Case Study," *Family Coordinator* 27, 1 (Jan. 1978): 55–58.

74. Shirley B. Klass and Margaret A. Redfern, "A Social Work Response to the Middle-Aged Housewife," *Social Casework* 58, 2 (Feb. 1977): 101–110.

75. See Vivian R. McCoy, Colleen Ryan, and James W. Lichtenberg, *Adult Life Cycle: Training Manual and Reader* (Lawrence, Kans.: Univ. of Kansas, 1978).

76. Sherod Miller, Elam W. Nunnally, and David B. Wackman, "A Communication Training Program for Couples," *Social Casework* 57, 1 (Jan. 1976): 9–18.

77. To facilitate the setting up of educational programs on separation and divorce, the Family Service Association of America has published its own workbook on how to structure such a program. See Betsy N. Callahan, *Separation and Divorce: Workshop Models for Family Life Education* (New York: FSAA, 1979).

78. Weiss in Caplan and Killilea (1976): 213–232.

79. Chiancola (1978): 497–498.

80. Sara F. Bonkowski and Brenda Wanner-Westley, "The Divorce Group: A New Treatment Modality," *Social Casework* 60, 9 (Nov. 1979): 552–557.

81. Beatrice (1979): 163–165.

82. Lilliam Messinger, Kenneth N. Walker, and Stanley J. Freeman, "Preparation for Remarriage Following Divorce: The Use of Group Techniques," *Amer. Jrnl. Orthopsychiatry* 48, 2 (Apr. 1978): 263–272.

Chapter 14. Guidelines for Intervention During Transitions

1. The most recent exposition of this view is presented in Margaret G. Frank, "Psychoanalytic Developmental Theory: A Study of Descriptive Developmental

Diagnosis," paper presented at the Clinical Conference sponsored by the Colorado Society for Clinical Social Work, Denver, Col., July 1980. Mimeo.

2. Carel B. Germain, "An Ecological Perspective in Casework Practice," *Social Casework* 54, 6 (June 1973): 326–327.

3. Alex Gitterman and Carel B. Germain, "Social Work Practice: A Life Model," *Social Service Review* 50, 4 (Dec. 1976): 602–605.

4. Helen H. Perlman, "Social Casework: The Problem-Solving Approach," in *Encyc. Social Work* (1977): 1292–1298.

5. See Golan, *Treatment in Crisis Situations* (1978): 61–72, 160–162, 176–177.

6. Lydia Rapoport, "Working with Families in Crisis: An Exploration in Preventive Intervention," *Social Work* 7, 3 (Sept. 1962): 48–56. Also Caplan, *Principles of Preventive Psychiatry* (1964): 56–88.

7. The latest version of this approach is found in William J. Reid, *The Task-Centered System* (New York: Columbia Univ. Press, 1978): 35–36.

8. A similar distinction is discussed by Reid in differentiating between "wants" and "problems." See ibid., 25–33.

9. See ibid., 139–141, for a fuller discussion of the concept of a task.

10. Golan, "Work with Young Adults in Israel," in Reed and Epstein, *Task-Centered Practice* (1977): 274.

11. Lydia Rapoport, "Crisis Intervention as a Mode of Treatment," in Robert W. Roberts and Robert H. Nee, eds., *Theories of Social Casework* (Chicago: Univ. of Chicago Press, 1970): 290.

12. Helen H. Perlman, *Relationship: The Heart of Helping People* (Chicago: Univ. of Chicago Press, 1979).

13. See ibid., 136–154.

Bibliography

ABARBANEL, ALICE. "Shared Parenting After Separation and Divorce: A Study of Joint Custody." *Amer. Jrnl. Orthopsychiatry* 49, 2 (Apr. 1979): 320–329.

ABRAHAMS, RUBY B. "Mutual Help for the Widowed." *Social Work* 17, 5 (Sept. 1972): 54–61.

AHRONS, CONSTANCE R. "The Coparental Divorce: Preliminary Research Findings and Policy Implications." Paper presented at Annual Meeting, National Council on Family Relations, Phila., Pa., Oct. 1978. Mimeo.

ALDOUS, JOAN. "The Making of Family Roles and Family Change." *Family Coordinator* 23, 3 (July 1974): 231–235.

————. *Family Careers: Developmental Change in Families.* New York: John Wiley & Sons, 1978.

ANKARLOO, BENGT. "Marriage and Family Formation." In Hareven, 1978: 113–133.

ANSBACHER, H. L., and R. R. ANSBACHER. *The Individual Psychology of Alfred Adler.* New York: Harper Torchbooks, 1956.

ANTHONY, E. JAMES, and THERESE BENEDEK, eds. *Parenthood: Its Psychology and Psychopathology.* Boston: Little, Brown, 1970.

ANTHONY, E. JAMES, and CYRILLE KOUPERNIK, eds. *The Child in His Family,* vol. 1. New York: Wiley-Interscience, 1970.

ANTONOVSKY, AARON. *Health, Stress, and Coping.* San Francisco: Jossey-Bass, 1979.

APPELBAUM, STEPHEN A. *The Anatomy of Change.* New York: Plenum Press, 1977.

APPLEBAUM, FLORENCE. "Loneliness: A Taxonomy and Psychodynamic View." *Clinical Social Work Jrnl.* 6, 1 (Spring 1978): 13–20.

301

ARLING, GREG. "Resistance to Isolation Among Elderly Widows." *Intl. Jrnl. Aging and Human Development* 7, 1 (1976): 67–86.

———. "The Elderly Widow and Her Family, Neighbors, and Friends." *Jrnl. Marriage and the Family* 38, 4 (Nov. 1976): 757–768.

ARONSON, ELLIOTT. "Dissonance Theory: Progress and Problems." In Robert Abelson et al., *Theories of Cognitive Consistency*. Chicago: Rand McNally, 1968.

ATCHLEY, ROBERT C. *The Social Forces in Later Life: An Introduction to Social Gerontology*. Belmont, Ca.: Wadsworth, 1972; 2nd ed., 1976.

———. "Adjustment to Loss of Job at Retirement." *Intl. Jrnl. Aging and Human Development* 6, 1 (1975): 17–27.

BAKER, FRANK. "The Interface Between Professional and Natural Support Systems." *Clinical Social Work Jrnl.* 5, 2 (Summer 1977): 139–148.

BAKKER, CORNELIS B. "Why People Don't Change." *Psychotherapy: Theory, Research, and Practice* 12, 2 (Summer 1975): 164–172.

BALDWIN, DORIS. "Poverty and the Older Woman: Reflections of a Social Worker." *Family Coordinator* 27, 4 (Oct. 1978): 448–450.

BALTES, PAUL B., and K. WARNER SCHAIE, eds. *Life-Span Developmental Psychology: Personality and Socialization*. New York: Academic Press, 1973.

BALTES, PAUL B., and SHERRY L. WILLIS. "Toward Psychological Theories of Aging and Development." In Birren and Schaie, 1977: 128–154.

BANE, MARY JO. "Marital Disruption and the Lives of Children." In Levinger and Moles, 1979: 276–286.

BARNHILL, LAURENCE R. "Healthy Family Systems." *Family Coordinator* 28, 1 (Jan. 1979): 95–108.

———, GERALD RUBENSTEIN, and NEIL ROCKLIN. "From Generation to Generation: Fathers-to-Be in Transition." *Family Coordinator* 28, 2 (Apr. 1979): 229–236.

BARRETT, CURTIS L., and HELEN NOBLE. "Mothers' Anxieties vs. the Effects of Long-Distance Moves on Children." *Jrnl. Marriage and the Family* 35, 2 (May 1973): 181–188.

BART, PAULINE B., and MARLYN GROSSMAN. "Menopause." In Notman and Nadelson, 1978: 337–354.

BAUBLITZ, JACINTH I. "Transitional Treatment of Hostile Married Couples." *Social Work* 23, 4 (July 1978): 321–323.

BEATRICE, DORY K. "Divorce: Problems, Goals, and Growth Facilitation." *Social Casework* 60, 3 (Mar. 1979): 157–165.

BECKER, HOWARD S. "Personal Change in Adult Life." In Neugarten, 1968: 148–158.

BEEBE, E. RICK. "Expectant Parent Classes: A Case Study." *Family Coordinator* 27, 1 (Jan. 1978): 55–58.

BELL, WILLIAM G. "Community Care for the Elderly: An Alternative to Institutionalization." *Gerontologist* 13, 3, Part I (1973): 349–354.

BENEDEK, THERESE. "Climacterium: A Developmental Phase." *Psychoanalytic Quarterly* 19 (1950): 1–27.

———. "Parenthood as a Developmental Phase." *Jrnl. Amer. Psychoanalytical Association* 7 (1959): 389–417.

———. "The Psychobiology of Pregnancy." In Anthony and Benedek, 1970: 137–152.

BERNARD, JESSIE. *The Future of Marriage*. New York: World, 1972.

BIBRING, GRETE L. "Some Considerations of the Psychological Processes of Pregnancy." *Psychoanalytic Study of the Child* 14 (1959): 113–121.

BINSTOCK, ROBERT H., and ETHEL SHANAS, eds. *Handbook of Aging and the Social Sciences*. New York: Van Nostrand Reinhold, 1976.

BIRREN, JAMES E., and K. WARNER SCHAIE, eds. *Handbook of the Psychology of Aging*. New York: Van Nostrand Reinhold, 1977.

BLENKNER, MARGARET. "Social Work and Family Relations in Later Life, with Some Thoughts on Filial Maturity." In Shanas and Streib, 1965.

BLOOM, BERNARD L., STEPHEN W. WHITE, and SHIRLEY J. ASHER. "Marital Disruption as a Stressful Life Event." *Psychological Bulletin* 85 (1978): 867–894.

BLOOM, MARTIN. "Social Prevention: An Ecological Approach." In Germain, 1979: 326–345.

———. *Life Span Development: Bases for Preventive and Interventive Helping*. New York: Macmillan, 1980.

BLOS, PETER. *The Adolescent Passage: Developmental Issues*. New York: International Universities Press, 1979.

BOHANNAN, PAUL. *Social Anthropology*. New York: Holt, Rinehart & Winston, 1963.

———, ed. *Divorce and After*. Garden City, N.Y.: Doubleday, Anchor Books, 1971.

BONKOWSKI, SARA E., and BRENDA WANNER-WESTLY. "The Divorce Group: A New Treatment Modality." *Social Casework* 60, 9 (Nov. 1979): 552–557.

BONNEFIL, MARGARET, and GERALD F. JACOBSON. "Family Crisis Intervention." *Clinical Social Work Jrnl.* 7, 3 (Fall 1979): 200–213.

BOWLBY, JOHN. "Grief and Mourning in Infancy and Early Childhood." *Psychoanalytic Study of the Child* 15 (1960): 9–52.

———. *Separation, Anxiety, and Anger*. New York: Basic Books, 1973.

———. "Affectional Bonds: Their Nature and Origin." In Robert S. Weiss, ed., *Loneliness: The Experience of Emotional and Social Isolation*. Cambridge: M.I.T. Press, 1973: 38–52.

———, and C. MURRAY PARKES. "Separation and Loss Within the Family." In Anthony and Koupernik, 1970: 197–216.

BRIM, ORVILLE G., JR. "Adult Socialization." In John A. Clausen, ed., *Socialization and Society*. Boston: Little, Brown, 1968: 182–226.

———. "Theories of the Male Mid-Life Crisis." *Counseling Psychologist* 6, 1 (1976): 2–9.

BRODY, ELAINE. "Aging and Family Personality: A Developmental View." *Family Process* 13, 1 (Mar. 1974): 23–37.

———. "Aging." In *Encyclopedia of Social Work*, 17th Issue, vol. 1. Washington, D.C.: National Association of Social Workers, 1977: 55–77.

BROOKS, LINDA. "Supermoms Shift Gears: Re-entry Women." *Counseling Psychologist* 6, 2 (1976): 33–37.

BROWN, CAROL A., ROSLYN FELDBERG, ELIZABETH M. FOX, and JANET KOHEN. "Divorce: Chance of a New Lifetime." *Jrnl. Social Issues* 32, 1 (1976): 119–133.

BÜHLER, CHARLOTTE. "The Developmental Structure of Goal Setting in Group and Individual Studies." In Charlotte Bühler and Fred Massarik, eds., *The Course of Human Life: A Study of Goals in the Humanistic Perspective*. New York: Springer, 1968: 27–54.

————. *The Way to Fulfillment: Psychosocial Techniques.* New York: Hawthorn Books, 1971.

BUSSE, EWALD J., and ERIC PFEIFFER, eds. *Behavior and Adaptation in Late Life.* Boston: Little, Brown, 1969.

BUTLER, ROBERT N. "The Life Review: An Interpretation of Reminiscence in the Aged." *Psychiatry* 26, 1 (Feb. 1963). Reprinted in Neugarten, 1968: 486–496.

CAINE, LYNNE. *Widow.* New York: Morrow, 1974.

————. *Lifelines.* New York: Dell, 1977.

CALLAHAN, BETSY N. *Separation and Divorce: Workshop Models for Family Life Education.* New York: Family Service Association of America, 1979.

CAMPBELL, A. "The American Way of Mating: Marriage, Si; Children, Only Maybe." *Psychology Today* (May 1975): 37–43.

CAMPBELL, JOSEPH, ed. *The Portable Jung.* Harmondsworth, Eng.: Penguin, 1971.

CAPLAN, GERALD. *Principles of Preventive Psychiatry.* New York: Basic Books, 1964.

————. *Support Systems and Community Mental Health.* New York: Behavioral Publications, 1974.

————. "The Family as a Support System." In Caplan and Killilea, 1976: 19–36.

————, and MARIE KILLILEA, eds. *Support Systems and Mutual Help.* New York: Grune & Stratton, 1976.

CARP, FRANCES. "Housing and Living Environments of Older People." In Binstock and Shanas, 1976: 244–271.

CARSMAN, EVALINE P. "Education as Recreation." In Troll, Israel, and Israel, 1977: 140–146.

CATH, STANLEY H. "Some Dynamics of the Middle and Later Years." *Smith College Studies in Social Work* 33, 2 (1963). Reprinted in Howard J. Parad, ed., *Crisis Intervention: Selected Readings.* New York: Family Service Association of America, 1965: 199–213.

————. "The Orchestration of Disengagement." *Intl. Jrnl. Aging and Human Development* 6, 3 (1975): 199–213.

CHEN, PEI N. "A Study of Chinese-American Elderly Residing in Hotel Rooms." *Social Casework* 60, 2 (Feb. 1979): 89–95.

CHERRY, SHELDON H. *For Women of All Ages: A Gynecologist's Guide to Modern Female Health Care.* New York: Macmillan, 1979.

CHESCHEIR, MARTHA W. "Social Role Discrepancies as Clues to Practice." *Social Work* 24, 2 (Mar. 1979): 89–94.

CHIANCOLA, SAMUEL P. "The Process of Separation and Divorce: A New Approach." *Social Casework* 59, 8 (Oct. 1978): 494–499.

CHIRIBOGA, DAVID, and LORAINE CUTLER. "Stress Responses Among Divorcing Men and Women." *Jrnl. of Divorce* 1, 2 (Winter 1977): 95–106.

CHODOROW, NANCY. *The Reproduction of Mothering.* Berkeley: Univ. of California Press, 1978.

CLAYTON, VIVIAN. "Erikson's Theory of Human Development as It Applies to the Aged: Wisdom as Contradictive Cognition." *Human Development* 18, 1–2 (1975): 119–128.

CLIFFORD, GLEN, and KATHERINE ODIN. "Young Adulthood: A Developmental Phase." *Smith College Studies in Social Work* 44 (Feb. 1974): 125–142.

COELHO, GEORGE V., DAVID A. HAMBURG, and JOHN E. ADAMS, eds. *Coping and Adaptation.* New York: Basic Books, 1974.

COHEN, JESSICA F. "Male Roles in Midlife." *Family Coordinator* 28, 4 (Oct. 1979): 465–471.

COHEN, STEPHEN Z., and BRUCE M. GANS. *The Other Generation Gap: The Middle-Aged and Their Aging Parents.* Chicago: Follett, 1978.

COLEMAN, JAMES, et al. *Youth: Transition to Adulthood.* Report of the Panel on Youth of the President's Science Advisory Committee. Chicago: Univ. of Chicago Press, 1974.

COLEMAN, SANDRA B. "A Developmental Stage Hypothesis for Non-Marital Dyadic Relationships." *Jrnl. Marriage and Family Counseling* 3, 2 (Apr. 1977): 71–76.

COMMITTEE ON WORK AND PERSONALITY IN THE MIDDLE YEARS, Social Science Research Council. *Progress Report:* June 1, 1974–Oct. 1, 1976. New York. Mimeo.

COLLINS, ALICE H., and DIANE L. PANCOAST. *Natural Helping Networks: A Strategy for Prevention.* Washington, D.C.: National Association of Social Workers, 1976.

CONSTABLE, ROBERT T. "Mobile Families and the School." *Social Casework* 59, 7 (July 1978): 419–427.

COOGLER, O. J., RUTH WEBER, and PATRICK C. MCKENRY. "Divorce Mediation: A Means of Facilitating Divorce Adjustment." *Family Coordinator* 28, 2 (Apr. 1979): 255–259.

CORMICAN, ELIN J. "Task-Centered Model for Work with the Aged." *Social Casework* 58, 8 (Oct. 1977): 490–494.

COTTON, WAYNE L. "Social and Sexual Relationships of Lesbians." *Jrnl. Sex Research* 11, 2 (May 1975): 139–148.

CUMMING, ELAINE. "Engagement with an Old Theory." *Intl. Jrnl. Aging and Human Development* 6, 3 (1975): 185–191.

―――――, and WILLIAM E. HENRY. *Growing Old: The Process of Disengagement.* New York: Basic Books, 1961.

CUMMING, JOHN, and ELAINE CUMMING. *Ego and Milieu.* New York: Atherton Press, 1966.

DALE, ARBIE M. *Change Your Job, Change Your Life.* New York: Playboy Press, 1977.

DATAN, NANCY, and LEON H. GINSBERG, eds. *Life-Span Developmental Psychology: Normative Life Crises.* New York: Academic Press, 1975.

DAVIDOFF, IDA. "'Living Together' as a Developmental Phase: A Holistic View." *Jrnl. Marriage and Family Counseling* 3, 3 (July 1977): 67–76.

DAVIS, JESSICA G. "Decisions About Reproduction: Genetic Counseling." In Notman and Nadelson, 1978: 33–54.

DAVITZ, JOEL, and LOIS DAVITZ. *Making It from 40 to 50.* New York: Random House, 1976.

DEAN, GILLIAN, and DOUGLAS GURAK. "Marital Homogamy the Second Time Around." *Jrnl. Marriage Family* 40, 3 (Aug. 1978): 559–570.

DEUTSCH, HELENE. *The Psychology of Women.* New York: Grune & Stratton, 1944.

DEUTSCHER, IRWIN. "The Quality of Postparental Life." In Neugarten, 1968: 263–268.

DOHRENWEND, BARBARA S., and BRUCE P. DOHRENWEND, eds. *Stressful Life Events: Their Nature and Effects.* New York: John Wiley & Sons, 1974.

DONOVAN, CORNELIA M. "Psychotherapy in Abortion." In Jules Masserman, ed., *Psychiatric Therapies* 15 (1975): 77–83.

DRAGASTIN, SIGMUND E., and GLEN E. ELDER, JR. *Adolescence in the Life Cycle: Psychological Change and Social Context.* Washington, D.C.: Hemisphere, 1975.

DUBERMAN, LUCILE. *Gender and Sex in Society.* New York: Praeger, 1975.

DUHL, FREDERICK J. "Changing Sex Roles—Concepts, Values, and Tasks." *Social Casework* 57, 2 (Feb. 1976): 87–92.

DUMONT, MATTHEW P. "Tavern Culture: The Sustenance of Homeless Men." *Amer. Jrnl. Orthopsychiatry* 37, 5 (Oct. 1967): 938–945.

_____. "Self-Help Treatment Programs." In Caplan and Killilea, 1976: 123–133.

DUVALL, EVELYN. *Marriage and Family Development,* 5th ed. Philadelphia: J. B. Lippincott, 1977.

DYER, EVERETT. "Parenthood as a Crisis: A Re-Study." *Marriage and Family Living* 25, 2 (May 1963). Reprinted in Parad, 1965: 312–323.

EATON, JOSEPH W., ed. *Migration and Social Welfare.* New York: Family Service Association of America, 1971.

EISDORFER, CARL, and M. POWELL LAWTON, eds. *The Psychology of Adult Development and Aging.* Washington, D.C.: American Psychological Association, 1973.

ELAIDE, MIRCEA. *Rites and Symbols of Initiation: The Mysteries of Birth and Rebirth.* New York: Harper & Row, 1958.

EPSTEIN, CYNTHIA F. *Woman's Place: Options and Limits in Professional Careers.* Berkeley: Univ. of California Press, 1971.

ERIKSON, ERIK H. *Childhood and Society.* New York: W. W. Norton, 1950.

_____. *Young Man Luther: A Study in Psychoanalysis and History.* New York: W. W. Norton, 1958.

_____. *Identity and the Life Cycle. Psychological Issues* 1, 1. New York: International Universities Press, 1959.

_____. *Insight and Responsibility.* New York: W. W. Norton, 1964.

_____. *Identity, Youth, and Crisis.* New York: W. W. Norton, 1968.

_____. "Life Cycle." In *Intl. Encyc. Social Sciences.* New York: Macmillan and The Free Press, 1968.

_____. *Gandhi's Truth: On the Origins of Militant Non-Violence.* New York: W. W. Norton, 1969.

_____, ed. *Adulthood.* New York: W. W. Norton, 1976.

ESCALONA, SIBYLLE. *The Roots of Individuality.* Chicago: Aldine Press, 1968.

ESTES, E. HARVEY, JR. "Health Experience in the Elderly." In Busse and Pfeiffer, 1969: 115–128.

FELDMAN, FRANCES L. *The Family in Today's Money World,* 2nd ed. New York: Family Service Association of America, 1976.

FILLENBAUM, GERDA G., and GEORGE L. MADDOX. "Work after Retirement: An Investigation into Some Psychologically Relevant Variables." *Gerontologist* 14, 4 (1974): 418–424.

FORD, CAROLINE S. "Ego-Adaptive Mechanisms of Older People." *Social Casework* 46 1 (Jan. 1965): 16–21. Reprinted in Sze, 1975: 599–608.

FRANK, MARGARET G. "Psychoanalytic Developmental Theory: A Study of Descriptive Developmental Diagnosis." Paper presented at Clinical Conference, Colorado Society for Clinical Social Work, Denver, Colo., July 1980. Mimeo.

FREED, ANNE O. "The Family Agency and the Kinship System of the Elderly." *Social Casework* 56, 10 (Dec. 1975): 578–586.

FREUD, SIGMUND. "Mourning and Melancholia." In James Strachey, ed., *The Complete Psychological Works of Sigmund Freud.* New York: Macmillan, 1964.

FRIED, BARBARA. *The Middle-Age Crisis*, rev. ed. New York: Harper & Row, 1976.

FRIED, MARC. "Grieving for a Lost Home." In Leonard J. Duhl, ed., *The Urban Condition: People and Policy in the Metropolis.* New York: Basic Books, 1963: 51–171. Reprinted in Alan Monat and Richard S. Lazarus, *Stress and Coping: An Anthology.* New York: Columbia Univ. Press, 1977: 375–388.

_____, PEGGY GLEICHER, LORNA FERGUSON, and JOHN HAVENS. "Patterns of Migration and Adjustment Among the Black Population of Boston." In Eaton, 1971: 117–141.

FRIEDMAN, EMANUEL A. "The Physiological Aspects of Pregnancy." In Notman and Nadelson, 1978: 55–71.

FUCHS, ESTELLE. *The Second Season: Life, Love and Sex for Women in the Middle Years.* Garden City, N.Y.: Doubleday Anchor Books, 1978.

GAITZ, CHARLES M. "Aged Patients, Their Families and Physicians." In Usdin and Hofling, 1978: 206–239.

GARFIELD, CHARLES A., ed. *Psychosocial Care of the Dying Patient.* New York: McGraw-Hill, 1978.

_____, and RACHEL O. CLARK. "The SHANTI Project: A Community Model of Psychosocial Support for Patients and Families Facing Life-Threatening Illness." In Garfield, 1978: 355–364.

GARTNER, ALAN, and FRANK RIESSMAN. *Self-Help in the Human Services.* San Francisco: Jossey-Bass, 1977.

GAYLORD, MAXINE. "Relocation and the Corporate Family: Unexplored Issues." *Social Work* 24, 3 (May 1979): 186–192.

GERMAIN, CAREL B. "An Ecological Perspective in Casework Practice." *Social Casework* 54, 6 (June 1973): 323–330.

_____. "General Systems Theory and Ego Psychology: An Ecological Perspective." *Social Service Review* 52, 4 (Dec. 1978): 535–550.

_____, ed. *Social Work Practice: People and Environments.* New York: Columbia Univ. Press, 1979.

GETTLEMAN SUSAN, and JANET MARKOWITZ. *The Courage to Divorce.* New York: Ballantine, 1975.

GITTERMAN, ALEX, and CAREL B. GERMAIN. "Social Work Practice: A Life Model." *Social Service Review* 50, 4 (Dec. 1976): 601–610.

GLICK, IRA O., ROBERT S. WEISS, and C. MURRAY PARKES. *The First Year of Bereavement.* New York: John Wiley & Sons, 1974.

GOLAN, NAOMI. "When Is a Client in Crisis?" *Social Casework* 50, 7 (July 1969): 389–394.

_____. "Crisis Theory." In Francis J. Turner, ed., *Social Work Treatment: Interlocking Theoretical Approaches.* New York: Free Press, 1974: 420–456.

_____. "Wife to Widow to Woman." *Social Work* 20, 5 (Sept. 1975): 369–374.

_____. "Work with Young Adults in Israel." In William J. Reid and Laura Epstein, eds., *Task-Centered Practice.* New York: Columbia Univ. Press, 1977: 270–284.

_____. *Treatment in Crisis Situations.* New York: Free Press, 1978.

_____. "Intervention at Times of Transition: Sources and Forms of Help." *Social Casework* 61, 5 (May 1980): 259–266.

————. "Using Situational Crises to Ease Transitions in the Life Cycle." *Amer. Jrnl. Orthopsychiatry* 50, 3 (July 1980): 542–550.

————. "Building Competence in Transitional and Crisis Situations." In Anthony N. Maluccio, ed., *Promoting Competence in Clients: A New/Old Approach to Social Work Practice*. New York: Free Press, 1981.

————. "The Influence of Developmental and Transitional Crises on Victims of Disasters." In Charles Spielberger and Seymour Saranson, eds., *Stress and Anxiety*, vol. 8. Washington, D.C.: Hemisphere Press, 1981.

————, and RUTH GRUSCHKA. "Integrating the New Immigrant: A Model for Social Work Practice in Transitional States." *Social Work* 16, 2 (Apr. 1971): 82–87.

————, and SHLOMO SHARLIN. "Utilizing Natural Help Systems to Intervene: How Young Couples in Israel Cope." Paper presented at 53rd Annual Meeting of Amer. Orthopsych. Assn., Atlanta, Ga., Mar. 5, 1976. Mimeo.

GOLDBERG, STANLEY B. "Family Tasks and Reactions in the Crisis of Death." *Social Casework* 54, 7 (July 1973): 398–404.

GOLDFARB, ALVIN I. "Institutional Care of the Aged." In Busse and Pfeiffer, 1969: 289–312.

GOLDSTEIN, EDA G. "Social Casework and the Dying Person." *Social Casework* 54, 10 (Dec. 1973): 601–608.

GOODMAN, NORMAN, and KENNETH A. FELDMAN. "Expectations, Ideals, and Reality: Youth Enters College." In Dragastin and Elder, 1975: 147–169.

GOULD, ROGER L. "The Phases of Adult Life: A Study in Developmental Psychology." *Amer. Jrnl. Psychiatry* 129, 5 (Nov. 1972): 521–531.

————. "Adult Life Stages: Growth Toward Self-Tolerance." *Psychology Today* 8, 9 (1975): 74–78.

————. *Transformations: Growth and Change in Adult Life*. New York: Simon & Schuster, 1978.

GREENE, MARTIN. "Loss of Mate—A Third Individuation Process." *Clinical Social Work Jrnl.* 4, 1 (Sept. 1976): 44–47.

GROLLMAN, EARL, ed. *Explaining Divorce to Children*. Boston: Beacon Press, 1969.

————. *Concerning Death: A Practice Guide for the Living*. Boston: Beacon Press, 1974.

GROSS, RONALD, BEATRICE GROSS, and SYLVIA SEIDMAN, eds. *The New Old: Struggling for Decent Aging*. Garden City, N.Y.: Doubleday Anchor Press, 1978.

GUBRIUM, JABER F. "Being Single in Old Age." *Intl. Jrnl. Aging and Human Development* 6, 1 (1975): 29–41.

GURIAN, BENNETT S., and MARJORIE H. CANTOR. "Mental Health and Community Support Systems for the Elderly." In Usdin and Hofling, 1978: 184–205.

GURIN, GERALD, JOSEPH VEROFF, and SHEILA FELD. *Americans View Their Mental Health*. New York: Basic Books, 1960.

GUTTMANN, DAVID, et al. *Informal and Formal Support Systems and Their Effect on the Lives of the Elderly in Selected Ethnic Groups*. Final Research Report. Natl. Catholic School of Social Service, Catholic Univ. of America, Jan. 1979.

GUZINSKI, GAY. "Medical Gynecology: Problems and Patients." In Notman and Nadelson, 1978: 181–202.

HALL, FRANCINE S., and DOUGLAS T. HALL. *The Two-Career Couple*. Reading, Mass.: Addison-Wesley, 1979.

HAMBURG, BEATRIX A. "Early Adolescence: A Specific and Stressful Stage of the Life Cycle." In Coelho, Hamburg, and Adams, 1974: 101–124.

HAMBURG, DAVID A., and JOHN E. ADAMS. "A Perspective on Coping Behavior: Seeking and Utilizing Information in Major Transitions." *Archives of General Psychiatry* 17 (1967): 277–284.

HANNAH, BARBARA. *Jung: His Life and Work.* New York: G. P. Putnam's Sons (Capricorn): 1976.

HAREVEN, TAMARA K., ed. *Transitions: The Family and the Life Course in Historical Perspective.* New York: Academic Press, 1978.

HARKINS, ELIZABETH B. "Effects of Empty Next Transition on Self-Report of Psychological and Physical Well-Being." *Jrnl. Marriage and the Family* 40, 3 (Aug. 1978): 549–556.

HASELKORN, FLORENCE, ed. *Family Planning: A Sourcebook of Readings and Case Materials.* New York: Council of Social Work Education, 1971.

HAVIGHURST, ROBERT J. *Human Development and Education.* London: Longmans, Green, 1953.

———. "A Social-Psychological Perspective on Aging." *Gerontologist* 8, 2 (Summer 1968): 67–71.

———. "History of Developmental Psychology: Socialization and Personality Development Through the Life Span." In Baltes and Schaie, 1973: 4–24.

———. "Social Roles, Work, Leisure, and Education." In Eisdorfer and Lawton, 1973: 599–618.

———, BERNICE L. NEUGARTEN, and SHELDON S. TOBIN. "Disengagement and Patterns of Aging." In Neugarten, 1968: 159–172.

HAYNES, JOHN M. "Divorce Mediator: A New Role." *Social Work* 23, 1 (Jan. 1978): 5–9.

HEYMAN, DOROTHY K., and DANIEL T. GRANTURCO. "Long-Term Adaptation by the Elderly to Bereavement." *Jrnl. Gerontology* 28 (1973): 359–362.

HILL, REUBEN. "Interdependence Among the Generations." In Hill et al., eds., *Family Development in Three Generations.* Cambridge, Mass. Schenkman, 1970.

HILTZ, S. ROXANNE. "Helping Widows: Group Discussions as a Therapeutic Technique." *Family Coordinator* 24, 3 (July 1975): 331–336.

HINTON, JOHN. *Dying,* 2nd ed. Middlesex, Eng.: Penguin, 1972.

HIRSCH, HYMAN. "Higher Education in Retirement: The Institute for Retired Professionals." *Intl. Jrnl. Aging and Human Development* 8, 4 (1977–78): 367–374.

HOBBS, DANIEL F., JR. "Parenthood as a Crisis: A Third Study." *Jrnl. Marriage and the Family* 27, 2 (Aug. 1965): 367–372.

———, and SUE P. COLE. "Transition to Parenthood: A Decade Replication." *Jrnl. Marriage and the Family* 38, 4 (Nov. 1976): 723–731.

———, and JANE M. WIMBUSH. "Transition to Parenthood by Black Couples." *Jrnl. Marriage and the Family* 39, 4 (Nov. 1977): 677–689.

HOFF, LEE ANN. *People in Crisis: Understanding and Helping.* Menlo Park, Ca.: Addison-Wesley, 1978.

HOFFMAN, DAVID L., and MARY L. REMMEL. "Uncovering the Precipitant in Crisis Intervention." *Social Casework* 56, 5 (May 1975): 259–267.

HONIG, ALICE S. "What We Need to Know to Help the Teenage Parent." *Family Coordinator* 27, 2 (Apr. 1978): 113–119.

HOROWITZ, NANCY H. "Adolescent Mourning Reactions to Infant and Fetal Loss." *Social Casework* 59, 9 (Nov. 1978): 551–559.

HUGHES, SALLY F., MICHAEL BERGER, and LARRY WRIGHT. "The Family Life

Cycle and Clinical Intervention." *Jrnl. Mar. Fam. Counseling* 4, 4 (Oct. 1978): 33–41.

HUNNICUTT, HELEN, and BARRY SCHAPIRO. "Use of Marriage Enrichment Programs in a Family Agency." *Social Casework* 57, 9 (Nov. 1977): 555–561.

IRESON, CAROL. "Girls' Socialization for Work." In Stromberg and Harkess, 1978: 178–200.

JACKSON, JACQUELYNE J. "Older Black Women." In Troll, Israel, and Israel, 1977: 149–156.

JACOBS, RUTH H., and BARBARA H. VINICK. *Re-Engagement in Later Life: Re-Employment and Remarriage.* Stamford, Conn.: Greylock, 1978.

JACOBSON, DORIS S. "Stepfamilies: Myths and Realities." *Social Work* 24, 3 (May 1979): 202–207.

JACOBY, ARTHUR P. "Transition to Parenthood: A Reassessment." *Jrnl. Marriage and the Family* 31, 4 (Nov. 1969): 720–727.

JAQUES, ELLIOTT. "Death and the Mid-Life Crisis." *Intl. Jrnl. Psychoanalysis* 46 (1965): 502–514.

JEFFERS, FRANCES C., and ADRIAAN VERWOERDT. "How the Old Face Death." In Busse and Pfeiffer, 1969: 163–181.

JENKINS, SHIRLEY. "Children of Divorce." *Children Today* 7, 2 (Mar.–Apr. 1978): 16–20, 48.

JESSNER, LUCIE, EDITH WEIGERT, and JAMES L. FOY. "Development of Parental Attitudes During Pregnancy." In Anthony and Benedek, 1970: 209–244.

JOHNSON, RALPH. "Marital Patterns During the Middle Years." Unpublished doctoral dissertation, Univ. of Minnesota, 1968.

JONES, STELLA B. "Geographic Mobility as Seen by the Wife and Mother." *Jrnl. Marriage and the Family* 35, 2 (May 1973): 210–218.

KALISH, RICHARD A. "The Onset of the Dying Process." *Omega* 1 (1970): 57–69.

———. *Late Adulthood: Perspectives on Human Development.* Monterey, Ca.: Brooks/Cole, 1975.

———. "Death and Dying in a Social Context." In Binstock and Shanas, 1976: 483–507.

———, and FRANCES W. KNUDTSON. "Attachment vs. Disengagement: A Life Span Conceptualization." *Human Development* 19, 3 (1976): 171–181.

KANTER, ROSABETH M. "Jobs and Families: Impact of Working Roles in Family Life." *Children Today* 7, 2 (Mar.–Apr. 1978): 11–15, 45.

———, DENNIS JAFFE, and D. KELLY WEISBERG. "Coupling, Parenting, and the Presence of Others: Intimate Relations in Communal Households." *Family Coordinator* 24, 4 (Oct. 1975): 433–452.

KAPLAN, DAVID, and NETTA GRANDSTAFF. "A Problem-Solving Approach to Terminal Illness for the Family and Physician." Paper presented at Second National Training Conference for Physicians on Psychosocial Care of the Dying Patient. Stanford Univ. Medical Center, June 2, 1977. Mimeo.

KAPLAN, MILDRED F., and ANNE GLENN. "Women and the Stress of Moving: A Self-Help Approach." *Social Casework* 59, 7 (July 1978): 434–436.

KARSON, MARTHA A., and ALBERT KARSON. "Counseling Couples in Their Sixties." *Social Work* 23, 3 (May 1978): 243–244.

KAY, EMANUEL. "The World of Work: Its Promises, Conflicts, and Reality." In *The Middle Years.* Washington, D.C.: American Medical Association, 1974: 63–69.

KELLY, JOAN B., and JUDITH S. WALLERSTEIN. "The Effect of Parental Divorce: Experience of the Child in Early Latency." *Amer. Jrnl. Orthopsychiatry* 46, 1 (Jan. 1976): 20–32.

_____. "Brief Interventions with Children in Divorcing Families." *Amer. Jrnl. Orthopsychiatry* 47, 1 (Jan. 1977): 23–39.

KENNISTON, KENNETH. "Youth, A (New) Stage of Life." *Amer. Scholar* 39, 4 (Autumn 1970): 631.

KERCKHOFF, RICHARD L. "Marriage and Middle Age." *Family Coordinator* 25, 1 (Jan. 1976): 5–11.

KESHET, HARRY F., and KRISTINE M. ROSENTHAL. "Fathering After Marital Separation." *Social Work* 23, 1 (Jan. 1978): 11–18.

KIEFER, WILLIAM. "A Preretirement Program in a Family Agency." *Social Casework* 59, 1 (Jan. 1978): 53–54.

KILLILEA, MARIE. "Mutual Help Organizations: Interpretation in the Literature." In Caplan and Killilea, 1976: 37–93.

KILPATRICK, ALLIE C., and EBB G. KILPATRICK, JR. "Retirement from the Military: Problems of Adjustment." *Social Casework* 60, 5 (May 1979): 282–288.

KIMMEL, DOUGLAS C. *Adulthood and Aging.* New York: John Wiley & Sons, 1974.

_____, KARL F. PRICE, and JAMES W. WALKER. "Retirement Choice and Retirement Satisfaction." *Jrnl. Gerontology* 33, 4 (1978): 575–585.

KIRSCHNER, CHARLOTTE. "The Aging Family in Crisis: A Problem in Living." *Social Casework* 60, 4 (Apr. 1979): 209–216.

KLASS, SHIRLEY B., and MARGARET A. REDFERN. "A Social Work Response to the Middle-Aged Housewife." *Social Casework* 58, 2 (Feb. 1977): 101–110.

KLEEMEIER, ROBERT W. "Leisure and Disengagement in Retirement." *Gerontologist* 4, 4 (Dec. 1964): 180–184. Reprinted in Sze, 1975: 661–669.

KLEIN, DONALD C., and ANN ROSS. "Kindergarten Entry: A Study of Role Transition." In Parad, 1965: 140–148.

KNOBLE, JOHN. "Living to the End: The Hospice Experiment." In Gross, Gross, and Seidman, 1978: 396–399.

KOHEN, JANET A., CAROL A. BROWN, and ROSLYN FELDBERG. "Divorced Mothers: The Costs and Benefits of Female Family Control." In Levinger and Moles, 1979: 228–245.

KOHN, JANE B., and WILLARD K. KOHN. *The Widower.* Boston: Beacon Press, 1978.

KOSBERG, JORDAN I. "The Nursing Home: A Social Work Paradox." *Social Work* 18, 2 (Mar. 1973): 104–110.

_____. "Social Work with Geriatric Patients and Their Families." In Prichard et al., 1977, 155–168.

KRANTZ, DAVID L. *Radical Career Change.* New York: Free Press, 1978.

KRESSEL, KENNETH, and MORTON DEUTSCH. "Divorce Therapy: An In-Depth Survey of Therapists' Views." *Family Process* 16, 4 (Dec. 1977): 413–443.

KRESSEL, KENNETH, MARTIN LOPEZ-MORILLAS, JANET WEINGLASS, and MORTON DEUTSCH. "Professional Intervention in Divorce: The Views of Lawyers, Psychotherapists, and Clergy." *Jrnl. of Divorce* 2, 2 (1978): 119–155. Reprinted in Levinger and Moles, 1979: 246–272.

KRUPP, GEORGE. "Maladaptive Reactions to the Death of a Family Member." *Social Casework* 53, 7 (July 1972): 425–434.

KÜBLER-ROSS, ELISABETH. *On Death and Dying.* New York: Macmillan, 1969.

————. *Death: The Final Stage of Growth*. Englewood Cliffs, N.J.: Prentice-Hall, 1975.

LAMB, MICHAEL E. "Fathers: Forgotten Contributors to Child Development." *Human Development* 18 (1975): 245–266.

LAMM, MAURICE, *The Jewish Way in Death and Mourning*. New York: Jonathan David, 1969.

LEADER, ARTHUR L. "The Place of In-Laws in Marital Relationships." *Social Casework* 56, 8 (Oct. 1975): 486–491.

LEBOVITZ, RUTH H. "Loss, Role Change, and Values." *Clinical Social Work Jrnl.* 7, 4 (Winter 1979): 285–295.

LEBOW, GRACE H. "Facilitating Adaptation in Anticipatory Mourning." *Social Casework* 57, 7 (July 1976): 458–465.

LEDERER, WILLIAM J., and DON D. JACKSON. *The Mirages of Marriage*. New York: W. W. Norton, 1968.

LEICHTER, HOPE J., and WILLIAM E. MITCHELL. *Kinship and Casework*, enlarged ed. New York: Russell Sage Foundation, 1978.

LeMASTERS, E. E. "Parenthood as Crisis." *Marriage and Family Living* 19, 4 (1957): 352–355. Reprinted in Parad, 1965: 111–117.

LEMON, ELIZABETH C., and SHIRLEY GOLDSTEIN. "The Use of Time Limits in Planned Brief Casework." *Social Casework* 59, 10 (Dec. 1978): 588–596.

LeSHAN, EDA J. *The Wonderful Crisis of Middle Age: Some Personal Reflections*. New York: David McKay, 1973.

LEUTZ, WALTER N. "The Informal Community Caregiver: A Link Between the Health Care System and Local Residents." *Amer. Jrnl. Orthopsychiatry* 46, 4 (Oct. 1976): 678–688.

LEVINGER, GEORGE. "A Social Psychological Perspective on Marital Dissolution." In Levinger and Moles, 1979: 37–60.

————. "Marital Cohesiveness at the Brink: The Fate of Applications for Divorce." In Levinger and Moles, 1979: 137–150.

————, and OLIVER C. MOLES. *Divorce and Separation: Context, Causes, and Consequences*. New York: Basic Books, 1979.

LEVINSON, DANIEL J., CHARLOTTE M. DARROW, EDWARD B. KLEIN, MARIA H. LEVINSON, and BRAXTON McKEE. "The Psychosocial Development of Men in Early Adulthood and the Mid-Life Transition." In D. F. Ricks, A. Thomas, and M. Roff, eds., *Life History Research in Psychopathology*, vol. 3. Minneapolis: Univ. of Minnesota Press, 1974: 241–258.

————. "The Periods in the Adult Development of Men: Ages 18 to 45." *Counseling Psychologist* 6, 1 (1976): 21–25.

————. *The Seasons of a Man's Life*. New York: A. A. Knopf, 1978.

LEWIS, ROBERT A. "A Developmental Framework for the Analysis of Premarital Dyadic Formation." *Family Process* 11, 1 (Mar. 1972): 17–48.

————. "Social Influences on Marital Choice." In Dragastin and Elder, 1975.

————, PHILLIP J. FRENEAU, and CRAIG L. ROBERTS. "Fathers and the Postparental Transition." *Family Coordinator* 28, 4 (Oct. 1979): 514–520.

LIDZ, THEODORE. *The Person: His and Her Development Throughout the Life Cycle*, rev. ed. New York: Basic Books, 1976.

————. "The Family as the Developmental Setting." In Anthony and Koupernik, 1970: 19–39.

LIEBERMAN, MORTON A. "Adaptive Processes in Late Life." In Datan and Ginsberg, 1975: 135–159.

LIFTON, ROBERT J. *Living and Dying*. New York: Praeger, 1975.

LINDEMANN, ERICH. "Symptomatology and Management of Acute Grief." *Amer. Jrnl. Psychiatry* 101 (Sept. 1944). Reprinted in Parad, 1965: 7–21.

LIPMAN, ALAN, and ROBERT SLATER. "Homes for Old People: Towards a Positive Environment." *Gerontologist* 17, 2 (1977): 146–156.

LIPNER, JOAN, and ETTA SHERMAN. "Hip Fractures in the Elderly—A Psychodynamic Approach." *Social Casework* 56, 2 (Feb. 1975): 97–104.

LIVSON, FLORINE B. "Coming Out of the Closet: Marriage and Other Crises of Middle Age." In Troll, Israel, and Israel, 1977: 81–92.

LOEWENSTEIN, SOPHIE F. "Preparing Social Work Students for Life-Transition Counseling within the Human Behavior Sequence." *Jrnl. Ed. Soc. Work* 14, 2 (Spring 1978): 66–73.

———. "Helping Family Members Cope with Divorce." In Sheldon Eisenberg and Lewis Patterson, eds., *Helping Clients with Special Concerns*. Chicago: Rand McNally, 1979: 193–217.

———. "Toward Choice and Differentiation in the Midlife Crises of Women." Simmons College School of Social Work, 1979: Mimeo.

LONG, LARRY H. "Migration and Resettlement Services." In *Encyclopedia of Social Work* 17, 2. Washington, D.C.: National Association of Social Workers, 1977: 914–919.

LONGFELLOW, CYNTHIA. "Divorce in Context: Its Impact on Children." In Levinger and Moles, 1979: 287–306.

LOPATA, HELENA Z. "Widowhood: Societal Factors in Life-Span Disruptions and Alternatives." In Datan and Ginsberg, 1975: 217–234.

———. "Contributions of Extended Families to the Support Systems of Metropolitan Area Widows: Limitations of the Modified Kin Network." *Jrnl. Marriage and the Family* 40, 2 (May 1978): 355–364.

———. "The Absence of Community Resources in Support Systems of Urban Widows." *Family Coordinator* 27, 4 (Oct. 1978): 383–388.

———. *Women as Widows: Support Systems*. New York: Elsevier, 1979.

LOWENTHAL, MARJORIE F. *Lives in Distress: The Paths of the Elderly to the Psychiatric Ward*. New York: Basic Books, 1964.

———, and DAVID CHIRIBOGA. "Transition to the Empty Nest: Crisis, Challenge or Relief?" *Archives of General Psychiatry* 26 (Jan. 1972): 8–14.

———., and BETSY ROBINSON. "Social Networks and Isolation." In Binstock and Shanas, 1976: 432–456.

———, and ALEXANDER SIMON. "Mental Crises and Institutionalization Among the Aged." *Jrnl. Geriatric Psychiatry* (Spring 1971): 163–187.

———, MAJDA THURNHER, and DAVID CHIRIBOGA. *Four Stages of Life: A Comparative Study of Women and Men Facing Transitions*. San Francisco: Jossey-Bass, 1975.

LYNCH, JAMES J. *The Broken Heart: The Medical Consequences of Loneliness*. New York: Basic Books, 1977.

———, COLLEEN RYAN, and JAMES LICTENBERG, eds. *The Adult Life Cycle*. Lawrence, Kans.: Division of Continuing Education, Univ. of Kansas, 1978.

MAAS, HENRY S., and JOSEPH A. KUYPERS. *From Thirty to Seventy: A Forty-Year*

5000

Longitudinal Study of Adult Life Styles and Personality. San Francisco: Jossey-Bass, 1974.

MACON, LILIAN B. "Help for Bereaved Parents." *Social Casework* 60, 9 (Nov. 1979): 558–561.

MADDOX, GEORGE L. "Retirement as a Social Event in the United States." In Neugarten, 1968: 357–365.

MAGID, D. TRACY, BARBARA D. GROSS, and BERNARD J. SHULMAN. "Preparing Pregnant Teenagers for Parenthood." *Family Coordinator* 28, 3 (July 1979): 359–364.

MALEFIJT, ANNEMARIE. *Religion and Culture.* New York: Macmillan, 1968.

MALUCCIO, ANTHONY N. "Promoting Competence Through Life Experiences." In Germain, 1979: 282–302.

MANASTER, GUY J. *Adolescent Development and the Life Tasks.* Boston: Allyn & Bacon, 1977.

MANTELL, JOANNE E., ESTHER S. ALEXANDER, and MARK A. KLEIMAN. "Social Work with Self-Help Groups." *Health and Social Work* 1, 1 (Feb. 1976): 86–100.

MARRIS, PETER. *Loss and Change.* New York: Pantheon, 1974.

MASTERS, WILLIAM H., and VIRGINIA E. JOHNSON. "Human Sexual Response: The Aging Female and Aging Male." In Neugarten, 1968: 269–279.

MAYER, NANCY. *The Male Mid-Life Crisis: Fresh Starts After Forty.* New York: Signet, 1978.

MAZOR, MIRIAM D. "The Problem of Infertility." In Notman and Nadelson, 1978: 137–160.

McCRACKEN, JAMES A. "The Company Tells Me I'm Too Old." *Saturday Review,* Aug. 7, 1976.

McNULTY, BARBARA. "Home Care for the Terminal Patient and His Family." In Prichard et al., 1977: 171–179.

MEDLEY, MORRIS L. "Marital Adjustment in the Post-Retirement Years." *Family Coordinator* 26, 1 (Jan. 1977): 5–11.

MERTON, ROBERT K., and ROBERT NISBET, eds. *Contemporary Social Problems,* 4th ed. New York: Harcourt Brace Jovanovich, 1976.

MESSINGER, LILLIAN, KENNETH N. WALKER, and STANLEY J. FREEDMAN. "Preparation for Remarriage Following Divorce: The Use of Group Techniques." *Amer. Jrnl. Orthopsychiatry* 48, 2 (Apr. 1978): 263–272.

MEYER, CAROL H. *Social Work Practice,* 2nd ed. New York: Free Press, 1976.

MILLER, IRVING, and RENEE SOLOMON. "The Development of Group Services for the Elderly." In Germain, 1979: 74–106.

MILLER, SHEROD, ELAM W. NUNNALLY, and DAVID B. WACKMAN. "A Communication Training Program for Couples." *Social Casework* 57, 1 (Jan. 1976): 9–18.

———. *Alive and Aware: Improving Communication in Relationships.* Minneapolis: Interpersonal Communication Programs, 1976.

MINAHAN, ANNE, and ALLEN PINCUS. "Conceptual Framework for Social Work Practice." *Social Work* 22, 5 (Sept. 1977): 347–352.

MINUCHIN, SALVADOR. *Families and Family Therapy.* Cambridge, Mass.: Harvard Univ. Press, 1974.

MONK, ABRAHAM. "Factors in the Preparation for Retirement by Middle-Aged Adults." *Gerontologist* 11, 4 (Winter 1971): 348–351, Part I.

MORRIS, SARAH. *Grief and How to Live with It.* New York: Grosset & Dunlap, 1972.

MURPHY, LOIS B. "Coping, Vulnerability, and Resilience in Childhood." In Coelho, Hamburg, and Adams, 1974: 69–100.

——, and ALICE E. MORIARTY. *Vulnerability, Coping, and Growth.* New Haven: Yale Univ. Press, 1976.

MYERHOFF, BARBARA. *Number Our Days.* New York: E. P. Dutton, 1978.

NADELSON, CAROL C. "'Normal' and 'Special' Aspects of Pregnancy: A Psychological Approach." In Notman and Nadelson, 1978: 73–86.

NELSON. L. M., and M. WINTER. "Life Disruption, Independence, Satisfaction, and Considerations of Moving." *Gerontologist* 15 (1975): 160–164.

NEUGARTEN, BERNICE L. *Personality in Middle and Late Life.* New York: Atherton Press, 1964.

——, ed. *Middle Age and Aging.* Chicago: Univ. of Chicago Press, 1968.

——. "The Awareness of Middle Age." In Neugarten, 1968: 93–98.

——. "Adult Personality: Toward a Psychology of the Life Cycle." In Neugarten, 1968: 137–147.

——. "Personality Change in Late Life: A Developmental Perspective." In Eisdorfer and Lawton, 1973: 311–335.

——. "Adaptation and the Life Cycle." *Counseling Psychologist* 6, 1 (1976): 16–20.

——. "Personality and Aging." In Birren and Schaie, 1977: 626–649.

—— and NANCY DATAN. "Sociological Perspectives on the Life Cycle." In Baltes and Schaie, 1973: 53–69.

——, and GUNHILD O. HAGESTAAT. "Age and the Life Course." In Binstock and Shanas, 1976: 35–55.

——, JOAN W. MOORE, and JOHN C. LOWE. "Age Norms, Age Constraints, and Adult Socialization." In Neugarten, 1968: 22–28.

——, VIVIAN WOOD, RUTH J. KRAINES, and BARBARA LOOMIS. "Women's Attitudes Towards the Menopause." In Neugarten, 1968: 195–200.

NEWMAN, BARBARA M., and PHILIP R. NEWMAN. *Development Through Life: A Psychosocial Approach.* Homewood, Ill.: Dorsey Press, 1975.

NOBLE, JUNE, and WILLIAM NOBLE. *How to Live with Other People's Children.* New York: Hawthorn Books, 1977.

NOTMAN, MALKAH H., and CAROL C. NADELSON, eds. *The Woman Patient: Medical and Psychological Interfaces,* vol. 1. New York: Plenum Press, 1978.

O'CONNELL, PATRICIA. "Developmental Tasks of the Family." *Smith College Studies in Social Work* 42, 3 (1972): 203–210.

O'NEILL, NENA, and GEORGE O'NEILL. *Shifting Gears: Finding Security in a Changing World.* New York: Avon, 1974.

ORY, MARCIA C. "The Decision to Parent or Not; Normative and Structural Components." *Jrnl. Marriage and the Family* 40, 3 (Aug. 1978): 531–539.

OXLEY, GENEVIEVE B. "A Life-Model Approach to Change." *Social Casework* 52, 10 (Dec. 1971): 627–633.

——. "Short-Term Therapy with Student Couples." *Social Casework* 54, 5 (Apr. 1973): 216–223.

PARAD, HOWARD J., ed. *Crisis Intervention: Selected Readings.* New York: Family Service Association of America, 1965.

PARENT, MARY K. "The Losses of Middle Age and Related Developmental Tasks." In Prichard et al., 1977: 146–153.

PARKES, COLIN MURRAY. "The First Year of Bereavement." *Psychiatry* 33 (Nov. 1970): 444–467.

———. "Psycho-Social Transitions." *Social Science and Medicine* 5 (1971): 101–115.

———. *Bereavement: Studies of Grief in Adult Life.* New York: International Universities Press, 1972.

———. "Evaluation of Family Care in Terminal Illness." In Prichard et al., 1977: 49–79.

PATTISON, E. MANSELL. "The Living-Dying Process." In Garfield, 1978: 133–168.

PECK, ROBERT C. "Psychological Developments in the Second Half of Life." In John E. Anderson, ed., *Psychological Aspects of Aging.* Washington, D.C.: APA, 1956: 42–54. Reprinted in Neugarten, 1968: 88–92.

PEPPERS, L. G. "Patterns of Leisure and Adjustment to Retirement." *Gerontologist* 16, 5 (1976): 441–446.

PERLMAN, HELEN H. *Social Casework: A Problem-Solving Process.* Chicago: Univ. of Chicago Press, 1957.

———. *Persona: Social Role and Personality.* Chicago: Univ. of Chicago Press, 1968.

———. "In Quest of Coping." *Social Casework* 56, 4 (Apr. 1975): 213–225.

———. "Social Casework: The Problem-Solving Approach." In *Encyclopedia of Social Work* 17, 1 (1977): 1290–1309.

———. *Relationship: The Heart of Helping People.* Chicago: Univ. of Chicago Press, 1979.

PFEIFFER, ERIC. "Psychopathology and Social Pathology." In Birren and Schaie, 1977: 650–671.

PILSECKER, CARLETON. "Help for the Dying." *Social Work* 20, 3 (May 1975): 190–194.

PINCUS, ALLEN. "Toward a Developmental View of Aging for Social Work." *Social Work* 12, 3 (July 1967): 33–41.

———. "Reminiscence in Aging and its Implications for Social Work Practice." *Social Work* 15, 3 (July 1970): 47–51.

PINCUS, LILY. *Death and the Family: The Importance of Mourning.* New York: Vintage, 1976.

POTTS, LEAH. "Counseling Women with Unwanted Pregnancies." In Haselkorn, 1971: 267–280.

POWELL, THOMAS J. "The Use of Self-Help Groups as Supportive Reference Communities." *Amer. Jrnl. Orthopsychiatry* 45, 5 (Oct. 1975): 756–764.

PRICHARD, ELIZABETH R., JEAN COLLARD, BEN A. ORCUTT, AUSTIN H. KUTSCHER, IRENE SEELAND, and NATHAN LEFKOWITZ. *Social Work with the Dying Patient and the Family.* New York: Columbia Univ. Press, 1977.

PROCHASKA, JANICE, and JANE R. COYLE. "Choosing Parenthood: A Needed Family Life Education Group." *Social Casework* 60, 5 (May 1979): 289–293.

RANSOM, JANE W., STEPHEN SCHLESINGER, and ANDRE P. DERDEYN. "A Stepfamily in Formation." *Amer. Jrnl. Orthopsychiatry* 49, 1 (Jan. 1979): 36–43.

RAPOPORT, LYDIA. "Working with Families in Crisis: An Exploration in Preventative Intervention." *Social Work* 7, 3 (Sept. 1962): 48–56.

———. "Crisis Intervention as a Mode of Brief Treatment." In Robert W. Roberts and Robert H. Nee, eds., *Theories of Social Casework.* Chicago: Univ. of Chicago Press, 1970: 267–311.

_____ and Leah Potts. "Abortion of Unwanted Pregnancy as a Potential Life Crisis." In Haselkorn, 1971: 249–266.

RAPOPORT, RHONA. "Normal Crises, Family Structure, and Mental Health." *Family Process* 2, 1 (1963). Reprinted in Parad, 1965: 73–87.

_____, and ROBERT N. RAPOPORT. "New Light on the Honeymoon." *Human Relations* 17 (1964): 33–56.

_____. "Further Considerations on the Dual-Career Family." *Human Relations* 24 (1971): 519–533.

RAPOPORT, ROBERT N., and RHONA RAPOPORT. "Work and Family Contemporary Society." *Amer. Soc. Review* 30 (1965): 381–394.

_____, eds. *Working Couples*. New York: Harper & Row, 1978.

RATHBONE-McCUAN, ELOISE. "Geriatric Day Care: A Family Perspective." *Gerontologist* 16 (1976): 517–521.

REICHARD, SUZANNE, FLORINE LIVSON, and PAUL G. PETERSEN. "Adjustment to Retirement." In Neugarten, 1968: 178–180.

REID, WILLIAM J. *The Task-Centered System*. New York: Columbia Univ. Press. 1978.

_____, and LAURA EPSTEIN. *Task-Centered Casework*. New York: Columbia Univ. Press, 1972.

_____, eds. *Task-Centered Practice*. New York: Columbia Univ. Press, 1977.

REISS, DAVID, and MARY ELLEN OLIVERI. "Family Paradigm and Family Coping: A Proposal for Linking the Family's Intrinsic Adaptive Capacities to Its Response to Stress." *Family Relations* 29, 4 (Oct. 1980): 431–444.

REITZ, ROSETTA. *Menopause: A Positive Approach*. Radnor, Pa.: Chilton, 1977.

REUL, MYRTLE R. "Migration: The Confrontation of Opportunity and Trauma." In Eaton, 1971: 3–22.

RHODES, SONYA L. "A Developmental Approach to the Life Cycle of the Family." *Social Casework* 58, 5 (May 1977): 301–311.

RICHARDS, ARLENE, and IRENE WILLIS. *How to Get It Together When Your Parents Are Coming Apart*. New York: Bantam, 1976.

RIEGEL, KLAUS F. "Toward a Dialectical Theory of Development." *Human Development* 18, 1–2 (1975): 50–63.

_____. "Adult Life Crises: A Dialectic Interpretation of Development." In Datan and Ginsberg, 1975: 99–128.

RILEY, MATHILDA, and JOAN WARING. "Age and Aging." In Merton and Nisbet, 1976: 355–410.

ROBERTSON, JOAN F. "The Significance of Grandparents: Perceptions of Young Adult Grandchildren." *Gerontologist* 16 (1977): 137–140.

_____. "Women in Midlife: Crises, Reverberations, and Support Networks." *Family Coordinator* 27, 4 (Oct. 1978): 375–382.

ROBINSON, BETSY, and MAGDA THURNHER. "Parental Caretaking: A Family Cycle Transition." Paper presented at 29th Annual Scientific Meeting of the Gerontological Society, New York, Oct 13–17, 1976. Mimeo.

ROSENBERG, BLANCA N. "Planned Short-Term Treatment in Developmental Crises." *Social Casework* 56, 4 (Apr. 1975): 195–204.

ROSENBERG, STANLEY D., and MICHAEL P. FARRELL. "Identity and Crisis in Middle-Aged Men." *Intl. Jrnl. Aging and Human Development* 7, 2 (1976): 153–170.

Rossi, Alice S. "Transition to Parenthood." *Jrnl. Marriage and the Family* 30, 1 (1968): 26–39. Reprinted in Skolnick and Skolnick, 1977: 351–362.

Rubin, Lillian B. *Worlds of Pain: Life in the Working Class Family.* New York: Basic Books, 1976.

———. *Women of a Certain Age: The Midlife Search for Self.* New York: Harper & Row, 1979.

Ruebsaat, Helmut J., and Raymond Hull. *The Male Climacteric.* New York: Hawthorn, 1975.

Russell, Betty, and Sylvia Schild. "Pregnancy Counseling with College Women." *Social Casework* 57, 5 (May 1976): 324–329.

Russell, Candyce S. "Transition to Parenthood: Problems and Gratifications. *Jrnl. Marriage and the Family* 36, 2 (May 1974): 294–301.

Russo, Nancy. "The Mothering Mandate." *Jrnl. Social Issues* 32, 3 (1976): 143–153.

Ryder, Robert G., John S. Kafka, and David H. Olson. "Separating and Joining Influences in Courtship and Early Marriage." *Amer. Jrnl. Orthopsychiatry* 41, 3 (Apr. 1971): 450–464.

Sander, Faye. "Aspects of Sexual Counseling with the Aged." *Social Casework* 57, 8 (Oct. 1976): 504–510.

Satir, Virginia. "You as a Change Agent." In Satir, Stachowiak, and Taschman, 1977: 37–62.

———, James Stachowiak, and Harvey A. Taschman. *Helping Families to Change.* New York: Jason Aronson, 1977.

Scherz, Frances H. "Maturational Crises and Parent-Child Interaction." *Social Casework* 52, 6 (June 1971): 362–369.

Schilling, Susan M., and Ellen J. Gross. "Stages of Family Therapy: A Developmental Model." *Clinical Social Work Jrnl.* 7, 2 (Summer 1979): 105–114.

Schmidt, David, and Edward Messner. "The Role of the Family Physician in the Crisis of Impending Divorce." *Jrnl. Family Practice* 2, 2 (1975): 99–102.

Schoenberg, Bernard, Arthur C. Carr, Austin H. Kitscher, David Peretz, and Ivan K. Goldberg, eds. *Anticipatory Grief.* New York: Columbia Univ. Press, 1974.

Schram, Rosalyn W. "Marital Satisfaction Over the Family Life Cycle: A Critique and Proposal." *Jrnl. Marriage and the Family* 41, 1 (Feb. 1979): 7–14.

Schwartz, Arthur N. *Survival Handbook for Children of Aging Parents.* Chicago: Follett, 1977.

Schwartz, Marc D. "Situation/Transition Groups: A Conceptualization and Review." *Amer. Jrnl. Orthopsychiatry* 45, 5 (Oct. 1975): 744–755.

Seelbach, Wayne C. "Correlates of Aged Parents' Filial Responsibility, Expectations, and Realizations." *Family Coordinator* 27, 4 (Oct. 1978): 341–350.

Seiden, Anne M. "The Sense of Mastery in the Childbirth Experience." In Notman and Nadelson, 1978: 87–106.

Shafer, N. "Helping Women Through the Change of Life." *Sexology* 36 (1970): 54–56.

Shanas, Ethel. "Living Arrangements and Housing of Old People." In Busse and Pfeiffer, 1969: 129–149.

———, and George L. Maddox. "Aging, Health, and the Organization of Health Resources." In Binstock and Shanas, 1976: 592–618.

SHANAS, ETHEL, and GORDON STREIB, eds. *Social Structure and the Family: Generational Relations*. Englewood Cliffs, N.J.: Prentice Hall, 1965.

SHAPIRO, JOAN. "Dominant Leaders Among Slum Hotel Residents." *Amer. Jrnl. Orthopsychiatry* 39, 4 (July 1969): 644–650.

SHAVIT, HANNA. "The Empty Nest as a Transitional Period for the Mother." M.A. Thesis, School of Social Work, Univ. of Haifa, 1979. Mimeo. (Hebrew).

SHEEHY, GAIL. *Passages: Predictable Crises of Adult Life*. New York: E. P. Dutton, 1976.

SHEPHARD, MARTIN. *Someone You Love Is Dying: A Guide for Helping and Coping*. New York: Charter, 1975.

SHERMAN, EDMUND, and EVELYN S. NEWMAN. "The Meaning of Cherished Personal Possessions for the Elderly." *Int. Jrnl. Aging and Human Development* 8, 2 (1977–78): 181–192.

SHNEIDMAN, EDWIN S., NORMAN L. FARBEROW, and ROBERT E. LITMAN. *The Psychology of Suicide*. New York: Science House, 1970.

SHUVAL, JUDITH. *Immigrants on the Threshold*. New York: Atherton Press, 1963.

SILVERMAN, ALIDA G., BEATRICE H. KAHN, and GARY ANDERSON. "A Model for Working with Multigenerational Families." *Social Casework* 58, 3 (Mar. 1977): 131–135.

SILVERMAN, PHYLLIS R. "The Widow as a Caregiver in a Program of Preventive Intervention with Other Widows." *Mental Hygiene* 54, 4 (Oct. 1970): 540–547.

———. "Widowhood and Preventive Intervention." *Family Coordinator* 21, 1 (Jan. 1972): 95–102.

———. "Anticipatory Grief from the Perspective of Widowhood." In Schoenberg et al., 1974: 320–330.

———. "Bereavement as a Normal Life Transition." In Prichard et al., 1977: 266–273.

———. *Mutual Help Groups: A Guide for Mental Health Workers*. Rockville, Md.: National Institute of Mental Health, 1978.

———. "Mutual Help: An Alternate Network." In *Women in Midlife—Security and Fulfillment*. Select Committee on Aging, U.S. House of Representatives. Washington, D.C.: U.S. Govt. Printing Office, 1978: 254–270.

———, and SUE ENGLANDER. "The Widow's View of Her Dependent Children." *Omega* 6, 1 (1975). Reprinted in Sara S. Cook, *Children Are Dying*. New York: Health Sciences, 1975: 60–77.

SILVERMAN, PHYLLIS R., DOROTHY MACKENZIE, MARY PETTTIAS, and ELIZABETH WILSON, eds. *Helping Each Other in Widowhood*. New York: Health Sciences, 1974.

SILVERMAN, PHYLLIS R., and HOPE G. MURROW. "Caregiving During Critical Role Transitions in the Normal Life Cycle." Paper presented at National Institute of Mental Health Continuing Education Seminar on Emergency Mental Health Services, Washington, D.C., June 1973. Mimeo.

SILVERSTONE, BARBARA, and HELEN K. HYMAN. *You and Your Aging Parent*. New York: Pantheon, 1976.

SIMONS, GUSTAVE. *Coping with Crisis*. New York: Macmillan, 1972.

SIMONS, RONALD L., and STEPHEN M. AIGNER. "Facilitating an Eclectic Use of Practice." *Social Casework* 60, 4 (Apr. 1979): 201–208.

SIMOS, BERTHA G. "Grief Therapy to Facilitate Healthy Restitution." *Social Casework* 58, 6 (June 1977): 337–342.

_____. *A Time to Grieve: Loss as a Universal Human Experience*. New York: Family Service Association of America, 1979.

SKOLNICK, ARLENE S., and JEROME H. SKOLNICK, eds. *Family in Transition*, 2nd ed. Boston: Little, Brown, 1977.

SLUZKI, CARLOS E. "Migration and Family Conflict." *In the Family* 3 (Mar. 1978): 1–3. Report of Workshops at Second Intl. Congress of Family Therapy, Jerusalem, 1977.

SNYDER, ALICE I. "Periodic Marital Separation and Physical Illness." *Amer. Jrnl. Orthopsychiatry* 48, 4 (Oct. 1978): 637–643.

SODDY, KENNETH. *Men in Middle Life*. London: Tavistock Publications, 1967.

SOLOMON, MICHAEL A. "A Developmental Conceptual Premise for Family Therapy." *Family Process* 12, 2 (1973): 179–188.

SPANIER, GRAHAM B., and ROBERT F. CASTO. "Adjustment to Separation and Divorce: A Qualitative Analysis." In Levinger and Moles, 1979: 211–227.

SPANIER, GRAHAM B., and WILLIAM SAUER. "An Empirical Evaluation of the Family Life Cycle." *Jrnl. Marriage and the Family* 41, 1 (Feb. 1979): 27–40.

SPENCE, DONALD L., and THOMAS LONNER. "The 'Empty Nest': A Transition Within Motherhood." *Family Coordinator* 20, 4 (Oct. 1971): 369–375.

SPIERER, HOWARD. *Major Transitions in the Human Life Cycle*. New York: Academy of Educational Development, 1977.

STEIN, PETER J. "Singlehood: An Alternative to Marriage." *Family Coordinator* 24, 4 (Oct. 1975): 489–503.

STEINZOR, BERNARD. *When Parents Divorce*. New York: Pantheon, 1969.

STEWART, WENDY ANN. "Psychosocial Study of the Formation of the Early Adult Life Structure in Women." Unpublished dissertation, School of Arts and Sciences, Columbia Univ., 1977.

STILL, HENRY. *Surviving the Male Mid-Life Crisis*. New York: Crowell, 1977.

STORR, ANTHONY. "C. G. Jung." *The American Scholar* 31 (1962): 395–403. Reprinted in Walter Katkovsky and Leon Gorlow, eds., *The Psychology of Adjustment: Current Concepts and Applications*. New York: McGraw-Hill, 1976: 81–92.

STREIB, GORDON F. "Older Families and Their Troubles: Familial and Social Responses." *Family Coordinator* 21, 1 (Jan. 1972): 5–19.

_____. "An Alternative Family Form for Older Persons: Need and Social Context." *Family Coordinator* 27, 4 (Oct. 1978): 413–420.

STRICKLER, MARTIN. "Crisis Intervention and the Climacteric Man." *Social Casework* 56, 2 (Feb. 1975): 85–90.

_____, and BETSY LASOR. "The Concept of Loss in Crisis Intervention." *Mental Hygiene* 54 (Apr. 1970): 301–305.

STROMBERG, ANN H., and SHIRLEY HARKESS, eds. *Women Working: Theories and Facts in Perspective*. Palo Alto, Ca.: Mayfield, 1978.

SUAREZ, JOHN M., NANCY L. WESTON, and NORMAN B. HARTSTEIN. "Mental Health Intervention in Divorce Proceedings." *Amer. Jrnl. Orthopsychiatry* 48, 2 (Apr. 1978): 273–283.

SUSSMAN, MARVIN B. "The Family Life of Old People." In Binstock and Shanas, 1976: 218–243.

Suszycki, Lee H. "Effective Nursing Home Placement for the Elderly Dying Patient." In Prichard et al., 1977: 185–197.

Sze, William C., ed. *Human Life Cycle*. New York: Jason Aronson, 1975.

Temes, Roberta. *Living with an Empty Chair: A Guide Through Grief*. Amherst, Me.: Mandala, 1977.

Tessman, Lora H. *Children of Parting Parents*. New York: Jason Aronson, 1978.

Thurnher, Majda. "Midlife Marriage: Sex Differences in Evaluation and Perspectives." *Intl. Jrnl. Aging and Human Development* 7, 2 (1976): 129–135.

———. "Goals, Values, and Life Evaluations at the Preretirement Stage." *Jrnl. Gerontology* 29, 1 (Jan. 1974): 85–96.

Tooley, Kay. "Antisocial Behavior and Social Alienation Post Divorce: The 'Man of the House' and His Mother." *Amer. Jrnl. Orthopsychiatry* 46, 1 (Jan. 1976): 33–42.

Troll, Lillian E. "The Family of Later Life: A Decade Review." *Jrnl. Marriage and the Family* 33 (1971): 263–290.

———. *Early and Middle Adulthood: The Best Is Yet to Be—Maybe*. Monterey, Ca.: Brooks/Cole, 1975.

———, Joan Israel, and Kenneth Israel, eds. *Looking Ahead: A Woman's Guide to the Problems and Joys of Growing Older*. Englewood Cliffs, N.J.: Prentice-Hall, 1977.

Turk, Ruth. *You're Getting Older, So What?* New York: Cornerstone, 1976.

Turner, Maureen F., and Martha H. Izzi. "The COPE Story: A Service to Pregnant and Postpartum Women." In Notman and Nadelson, 1978: 107–122.

Tuzil, Teresa J. "The Agency Role in Helping Children and Their Aging Parents." *Social Casework* 59, 5 (May 1978): 302–305.

Tyhurst, James. "The Role of Transitional States—Including Disasters—in Mental Illness." *Symposium on Preventive and Social Psychiatry*. Washington, D.C.: Walter Reed Army Institute of Research, 1957: 149–169.

Tyhurst, Libuse. "Displacement and Migration: A Study in Social Psychiatry." *Amer. Jrnl. Psychiatry.* 107 (1951): 561–568.

Usdin, Gene, and Charles J. Hoflin, eds. *Aging: The Process and the People*. New York: Brunner/Mazel, 1978.

Vaillant, George E. "Natural History of Male Psychological Health. II. Some Antecedents of Healthy Adult Adjustment." *Arch. Gen. Psychiat.* 31, 1 (July 1974): 15–22. "III. Empirical Dimensions of Mental Health." *Archives of General Psychiatry* 32, 4 (Apr. 1975): 420–426.

———. *Adaptation to Life*. Boston: Little, Brown, 1977.

———, and Charles McArthur. "Natural History of Male Psychological Health. I. The Adult Life Cycle from 18 to 50." *Seminars in Psychiatry* 4, 4 (Nov. 1972).

Van Gennep, Arnold. *Les Rites de Passage*. Paris, 1908. Translated as *The Rites of Passage*. Chicago: Univ. of Chicago Press, 1960.

Vinick, Barbara H. "Remarriage in Old Age." *Family Coordinator* 27, 4 (Oct. 1978): 359–363.

Visher, Emily, and John S. Visher. *Stepfamilies: A Guide to Working with Stepparents and Stepchildren*. New York: Brunner/Mazel, 1979.

Waletzky, Lucy R. "Husbands' Problems with Breast Feeding." *Amer. Jrnl. Orthopsychiatry* 49, 2 (Apr. 1979): 349–352.

WALKER, KENNETH N., JOY ROGERS, and LILLIAN MESSINGER. "Remarriage after Divorce: A Review," *Social Casework* 58 (May 1977): 276–285.

WALKER, KENNETH M and LILLIAN MESSINGER. "Remarriage after Divorce: Dissolution and Reconstruction of Family Boundaries." *Family Process* 18, 2 (June 1979): 185–192.

WALLERSTEIN, JUDITH S., and JOAN B. KELLY. "The Effects of Parental Divorce: The Adolescent Experience." In E. James Anthony and Cyrille Koupernik, eds., *The Child in His Family: Children at Psychiatric Risk*, vol. 3. New York: John Wiley & Sons, 1974.

———. "Effects of Parental Divorce—Experiences of the Pre-School Child." *Jrnl. Amer. Academy of Child Psychiatry* 14, 4 (Autumn 1975): 600–616.

———. "Effects of Parental Divorce—Experiences of the Child in Later Latency." *Amer. Jrnl. Orthopsychiatry* 46, 2 (Apr. 1976): 256–269.

———. "Divorce Counseling: A Community Service for Families in the Midst of Divorce." *Amer. Jrnl. Orthopsychiatry* 47, 1 (Jan. 1977): 4–22.

———. "Children and Divorce: A Review." *Social Work* 24, 6 (Nov. 1979): 468–475.

———. *Surviving the Breakup: How Children and Parents Cope with Divorce*. New York: Basic Books, 1980.

WARD, RUSSELL A. "Limitations of the Family as a Supportive Institution in the Lives of the Aged." *Family Coordinator* 27, 4 (Oct. 1978): 365–373.

WARREN, DONALD. "Neighborhood Structure and Riot Behavior in Detroit: Some Exploratory Findings." *Social Problems* 16 (1969): 464–484.

WASSERMAN, SIDNEY. "The Middle Age Separation Crisis and Ego Supportive Casework Therapy." *Clin. Soc. Work Jrnl.* 1, 1 (Spring 1973): 38–47.

WATZLAWICK, PAUL, JOHN H. WEAKLAND, and RICHARD FISCH. *Change: Principles of Problem Formation and Problem Resolution*. New York: W. W. Norton, 1974.

WEAKLAND, JOHN H., RICHARD FISCH, PAUL WATZLAWICK, and ARTHUR M. BODIN. "Brief Therapy: Focused Problem Resolution." *Family Process* 13, 2 (June 1974): 141–167.

WEISS, ROBERT S., ed. *Loneliness: The Experience of Emotional and Social Isolation*. Cambridge: M. I. T. Press, 1973.

———. "The Contributions of an Organization of Single Parents to the Well-Being of Its Members." *Family Coordinator* 22, 3 (July 1973): 321–326.

———. *Marital Separation*. New York: Basic Books, 1975.

———. "Transition States and Other Stressful Situations: Their Nature and Programs for Their Management." In Caplan and Killilea, 1976: 213–232.

———. "The Emotional Impact of Marital Separation." *Jrnl. Social Issues* 32, 1 (1976): 135–145. Reprinted in Levinger and Moles, 1979: 201–210.

———. "Issues in the Adjudication of Custody When Parents Separate." In Levinger and Moles, 1979: 324–336.

———, EDWIN HARWOOD, and DAVID RIESMAN. "The World of Work." In Merton and Nisbet, 1976: 605–537.

WEISSMAN, MYRNA M., and EUGENE S PAYKEL. "Moving and Depression in Women." *Society* 9 (July/Aug. 1972). Reprinted in Weiss, 1973: 154–164.

———. *The Depressed Woman: A Study of Social Relationships*. Chicago: Univ. of Chicago Press, 1974.

WEISSMAN, MYRNA, CYNTHIA PINCUS, NATALIE RADDING, ROBERTA LAWRENCE, and RISE SIEGEL. "The Educated Housewife: Mild Depression and the Search for Work." *Amer. Jrnl. Orthopsychiatry* 43, 4 (July 1973): 565–573.

WENTE, AREL S., and SUSAN B. CROCKENBERG. "Transition to Fatherhood: LaMaze Preparation, Adjustment Difficulty, and the Husband–Wife Relationship." *Family Coordinator* 25, 4 (Oct. 1976): 351–357.

WESTON, NANCY L., and NORMAN B. HARTSTEIN. "Mental Health Intervention in Divorce Proceedings." *Amer. Jrnl. Orthopsychiatry* 48, 2 (Apr. 1978): 273–283.

WHITE, ROBERT W. "Strategies of Adaptation: An Attempt at Systematic Description." In Coelho, Hamburg, and Adams, 1974: 47–68.

––––––. *Lives in Progress*, 2nd ed. New York: Holt, Rinehart, & Winston, 1975.

WIJNBERG, MARION, and MARY C. SCHWARTZ. "Competence or Crisis: The Social Work Role in Maintaining Family Competency During the Dying Period." In Prichard et al., 1977: 97–112.

WILLIAMS, JUANITA H. *Psychology of Women: Behavior in a Biosocial Context.* New York: W. W. Norton, 1977.

WINNICOTT, DONALD W. "The Mother–Infant Experience of Mutuality." In Anthony and Benedek, 1970: 245–258.

WISEMAN, REVA S. "Crisis Theory and the Process of Divorce." *Social Casework* 56, 4 (Apr. 1975): 205–212.

WITKEN, LYNN. "Group Helps Widowed Parents Deal with Children's Grief." *Practice Digest* 2, 2 (Sept. 1979): 27–28.

––––––, *Women in Transition: A Feminist Handbook on Separation and Divorce.* New York: Charles Scribner's Sons, 1975.

WOOD, VIRGINIA. "The Older Woman Alone." Paper presented at Forum on Aging: Problems, Patterns, and Prospects. Calif. State Univ., Fresno, Mar. 22, 1979. Mimeo.

––––––. Operational Grant Proposal on Multidisciplinary Project on Aging Women, Faye McBeath Institute on Aging and Adult Life, Univ. Wisconsin-Madison, 1977. Mimeo.

––––––, BETH HOWE, and MARY WYLIE. "Growing Old Single." Faye McBeath Institute on Aging and Adult Life, Univ. Wisconsin: Madison, 1978. Mimeo.

WOODSON, ROBERT. "Hospice Care in Terminal Illness." In Prichard et al., 1977: 365–385.

WOODY, JANE D. "Preventive Intervention for Children of Divorce." *Social Casework* 59, 9 (Nov. 1978): 537–544.

WOOLEY, PERSIA. *Creative Survival for Single Mothers.* Millbrae, Ca.: Celestial Arts, 1975.

YATES, MARTHA. *Coping: A Survival Manual for Women Alone.* Englewood Cliffs, N.J.: Prentice-Hall, 1976.

YOUNG, CRISTABEL M. "Work Sequences of Women During the Family Life Cycle." *Jrnl. Marriage and the Family* 40, 2 (May 1978): 401–411.

ZIMMERMAN, MARY K. *Passage Through Abortion.* New York: Praeger, 1977.

Index

geographical moves and migrations, 223–227

health impairment, 213–221

institutionalization, path to, 221–230

Ford, Caroline, 227, 228

Freud, Sigmund, 43, 174

Fried, Barbara, 117

Fried, Marc, 104

Friends, as natural help system, 246–247

G

Gaitz, Charles, 218, 219

Gans, Bruce, 141

Gaylord, Maxine, 105

Gennep, Arnold van, 23–24

Geographic moves and migrations, 3–4, 14, 46, 99–114

actual migration, 105–107

adjustment period, 107–114

aging persons and, 206, 223–227

breaks with past, 104–105

decision making, 103–104

Germain, Carel, 5, 262

Gettleman, Susan, 147, 152

Gitterman, Alex, 262

Going together, 163

Gould, Roger, 40–41

Grandparent, role of, 225

Greene, Martin, 178

Grief, 104, 170–180

Group identity, 104

Group services, 257–259

Gubrium, Jaber, 209

Gurin, Gerald, 242

H

Hall, Douglas, 103

Hall, Francine, 103

Hamburg, Beatrix, 50

Hamburg, David, 19

Harkins, Elizabeth, 132

Havighurst, Robert, 15, 27–28, 53, 62, 268

Health impairment, 213–221

Helping process, 266–270

Hill, Reuben, 245

Hobbs, Daniel, 80, 81

Hoff, Lee Ann, 250

Homosexuality, 121

Honeymoon, 70–73

Hull, Raymond, 136

Hypochondriasis, 216

I

Immigration, 107, 112–114, 266

Income management, 108, 110–111

Incorporation, 24

Individuation, 25, 119–122

Inner change, 17–19

Institutionalization, path to, 221–230

Intergenerational cogwheeling, 5–6

Intervention, guidelines for, 261–271; see also Sources and forms of help during transitions

approaches to practice, 261–265

client-worker relationship, 270–271

helping process, 266–270

nature of transitional problems, 265–266

J

Jackson, Don, 67

Jacobson, Doris S., 166

Jacobson, Gerald F., 255

Jaques, Elliot, 118, 120

Johnson, Virginia, 134

Joint custody, 156

Jones, Stella, 108

Jung, Carl, 25, 119

K

Kafka, John, 68

Kay, Emanuel, 60

Kelly, Joan, 157, 255, 256

Kenniston, Kenneth, 49

Kerckhoff, Richard, 115

Keshet, Harry, 158

Kirschner, Charlotte, 224

Kosberg, Jordan, 226, 234

Kressel, Kenneth, 257

Kris, Ernst, 85

Krupp, George, 178

Kübler-Ross, Elisabeth, 171, 230, 231, 233, 237

L

Labor, 89

Lamaze, Fernand, 90

Late adulthood, 13, 190–192; see also Widowhood

entering, 196–197

final years: see Final years

leaving mid-adulthood, 191, 192–195

retirement: see Retirement